Keech

NB Fenno
criticism in
Home Style.

Je näher man ein Wort ansieht,
desto ferner sieht es zurück.
—KARL KRAUS

The

Concept

Of Representation

Hanna Fenichel Pitkin

THE CONCEPT OF
REPRESENTATION

UNIVERSITY OF CALIFORNIA PRESS
Berkeley, Los Angeles, London 1972

University of California Press
Berkeley and Los Angeles, California

University of California Press, Ltd.
London, England

Copyright © 1967, by
The Regents of the University of California
First Paperback Edition 1972

ISBN: 0-520-02156-8
Library of Congress Catalog Card Number: 67-25052
Printed in the United States of America

Contents

1

Introduction

Being concerned with representation, this book is about an idea, a concept, a word. It is primarily a conceptual analysis, not a historical study of the way in which representative government has evolved, nor yet an empirical investigation of the behavior of contemporary representatives or the expectations voters have about them. Yet, although the book is about a word, it is not about mere words, not merely about words. For the social philosopher, for the social scientist, words are not "mere"; they are the tools of his trade and a vital part of his subject matter. Since human beings are not merely political animals but also language-using animals, their behavior is shaped by their ideas. What they do and how they do it depends upon how they see themselves and their world, and this in turn depends upon the concepts through which they see. Learning what "representation" means and learning how to represent are intimately connected. But even beyond this, the social theorist sees the world through a network of concepts. Our words define and delimit our world in important ways, and this is particularly true of the world of human and social things. For a zoölogist may capture a rare specimen and simply observe it; but who can capture an instance of representation (or of power, or of interest)? Such things, too, can be observed, but the observation always presupposes at least a rudimentary conception of what

representation (or power, or interest) *is*, what *counts as* representation, where it leaves off and some other phenomenon begins.
Questions about what representation is, or is like, are not fully
separable from the question of what "representation" means.
This book approaches the former questions by way of the latter.

But one would hardly recommend that all social or political
concepts be treated to a book-length analysis. The singling out
of representation for such treatment must rest on the concept's
importance and ubiquity, on the one hand, and on its complexity
and its consequent role in long-standing theoretical confusions
and controversies, on the other. The confusions invite clarification; the importance of the concept seems to make clarification
worth while.

That representation is today a significant and widely used
concept need hardly be argued. In modern times almost everyone wants to be governed by representatives (although not necessarily by a conventional representative government); every
political group or cause wants representation; every government
claims to represent. At the same time we are troubled by the difference between sham and real representative institutions, and
by the many competing ways in which representation can be institutionalized. The whole issue of representation has recently
been reopened in the United States by the Supreme Court's action
in *Baker vs. Carr*, and the resulting concern with legislative apportionment.[1]

No doubt the contemporary popularity of the concept depends
much upon its having become linked with the idea of democracy,
as well as with ideas of liberty and justice. Yet through much
of their history both the concept and the practice of representation have had little to do with democracy or liberty. Representation need not mean representative government. A king can
represent a nation, as can an ambassador. Any public official
can sometimes represent the state. Thus institutions and practices which embody some kind of representation are necessary
in any large and articulated society, and need have nothing to
do with popular self-government.

The concept of representation, particularly of human beings
representing other human beings, is essentially a modern one.
The ancient Greeks had no corresponding word, although they

elected some officials and sometimes sent ambassadors—activities which *we* might say involve representation.[2] The Romans had the word *repraesentare*, from which our own "representation" derives by way of Old French; but they used it to mean the literal bringing into presence of something previously absent, or the embodiment of an abstraction in an object (say, the embodiment of courage in a human face or in a piece of sculpture). They did not apply it to human beings acting for others, or to their political institutions. Such uses began to emerge in Latin in the thirteenth and fourteenth centuries, in English even later, as persons sent to participate in church councils or in the English Parliament came gradually to be thought of as representatives.[3] Initially, neither the concept nor the institutions to which it was applied were linked with elections or democracy, nor was representation considered a matter of right.

In England, to take the classical example, the calling of knights and burgesses to meet with the king's council seems to have begun as a matter of royal convenience and need.[4] Far from being a privilege or right, attendance at Parliament was a chore and a duty, reluctantly performed.[5] Only with the passage of time did parliamentary representation begin to be used as a device for furthering local interests, as a control over the power of the king. By the seventeenth century, the right to elect a member of Parliament could be claimed for even "the poorest hee that is in England," although many still disputed the claim.[6] From this tradition, in turn, came the rallying cry of the American Revolution, that "taxation without representation is tyranny."[7] Representation had become one of the sacred and traditional "rights of Englishmen," worth fighting for; with the American and French revolutions it was transformed into one of the "rights of Man."[8] Thus representation came to mean popular representation, and to be linked with the idea of self-government, of every man's right to have a say in what happens to him. And that is how it became embodied in our institutions.

Considering the importance of the concept, and the frequency with which it is used by writers on politics, there has been surprisingly little discussion or analysis of its meaning. Perhaps it is one of those fundamental ideas so much taken for granted that they themselves escape close scrutiny; or perhaps its com-

plexity has discouraged analysis. Hobbes is the only major political theorist who gives a fully developed, systematic account of
its meaning; other theorists' views must be garnered from casual
remarks or read between the lines. Even John Stuart Mill, who
devotes an entire book to representative government, does not
consider it necessary to explain what representation is or means.[9]
Yet the literature is full of obvious disagreements over its
meaning. Some theorists offer definitions which directly contradict those offered by others or (even worse) bear no relationship to them. There are few attempts to account for these
confusing discrepancies, and, as a result, discussions of representation are marked by long-standing, persistent controversies
which seem to defy solution. Hobbes, for example, holds that
every government is a representative government in that it represents its subjects; and many more recent writers share his view.
On the other hand, the tendency in this century has been to dis-
parage the representativeness of so-called indirect democracies
as mythical or illusory. Writers point out that all governments use propaganda to manipulate their subjects; that, conversely, even totalitarian dictators have (and must have) popular
support. They argue that no government really represents, that
a truly representative government does not exist. Yet political
scientists and laymen alike talk about representative government as distinct from other forms. Are all governments representative, or none, or some? Surely there is need for clarification
here.

Another vexing and seemingly endless controversy concerns
the proper relation between representative and constituents.
Hobbes suggests that the representative is free to do whatever
he pleases (at least so far as his constituents are concerned). The
majority of theorists argue that the representative must do what
is best for those in his charge, but that he must do what he thinks
best, using his own judgment and wisdom, since he is chosen to
make decisions for (that is, instead of) his constituents. But a
vocal minority maintain that the representative's duty is to reflect accurately the wishes and opinions of those he represents.
Anything else they consider a mockery of true representation.
The truth may lie somewhere in between, but if so, where does
it lie, and how is one to decide?

Faced with such disagreements, one could perhaps select a particular position and defend it as correct, dismissing the rest; or one could dismiss them all and propose a new and still better position. But that will not help to explain how so many intelligent, profound thinkers could have been so completely wrong. Even more, it will not explain the plausibility of their views to us, the fact that we are able to follow their arguments and are tempted by their definitions. Reading any one of them in isolation, we are inclined to accept his view; the difficulties become apparent only when we go on to other, equally plausible but incompatible arguments. Finally, claiming to single out the one right definition will not explain the timeless quality of the theorists' disputes, the way they persist and recur without resolution.

Alternatively, then, we might conclude that representation has no fixed meaning, that the various theorists disagree because they are in fact talking about different things. Perhaps the concept has evolved, and that is why earlier writers disagree with later ones. Or perhaps, if the meaning is not fixed, each writer is free to use the concept as he pleases, assigning whatever meaning he chooses. Now, of course this is true in a sense; every writer is free to use and define his terms as he wishes. But he cannot use words as he wishes and still communicate with others, still speak of precisely that state of affairs he has in mind.[10] Nor does the political philosopher usually think of himself as redefining words or giving them new meanings, but rather as explaining the meanings they already have. Even redefinition has its difficulties. Both writer and reader are likely to forget that the word has been redefined, and to start thinking of it in its old meaning. And even a redefinition, to be intelligible, must be expressed in words with familiar meanings. A writer may, indeed, redefine a term; he must do so if he does not want it to mean what it usually means. But that is not what most writers on representation have done.

Still another possibility might be to conclude that the difficulty comes from the word itself. Some recent commentators have maintained that "representation" is vague or "ambiguous," that it "may sometimes be one thing, sometimes the other," that it is "used in various senses in different connections."[11] And with such judgments they abandon further effort, or resign themselves to compiling a list of the definitions offered by others.[12] H. B. Mayo, having noted that "theories of representation are something of a morass," even recommends that we simply abandon the word and stop using it because of its complexity.[13] But he has continued to use it just the same, as if he knew perfectly well what it meant. Apparently it is not easy simply to abandon a part of our conceptual framework.

Recent work in philosophy suggests that, even if we know perfectly well how to use a word, use it unhesitatingly and correctly, and understand others who use it, we may yet be unable to define it completely and explicitly, to *say* what we know. But if that is true of representation, we may not be quite so hopelessly trapped in the verbal morass. For philosophy has produced tools and techniques to deal with such cases—ways of making explicit the inarticulate working knowledge of our language that we all have.

For this purpose I have used some of the methods of that school in contemporary philosophy known variously as "ordinary language philosophy," "Oxford philosophy," or "linguistic analysis," and particularly the work of the late J. L. Austin.[14] That means, first, that I have attended carefully to the way in which we ordinarily use words when we are not philosophizing or wondering about their meanings. It means, further, attending not merely to "representation" itself, but to the entire family of words on the root "represent-," including "representative" (both noun and adjective), "represent," "misrepresent," "misrepresentation," and "representational." And it means attending to fine distinctions between such words and their close synonyms: the difference between representing and symbolizing, or between a representative and an agent. For the borderlines of what "representation" means are set, at least at crucial points, by what we might have said instead but did not—by the available alternatives.

Finally, this method means that, although this is a study in political theory and my interest (like that of most of the theorists discussed) is primarily in political representation, I have looked beyond political contexts to all the areas of human life in which this family of words is used. Behind this approach lies the basic assumption that the various uses of a single family of words are related. Even a new application of a word must make sense to the speakers who use it: they must have a reason for thinking of *that* as an instance of representation. Thus we learn what representation is, not merely from the history of representative government, but also from knowing about representational art, knowing how to pick out a representative example, knowing how an actor represents a character on the stage, knowing how contract law treats the making of representations.

Attention to such nonpolitical contexts is hardly new in the study of representation. Many theorists invoke and develop one or another analogy; indeed, the literature might almost suggest that indiscriminate use of improper analogies has been the cause of all the confusion. Accordingly, some modern commentators have warned against using nonpolitical examples to explain political representation, since "the similarities are mainly verbal."[15] But my assumption has been that analogies and nonpolitical uses of the word are misleading only where they are misused, especially where one analogy or context is taken as definitive, to the exclusion of all others. In that case, we need systematic study and clarification of all the word's uses and the contexts in which it can be used. Such a systematic study has not, to my knowledge, been undertaken before.

This book, however, is not merely a conceptual analysis, an exercise in language philosophy. It attempts to be also, and at the same time, a study in the history of political thought, tracing the treatment of representation by major political theorists. For, with all due attention to its nonpolitical uses, "representation" remains to some extent a technical, political word; and political theorists are still among the most persistent and important "talkers about" it. To be meaningful for political theory, whatever language philosophy can reveal about the concept must be applied to their views and problems.

In philosophy itself, the function of the linguistic analysis of concepts is often taken to be the clearing up of certain characteristic "muddles" or philosophical pseudo-problems arising out of the misuse of ordinary words. Consequently philosophers have disputed about whether, if all terms were properly and completely analyzed, philosophy would disappear. Whatever the merits of that dispute, the situation in political theory is somewhat different. For political theory is not confined to philosophical puzzles; its problems are only partly or sporadically philosophical or conceptual. It may even be that such problems, rather than being the substance of the political theorist's work, only get in the way of that work and confuse it. Thus the removal of these problems might clear the way for progress on other work. In any case, my application of these techniques has not been confined to the identifying of "misuses" or the removing of needless puzzles. Rather, the language-philosophical approach and assumptions pervade my work in a more general way, and are useful at different points for a variety of purposes.

The confused state of representation theory does not seem to me a cause for despair; nor do I think that we should abandon the concept, that it lacks a fixed meaning, is vague, or differs in this regard from our other concepts. It *is* "used in various sense in different connections," but it does not follow that the word can be (correctly) used in various senses in any given connection; in a particular context, the appropriate use of the word may be obligatory. "A varied usage is not the same thing as a vague usage"; quite the opposite: "the need for making distinctions is exactly contrary to the vagueness which results from failure to distinguish."[16] In that case, however, the problem is not to state the correct meaning of the word, but to specify all the varieties of its application to various contexts.

Thus my first working assumption has been that representation does have an identifiable meaning, applied in different but controlled and discoverable ways in different contexts. It is not vague and shifting, but a single, highly complex concept that has not changed much in its basic meaning since the seventeenth century. There is, indeed, no great difficulty about formulating a one-sentence definition of this basic meaning, broad enough to cover all its applications in various contexts. Several commentators have done so, and in that sense one correct definition can be singled out: representation means, as the word's etymological origins indicate, *re-presentation*, a making present again.[17] Except in its earliest use, however, this has always meant more than a literal bringing into presence, as one might bring a book into the room. Rather, representation, taken generally, means the making present *in some sense* of something which is nevertheless *not* present literally or in fact. Now, to say that something is simultaneously both present and not present is to utter a paradox, and thus a fundamental dualism is built into the meaning of representation. It has led some writers—notably a group of German theorists—to regard the term as shrouded in mystery, a *complexio oppositorum*.[18] But there is no need to make mysteries here; we can simply say that in representation something not literally present is considered as present in a nonliteral sense.

Such a formulation directs us toward two further questions: first, in what sense can something be considered as present although in fact it is not? And, second, who is doing the "considering"? On whose view does the existence of representation depend? Hans Wolff has said:

the manner and type of representation depend completely on how it is conceived. The making present of A by [B] is merely a formula; what is important is how that is to be understood, what it means, under what circumstances and assumptions it is possible, and how it is justified. For it is a matter . . . of a mere conceptual construct, particularly a construct of group opinion and ideology. If A is absent, he is not present; he is merely thought, conceived, imputed to be present in [B]. Such a conception can force itself upon one, it can be institutionalized or given by an unquestioned tradition or a general conviction. But there is nothing to prevent anyone denying it, rejecting the group opinion, or being unbelieving.[19]

Since representation is a human idea, it may be asserted or assumed by some and questioned by others. This has led some theorists to a kind of "reductionist realism," to the assertion that representation exists if and only if people believe in it. That is surely true, in a way, but it must not be permitted to obscure further rational inquiry. If one asks which people must believe in political representation for it to exist, writers slip all too easily into the "democratic" answer: the people who are represented, of course. A man is represented if he feels that he is, and not if he does not. This view leads one to concentrate on questions of social psychology: What makes men feel represented—identification? marching bands? voting? I want to ask, rather: When should men feel that they are represented? When would it be correct to say that they are represented? Or again, What would count as evidence that they are represented? It seems likely that men who are in fact represented will feel represented; but they need not, and some may have the illusion of being represented when an objective observer would say that they are not. So I will ask not what *causes* people to have a psychological feeling of being represented, but what *reasons* can be given for supposing someone or something is being represented. This is simply the question of what representation means.

But the single, basic meaning of representation will have very different applications depending on what is being made present or considered present, and in what circumstances. Not just anything can be represented anywhere and when, and being made present in a representative sample is very different from being represented by a symbol on a map. That is why, although it is easy to formulate a single, basic definition, a number of astute theorists have formulated incorrect definitions. And that is also why the single, basic definition is not much help. What we need is not just an accurate definition, but a way of doing justice to the various more detailed applications of representation in various contexts—how the absent thing is made present, and who considers it so.

My second working assumption has been that if *that* can be done, it will account for many of the wide disagreements among theorists about the meaning of representation. For even incorrect theories or definitions are seldom invented out of whole cloth; they are built up, like pearls, around a grain of truth. Only, in philosophy, the grain is valuable; the deposit of pearl around it is what gives trouble. If we discover the grains of truth in the conflicting theories of representation, perhaps they will turn out not to be in conflict after all. Perhaps the theories are incorrect extrapolations from correct beginnings, each based on what representation is like in some particular context. That would help to explain how intelligent writers could disagree about them, and why we are still tempted by their arguments.

We may think of the concept as a rather complicated, convoluted, three-dimensional structure in the middle of a dark enclosure. Political theorists give us, as it were, flash-bulb photographs of the structure taken from different angles. But each proceeds to treat his partial view as the complete structure. It is no wonder, then, that various photographs do not coincide, that the theorists' extrapolations from these pictures are in conflict. Yet there is something there, in the middle in the dark, which all of them are photographing; and the different photographs together can be used to reconstruct it in complete detail. We must determine from which angle each was taken to reconcile the differences among them, and sort out a theorist's extrapolations from his original photograph.[20]

This metaphor suggests why the solution does not lie in presenting one more photograph. Even a correct definition is not much help for what troubles representation theory. What is necessary is to interpret each view by identifying its angle of vision, or (to speak less metaphorically) by identifying the context for which it is correct and exploring the assumptions and implications imposed by that context. This process discloses the meaning of representation as no single definition can, by making explicit the knowledge we already have about how the word is used. And knowing how the word is used is a vital element in knowing what the thing is.

The next five chapters survey some of the main views of the concept that theorists of representation have developed explicitly or used implicitly. A discussion of Thomas Hobbes serves both to introduce his particular view and to demonstrate the difficulties inherent in any such plausible but partial, and hence incorrect, definition. Hobbes' definition is essentially *formalistic*, conceiving of representation in terms of formal arrangements which precede and initiate it: *authorization*, the giving of authority to act. From this view we turn to one which is diametrically opposed, yet equally formalistic, defining representation by certain formal arrangements that follow and terminate it: *accountability*, the holding to account of the representative for his actions. Both these formalistic views take it for granted that representation must be done by human beings; but in chapters 4 and 5 we consider views of representation as a *standing for* rather than an *acting for*, a phenomenon which may be accomplished equally well by inanimate objects. We examine, first, *descriptive* representation, the making present of something absent by resemblance or reflection, as in a mirror or in art; and then *symbolic* representation, in which no resemblance or reflection is required and the connection to what is represented is of a different kind. Each of these kinds of representing by standing for brings with it a corresponding notion of activity, the *making* of a descriptive representation or the *creation* of a symbol. Chapter 6 deals with a view which again links representation with activity—not a making of representations or symbols, but an *acting for* others, and not just the formalistic trappings that surround action, but the substance of the activity itself. The remainder of the book is concerned with problems connected with this view, particularly the controversy over the proper relation between a representative and those for whom he acts. This controversy is introduced in chapters 6 and 7, and further explored in the ideas of Edmund Burke, in Chapter 8; and of Liberalism, in Chapter 9. A concluding chapter then reviews what has been said about this controversy and about the various views of representation, and assesses their meaning in relation to political life.

It is impossible for me to do justice here to the many people who have helped me in the very lengthy development of this book, and of the doctoral dissertation on which it is based. I am deeply grateful to Sheldon S. Wolin, whose ideas have influenced my work beyond measure, and who read and criticized my manuscript with painstaking care. I am equally grateful to Stanley L. Cavell, who introduced me to the new way of doing philosophy, and spent many hours trying to bring clarity and depth to my thinking about representation. I am no less grateful for the help of John H. Schaar, who gave generously of his time and patience, and whose critical sense was invaluable to me. My thanks go also to Thomas P. Jenkin, in whose seminar my attention was first directed to the concept of representation, and who later read parts of this manuscript and made helpful suggestions. I am grateful to the Social Science Research Council for the award of a fellowship which, as William York Tindall says, "enabled me to complete this thing in peace or something like it."[21]

Acknowledgement is gratefully made to the *American Political Science Review* for permission to reproduce, in somewhat altered form, the article which is the basis of Chapter 2; and to Basil Blackwell, Publisher, Oxford, for permission to use passages from *The Federalist*, edited by Max Beloff. Grateful acknowledgement is likewise made for the use of passages reprinted by permission of the publisher from *Burke's Politics*, edited by R. J. S. Hoffman and P. Levack, copyright, 1949 by Alfred A. Knopf, Inc.

2

The Problem
of Thomas Hobbes

If philosophy begins in wonder, a discussion of the concept of representation had better start by giving the reader something to wonder about. And there is no better way to do so than to begin with the first extended and systematic discussion of representation in English. That discussion, by the seventeenth-century British political theorist, Thomas Hobbes, raises most of the interesting questions about representation, and reveals enough of its difficulties to initiate some serious wondering.

Hobbes is not usually thought of as a representation theorist. Very few of the classical commentaries on his thought even acknowledge that he mentions the word, and the index to Molesworth's standard edition of Hobbes' English works contains no reference to it.[1] Yet representation plays a central role in Hobbes' main political work, and he brings to bear on the concept all the power of his lucid vision and intellectual rigor. The view he develops is both temptingly plausible and peculiarly deficient. Because it is plausible, it has tempted other astute thinkers since Hobbes' time and can tempt us as well. Because it is deficient, it can be used as a springboard into a more extended study of what representation is and means.

Hobbes' discussion of representation is confined almost entirely to chapter 16 of his major work, *Leviathan*. Thus the context is one of political rather than, say, esthetic thought. The *Leviathan* is the last of three works of political theory whose argument in other respects runs closely parallel; yet only in the *Leviathan* is representation introduced.[2] Hobbes' analysis of the concept was a discovery for him, a discovery which fitted into the structure of a difficult political-philosophical argument he had formulated twice before; and it seemed to him to enhance and strengthen that structure.

In chapter 16 of the *Leviathan*, called "Of Persons, Authors and Things Personated," Hobbes' analysis of representation proceeds from the notion of a person, to a distinction between "natural" and "artificial" persons, and finally to the classifying of a representative as a kind of artificial person.[3] We are not simply to equate "person" with "human being," for the chapter begins: "A person, is he, whose words and actions are considered either as his own or as representing the words or actions of an other man, or of any other thing, to whom they are attributed, whether truly or by fiction."[4] A person, then, is a "he" with words and actions, so that one can speak of his ("whose") words and actions. A person is a thing that we may observe speaking words or performing actions. But we do not always consider the words we hear spoken or the actions we observe performed as "his own"; sometimes we consider them as representing the words or actions of someone or something else.

Hobbes distinguishes two kinds of persons to correspond to these two possibilities: natural and artificial. A natural person is one whose words and actions are considered his own; a feigned or artificial person is one whose words and actions are considered those of someone else. Some if not all artificial persons are representatives; so it is important to understand what Hobbes has to say about the artificial person. The modern reader is liable to a confusion (to which some commentators have succumbed) as to just what is "artificial" about an artificial person.[5] Modern legal terminology distinguishes between natural persons, that is, human beings, and fictitious persons like corporations. A corporation, although not a human being, may be treated like one in law: it may be sued in court, and it is responsible for the authorized actions of its officers. But this is not the way in which

Hobbes draws the distinction. If the treasurer of a corporation, acting in his official capacity, makes out a check, we would regard him as a natural person, and the corporation as an artificial one responsible for his action. But for Hobbes the treasurer would be an artificial person, his actions "owned" by the corporation. In modern legal terminology the fictive element in the idea of a fictitious person is that a group of men associated by a legal agreement are (like) a human being. In Hobbes' terminology the fiction or artifice about an artificial person is that the actions he is performing are not (considered) his own but those of someone else.

But this seems an odd thing to say. What can it mean to say that sometimes a person's words and actions are not considered his own? When are someone's actions not his own? When might we spontaneously say such a thing?

One does talk that way sometimes about words; so perhaps that is the place to begin. A student who mouths phrases he has memorized, but the meaning of which he obviously does not understand, may be admonished to put it in his own words. Thus sometimes a man's words are not his own; he has spoken them, but the work of composition was done by Hegel and not by this sophomore student. Or we may treat a speaker's ideas in this way: a radio commentary may be preceded by the disclaimer, "The views expressed are the speaker's own, and do not necessarily reflect the views of our sponsor." Here the intent seems to be to underline the sponsor's refusal to take responsibility for what is said.

But is there a corresponding notion for action? A person under hypnosis does what he is ordered to do by the hypnotist. A person "possessed" by the devil or by spirits does their bidding. A puppet goes through certain motions in response to the pull of the strings. But in none of these cases would one really say "his actions are not his own." One might say that his actions were not under his own control, or that he did not know what he was doing, or that he performed them not of his own volition. In the case of the puppet it might be denied that he was performing actions at all.

When are our actions not our own? When does one say of

any object or concept, X, "His X is not his own" or "My X is not my own"? Even such a formulation is rare, but it does occur when the context supplies some sense of the possessive other than ownership, to contrast with it. "His house is not his own" might mean the house in which he lives belongs to someone else. "Since I took this job, my life is not my own"; I live the life, but I have no rights of ownership, no choice or control over what I do. A boy who shares the family pet with the other children may complain, "Gee, I wish I had a dog of my own." He has the use of a dog, but not the exclusive rights and prerogatives that ownership would bring. In the situation above, where the student's words were not his own, this criterion is fulfilled. They were his words in the sense that he spoke them, but not his own in the sense that he did not invent the sentences he used and should not be credited with them.

One would suppose that Hobbes has this sort of thing in mind with regard to actions. "My" things are not "my own" if I have possession of them but they are owned by someone else, or, conversely, if I have technical ownership but no practical control. My words are not my own if what comes out of my mouth is someone else's composition. Then, presumably, my actions are not my own if what I am seen to be doing is—what? owned by someone else? composed by someone else? Apparently Hobbes is thinking as if there were something which is related to actions as ownership is to property, or authorship is to groups of words.

The analogous idea for actions is authority, which Hobbes defines as the right to perform the action.

That which in speaking of goods and possessions, is called an owner, and in latine dominus, in Greek κύριος, speaking of actions, is called author. And as the right of possession, is called dominion; so the right of doing any action, is called AUTHORITY. So that by authority is always understood a right of doing any act; and done by authority, done by commission, or license from him whose right it is.[6]

And much later in the *Leviathan* Hobbes writes, "for every act done, is the act of him, without whose consent it is invalid."[7]

Hobbes calls the man who actually performs an action the "actor," and the one by whose authority he acts, who gave him

the right to act, the "author." The idea seems to be that when
we see someone perform an action, just as when we see someone driving an automobile, we do not yet know who "owns"
that action or that automobile. The man who owns the automobile is the one who paid for it and in whose name it is
registered. The man who owns the action is the author, the one
who authorized it, who had the right to do it, without whose
consent it is invalid. The owner of an automobile may drive it
himself, or he may turn it over to someone else to drive, or it
may be driven without his knowledge or permission. Similarly,
the man who has the right to perform an action may perform
it himself, or he may authorize someone to do so, or someone
may perform the action without the right to do so, through
fraud or pretense.

A person, then, is a performer of actions or speaker of words,
like the driver of a car. But the question of ownership—of the
action or the vehicle—remains open. Explicitly, Hobbes defines
both in terms of having a right: the "right of ownership" over the
car, the right to perform the action. But if we consider the kind
of situation in which it becomes important who owns a car, we
see that there is more to ownership than rights. An equally important aspect is responsibility, as for damage caused by the
car. And the responsibilities of ownership are relevant to actions
as well. It is in this sense that one "owns up to" a misdeed.
Hobbes is very much interested in the responsibility borne by
the owner of an action. As soon as he has asserted the parallel
between authority and ownership, he makes a sudden jump from
the rights to the responsibilities involved. The former passage
closes: "So that by authority, is always understood a right of
doing any act; and *done by authority*, done by commission, or
license from him whose right it is."[8] The text then continues:
"From hence it followeth, that when the actor maketh a covenant by authority, he bindeth thereby the author, no less than
if he had made it himself; and no less subjecteth him to all the
consequences of the same." Not only is it the author who is
bound by any covenant made on his authority; but he is responsible also for any breaches of the law of nature he has authorized:
"When an actor doth any thing against the law of nature by

command of the author, if he be obliged by former covenant to obey him, not he, but the author breaketh the law of nature; for though the action be against the law of nature; yet it is not his."[9] The action is not his because it is owned by the author.

There is a significant passage at the end of the chapter: "Of authors there be two sorts. The first simply so called; which I have before defined to be him, that owneth the action of another simply. The second is he, that owneth the action, or covenant of another conditionally; that is to say, he undertaketh to do it, if the owner doth it not, at, or before a certain time. And these authors conditional, are generally called SURETYES."[10] If we interpret this passage according to Hobbes' explicit definitions, ownership of actions is authority, which is the right to do the action. Then this passage would refer to situations in which a man has the right to perform a certain action only if someone else does not do it (by a certain time). There are such situations, but this passage is clearly not about them, nor would we call such a man a surety. This passage concerns conditional ownership in the sense of conditional *responsibility*; it concerns not the right to act but the obligation to act.

Hobbes recognizes two aspects of authority, or what it means to own an action. He defines it as the right to perform the action, but apparently regards it equally as responsibility for the action (as if one had done it oneself). This duality is reflected in two alternative ways of describing the authorization process. Sometimes Hobbes speaks as if a man who has the right to do an action commissions someone else to do it for him. At other times, Hobbes describes a man making himself owner of, making himself responsible for, what someone else is going to do.[11] In both situations the rights and privileges accrue to the one who is authorized, the obligations and responsibilities to the one who authorizes. It follows that representation is such a relationship of rights and responsibilities, for a representative is an artificial person: "to personate, is to act, or represent himself or another; and he that acteth another, is said to bear his person, or act in his name; . . . and is called in divers occasions, diversly; as a representer, or representative, a lieutenant, a vicar, an attorney, a deputy, a procurator, an actor, and the like."[12]

The fact that Hobbes' definition places all the rights at the representative's disposal and all the burdens on the represented is partially obscured by a distinction he draws between limited and unlimited authorization. But careful study of the distinction shows that it leaves his fundamental position unchanged: the representative, as such, is free. Hobbes says that men may give authority either "without stint" or in limited amounts, restricting the representative "in what, and how far, he shall represent them."[13] Thus it is possible to talk about limits on, or standards for, what a representative may do, even within the Hobbesian system. But they are always limits of the *ultra vires* kind, the limits on what he *can* do as representative. Outside the limits he simply does not represent. Within the limits he represents, and this *means* that he has a special right and no special obligations; someone else bears the responsibility for his action. In the Hobbesian system it is possible sometimes to authorize without limitations, creating a total representative, who in every sense and any situation may do as he pleases and bind you with his action.

But the pattern of bound author and free actor is only the most general one in Hobbes' analysis. A number of variations on this theme are possible, and it is in the variations that the difficulties of the Hobbesian definition begin to emerge. The variations concern certain special kinds of artificial persons: the guardian, the fraud, the stage actor. Hobbes says of artificial persons that "some have their words and actions owned by those whom they represent. And then the person is the actor; and he that owneth his words and actions, is the author: in which case the actor acteth by authority."[14] Some artificial persons fit this basic model; what of the rest? Unfortunately, Hobbes never follows up on that "some" explicitly; so whatever else can be said must be inferred from his argument. Reviewing what we know about artificial persons so far, we have:

A person, is he whose words and actions are considered either as his own, or as representing the words and actions of an other man, or of any other thing, to whom they are attributed, whether truly or by fiction.

And when they are considered as representing the words and actions of another, then is he a feigned or artificial person.

Of persons artificial, some have their words and actions owned by those whom they represent.

If we take these passages literally, there are only two possibilities for the remaining artificial persons, those whose actions are neither their own nor owned by those whom they represent. Either their actions are owned and authorized by someone other than the one they represent, or their actions are not authorized by anyone other than themselves. Both categories exist in the Hobbesian system, and both raise difficulties.

The actions of some artificial persons are authorized not by the one they represent but by a third party. This is the case with the representatives of inanimate objects or irrational beings. Hobbes writes: "There are few things, that are incapable of being represented by fiction. Inanimate things, as a church, an hospital, a bridge, may be personated by a rector, master or overseer. . . . Likewise children, fooles and mad-men that have no use of reason, may be personated by guardians, or curators."[15] But inanimate objects, children, and madmen cannot be authors and cannot authorize, because they "have no use of reason." Rationality is crucial here for Hobbes: one can be obliged only if he is capable of knowing his obligation and capable of having sufficient motive to perform the action it prescribes.[16] Both of these conditions presuppose rationality; in its absence one cannot be obligated, and hence cannot enter into valid agreements, like the authorization of a representative. Someone who cannot be held responsible for his own acts cannot assume responsibility for the acts of another. When inanimate objects, children, or lunatics are represented, therefore, authority must come from elsewhere. Although inanimate objects cannot authorize their actors, "yet the actors may have authority to procure their maintenance, given them by those that are owners, or governors of those things. . . . Likewise children, fooles and mad-men . . . can be no authors . . . yet . . . he that hath right of governing them, may give authority to the guardian."[17]

Such situations apparently are examples of representation by fiction. ("There are few things, that are uncapable of being represented by fiction.") What fiction is it that Hobbes speaks of here? It cannot be merely the fiction which is operative in every case where an artificial person acts: the fiction that his

actions are not his own. But it may be related to the fiction referred to in the definition of a person. There Hobbes says the
attribution of an action may occur "truly or by fiction." The
case of the representation of inanimate objects suggests the
following interpretation: when a person's actions are considered
as truly representing those of another, it is because the latter has
authorized them. And when a person's actions are considered
those of another by fiction, it is because a third party, someone
other than the person who is represented, has authorized them.

But why, in such a case, should we say that the artificial person represents the inanimate object, the child, or the lunatic?
Why should he not be considered simply the representative of
the man who authorized him, of the "owner or governor" of the
object, child, or lunatic? We have here two situations. In one
situation a man who happens to be the owner or director of a
hospital, say, authorizes someone to represent him personally;
the latter becomes representative of the director. In the other
situation the same man authorizes someone to represent the
hospital; the latter becomes representative of the hospital. In
both situations control over the action, the doing of the action,
is in the hands of one or both of those men. In both situations
responsibility for the action and obligations arising out of it rest
on the author. (And in neither situation is the author the hospital, since inanimate things cannot be authors.) What difference
is there between the two cases to justify the differing ways in
which we would describe who is represented? Nothing in Hobbes'
explicit analysis of authorization can account for the difference,
yet clearly there is one.

To account for this difference, we might want to argue that
children and hospitals can have rights and obligations after all.
Then the representative of a hospital is someone who can incur
obligations for it, spend its funds; and the representative of the
hospital director is someone who can spend that man's personal
funds. From such an argument Hobbes has cut himself off by
maintaining that the obligations arising out of an action always
fall on the author, and that inanimate objects cannot be authors.
But we might also want to say that the two representatives are
supposed, expected, obligated to do different things. The one
should look after the interest or welfare of the hospital; the other,

after the interest or welfare of its director. And this suggestion does find an echo in Hobbes; for the authority given to the representatives of inanimate objects or children is "authority *to procure their maintenance*."

This example from Hobbes' own text cannot be fully explained on the basis of his account of representation. Given Hobbes' assumptions, the only way to explain the difference between the representative of a hospital and the representative of the hospital's director is that they are supposed to do different things, procure different maintenances. This suggests that something is missing from Hobbes' definition, something related to what a representative is supposed to do, whose interest he is supposed to pursue. We shall return to this problem.

Besides the artificial persons authorized by someone other than the one they represent (by a third party), there are artificial persons who are not authorized by anyone but themselves. This may at first seem paradoxical, since if they are authors of their own actions they must be natural persons by definition. But such a category nevertheless exists for Hobbes. They are persons who, in one way or another, pretend to be authorized by someone else, but in fact are not. This suggests an alternative interpretation of the assertion that we may attribute a person's action to someone else "truly or by fiction." It may be that when the actor is authorized we attribute his action to another truly; but when he is not, we attribute it by fiction.

The simplest and most obvious example of an unauthorized artificial person of this kind is the fraud or swindler. A contract made by an authorized representative obliges the author as if he had signed it himself. But if someone fraudulently pretends to have authority, and so makes a contract with a third party, then of course the alleged author is not bound by it. "When the authority is feigned, it obligeth the actor only."[18]

But Hobbes introduces a further troubling example—that of the stage actor, who is in certain respects like the swindler, but whose case fits neither the standard author-actor pattern nor either of the variations. The stage actor is introduced when Hobbes uses the familiar theme of fiction or artifice to say something more about what a person is. Since a person performs actions or does things, he is an actor; but an actor is also some-

one who appears on the stage in a play, and there the element
of fiction or artifice is very evident.

Etymologically, Hobbes argues, "person" derives from the
Latin *persona*, which "signifies the disguise, or outward appearance of a man, counterfeited on the stage; and sometimes more
particularly that part of it, which disguiseth the face, as a mask
or vizard."[19] Like a mask on the stage, the person performing an
action may not be "real"; that is, he may be only a "front" for
the one who is the real "owner" of the action. The implication is
that the person performing the action, like a mask on the stage,
is always a false front; but sometimes the face behind the mask
is the same one that the mask depicts. "So that a person, is the
same that an actor is, both on the stage and in common conversation; and to personate, is to act, or represent *himself, or
another*."[20] In this last statement Hobbes finds the same duality
in yet a third word, "represent." First, a person is a human being
in ordinary conversation, but, at least etymologically, a person
is a mask. Second, an actor is one who performs actions but
also an actor is a performer on the stage ("perform" itself follows
this dual usage, although Hobbes does not exploit it). But, third,
"to personate is to act or *represent* himself or another." The
actor represents a character on the stage; the man who acts
represents someone in ordinary life. We might say that the latter
is true only when a man acts in his capacity as representative of
someone else. Hobbes is suggesting that every act is an act of
representation—if not of someone else, then of oneself.[21]

Hobbes chooses to illustrate the Latin use of *persona* by a
quotation from Cicero: "he that acteth another, is said to bear
his person, or act in his name; in which sense Cicero useth it
where he says, *Unus sustineo tres personas; mei, adversarii, et
judicis*: I bear three persons; my own, my adversary's and the
judge's."[22] This passage, although Hobbes (who seldom cites
his sources) does not tell us so, is from Cicero's essay "On the
Character of the Orator," in which he lets Antony describe his
technique for preparing to argue a legal case. First, says Antony,
he hears his client's story in private, and presents his opponent's
case to him to draw out all the details and discover inconsisten-
cies. "Itaque cum ille discessit, tres personas unus sustineo
summa animi aequitate, meam, adversarii, iudicis." He plays

three roles, or imagines himself in three roles, in order to see what arguments and questions would occur to each: himself, his adversary, and the judge. He puts himself in their places, like the detective trying to outguess the criminal by asking himself, "What would I do if I were he?"

The use of *persona* here is a little wider than as a mask or visard, or even the disguise or outward appearance of a man on the stage. Antony pretends to be his adversary and his judge, not on the stage but to himself. Mentally he puts on their masks. And he may, indeed, assume a typical stance or facial expression of the man he is "playing" to aid himself psychologically in identifying, in imagining the other's thoughts and arguments. But what is the connection or relationship between what Antony does in preparing a case, what an actor does on the stage, and what a representative does? Recall the context in which Cicero's Antony entered the discussion. Hobbes had said "person" derives from *persona*, and that therefore a person is an actor in both senses of the word, and "he that acteth another is said to bear his person, or act in his name; in which sense Cicero. . . ." Does Antony act in the name of adversary and judge? Surely not; they do not even know of his little charade, and it will not have "official" consequences, as an action in the name of a judge might have. Does Antony bear the persons of adversary and judge? Perhaps. This phrase is more difficult, since it is no longer in common usage. Certainly we can agree that he "acteth another," if only to himself, mentally, in the same metaphorical sense as (above) he puts on a mask.

Cicero's Antony, an actor on the stage, and a representative are all artificial persons to Hobbes, while they perform those specific actions. By definition, this means that their actions are considered not their own but those of someone or something else. But the only concept of ownership of actions Hobbes has given us refers to authority to perform the action—the right to do it, and responsibility for it. Surely this does not apply to a stage actor or to Antony "bearing three persons." No one has authorized their actions, neither the person(s) they represent nor any third party.

Could one argue that they are self-authorized, that their authority is feigned, like that of a fraud or swindler? It is tempting

to do so, for the element of artifice is similar, and Hobbes may
well have assumed such an argument. But it simply is not true
that the stage actor and the legal agent both pretend to something
which is false for the one and true for the other. There are, of
course, situations in which a man pretends to be authorized when
he is not; and we may compare such an activity to what goes on
in a theater performance. A good actor, for instance, might be
more successful at such deception than a poor one.

But such a situation is noticeably different from what ordinarily goes on on the stage, or when someone is acting a part.
Ordinarily the actor in a play does not claim or even pretend to
be the authorized representative of anyone. He does not pretend
to act on authority of Hamlet, but to *be* Hamlet. His entire manner and appearance are directed to creating the illusion that he
is someone else, someone whom he is playing or, as we say,
representing on the stage. Conversely, an authorized representative does not, under ordinary circumstances, pretend to *be* the
person he represents. The agent of the king does not dress or
behave like the king, or try to pass himself off as his royal majesty. The West-coast representative of a national corporation
does not try to pass himself off as that corporation itself. Nor, of
course, does a Congressman pretend to be a large number of
citizens. Thus Hobbes' definition of the ownership of actions
and of authority seems too narrow; again his examples require
more than he says explicitly.

What would be a more satisfactory account of Hobbes' own
example of a theater performance? There is, surely, a sense in
which the actions of a performer on the stage are to be considered "not his own." This seems to mean that there are re-
strictions on his actions, or expectations to which he conforms.
His actions are not his own because they are not characteristic
of him, do not express his own feelings or manners. He is deliberately conforming to the playwright's script and to his role.
One may say that his words are not his own but Shakespeare's;
more frequently one would say that his words and actions are not
his own but Hamlet's. The role is an external standard for the
actor even if it is self-imposed (as it usually is), even though
the actor himself helped shape the role, or even if the actor himself wrote the play.

The actor "represents" someone on the stage, and his actions are not his own but someone else's, in a sense different from any of those in Hobbes' account of authorization. The stage actor's situation is defined not by prior giving of right or accepting of responsibility, nor by pretense to these, but by the content and manner of what he does and how he acts. This is seen even more clearly in the example of Antony's situation as portrayed by Cicero. Of course it is Antony who acts, and he is neither authorized nor pretending to be. And he could put any words or thoughts he liked into the mouths of his adversary and judge while he played them; he is alone and no one cares about his fantasies. But to achieve his purpose of preparing an effective legal argument, he must play these men well, play them as they are. He must think as they would think, fit his actions and words to the external but self-imposed standard of their character and reactions.

Hobbes comes back to the passage from Cicero in his "Letter to Bishop Bramhall," while defining "person" for a theological argument.[23] He appends the following explanation to the citation: "In the same sense we use the word [person] in English vulgarly, calling him that acteth by his own authority, his own person, and him that acteth by the authority of another, the person of that other." The American reader should be reminded here of the British usage, "He's not his own man." or the terming of a servant or vassal as, "———'s man."[24] But here again the defining element in the situation is not, as Hobbes alleges, who has the right to act and who is responsible for the action. or at least not primarily. The crucial element is who has control over the action. He is not his own man—why? Because he is not free to do as he likes, or because he has been well paid or otherwise brought into line to do someone else's bidding.

A further aspect of the ownership of actions thus emerges from a study of some of Hobbes' examples; it is an aspect involving control over action, or limitation on it. Apparently Hobbes sometimes defines representation by the way in which an action is performed, or by standards or expectations to which it must conform, rather than by any agreement concerning the right to do it or responsibility for it. This additional aspect of representation was seen first in the account of the representation

of inanimate objects; now it reappears in the discussion of stage
acting and of Antony preparing his legal argument.

This aspect of ownership may be found in almost all the examples used in our earlier abstract discussion of ownership as
distinct from possession. The "views expressed are the speaker's
own." Hence the sponsor should not be held responsible for
them, but why not? Because the speaker is the only one who has
sufficient control over what he says. Or, again, the boy who
wants a dog of his own and the man who complains that his life
is no longer his own are seeking the control and the freedom
which go with ownership. The same element exists in the concept of authority. For an author is not only someone with authority, who can authorize; he is also the one who writes or
composes or originates something—who controls its development
or outcome or final form.[25] When a student is admonished to put
something he has just parroted by rote, into his own words, it
is the act of authorship that was missing. The author of an action,
like the author of a book, is the one to whom credit or blame
accrues. Surely it is because he wrote and created the book, or
planned and controlled the action.

Nor is the Hobbesian notion of limited authorization any help
here. The stage actor and Antony have no elaborately limited
authority, nor do they pretend to have it. Authority, rights, and
responsibilities are irrelevant to the way (sense) in which they
represent. Similarly, in representing inanimate objects, children,
or lunatics, limited authorization is no help. One can imagine a
man giving limited authority to someone to "procure the maintenance" of an incompetent. But this does not explain why he is
then the representative of the incompetent instead of the
(limited) representative of the person who authorized him.

These examples suggest the inadequacy of the Hobbesian
definition, and point toward the nature of this inadequacy. Representing does not mean merely acting with authority from another. There may be such relationships, but they are not what
representation is normally like, and they are not what "representation" means. Although Hobbes defines it in this way, his
own use of the word does not always conform to the definition.

The use which Hobbes makes of representation in the political
argument of the *Leviathan* further substantiates what has been

said so far.[26] Hobbes, for the most part, uses the term in accord with his definition; yet at crucial points his argument takes advantage of those aspects of representation which the definition omits.

The *Leviathan* attempts to explain and justify political obligation, and to do so in so firm and unequivocal a manner, as to leave no possibility of anarchy, rebellion, revolt, or civil war. Hobbes begins with an examination of what the world would be like (is like?) in the absence of political obligation, in the absence of civil society, in man's "natural condition." What becomes crucial, therefore, is the transition from this state of nature to "civil society," in which government and political obligation exist.

Having once postulated man into the state of nature, it is no easy thing to get him out of it into civil society. The very characteristics which define the absence of society seem to make its founding virtually impossible. For the state of nature is to Hobbes a state of war, the struggle of each man with every other for survival. There is no mutually recognized authority, no mutual trust. Obligation is not completely absent, for man is bound by the law of nature, which dictates self-preservation and all that logically follows from it. Thus man is obliged even in the state of nature to "endeavor peace"—that is, to act peacefully whenever he can do so safely, to make a contract if he can, to keep his contracts when he can do so safely.[27] But such opportunities are relatively rare in the state of nature, and self-preservation will usually imply striking first, looking after one's own needs, and trusting no one.

To get men out of this situation Hobbes uses not only the device of the social contract but also (as is less frequently recognized) his concept of representation. Men create a commonwealth by contracting each with every other, to authorize one among them to represent them all.

A commonwealth is said to be instituted, when a multitude of men do agree, and covenant, every one with every one, that to whatsoever man, or assembly of men, shall be given by the major part, the right to present the person of them all, that is to say, to be their representative; every one . . . shall authorize all the actions and judgments, of that man, or assembly of men, in the same manner, as if they were his own.[28]

This action welds the multitude of men who make the contracts and do the authorizing into a single, lasting whole, "the person of them all." The sovereign represents that single, public person; indeed, it is because he represents it that it can be considered a unit.

A multitude of men, are made *one* person, when they are by one man, or one person, represented; so that it be done with the consent of every one of the multitude in particular. For it is the *unity* of the representer, not the *unity* of the represented, that maketh the person *one*. And it is the representer that beareth the person, and but one person; and *unity*, cannot otherwise be understood in multitude.[29]

The authorization given to the sovereign is unlimited; anything he does is to be taken as done by his subjects; and any decision he makes is binding on them. Each man who contracts "authorizes *all* the actions and judgments" of the representative "as if they were his own."

At one point Hobbes does seem to imply that the authorization given to the sovereign representative is not unlimited, for he says that the subjects acknowledge themselves to be authors of what the representative says and does "*in those things* which concern the common peace and safety; and *therein* to submit their wills, every one to his will."[30] But Hobbes makes it abundantly clear that the sovereign is the only judge on earth of what things concern "the common peace and safety." And most of the time he says explicitly, as in the last passage but one quoted above, that the subjects authorize all the sovereign's actions, that his authority has no bounds, and that he is "their representative unlimited."[31]

Thus there are no limits on the actions of the sovereign as representative; anything he chooses to do binds his subjects as if they had chosen it themselves. This is merely an application of the authorization definition. But, although the subjects have no claim on their representative, have committed themselves to him totally in advance, the sovereign nevertheless does have duties, which he must interpret in the light of his own conscience, and for which he is responsible to God. In the first place he has all the duties to obey the law of nature which any man in the state of nature has. For the sovereign has contracted with no one, and remains himself in the state of nature. But Hobbes goes on to say that some of the sovereign's duties derive from the purposes for which his subjects formed civil society and authorized him. "The office of the sovereign, be it a monarch, or an assembly, consisteth in the end, for which he was trusted with the sovereign power, namely the procuration of the *safety of the people*; to which he is obliged by the law of nature, and to render an account thereof to God, the author of that law, and to none but him."[32]

Hobbes is not saying that the sovereign's authorization extends only to actions which promote the safety of the people, that his authorization is limited. Rather, the sovereign is, like all men, subject to the law of nature, which commands men to found and maintain civil society and to endeavor peace whenever it is safe and possible to do so. But a sovereign is a man in a very powerful position, whose actions will have great consequences for the life or death of the commonwealth, and whose safety is more secure than that of most men. Hence, if one happens to have the "office" of sovereign, one's obligation under the law of nature becomes greatly enlarged in scope, because there is much more one can safely do. The important point to recognize is that the duties of the sovereign are his duties qua sovereign and not qua representative. A Hobbesian representative cannot have duties qua representative; if he does something outside his authorization he is not representing at all, but has exceeded the limits. And the sovereign's authorization has no limits.

Consequently, although the sovereign has duties, they are not duties *to* his subjects, and a subject can never justifiably disobey or criticize his sovereign on the grounds that the latter is violating his duty. Hobbes supports this allegation with the argument that the sovereign has no obligation to the subjects. The only way in which he could have acquired an obligation to other people (as distinct from obligations to God) is by covenanting. And he has not covenanted; he has only been the beneficiary of the covenants among his subjects.[33]

But even if the sovereign had obligations to his subjects in this sense, he could never commit a breach of them, because the subjects have authorized in advance all he shall do. They have agreed that his actions shall be regarded as their own, as if they

had done them. So, if they were later to complain about something he did, or refuse to obey one of his commands, they would
be complaining of themselves or refusing themselves. This is
the point of Hobbes' famous dictum that the criminal is author
of his own punishment; his punishment, then, can be no injury
to him. Hobbes uses "injury" here to mean a wrong, a breach
of obligation, and not mere physical harm, which he calls "damage."

> For he that doth any thing by authority from another, doth
> therein no injury to him by whose authority he acteth: But by
> this institution of a commonwealth, every particular man is
> author of all the sovereign doth; and consequently he that com-
> plaineth of injury from his sovereign, complaineth of that whereof
> he himself is author; and therefore ought not to accuse any man
> but himself; no nor himself of injury; because to do injury to
> one's self, is impossible.[34]

In particular, the sovereign cannot default on any obligation to
his subjects, because the very act of ignoring the obligation
would release him from it, since the subjects have agreed that
he shall will for them.

> Whatsoever is done to a man, conformable to his own will
> signified to the doer, is no injury to him. For if he that doeth it,
> hath not passed away his original right to do what he please, by
> some antecedent covenant, there is no breach of covenant; and
> therefore no injury done him. And if he have; then his will to
> have it done being signified, is a release of that covenant: and so
> again there is no injury done him.[35]

Authorization constitutes such a signification of will; since the
sovereign wills for his subjects, all his actions are "conformable
to" their wills. Thus he can never be guilty of neglecting an obligation to his subjects.[36]

Now this kind of paradoxical argument—that a sovereign
has duties which no man can claim against him—is always in
danger of being misunderstood in one direction or the other.
Hobbes is always at pains to emphasize that the subjects have
no claim on the sovereign. It is apparent that every time he
mentions that the sovereign has duties, he invites such a claim
and must then refute it. Yet the danger of misunderstandings in
the opposite direction is equally great. The literature of Hobbism

abounds with critics who argue that a sovereign bound by duty
which his subjects cannot claim, is not bound at all, that the
duties of Hobbes' sovereign are mere sophistry. Hobbes wants
to emphasize the duties of the sovereign because they demonstrate the desirability and general benefit of his rule; at the same
time, the security basic to his system would be shaken if subjects
could presume to judge or even to question the acts of the
sovereign.

Representation does not do away with the difficulty of conveying this idea, or the danger of misunderstanding, but it helps to
some extent. For representation implies standards for, or limits
on, the conduct of the representative. When Hobbes calls his
sovereign a representative, he implies that the man is to *represent*
his subjects, not merely do whatever he pleases. The concept
itself contains the idea that the sovereign has duties. At the same
time, Hobbes' definition of representation—the one-sided assumption of obligations by the man who is represented—ensures
that in the last analysis these duties cannot be claimed. By referring to the definition of authorization, Hobbes could defeat any
allegation that subjects might resist the sovereign if he did not
represent them as he should. Indeed, within the framework of
Hobbes' explicit definition, there is no such thing as not representing a person as one should.

Not only does the term "representative" remind the reader
that the sovereign has duties, but it has certain implications for
the nature or content of those duties. The implications again derive from those very aspects of representation which Hobbes
omitted from his definition. Hobbes does say that it is part of the
sovereign's duties to look after the safety of the people, and this
seems to be related to one aspect of what we expect from a representative. In chapter 16 of the *Leviathan*, the representative of a
child or madman or inanimate object is said to be authorized to
"procure their maintenance." And this standard for his conduct is
what distinguishes the representative of a child, authorized by
its guardian, from the personal representative of that guardian.
It can be argued that the duties of the sovereign, although they
do not derive from his authorization, nevertheless correspond
to "procuring the maintenance" of his subjects, at least in a
general way.

Calling the sovereign a representative arouses other expectations in the reader which the Hobbesian system does not fulfill. When we look at the Hobbesian political structure as a whole we are most aware of how partial, formal, and empty of substance his concept of representation is. A sovereign given complete power in perpetuity, with no obligation to consult the wishes of his subjects and no duties toward them which they can claim—surely nothing could be farther from what we ordinarily think of as representation or representative government! We read the *Leviathan* and feel that somehow we have been tricked.[37]

Indeed, some commentators argue that this was actually Hobbes' intention, that representation was part of Hobbes' "public theme," to deceive the foolish multitude and mislead the casual reader.[38] The casual reader would be deluded into thinking he was really getting representation; only the wise few might penetrate this façade to Hobbes' true position. Other commentators attribute no evil motives, but regard the disparity between claim and fulfillment in Hobbes' system as a sign of failure, occurring despite his "feeble efforts . . . to keep alive the representation on which the original contract was based."[39]

In one sense, representation does function for Hobbes as a "persuasive definition."[40] By calling the sovereign a representative, he implies that the sovereign will in fact represent—take care of, consult—his subjects. True, this implication is vitiated by the authorization definition Hobbes gives, but it is there nevertheless.[41] By labeling his political system representation, Hobbes suggests that it has good or desirable attributes. This is not a redirection of our attitudes apart from the meaning of the concept; quite the opposite, it is because we know what representation means that we are attracted to a political system based on it. Had Hobbes merely reiterated that his sovereign is "good, and good for you," he might have affected some attitudes, but he could not have invoked the special information about the sovereign that is implied by calling him a representative.[42]

It might be that Hobbes, wishing to advocate political absolutism out of an excessive fear of anarchy, cleverly gave a partial definition of representation and used it in his argument to deceive. But he may have believed his definition to be complete and correct. Any number of theorists since Hobbes have adopted an authorization definition very much like his. Are they, too, trying to mislead?

It seems to me more likely that Hobbes was sincere in thinking that he really had grasped the nature of the concept. His definition is not so much false as incomplete. It stresses only the formal aspects of what it means to represent someone; but the formal aspects are often very important. They are, for example, the very heart of the law of agency. A legal agent represents just to the extent that his actions are binding on his principal as if the principal himself had acted. When we deal with agency, this is the aspect of representation that seems central. In other contexts it may seem more important whether the representative has been acting in such a way that he deserves to be called a representative, apart from whether the principal is technically bound. This is what happens to most modern readers of the *Leviathan*; they suddenly want to say, "Oh, well, call the sovereign a representative if you like, but it's sheer hypocrisy. He doesn't really represent the people at all."

There is something ironic about Hobbes' use of the concept in his political argument: the very problems that he solves formally, on a logical plane, by his authorization view, can be solved empirically by the aspects of representation he overlooked. At least they can be solved in some measure in a practical way, but this was not enough for Hobbes.

Hobbes set himself the problem of creating a lasting union out of a multitude of separate men with separate conflicting wills. He made this a formal problem, and solved it with his theory of representation. But behind this verbal game lies a real problem of the creation of political consensus, the peaceful settlement of disputes, the development of community. In the solution of these actual political problems, representation (in its full sense) can play an important part. Hobbes was troubled by the people's inability to give their sovereign sufficient power to terrify them into conformity. The authorization view of representation helped solve this formal problem. But behind the formal problem lies the real need to enlist the capacities of citizens for positive political action, the problem of participation, the problem of creating motives for obedience and coöperation with a government. Here again representative institutions can make a contribution, and have sometimes done so. Behind Hobbes' logical formulae lies the practical difference between being ruled by one's own representative(s) and being ruled by some other authority.

But the help that real representation gives in solving political problems is contingent. It is uncertain; it does not always succeed; it cannot eliminate conflict, but can at most provide a structure for solving conflict. Hobbes set his goals much higher: he sought the logical or deductive guarantee of unity and peace. For this purpose, the authorization view is much more suitable. Whether he adopted the definition to serve his political argument, or introduced representation because he genuinely thought this is what it meant, the concept and the political theory are correlative. What we find omitted from the one, is what disturbs us about the other.

Hobbes' treatment of the concept of representation is puzzling in a number of ways. He is at pains to give a clear definition, yet he produces examples of representation that do not fit the definition. Was he simply being inconsistent? Perhaps the definition was intended to be stipulative and new, intended to differ from what the word had previously been used to mean. And perhaps the examples which do not fit under it are occasional lapses back to more common usage. But there is no sign that Hobbes intended to *re*define the word, and a good deal of evidence that he did not, that he thought he was clearly explaining what the word already meant. He never presents his definitions with expressions such as "let us call" or "I propose to call," but purports rather to tell us what a thing "is called" or what "we call" it.

Then, too, his definition fits well into his political argument. Is this, as some commentators have suggested, because he deliberately gave us a false definition that would strengthen his argument? Or was he simply mistaken about what representation means? Could so careful and astute a thinker make such a mistake?

But his definition is not just wrong, not obviously wrong. Any number of other theorists have adopted similar views about representation. And the argument of chapter 16 of the *Leviathan* is very convincing; anyone can be led to accept Hobbes' definition by following his argument step by step—except, of course, for the damaging counterexamples. So the definition seems right, and tempts us; yet the counterexamples seem right too, and we recognize them as instances of what we, too, would call "representation." But when we see the final result of the definition embodied in a Hobbesian political system with an absolute sovereign, we feel that something has gone wrong, that representation has somehow disappeared while our backs were turned. Can Hobbes' definition, then, be both right and not right? Perhaps in a sense it can, if it is a true but partial view of representation, a true view of a part of the concept's meaning, and therefore false if taken to define the whole meaning. I suggest that Hobbes developed too narrow a perspective on representation by approaching it from only one angle, by taking into account only one kind of representing.[43]

3

Formalistic Views
of Representation

Perhaps the most curious thing about Hobbes' problematic treatment of representation is that it cannot be dismissed as his private idiosyncrasy, of interest perhaps to Hobbes scholars but essentially a deviation from the more reasonable main line of scholarship. Rather, it is the first, and in a way the most fully developed, version of a view of representation which continues to appear from time to time in the history of political thought, and which is held (often in unexamined form) by a number of modern political scientists. By following their approach to the concept, starting from their kind of examples, we can induce that view in ourselves. Whenever it appears and however it is articulated, its basic features are those of the Hobbesian argument, and eventually it encounters the same difficulties. Because it defines representation in terms of the giving and having of authority, I shall call it the "authorization view," and theorists who hold or develop it I shall call "authorization theorists." The authorization view is one of several different ways of seeing representation, each tempting because it is partly right, but each wrong because it takes a part of the concept for the whole.

The basic features of the authorization view are these: a representative is someone who has been authorized to act. This means that he has been given a right to act which he did not have before, while the represented has become responsible for the consequences of that action as if he had done it himself. It is a view strongly skewed in favor of the representative. His rights have been enlarged and his responsibilities have been (if anything) decreased. The represented, in contrast, has acquired new responsibilities and (if anything) given up some of his rights. The authorization view concentrates on the formalities of this relationship; it is what I shall call a "formalistic" view. It defines representing in terms of a transaction that takes place at the outset, before the actual representing begins. To the extent that he has been authorized, within the limits of his authority, anything that a man does is representing. One can speak of limits or restraints on the conduct of a representative, but they are always coextensive with the limits of the authority he has been given. Representation is a kind of "black box" shaped by the initial giving of authority, within which the representative can do whatever he pleases. If he leaves the box, if he exceeds the limits, he no longer represents. There can be no such thing as representing well or badly; either he represents or he does not. There is no such thing as the activity of representing or the duties of a representative; anything done after the right kind of authorization and within its limits is by definition representing.

Such a view is shared by many political theorists and political scientists. We shall consider three versions: one developed by a succession of German theorists and centering on the concept of *Organschaft*, a second undertaking an account of democratic representative government, and a third articulated in the work of Eric Voegelin.

Unlike Hobbes, the *Organschaft* theorists start from the group rather than from the isolated individual; instead of being the agent of an individual, the representative becomes an organ of the group. The best known of the writers who develop such views (though he himself does not use the term *Organschaft*) is undoubtedly Max Weber. Weber says that by "representation" we mean primarily a state of affairs in which "the action of certain members of a group is ascribed to the rest; or that the rest are supposed to, and do in fact, regard the action as "legitimate" for themselves and binding on them."[1] When he later expands on this definition, Weber says that a social relationship may be such that each member's action is ascribed to all the other members, or that the action of certain specified members is ascribed to the rest, "so that the benefits accrue to them and the consequences fall upon them."[2] When each member's actions are ascribed to all, we have not representation but "solidarity," as exemplified in vendettas, blood feuds, or reprisals.[3] True representation exists only where certain select members have authority to act for the group, but other members do not.

Weber's argument differs only slightly from that of the conventional *Organschaft* theorists. Hans Wolff, for example, defines a representative as a person "from whose behavior rights and duties accrue to the group. A representative acts for the group with the result that his behavior is ascribed to the group."[4] Like Weber, Wolff distinguishes the case where every member's actions are ascribed to all, from that where certain members are designated to act for the rest; but he regards both as instances of representation. When only certain members can act for the group, however, it is a more highly developed form of representation: *Organschaft*.

The doctrine of *Organschaft* has roots in the French Revolution and appears in some nineteenth-century writers.[5] But it was developed mainly by Gierke and Jellinek, and had a vogue on the Continent in the early decades of this century.[6] It argues that an official, a representative, is the specialized "organ" of a group. This argument has obvious affinities with what we more generally call organic political theory, the idea that (some) groups of people are (like) living organisms. Most of the *Organschaft* writers, however, are not interested in this kind of metaphor, but in questions of sovereignty and the legal status of government agents. For them it is more a theory of officialdom than of organism.

Conceived in this way, all government officials, all organs of the state, are representatives, and representation is necessary in any complex society. A group may need to have services performed for it that can only be done by the action of individuals. One need not be an *Organschaft* theorist to see that "some form of representation seems to be necessary in any social group whose decisions must be carried out by particular individuals."[7] In this

sense, anyone who performs a function for the group may seem to
be its representative, for his actions may be attributed to it and are
binding on it. The postman delivers mail for the United States
government, and the government is responsible for damage he
does in the line of duty. Judges represent the state in this way. So
do ambassadors. Even the voter may be seen as an organ or agent
of the state, whose special function is the selection of other
organs; thus even the voter is a representative.[8] Obviously, representatives defined in this manner need not be elected to office.
The manner of their selection is irrelevant so long as they become
organs of the group. Elected representatives are no different in
status here than those chosen in some other way.[9]

But at this point the *Organschaft* theory encounters a problem
very similar to the difficulties in Hobbes' argument. We note
that not all government officials are ordinarily called representatives. Rather, certain ones, particularly ones who are elected to
a legislature (but perhaps also an elected executive), are given
this designation. And it is not just any government agency that
we speak of as a representative body. But given the authorization definition, there seems to be no way to account for the
distinction, no way to explain how elected legislators and legislatures are more truly or more fully representatives than other
officials.

Several of the *Organschaft* theorists recognize this difficulty
and try to deal with it. Jellinek suggests that, whereas other state
organs act for the state "outward," in its dealings with other
states and foreigners, the representative legislature is the state's
official voice "inward," toward its own citizens.[10] But this account
does not give any reason why one function is any more truly
representing than the other. Jellinek suggests that the state
organs which we conventionally call representative(s) are "secondary" organs. That is, for every such organ there is another
organ which is "primary" to it and which it represents. For
example, the people themselves are a primary organ of the state,
and a representative legislature is their secondary organ. Unfortunately, Jellinek is far from clear about what this means. Presumably a secondary organ's actions are ascribed not only to
the whole state but also to its corresponding primary organ. But
why are some actions ascribed twice rather than once? Sometimes

Jellinek implies that the primary organ must have the right to appoint or supervise or receive an accounting from the secondary organ.[11] But more frequently he says that this is unnecessary, that only the legal attribution is required: the legislature's will is officially attributed to the people.[12] Selection by another organ cannot be the criterion, for every state official is selected or appointed in some way by someone; even voters must be registered. So we are left with the puzzle of why certain organs represent not merely the state but also another organ, as well as the more fundamental question why such double representing is more truly representation than single representing is.

The explanation most commonly given by *Organschaft* theorists is that the organs we conventionally call representative(s) have a unique function in the state. Their function is to will; they are the state's willing-organ, just as the sovereign was for Hobbes.[13] But the *Organschaft* theorists never succeed in making clear why the attribution of will should be more significant in this respect than the attribution of other actions.

For Hobbes, any government was representative, and though we can see his point we would not really want to call his kind of sovereign a representative. In much the same way, the *Organschaft* theorists show us a sense in which every state agent represents, but they are uncertain how to distinguish representative agencies from the rest. Most modern political scientists would demand of a definition of representation precisely that it should distinguish representative government from other forms, and representatives from other government agents.[14] But a number of them attempt to derive these distinctions from an authorization view.

If we look beyond systematic arguments to asides, casual comments, and brief definitions, we find a variety of recent English and American political scientists and theorists adopting the authorization view. Writers from Edward Sait to Avery Leiserson, from Sir Ernest Barker to Karl Loewenstein, from John Plamenatz to Joseph Tussman, are in fundamental agreement with the Hobbesian definition. Representation, they tell us, "occurs whenever one person is authorized to act in place of others"; to represent means "to act with binding authority in the name of" others; even an elected body is truly representative only if it "has representative authority," which means authority "to deliberate and decide" for others.[15] The essence of representation "is that the representatives—whatever the manner of their investiture—are authorized in advance to act conjointly in behalf of their constituents and bind them by their collective decisions."[16] Authority given in advance, the representative's actions binding on those for whom he acts—the familiar elements are there.

For the theorist of representative democracy working from an authorization definition, the crucial criterion becomes elections, and these are seen as a grant of authority by the voters to the elected officials. Normally this grant of authority is limited as to time, so that the officials' status as representatives ends when the time comes for new elections. In each election, voters grant authority anew, name representatives anew, though of course they may reauthorize the same individuals for another term. The definitive election is the one which puts a man into office, for it is that election which gives him authority and makes him a representative. Elections are acts of "vesting authority."[17]

Thus Tussman has argued:

The essence of representation is the delegation or granting of authority. To authorize a representative is to grant another the right to act for oneself. Within the limits of the grant of authority one is, in fact, committing himself in advance to the decision or will of another. . . .

The fact that our rulers are elected does not make them any less our rulers. . . . To say that we send our representatives to Congress is not to say that we have sent our servants to the market. We have simply designated the person or persons to whose judgement or will we have subordinated ourselves. Nor does the fact that at a later date we must redesignate a representative alter that fact that an act of subordination has occurred.[18]

Similarly, Plamenatz sees representing as "acting with the consent of someone else," which means two things.[19] First, a man acts with the consent of another if his right "to act in a certain way is conditional upon another man's having expressed the wish that he should act in that way." And second, the represented must at least share in responsibility for the actions taken in his name by the representative; only then can it "truly be said of the latter that he is acting with the former's permission," and

represents him.[20] Thus representative government again can be
defined as "a form of government whereby the governed can be
said to be responsible for their governors' actions."[21]

But these writers, too, face a difficulty. Their definitions of
representation do not require that authority be given only for
a limited time or that elections be held regularly. One could
stipulate that a government is a representative government only
if the acts of authorization occur reasonably often and hold for
only a limited time; but there is nothing in the meaning of representation as these theorists have defined it that could justify or
explain such a stipulation. As Hobbes saw, there is no reason
why men could not give unlimited authority at the outset for
an indefinite period of time, thus making any government that
is initially elected, representative forever, or at least for the life-
times of the ruler and the voters. None of these writers succeeds
in dealing with this possibility, although none of them would
accept a lifetime dictatorship as a representative government.

A third version of the authorization view is given in Eric
Voegelin's *New Science of Politics*, which proposes a classical
authorization definition, but proceeds beyond it to a different
view. The latter, again, bears close affinity to the difficulties in
Hobbes' argument; so Voegelin's work is another illustration of
the problematic tension between the authorization view and its
as yet undefined missing elements.

Voegelin begins with the everyday sense of representation, by
which ordinary people "in political debate, in the press, and in
the publicist literature" distinguish "conventionally so-called"
representative governments from other forms.[22] One can list
such governments and specify their main common features: an
elected legislature, perhaps an elected executive. Voegelin refers to this notion of representation as "descriptive," and labels
it the "elemental type" of representation.[23] But he urges that it
is necessary to go beyond this elemental level. On principle it is
necessary because the common-sense terms used by the participants in a political system "in political reality" often cannot be
"critically clarified" to the point where they are "of any cognitive
use in science."[24] And this principle may be illustrated at a more
practical level by noting that the common-sense notion of representation leaves one in doubt about whether a government like

that of the Soviet Union, which has the necessary outward features, is really a representative government, whether its constitution and elections are genuine, whether its representative institutions are "meaningful."

So Voegelin proceeds to a second sense or "type" of representation, which he calls the "existential" sense.[25] While one may be in doubt whether the Soviet government represents the people, he says, there can be no doubt that it is the effective, authoritative leader of the Soviet Union, who "represents the Soviet society as a political society in form for action in history."[26] Such authoritative leadership by a few emerges only gradually, as a society differentiates itself and organizes for action. Clearly, what Voegelin means by existential representation is very much an authorization view.

As a result of political articulation we find human beings, the rulers, who can act for the society, men whose acts are not imputed to their own persons but to the society as a whole—with the consequence that, for instance, the pronunciation of a general rule regulating an area of human life will not be understood as an exercise in moral philosophy but will be experienced by the members of the society as the declaration of a rule with obligatory force for themselves. When his acts are effectively imputed in this manner, a person is the representative of a society.[27]

Such representation does not require election. A hereditary monarch can be such a representative; an undemocratic parliament can be such a representative. Only under certain historical circumstances is there a democratizing downward expansion of representation: "when articulation expands throughout society, the representative will also expand until the limit is reached where the membership of the society has become politically articulate down to the last individual, and correspondingly, the society becomes the representative of itself."[28] Hobbes would say: authority may be given to one man, or a council of men, or to all the people assembled.

As with Hobbes, also, Voegelin's concept is based on the need for social action. A society can exist as a society only when it has a representative to act for it: "the historical existence of a political society was consistently expressed in terms of acquisition, possession, or loss of the *rex*, of the royal representative.

To be articulated for action meant to have a king; to lose the king meant to lose fitness for action; when the group did not act, it did not need a king."[29] Then it ceased to exist as a group. Voegelin would no doubt agree with Hobbes that a representative which cannot act is no representative at all.

But Voegelin does not find this authorization view sufficient, either. For the imputation of the authorized representative's actions to the society as a whole will take place effectively only if he acts in accord with the basic directive idea of the group, what one might call the spirit of the nation. And this leads Voegelin to the "transcendental" type of sense of representation, the sense in which a society is or can be "the representative of something beyond itself, of a transcendent reality," "a transcendent truth."[30] This kind of representing is not confined to societies; the theorist or philosopher can also "represent a truth" in this way, and if a Greek tragedy succeeds in arousing a sense of participation and identification in the spectators, its hero undergoes "representative suffering" for them all.[31] Voegelin maintains that the authoritative representative of a society is effective in his role only if he represents a transcendent truth or order appropriate to that society: "the ruler himself represents the society *because* he represents the transcendent power which maintains cosmic order."[32]

The transcendental type plays a complex but central role in the development of Voegelin's major thesis about history, societies, and religious awareness; and that thesis is precisely what Voegelin's discussion of representation is intended to illuminate. But for our purposes, we need not consider that thesis; we need only consider his three definitions of "representation" and their relationship. The second, or authorization, definition is supposed to grow out of the first, or common-sense definition, as the critical scientist refines the terminology of the marketplace into a cognitive tool.[33] Concerning the relationship between the authorization view and his transcendental type, Voegelin tells us that they both "refer to aspects of one problem." So the authoritative representative is the society's "active leader in the representation of truth"; "a government by consent of the citizen-body" presupposes political awareness to the point where the citizens "can be made active participants in the representation of truth through

Peitho, through persuasion"; the problem itself was discovered only when man discovered his psyche as capable of representing a transcendent truth; and the philosopher who first made this discovery "became as a consequence the representative of the new truth."[34]

Voegelin thinks that his three definitions are related, that each refers to something called "representation." But the three types are really very different. If we took his authorization view as definitive—that a representative is someone whose acts are imputed to a group so that they impose obligations on that group— there would be no reason why a government with an elected legislature should be called a "representative" government, and there would be no sense in which anyone could represent a transcendent truth. What would "representing a transcendent truth" mean, if representing meant acting for others with binding authority? That the society's actions are accepted by the transcendent truth as binding norms on it?

Voegelin, seeing both the validity of the authorization view and its shortcomings, supplements it with a "type" of representation related to the "conforming to some external limits or standard" that is missing from Hobbes' definition. But Voegelin does not relate the various definitions to each other; he does not explain how a single concept can have several seemingly incompatible yet correct definitions. That need not be a criticism of Voegelin's work; the concept of representation is not his real interest in *The New Science of Politics* but only a means to that interest. But for our purposes his work poses again and most sharply the problems we first encountered in Hobbes: the need to account simultaneously for both the plausibility and the inadequacy of the authorization view.

The authorization view, then, seems to be far more than a random mistake about representation. Surely so many theorists of different kinds could not all simply happen to see the concept in the same incorrect way. If we approach the idea of representation from a certain direction, the authorization view will arise quite naturally. If, for example, we begin to wonder what the crucial difference is between a businessman contracting for himself and an agent contracting for another, our answer will quite naturally be in terms of who is bound by the action. This may lead us to think about the difference between authorized and fake agents, and to identify this capacity to act for another and bind him with authority, with having been authorized. Or again, if we think about organizations and wonder how a spokesman for a group is different from someone speaking only for himself, some version of the authorization view is almost bound to emerge.

So there is nothing mysterious about the attractiveness of the authorization view; it is a definition abstracted from and founded on (certain kinds of) ordinary, valid examples of representation. Yet the various versions of this view continue to run into difficulties, either explicitly, in the recognition of the authorization theorist himself, or implicitly in some of his own examples and arguments, or (if he has been very careful or very brief) in further arguments related to what he has said.

Seeing the validity of the authorization theorist's examples of representation, we are likely to overlook the fact that there are other and different things which we also call representing, and with equal naturalness. Working only from authorization examples, we are likely to impose on ourselves, or accept with a theorist, fundamental unexamined assumptions so obvious that we do not notice them, yet very restrictive indeed. We are led to assume, for example, that representation must have to do with the activities of people, that it is an arrangement among people concerning actions and their consequences. And of course that is true, but only sometimes. But we also speak of a representative case, a representative sample, representational art, a work "representing someone's best efforts," a painter "representing his subject" in a certain way, a flag representing the nation, symbols on a map representing iron-ore deposits. No definition formulated in terms of agreements, rights, obligations, authority, and actions can explain why the word "represent" should have anything to do with such things—why these, too, should be instances of representation. The authorization view seems to explain some uses of the nouns "representation" and "representative" and the verb "to represent," but it cannot account for other words in the same family. It cannot tell us what "misrepresenting" or "misrepresentation" might be, nor can it explain the noun "representativeness" or the adjective "representative" where it is more or less synonymous with "typical."

Is there any harm in missing such examples and terms, in restricting our view and definition to a subcategory of representation, the representing of people by other people in action? Why should the political theorist have to concern himself with art or mapmaking or mathematical sampling theory, when he is really interested in people and social arrangements? The answer would seem to be that the restrictive assumption causes us, and the authorization theorist, to mistake what representing is like even when it does refer to actions and consequences. It results in a view which encounters precisely those difficulties with regard to *acting for others* that have been plaguing the authorization theorists. It results in a formalistic view stressing only the representative's capacity to bind others, not his obligation to conform to some external standard or act in accord with special considerations.

To discuss what happens here, we may make use of a distinction drawn by A. Phillips Griffiths, between ascribing one man's action to another, and ascribing the consequences of action.[35] While not himself an authorization theorist, Griffiths distinguishes, among several senses of representation, one that he calls "ascriptive," which is essentially an authorization view. An ascriptive representative is one whose actions are "grounds for ascribing either acts, or status, such as being married, which normally presupposes acts" to another.[36] He acts, but his actions or the changes in status that result from them are ascribed to someone else whom he represents.

Griffiths marks an important distinction between the ascription of actions themselves and the ascription of what he calls the "normative consequences" of actions. Some actions, he says, require bodily movements for their doing, and hence can only be done in person.

For example, it is impossible for a man to eat unless he swallows, or to sing unless he makes sounds. On the other hand, many acts may be ascribed to a person where no particular movements of his body are essential; for example, getting married, entering into a contract, insulting someone, trespassing. Essential to such actions is not the physical movements which they may happen to involve but the acquisition of certain rights, obligations, commitments, etc.[37]

The former kind of actions have only causal consequences, "like poisoning oneself or satisfying one's hunger or waking the baby."[38] The consequences of the latter kind of actions are changes in rights, obligations, or status; these are what Griffiths calls normative consequences.[39] Even actions which require personal bodily movements and have causal consequences may nevertheless also

contingently have certain normative consequences, and the principal can still be spoken of as being committed to these. For example, it is a contingent normative consequence of begetting children that one is responsible for their care and upbringing. Under no system of representation would it be possible for the physical act of begetting the child to be attributed to me in virtue of the same act on the part of my representative; but I might under some system of representation thereby become responsible for looking after the child as if it were my own.[40]

It is thus important to distinguish between the ascription of one man's action to another, and the ascription of the normative consequences of that action. The former can occur, can make sense, only with respect to actions like getting married, which do not have to be done in person. It makes no sense to ascribe A's singing or eating or sleeping to B; one man cannot do these things for another. But the normative consequences of any action can be so ascribed—either the direct changes in status, obligations, and so on of an action like getting married, or the "contingent" normative consequences of physical actions. Hence Griffiths argues that the ascription of normative consequences is "more fundamental" than the ascription of an action itself, both because all actions permit the former but only some actions the latter, and because the "essential function" of ascriptive representation is that the consequences of A's action should fall on B.[41] We ascribe one man's action to another in order to ascribe its normative consequences to him. About this, Griffiths is, though in a sense right, wrong in an important way, as we shall see.

Applying Griffiths' distinction to the authorization theorists, we might say that they define representing in terms of any or all of four different ideas, assuming them to be more or less coextensive when, in fact, they are not. Authorization theorists thus tend to confuse: (1) having one's actions attributed to another; (2) having the normative consequences of one's actions attributed to another; (3) having been given the right to act by another; and (4) having authority, particularly authority over another, the right to command him.

The first of these, the ascription of actions—wanting to say simultaneously that A did it and yet that it was B's action—is what representation means *in the context of actions.* But this may or may not be connected with the ascription of normative consequences, the right to act, or authority. All of these can be occasions or reasons for the ascription of actions, but none of them need be; and there are other occasions for the ascription of actions as well.

Many of the authorization theorists begin with the attribution of one man's actions to another. This clearly is what Hobbes means by speaking of the "ownership" of actions: a representative is someone whose actions are not his "own" but ascribed to another. Similarly, Weber defines representation as the fact that some men's actions are ascribed to a group rather than just to themselves. And Voegelin speaks of representatives (in the "existential" or authorization sense) as men whose actions are imputed not to themselves but to others. But they then try to explicate what this means in terms of ideas two, three, and four. Yet these ideas are by no means coextensive or identical in meaning.

Not every ascription of the normative consequences of A's actions to B is an occasion for saying that A represents B. On this point Griffiths is as wrong as the authorization theorists. He suggests that a union negotiator is considered to represent his union because his actions (agreeing to a contract, say) have normative consequences for the union. "We sometimes speak of trade unionists as accepting a wage settlement when their representatives have done so. . . . We more often say however that . . . the trade unionists are committed to observing the wage agreement by the action of their representatives."[42] But one does not need to be a union's representative to bring down normative consequences on it through one's actions. A judge may issue a judicial injunction binding on the union; yet we do not say that he is the union's representative or represents it when he does so. How is the judge different from the union negotiator? Both have authority to bind the union, but only one of them represents the union in his actions. Only the union negotiator's action is itself ascribed to the union; only when he acts can we say that the union has acted. We do not need to ascribe action in the case of the judge; thus in some situations we can ascribe normative consequences without invoking representation at all. But the normative consequences brought down on the union by the judge's action are not the kind of normative consequences that normally would fall on the one who performs the action. Injunctions do not normally impose obligations on the judge who issues them; they are a way for him to impose legal obligations on others. But the signing of a document normally has normative consequences for the signer himself; if in this case we want them to fall instead on the union (or need to explain how they fall instead on the union), we say that the signer acted for the union and not for himself, that he represented it. But then the action is ascribed, along with its normative consequences. Thus the ascription of the action is what is fundamental here; the ascription of consequences is but one kind of occasion or reason for ascribing an action whose consequences normally would fall on the actor himself.[43]

Similarly, not every instance of A's giving B the right to act involves representation, nor need it involve the ascription of normative consequences. If one man gives another the right to hunt on his land, say, he has surely given him a right the other did not have before, but he has not made the other his representative. Or again, a police commissioner may issue licenses to peddlers, giving them the right to sell their wares in the community; but the peddlers do not become his representatives, nor need any normative consequences of their actions fall on him. Or a man may give another the right of access to his safe-deposit box; this may entail making the other his representative for this purpose, but it need not entail any normative consequences for the first man. Again, we invoke representation only if the transfer of rights is such that the action is to be ascribed to another; this happens most typically when one man gives another the right to do something which normally each must do for himself. Thus, where an authorization theorist like Hobbes speaks of a transfer of rights, he has in mind one particular kind of example: transferring the right to act in your name, make commitments on your behalf, sign your signature.

This may be because, for so many of the authorization theorists, the ultimate concern is neither with rights nor with normative consequences in general, but particularly with political authority, authority over others, the right to command. Defining representation in terms of authority, they tend to assume that all authority is representative and that every representative is in authority over those for whom he acts. This is very clear in Hobbes, whose representation argument serves mainly to reinforce absolute sovereignty. But Weber, too, works his way toward examples in which a group regards one member's actions as "legitimate for" and "binding on" them all; and the *Organschaft* theorists generally focus on one state organ—the "willing organ" that makes binding decisions for the rest. Voegelin's "existential" representative, similarly, is the effective political sovereign of a nation. And even the authorization theorists concerned with representative democracy stress the representative's authority over his constituents, his power to make laws for them.

Yet the assumption they make by generalizing from these cases to all of representation is simply false. Some representatives do have authority over those they represent, but others do not.[44] Often, indeed, the represented may have authority over the one who acts for him: an employee representing a corporation, a servant representing his master, a hired factor representing a businessman. Furthermore, it is possible to have authority over others without representing them. An army officer has authority over his men and can issue commands binding on them, yet he is not thereby their representative. The same is true of a teacher and his class. And, as we have already seen with regard to a judicial injunction, the same is true generally of a judge and the parties before him. Authority over others, the right to give orders, is one thing; representation is another. Sometimes the two go together, but at other times they do not.

Authority, the transfer of rights, the ascription of normative consequences can each sometimes be the occasion or reason or point of speaking about representation. But each of them may also occur when no representation is involved. We speak of representation in connection with authority or rights or normative consequences only where the action is to be ascribed to someone other than the one who acts—someone who is under authority, or gave him the right to act, or is to bear the normative consequences. But, there are other very different reasons or occasions for ascribing one man's action to another and invoking representation—reasons unconnected with any of these elements of the authorization theorist's definition. We may, for example, pretend that it is not A but B who is acting in a theater performance; the ascription may be a way of expressing the fact that the actor is playing a role. Or we may find that a man is acting on orders from another, is merely a "front man" for him; to express this idea we may speak of representation. Or one man may be acting on behalf of another, furthering his interest; or he may act for and advance some abstract cause or principle. In the right circumstances that, too, can be representation.

In comparison with such occasions for ascribing actions, rights and normative consequences seem formal, for these occasions are concerned with the substantive content of what the representative does or how he does it. They seem to be related, on the one hand, to the persistent difficulties the authorization theorists encounter, for instance, in Hobbes' examples of representing which cannot be accounted for under his authorization definition. On the other hand, such "substantive" occasions for ascribing actions and invoking representation seem related also to the kinds of representing by inanimate objects which the authorization view completely ignores because of its focus on action, rights, and responsibilities. Thus the different senses of representation may not be as separate or separable as might be supposed. By restricting their view to persons and actors and ignoring other uses of the word, the authorization theorists seem to have arrived at an incomplete and distorted view even of what they do look at, even of representation with regard to actions. A blindness to the way in which symbols or paintings represent seems correlated with an excessively formal view of the way in which people represent—a view that makes it impossible to speak of the obligations of a representative as such, or to judge his actions in relation to his role. If representing means merely acting with special rights, or acting with someone else bearing the consequences, then there can be no such thing as representing well or badly.

The formality of the authorization view may be demonstrated most clearly by considering a view which, while diametrically opposed to authorization in one sense, is equally formal and empty of substantive content. This view defines representation in terms not of authority but of accountability. I shall call it the "accountability view," and speak of those who express or develop it as "accountability theorists." It is not an important strand in the literature of representation; so far as I know, no writer has discussed it at length or developed it into a theoretical system, as Hobbes does with authorization. The view crops up here and there, often articulated without much attention or thought, thrown out in passing while the theorist pursues some other point. But, as with authorization, one can make a case for accountability, one can be led to accept it as definitive of representation, if one approaches that concept from a certain angle and with certain questions in mind. The inadequacies of accountability are more striking than those of authorization, but it has a certain tempting rightness all the same.

For the accountability theorist, a representative is someone who is to be held to account, who will have to answer to another for what he does. The man or men to whom he must eventually account are those whom he represents. "Representation, if it means anything," a contemporary political scientist and educator tells us, "means that the representative must be responsible to the represented."[45] And even Carl Friedrich agrees that "if A represents B, he is presumed to be responsible *to* B, that is to say, he is answerable to B for what he says and does."[46] In a sense, then, this view is diametrically opposed to that of the authorization theorist. For the latter, being a representative means being freed from the usual responsibility for one's actions; for the accountability theorist, being a representative means precisely having new and special obligations.[47] Whereas authorization theorists see the representative as free, the represented as bound, accountability theorists see precisely the converse. The authorization theorist defines representative democracy by equating elections with a grant of authority: a man represents because he has been elected at the outset of his term of office. The accountability theorist, on the contrary, equates elections with a holding-to-account: an elected official is a representative because (and insofar as) he will be subject to reëlection or removal at the end of his term. "In every kind of government power must exist and be trusted somewhere," a political scientist writes, but the distinguishing characteristic of representative government "is to hold the trusteeship to steady account for its behavior."[48]

The accountability theorists often seem to be led to their views by asking how representative government differs from other forms, and seeking the answer in terms of the point or purpose of having regular elections. Thus they may equate representative government with popular sovereignty, which

does not mean that the voters actually decide legislative policy, but it does mean that political rulers should be accountable to the voters at periodic elections. The trouble with Burke's idea of representation is that it does not acknowledge the importance of accountability. . . .

The role of the electoral body as the source of sovereign power is to give or withhold consent. This power is not one of instructing political leaders on specific policies, but holding them accountable at periodic elections.[49]

For these writers, the meaning of representative democracy "is that the agents, the personnel of government, are held responsible to the society as a whole."[50] A recent article on metropolitan government asks: "Do the residents of our new metropolitania . . . want to be served by authorities not politically accountable to them, *and so* to be governed without representation?"[51] And it makes clear that direct election is not necessarily coextensive with representation in this sense. It examines alternative means for selecting governors for metropolitan areas—direct election, indirect election, appointment by various agencies, and combinations of these—and asks "whether actual accountability to the metropolitan community is achieved by state-local appointment."[52] Accountability to the governed is what defines representation, whether it be achieved by elections or by other means.

It is easy to see from what direction or point of view the accountability theorists approach representation. Typically, their view does not develop as an independent, spontaneous, and general definition; rather, it is meant to correct a false view which they have encountered (or perhaps themselves generated). They introduce accountability as a response and a corrective to the authorization view. Looking at Hobbes' sovereign, they want to object, "That isn't representation; it's the very opposite of what representation means." And in that objection they find their definition. The accountability theorists are usually engaged in trying to distinguish "true" or "genuine" or "real" representation from something that has only the outward trappings, that looks like representation in a formal way but is not. Thus their view may emerge as they try to distinguish representative government from other effective governmental forms; often it is linked with a discussion of necessary distinguishing features—genuine free elections, a real choice of candidates, free communications, and so on.[53] Or the accountability view may be used to distinguish "real" representation from the "fraudulent" claim that even those who are not allowed to vote are "virtually" represented.[54] The view is intended as a corrective to theories or examples of representation which, like the authorization view, give the representative authority and new rights but place no obligations or controls on him. Objecting to this, accountability theorists assert that, quite the contrary, genuine representation exists only where there are such controls—accountability to the represented; indeed, it is identical with such controls.

But the accountability theorists' real interest is not in the controls or accountability which they impose on the representative; those are merely a device, a means to their ultimate purpose, which is a certain kind of behavior on the part of the representative. The point of holding him to account after he acts is to make him act in a certain way—look after his constituents, or do what they want. "One is held responsible in order that he may *become* responsible, that is, responsive to the needs and claims of others, to the obligations implicit in his position."[55] In genuine representation, the representative must eventually be held to account so that he will be responsive to the needs and claims of his constituents, to the obligations implicit in his position. That is what these theorists find missing from the authorization view, and what their definition is intended to supply.

That is the intention; but their definition does not and cannot succeed in accomplishing it. For the definition they give is just as formal as the one they reject, and makes it just as impossible to speak of "obligations implicit in the position" of a representative.

Where the one group defines a representative as someone who has been elected (authorized), the other defines him as someone who will be subject to election (held to account). Where the one sees representation as initiated in a certain way, the other sees it as terminated in a certain way. Neither can tell us anything about what goes on *during* representation, how a representative ought to act or what he is expected to do, how to tell whether he has represented well or badly. Such questions do not even make sense in terms of formalistic definitions like the authorization and accountability views.

One might say that the accountability view is a practical or empirical hypothesis, mistakenly disguised as a conceptual view. Accountability theorists mean to say that a man who will be held to account for what he does, and knows that he will, is most likely to act responsibly and respond to the desires of those to whom he must account. And that may well be true, assuming that he wants to please them (to be reëlected). But if representation is defined as action for which one will be held to account, and the represented as the one to whom the accounting must be given, nothing follows about any kind of duty, obligation, or role for the representative. On the basis of such a definition, a representative who acted in a completely selfish and irresponsible manner could not be criticized as long as he let himself be removed from office at the end of his term.

We are thus confronted by two definitions, diametrically opposed and yet both equally formal. From the accountability theorist's point of view, Hobbes and Weber and Voegelin have simply and inexplicably missed the meaning of representation. From the authorization theorist's point of view the same is true of accountability theorists. What are we to make of such flagrant conceptual polarities? Are we to adopt one position and ignore the other? But each has a certain plausibility, and we can sympathize (separately) with the arguments of each. At any rate, each of them, and both together, point beyond themselves, in the sense that they cannot yet be the whole story about representation; they could at most be two pieces in an incomplete jigsaw puzzle. This possibility is further underlined by the limitations of both views. Both are meaningful only if we assume that representation is activity and that both representative and represented are human beings. Yet we know that sometimes inanimate objects (are said to) represent, and that sometimes men (are said to) represent an interest or a cause or some other abstraction. At this point, we still lack an explanation of what that might mean. And both views are formalistic, in the sense that their defining criterion for representation lies outside the activity of representing itself—before it begins or after it ends. Indeed, they recognize no such thing as "the activity of representing"; to represent simply means to act after authorization or to act before being held to account.

If we attempt to penetrate beyond the formalities of representation to its substantive content, two directions of inquiry are open to us. We may ask what a representative does, what constitutes the activity of representing. Or we may ask what a representative is, what he must be like in order to represent. The distinction may be expressed by contrasting the two German words, *vertreten*, to act for another, and *darstellen*, to stand for another.[56] These two further senses of, or questions about, representation are often intertwined, but their implications and consequences are very different; so they are best considered separately. Thus we shall turn first to two kinds of *darstellen*, descriptive and symbolic standing for something or someone; the discussion of the activity of representing will commence in Chapter 6.

4

"Standing For":
Descriptive Representation

An entirely different view of representation emerges for writers who approach the concept from a different angle, with other problems and questions in mind. Consider the many political scientists, statesmen, theorists, and philosophers concerned with the proper composition of a legislative assembly—with constituencies and apportionment, with suffrage and party organization, with electoral systems and voting. Their investigations sometimes lead them to formulate their ideas in terms of what a representative legislature should, by its very nature, be like. What such an approach often produces, is the view that a representative body is distinguished by an accurate correspondence or resemblance to what it represents, by reflecting without distortion. This view can then be articulated through a variety of familiar examples and expressions.

True representation, these writers argue, requires that the legislature be so selected that its composition corresponds accurately to that of the whole nation; only then is it really a representative body. A representative legislature, John Adams argues in the American Revolutionary period, "should be an exact portrait, in miniature, of the people at large, as it should think, feel, reason and act like them."[1] And though his views become more conservative later, he still holds, in his *Defense* of the new Constitution, that in a "representative assembly," as in art, "the perfection of the portrait consists in its likeness."[2] In the same vein, James Wilson argues at the Constitutional Convention, that, as "the portrait is excellent in proportion to its being a good likeness," so "the legislature ought to be the most exact transcript of the whole society," "the faithful echo of the voices of the people."[3] Even Edmund Burke maintains that "the virtue, spirit and essence" of a representative body lies "in its being the express image of the feelings of the nation."[4]

Other writers require that the legislature be a "mirror" of the nation or of public opinion, that it "mirror" the people, the state of public consciousness, or the movement of social and economic forces in the nation.[5] Representative government, they tell us, means "accurate reflection" of the community, or of the general opinion of the nation, or of the variety of interests in society.[6] Representation should secure in the government a "reflex" of the opinion of the entire electorate.[7] Hence Sidney and Beatrice Webb judge the British House of Lords to be "the worst representative assembly ever created, in that it contains absolutely no members of the manual working class; none of the great class of shopkeepers, clerks and teachers; none of the half of all the citizens who are of the female sex."[8]

This approach to the concept of representation is very different from the formalistic authorization and accountability views. For these writers, representing is not acting with authority, or acting before being held to account, or any kind of acting at all. Rather, it depends on the representative's characteristics, on what he *is* or is *like*, on being something rather than doing something. The representative does not act for others; he "stands for" them, by virtue of a correspondence or connection between them, a resemblance or reflection. In political terms, what seems important is less what the legislature does than how it is composed.

The major features of this view are most clearly developed among the advocates of proportional representation. Indeed, it may be argued that the "fundamental principle" of proportional representation is the attempt to "secure a representative assembly reflecting with more or less mathematical exactness the various divisions in the electorate."[9] Such an assembly, proportionalists maintain, must be "the most exact possible image of the country."[10] It must "correspond in composition with the community," be a "condensation" of the whole, because "what you want is to get a reflection of the general opinion of the nation."[11] Other proportionalists invoke the metaphor of a map, apparently first articulated in a speech before the Estates of Provence in 1789 by Mirabeau (himself no advocate of proportional representation). "A representative body," he said, "is for the nation what a map drawn to scale is for the physical configuration of its land; in part or in whole the copy must always have the same proportions as the original."[12] Mirabeau's metaphor was picked up and elaborated a few years later by the Swiss legal theorist, Bluntschli:

Truly, as the map represents mountains and valleys, lakes and rivers, forests and meadows, cities and villages, the legislative body, too, is to form again a condensation of the component parts of the People, as well as of the People as a whole, according to their actual relationships. The more noble parts may not be crushed by the more massive ones, but the latter may not be excluded either. The value of each part is determined by its significance in the whole and for the whole. The relationships are organic, the scale is national.[13]

And this passage, in turn, seems to have been adopted by at least two advocates of proportional representation (both of whom mistakenly attribute it to Mirabeau himself).[14] One of them then commends his own proposed electoral system because it "will represent the whole community and be a miniature picture of the different opinions which for the time being exist in the minds of the people."[15]

The proportionalists make explicit that it is a view of representation they are articulating; resemblance, reflection, accurate correspondence are vitally necessary in a legislature precisely because these things are what representation means. Without them, no true representation is possible, no legislature can be representative. "Does the Chamber of Representatives have to represent the electorate? That is the whole question. If so, all opinions, the most absurd ones, the most monstrous ones, even, must have representatives in a number proportional to their strength in the electorate."[16] The famous Thomas Hare himself, inventor of the best-known proportional system, argues that "a perfect representation is plainly inconsistent with the exclusion of minorities," because the correspondence must be accurate.[17] Others commend electoral reforms so that "the 'representative' body, so called, is sure to be representative in reality," to be "eminently representative," to be "truly representative," or to be "representative in fact as well as in name."[18]

Not all proportionalists argue in terms of the meaning of representation, or use such colorful metaphors.[19] But many do, and it seems natural for them to do so, since they are interested in the composition of the legislature, the presence in it of spokesmen for all groups in proportion to their number in the electorate. What matters is being present, being heard; that is representation. A representative body, said John Stuart Mill, is "an arena" in which each opinion in the nation "can produce itself in full light."[20] Other proportionalists speak of the right of each man to "appear by deputy" in the legislature; "appearing" is what matters.[21]

Of course even the proportionalists are interested in what the legislature does; they care about its composition precisely because they expect the composition to determine the activities. But they often conceptualize those activities as a giving of information about constituents' views, on analogy with the activities of the artist or map-maker. The function of a representative assembly, they say, is to depict or present or reflect popular opinion; often they explicitly contrast this "talking" function of the assembly with the function of acting or making policy, which they ascribe to the executive. And the executive they somehow do not think of as "representing." Thus, while it is not strictly true, as one commentator charges, that Mill "did not consider" the function of Parliament, it is true that he and other proportionalists see that function as one of talking rather than actively governing.[22] Legislatures should not and cannot govern because they are unfit for political action; their task is to debate and criticize the action of government: "Instead of the function of governing, for which it is radically unfit, the proper office of a representative assembly is to watch and control the government: to throw the light of publicity on its acts."[23] This is precisely why Mill thinks that all opinions and interests must be represented accurately: so that all possible views and criticisms will come to light.

Other proportionalists, too, tend to distinguish between representation, on the one hand, and activity—government, lawmaking. decision-making—on the other.[24] They often argue that, although decisions must be made by majority rule, minorities have a right to representation, to be heard in the legislature. This argument is found in Mill, but it appeared already in the writings of one of the earliest proportionalists, who allowed the majority the right to govern "but insisted that the total community, by reference to all the interests which went into making up the community, had the right to participate in the *deliberations*, that is, the representation."[25] Thus representation is one thing, and governing another. "The right of representation" must not be confused with "the right of decision"; majority rule is applicable as "an instrument of action" but not as "an instrument of representation."[26]

Their seeming neglect of political action is what has made the proportionalists most vulnerable to critical attack. Critics charge that their zeal for accurate reflection in the composition of the legislature has made them blind to the importance of its governing activities. Hence they have failed to notice that proportional representation can make these activities impossible. The critics charge that a proportional system atomizes opinion, multiplies political groupings, increases the violence of faction, prevents the formation of a stable majority, and hence prevents the legislature from governing, which is its major task. These criticisms appear as early as Walter Bagehot's reply to Mill, which stresses Parliament's task of governing, or at least of selecting and supporting a government.[27]

The critics attack the proportionalist's reliance on electoral devices; they challenge the view of a legislature as passive; they question whether there is a fixed "something" in the nation which can be reflected. But the one thing they do not challenge is the proportionalist's view of what representation is, or means. They, too, take it for granted that to represent means to resemble or reflect accurately. Thus they are forced to urge sacrificing "accurate representation" for the sake of effective government. "Unity of action is of more consequence than variety of opinion.

The idea, indeed, of representation may be, and often is, carried much too far."[28] Besides having "representative functions," they say, a legislature must *also* support a stable government.[29] Thus they conclude that proportionalism "assures adequate representation but only at the cost of weakening government, while the majority system secures adequate government but only at the price of withholding adequate representation."[30] Similarly, F. A. Hermens, perhaps the proportionalists' most active contemporary critic, attacks them by questioning whether it is "the object of representative bodies" to represent. He argues, instead, that "parliaments have primarily become agents for the constitution and control of governments; properly we might call them intermediate agents of government rather than 'representative' bodies. . . . [Thus a modern parliament] . . . should not be constituted in such a way as merely to 'represent' the voters, but on a basis which will assist it in fulfilling the great tasks it has to fulfill."[31] Even Walter Bagehot, that classical opponent of proportionalism, felt compelled to acknowledge that it alone would produce "genuine representatives." And Bagehot conceded that without proportional voting, voters whose candidate lost the election were "by law and principle misrepresented."[32]

There is something so compelling about the view that representation means accurate reflection, once it has been articulated, that the critics have accepted it unchallenged. Thus they are forced to an admission which seems damaging to their cause: that representation must be sacrificed—for something more important, no doubt, but sacrificed nonetheless. Yet we know, from our discussion of the authorization theorists, that representation does not have to be defined in terms of accurate resemblance or reflection or correspondence. For Hobbes the concept is so intimately connected with action and governing that an assembly in which each member has a veto power "*is no representative at all*," because it might be paralyzed and unable to act, that is, represent.[33] A representative must first of all be capable of effective action. Yet the opponents of proportional representation never think to argue on such grounds.

The critics accept the proportionalists' definition because it strikes them as correct and convincing, as it may strike us unless we have thought about other definitions or counterexamples.

Like the authorization definition, it is, by itself, plausible and tempting; it is a definition we might formulate if we approached representation from a certain direction and with the appropriate concerns. Like the authorization definition, it is not false, but rather a partial truth, a part of the truth about what "representation" means. The proportionalists' analogies—the picture and the map—are sometimes said to represent or to be representations; we are accustomed to say that the artist represents the visible world on canvas, that there is such a thing as "representational art."

But perhaps we should not assume too readily that we know what kind of "representation" this is, what the word means in such a context. What, for example, distinguishes representational art? The proportionalists' stress on accuracy of correspondence makes it seem obvious that representation in art is also a matter of accuracy. And of course there have been periods in the history of art when teachers and critics and even painters held the purpose of art to be the accurate depiction of the visible world, the more accurate the better. That is why the makers of the American Constitution assumed that "the portrait is excellent in proportion to its being a good likeness."

But accuracy of depiction has not always been seen as the goal or measure of art—even of art that depicts recognizable scenes and objects; in the Western tradition the idea that the artist should paint what he sees dates only from the Renaissance.[34] Even where accurate rendering is the goal, the very standards of what counts as accurate rendering vary with time and place and school. The history of art and art criticism demonstrates that artistic representation has always been a matter of style and convention, as well as of skill. A painting is not a photograph, and even photographs are not much like the objects they depict. Even in paintings of the most painstaking accuracy, even in *trompe-l'oeil*, the artist does not reproduce reality, but combines paint in complex ways on canvas. This is something an artist has to learn to do, and a viewer has to learn to read.

A representation is never a replica. The forms of art, ancient and modern, are not duplications of what the artist has in mind any more than they are duplications of what he sees in the outer world. In both cases they are renderings within an acquired medium, a medium grown up through tradition and skill —that of the artist and that of the beholder.

To say of a drawing that it is a correct view of Tivoli does not mean, of course, that Tivoli is bounded by wiry lines. It means that those who understand the notation will derive *no false information* from the drawing.[35]

Some paintings give more accurate information than others, are more like photographs; but there is always a notation to be read, and even a photograph can be misread.

But it is not accuracy of depiction or correspondence which defines representational art. A painting is not more representational or less representational depending on how accurate it is. An Audubon or a Constable is not more representational than a medieval madonna or a Greek statue, nor is a photograph the most representational of all. Even a crude resemblance is sufficient to constitute a representation. Thus the simplest, childish outline drawing of a stick man or a box house is a representation.[36] And when we read that the Egyptian alphabet was based on "representational signs," we do not expect or require that the hieroglyphs have any but the faintest indications or resemblance to what they stand for.[37] "The only characteristic that a picture must have in order to be a picture of a certain thing is an arrangement of elements analogous to the arrangement of salient visual elements in the object."[38] Thus we can, if necessary, demonstrate the correspondence part by part to show that the picture is representational, is *of* something. ("Look, that is the door, and that is the roof; it's a house.")

What is necessary to make a representation is not accuracy of depiction of something visible, but simply depiction of something visible, the intention to depict. The point at which we might begin to debate degrees of "representationality" in art, or whether a particular painting is or is not representational, is not where paintings become crude or inaccurate, but rather where we begin to doubt whether any pictorial resemblance to something visible is intended. Thus we could debate whether "Nude Descending a Staircase" is or is not representational (although I think it is). The Picasso and Braque abstractions in which there is one recognizable object (say, a guitar) can be spoken of as containing representational elements. In contrast, nonrepresentational art is precisely art which is not intended to correspond to the appearance of any physical objects or scenes. It may contain leaflike or boxlike shapes, but it is not a painting *of* leaves or boxes; the resemblance is irrelevant.[39] Thus, although a painting must be representational before the question of accurate depiction can arise, it is not accuracy that makes it representational.

Furthermore, representation seems to require a certain distance or difference as well as resemblance or correspondence. "If we could make a genuine tree, as pins are made in the factory on the model of those which exist already, it would not be called a representation."[40] It is difficult to be clear about this, because of our ordinary way of talking about pictures of objects. For, ordinarily, pictures of things, especially pictures of simple objects, although they are representations of those objects, do not (are not said to) "represent" them. We do not point to a picture of a tree or a house or a table and say, "This represents a tree (a house, a table)." We are likely to say, "This is a tree." (We sit over the picture book with our child and say, "What's that?" "A rabbit." "Right! And that?") "This represents a tree" is what we might say about a patch of color or squiggle of line that is intended to indicate a tree but does not look like one. Of course we do not mean that the picture-book rabbit should be fed real carrots, that the picture-book tree would benefit from a glass of water poured over its roots. Yet they are (in some sense) a rabbit and a tree. So in learning to draw a child will learn how to "make" a tree, although in nature that privilege may be reserved for Joyce Kilmer's God.

We are more likely to use the verb "represents" about complex pictures of whole scenes or events. Thus we might say of a painting that it "represents the Annunciation." Or we may speak of "two pieces of Holbein representing the triumph of riches," "monuments [that] represent them like themselves," "wallpaper representing spacious Tyrolese landscapes."[41] I am not sure why such complex representations (sometimes) do represent, and simple ones do not (are not said to); the reason may be connected with the sense in which the *artist* represents. A representation may resemble very crudely, but the resemblance must be intentional. In this sense pictures are representational insofar as the artist was alleging something about the visual appearance of what he depicted, about the way it looked or the way he imagined it to look. Representation here means the action or activity of the artist, something very close to "presentation" or "rendering." Each artist who has painted a picture of the Crucifixion has represented it in a particular way. We say that the artist represents Christ as a chubby baby, or represents philosophy as a woman with her head in the clouds, or represents death as a hooded skeleton. He is alleging something about what they look like, presenting their appearance in a certain way, perhaps as he imagines it.

This kind of presenting by the artist can use nonrepresentational symbols also, or representational figures that are not supposed to resemble what they stand for. Thus the artist may represent Christ by a fish or even by a nonrepresentational sign. So this kind of representing does not seem unique to representational art. But it is important to distinguish here between "representing as" and "representing by." In some contexts it does not seem to matter whether we say the artist "represents the Holy Ghost *as* a dove" or "represents the Holy Ghost *by* a dove." But that is because the dove is now both symbol and appropriate depiction. But it is not a matter of indifference whether we say that the artist "represents Christ by a fish" or "represents Christ as a fish." The latter sounds distinctly odd, for it suggests that he wants us to think of Christ as looking like a fish. The connection with representational art, then, would have to be in the activity of "representing as" rather than "representing by"; it would involve alleging something about the appearance of a thing, not merely referring to it.

This sense of representation is very close to "making representations to someone," or "representing oneself to be starving": the allegation that certain facts are so, which plays an important role in the law, where a representation is "a statement of fact made during preliminary negotiations toward a contract, seriously affecting the inclination of one party to enter into it."[42] In legal terminology this kind of representing means "to describe or *portray in words*; to declare, set forth, exhibit to another mind in language."[43] If the allegations or statements are false, they constitute "misrepresentation," and a contract made on the basis of them may be invalidated.[44] The courts have even gone so far as to say that such representation need not be in words, but simply "means to exhibit, expose before the eyes," so that "any conduct capable of being turned into a statement of fact is a representation."[45]

Besides its similarity to allegations about facts, the way in which an artist represents is closely related to the way in which an actor represents a character on the stage. And here we encounter the same duality between "represents" and "is" that we found with regard to pictures of simple objects. For if we are merely identifying the part an actor plays, who he is supposed to be, we say simply, "He is Hamlet." In the same way we would identify a piece of scenery: "That is the castle gate"; whereas we could say of a chair temporarily serving as a substitute for a piece of scenery, "That chair represents the castle gate." Again, as with the picture of a tree which simply "is a tree," the scenery and the character of Hamlet lack the distance or difference that representation requires; they *are* what they are supposed to be. But in another sense the actor represents Hamlet, and the whole company represents the play *Hamlet* on the stage. This refers to their activity of presenting the play and the character in a certain way. Thus an actor might worry about "how to represent Hamlet" on television, not about "how to be Hamlet." And a director might worry about how to represent *Hamlet* in central staging. The word here is again very close to "present."

When we say that a picture represents the Crucifixion, or that wallpaper represents Tyrolese landscapes, we may be expressing a metaphorical analogy with what the artist does. We may be saying that the painting, although it is inanimate, nevertheless shows (represents) the Crucifixion in a certain way, makes allegations (representations) about what it looked like. Although we would not say of a picture of a tree that it "represents a tree," we might easily say that it "represents a tree as being very fragile and almost translucent."

The artist, and by analogy the representational work of art, presents a part of the world as being or looking a certain way, makes allegations about it. Hence the painting can yield information to someone who understands the stylistic conventions. Art, as distinct from technical illustration, is not intended primarily as a source of information about depicted scenes, nor do we judge it by such standards. Yet what makes it representational is an intended visual correspondence of parts such that one could gather information from it. That is why even an astute esthetic philosopher, whose message is precisely that art is not a matter of accuracy and information, can nevertheless say (I think, correctly) that artistic representation means that someone who understands the notational system can gather from the painting information about what is depicted.[46] Here as elsewhere, representation means a presenting again, a presenting of something not present. In art, the absent thing is presented visually, and there is a correspondence of visible features, part by part.

In this sense, a map or a blueprint is as much of a representation as a painting is—in a way even more so, since maps and blueprints really are used to convey information about what they depict, although not primarily about its appearance. "A picture is a picture of a certain house because of a close correlation between the parts of the picture and certain visual features of the house. A blueprint of the same house is correlated with structural features of the house. Either the blueprint or the picture could be said to be a representation of the house."[47] And maps and blueprints, like paintings, need to be read; to understand the information they contain, we need to understand the style, the notation, the code that is used. A blueprint or map is not representational, although it is a representation. Most map-makers' signs and symbols are arbitrary and in themselves "meaningless." Only occasionally does the map-maker use representational signs or elements, as when he indicates camping places by a small triangle, a stylized representation of a tent. But most map signs are conventional, and map-making is a "representing by" rather than a "representing as."

With a map, we may feel that we have arrived at a kind of representation that will serve the purposes of political theorists who want to stress accuracy of correspondence as defining representation. A map is judged by its accuracy. Yet even here we require difference along with the correspondence. "A map *is not* the territory it represents, but, if correct, it has a *similar structure* to that territory."[48] Furthermore, there are many kinds of maps for many different purposes. Some show certain features of the land; some show others. Many are flat; some are topographical.

Some show invisible things like economic trade regions or dialect distribution. With any map the question of accuracy can be raised, but again it is likely to be misleading. Korzybski argues: "If the map could be ideally correct, it would include, in a reduced scale, the map of the map; the map of the map, of the map; and so on endlessly."[49] But a map is not more correct or more accurate just because it is more detailed, and certainly a map showing economic trade regions is neither more nor less correct than one showing speech dialects or highways. A Mercator projection map of the world is not less accurate or correct than one which breaks up the surface of the globe like slices of orange peel. It depends on the purpose for which the map is to be used, and on knowing how to read what it shows. A map, like a representational painting, conveys information only to someone who knows the "style." And, as in artistic representation, the information is conveyed by a systematic part-by-part correspondence between the map and what it depicts—the kind of isomorphism, feature by feature, which mathematicians call "mapping."

With the notion of a mirror, we seem to come still closer to the ideal of perfect accuracy—the map which is accurate for every conceivable purpose. While pictures and maps and blueprints are static, remaining unchanged once they are completed, the mirror faithfully shows the changing scene before it at each moment. Thus it seems not merely accurate, but accurate over time; without itself changing in any way, it reflects change automatically. One need only make sure that the mirror is not warped, that the glass does not distort the image. Even a mirror, however, can reproduce only visual features; it cannot show structure as a blueprint can, or abstract relationships as on a map. Even a mirror image is not easily confused with the thing itself. I am not even sure that we would call a mirror image a representation at all; that locution sounds somewhat odd to me. Similarly it sounds odd to say that the mirror "represents" my face, or "represents me as looking surprisingly old." Somehow "presents" or "shows" seems more natural here, as if the image is so much like the original, so faithful and accurate, that it is not a re-presentation at all.

The metaphors of portrait, map, and mirror have this in common: all are renderings of an "original" in a medium different from it—a picture of physical objects or scenes on canvas, a map of a geographic territory on paper, a two-dimensional reflection of physical bodies on glass. But a similar view can be developed using examples in which the representing is done by something of the same kind as the original—a miniature or condensation of the original, or a part of the original that can be used to stand for the rest. We turn now to a few examples, and the terms that go with them: the adjective "representative" and the noun "representativeness."

The idea that a representative assembly should be a condensation of the whole nation is a venerable one, appearing as early as the Monarchomachs, whose ideal legislature was an *epitome regni*, or *regni quasi epitome*.[50] In American thought, too, both proportionalists and others have suggested that "the representative body in a State may be said to be an epitome or abridgement of the whole civil body or community," that it is a "condensation" of the whole, a "miniature" of the electorate.[51] The proportionalists' metaphor of the perfect map is quite similar: a legislature should be a miniature in the sense that it should have members to correspond to each feature of the national landscape. But there are other ways of conceptualizing the representative assembly as a condensation of the whole. Some theorists think of it as a representative sample of the whole nation, whether chosen mathematically or by lot. And others see it as a body composed entirely of representative men.

A number of writers who desire a legislature that is "an average sample of ordinary men" conclude quite reasonably that this might be achieved by a randomizing process of selection.[52] "Selection by lot, or a controlled random sample, would be best calculated to produce the microcosm of the whole body of the people."[53] Choice by lot, they say, "would secure the same probability of impartial judgement that is expected of jurors. . . . [and] be likely to secure a more accurate reflection of the popular will."[54] Even more common than the idea of selection by lot is that of genuine random sampling, no doubt because of the power of that technique in scientific research and because it is familiarly linked with representation in the idea of the representative sample. Thus it is easy to suppose that a legislature must be a representative sample in order to represent truly. Already in the early 1920's one can find references to "representation by sample," the idea that in a democracy public officials may be selected "to use their judgment as fair samples of the people, on the supposition that their opinion will be the same that the public itself would form, if it could spend time enough to examine the matter thoroughly."[55] Probably the most extensive attempt to identify representation with sampling is made by Marie Swabey:

the principle of sampling in democratic theory is that a smaller group, selected impartially or at random from a larger group, tends to have the character of the larger group. Accordingly a part, if properly chosen, may be taken as truly representative of the whole and substituted for it . . . Throughout modern "representative" democracy this principle of the valid substitution of the part for the whole is central.[56]

Swabey argues that the principle of sampling is displayed on no less than three levels in a modern representative government. First, the voters are to be considered a sample of all the people: "the government finds it necessary to interpret the recorded opinion of those who vote at election as a fair, trustworthy sample of what the opinion of the general public would be if they expressed it."[57] Second, the majority of the voters are to be taken as a sample of all the voters, yielding a novel interpretation of majority rule: "Having learned that the chances which give the mean character of a collection are more numerous than those representing the extremes, we tend to believe that the type of vote that occurs most frequently in the election is probably representative of what most of the people want."[58] Finally, the public officials who are elected are to be regarded as a sample of the nation:

the office-holders selected by this majority belong to the same average type. According to the general assumption, the average or mediocre man is the kind of "sample" that most truly represents the public . . . What there is most of in a collection is held to picture it more accurately than any other part . . .

In other words, elections are held for the more or less conscious purpose of choosing for office men to represent "fair samples" of the public in general.[59]

Several contemporary political scientists have adopted Swabey's view of representation, despite its obvious difficulties.[60] It

is not clear whether Swabey offers her views as an interpretation
of how elective democracy actually works or as an ideal toward
which it should strive. But much light can be shed on its difficulties as an interpretation, by taking it seriously as an ideal. Although elections may send average men to office, they need not
do so; although voters, or the majority of them, or elected officials may be something like a sample of the nation, they are
certainly not an accurate or truly random sample. It is instructive
to imagine what our political system would be like if, instead of
elections, we actually conducted random samplings of the population, making Congress a "truly representative" body. Such a
change would mean an end to political parties, to professional
politicians, to the regarding of elections as an occasion for reviewing policy or authorizing or holding to account.[61] Insofar
as such a system would differ from present practice, Swabey's
interpretation of present practice is misleading; insofar as the
differences involve parts of what representation means, the representative sample is a misleading model for understanding political
representation (misleading, again, because it is only a partial
account of what it means to represent).

The theorists considered so far in this chapter seem to be
concerned mostly with the representative assembly as a whole,
and they work from the metaphors of picture or map or mirror
or sample. It would be rather awkward to think of a single, isolated representative as a picture or map or even sample of his
constituency, although he might be said to "mirror" or "reflect"
it.[62] But other theorists within the descriptive view work from
the adjective "representative" (in the sense of "typical") and
the concept of representativeness rather than from metaphors,
and consequently can deal with the individual representative just
as well as with a representative assembly. For them, indeed, it is
the representativeness of each member that makes an assembly
truly representative as a whole, that defines representation.

Many textbooks of political science discuss the characteristics
of elected legislators under some such rubric as "The Representativeness of Representative Assemblies."[63] From this it would
be easy to assume that the two appearances of virtually the same
word must mean the same, and thus to interpret the latter in
terms of the former. Consider, for example, a pioneer study in

empirical political science entitled "The Representativeness of Elected Representatives."[64] Attempting to correlate the characteristics of state legislators with those of their constituents, the study takes it as obvious that the degree of such correlation measures "the extent to which they represent their constituents," while the specific characteristics on which there is high correlation show "the respects in which legislators *actually represent*."[65] To represent means to be representative in the sense of having representative (typical) characteristics. Seen in this way, elections "appear to be a method of finding persons who possess this representative quality."[66]

But only a few writers remain at this simplistic level; most of them soon discover the serious difficulties in the way of simply identifying representing with representativeness. Not many people, after all, seriously think that the best legislator is one who is typical and average in every conceivable respect, including intelligence, public spiritedness, and experience. Even the author of the empirical study mentioned above, despite his identification of being-like-one's-constituents with "actually" representing, concedes that a good representative will and should be typical only in certain respects.[67] At most one can say that representativeness "*may* apply" in representative government. "A typical farmer— one who owns an average farm, who farms it as most farmers do, who thinks along the same lines as most of his fellows—might be sent to the legislature to represent a farming district. His attitude toward problems facing the legislature would be representative of the general farm attitude."[68] Here three different ideas are identified: being representative (typical), being elected Representative, and having a representative attitude. The passage avoids a common pitfall by recognizing that voters do not always elect typical men; but it does not help us to understand the relationship among the different senses of the word. A recent textbook in American government expresses uneasiness about this relationship by discussing the characteristics of Congressmen under the heading "How Well Does Congress 'Represent' the American People?"[69] The quotation marks around "represent" convey a certain awareness that characteristics, representativeness, may not be the whole measure of how well an assembly represents.

Many attempts have been made to grapple with this difficulty, to explain what the relationship between representativeness and political representation might be if the two are not the same, the former not a direct and complete measure of the latter. One possibility is to concede the whole concept of representation, and admit that the ideal legislature should not represent. This solution parallels the position taken by the critics of proportional representation: "represent" does mean "be as much like as possible," so representation is not desirable in politics. One critic of American democracy sneers that "our legislatures are indeed representative enough" in being "composed of a fair average of men in the various walks of life. But they are indicative rather of that average—a somewhat indifferent mean—than of great ability and experience in social and economic life."[70]

Another alternative is to argue that "representativeness" does not mean likeness or typicalness at all. In a recent article the meaning of representativeness is approximated to that of institutionalized political representation rather than the other way around. The authors argue that when we speak of a nonelected body as a representative group, we mean that its members would have been elected if membership had been elective. "An appointed commission may approvingly be called a body of 'representative' citizens, or may be attacked as 'unrepresentative,' depending on whether its members might conceivably have been chosen had they been subject to election rather than appointment."[71] The vagaries of meaning encountered in our concept have made us suspicious of such solutions. Representing and representativeness need not mean exactly the same thing: the former is not just being typical; the latter is not just being electable. Hobbes' definition could never explain the representativeness of a representative sample; on the other hand, a representational painting is not one that has been or could be elected.

The most elaborate of the unsuccessful struggles to resolve these difficult questions is found in the works of De Grazia and Gosnell. Both begin by defining representation as a condition which exists when the desires of the constituent are being fulfilled by a power-holder.[72] De Grazia and Gosnell recognize that constituents can be satisfied either by the power-holder's actions or by his characteristics; and they want to equate the latter with representativeness, with the power-holder's having representative (typical) characteristics. Seeing that the same word root is involved, they correctly assume that there must be a connection, and struggle to specify what it might be.

Gosnell says that voters may support a candidate because they like "his picture with a pretty wife and child," and desire "a handsome family to represent them." This is both true and in accord with his definition: if handsomeness is what that voter desires, then a handsome candidate represents him. But then Gosnell proceeds to treat this as an instance of *likeness* of characteristics. "One of the primitive, liberal and persistent meanings of the term 'representation' is to 'present again.' . . . A person may . . . see a remarkable similarity to himself in the physiognomy and social characteristics of his representative. In fact, he sees a mirroring of himself. He will feel as though he himself were present in the seat of power."[73] The fact that voters' desires are sometimes satisfied by representativeness in the candidate may, indeed, be linked to the sense in which representing means accurate mirroring. But then one must explain how or why a voter satisfied by a candidate unlike him (more handsome for instance) is also a case of representation, or how the two cases are related. This Gosnell fails to do.[74]

The same difficulty is encountered by De Grazia. He notes that voters often demand that their representative possess "some large measure of identity of characteristics with the group qualities," so that representation "may be regarded as a consensus of characteristics between politically unequal parties of which one is the representative and the other constituent."[75] Such identity of characteristics may be found also in systems with other means of recruitment than elections, as when a dictator "resembles the masses in origin, traits and behavior." But then De Grazia continues: "*Furthermore*, so-called democracies have been known to select representatives by reason of their *superior* class position rather than to reject them because of it. The society's norms for representation may have demanded special *differences* rather than identity."[76] This is undoubtedly true, but then one can no longer say simply that representation means "identity of characteristics." De Grazia tries to save the notion of identity of reflection even here, by arguing that in this situation the representative "mirrors social norms."[77] But mirroring social norms can no longer mean being a typical member of the society, when the norms "demand special differences rather than identity." A German theorist has suggested that in the latter case we have not someone who is typical of the group but someone who is "ideal-typical," who corresponds to the group's ideal.[78] But while voters are sometimes pleased by typicalness, sometimes by ideal-typicalness, the latter is not representativeness, is not "identity of characteristics."

The matter is complicated still further when De Grazia mentions examples in which a ruler pretends to have representative characteristics, as when Huey Long took off his silk pajamas to don an old-fashioned nightgown before permitting himself to be photographed in bed.[79] And another political scientist adds that identity of characteristics can be achieved at a psychological level in the mind of the voter if he identifies with the officeholder: "The legislator is representative first, because voters tend to select men of their own 'kind' to office, even though the similarity in kind may be based in the voter's 'identification' of himself with the social, economic, or intellectual attributes of the office holder."[80] But this can bridge the gap between representing and representativeness only if we are willing to say representativeness means "being *thought by the voters* to share the voters' characteristics." This again is simply not true; representativeness can show up in all sorts of contexts where there are no voters—with regard to inanimate objects, representative samples, and so on.

But if none of these discussions is satisfactory, what can be said to clarify representativeness and its relationship to representing? Why do we use the same root word for both? The dictionary tells us that "representative" in the sense of "representativeness" means "typical of a class, conveying an adequate idea of others of the kind." Thus, as with representational art, and map, and sample, it is a matter of being able to draw correct conclusions from A about B. But an idea "adequate" for what purpose? Here we encounter the same possibility of ambiguity as with the map.

There is also, despite the dictionary, a certain difference between typicality and representativeness, but it is subtle and not easy to demonstrate. If we need to select a few representative poems from the works of a certain poet (perhaps for teaching purposes), we might want his most typical or average or characteristic poems; but we might prefer those that show him at his very best, the outstanding ones. Thus, in *Representative Men*, Emerson was concerned neither with the average man-in-the-street nor with the typical, but with what he himself called "great men."[81] It seems to be a matter of the purpose for which the examples are selected.

The difference between being representative and being typical shows up most clearly, however, in a collection containing several major varieties of objects. Suppose that we are to pick not a single representative object but a representative group of objects from such a collection. For most purposes we would pick one object of each of the major varieties in the collection, to make up our representative group. If we were interested also in the relative proportions of each variety in the collection, we would have to select different numbers of objects from each variety instead of just one. But in either case our representative group would not be "typical" of the collection, for there is no "type" to which it could conform. Here again we have the element of isomorphism or part-by-part correspondence: one object to represent each variety, with the group of objects being representative of the whole collection. In this respect, representativeness is related to the metaphors of map and condensation. And what constitutes a representative example (or sample) depends on what we want to know about the thing it stands for; it depends on our purposes.

Despite their various assumptions and implications, the metaphors of picture and map and mirror, of miniature and sample, and the concept of representativeness all seem to have this in common: they involve a representing very different from that defined by the formalistic theorists, primarily a "standing for" something or someone absent by some correspondence of features. They constitute generally what we may call (following Griffiths) "descriptive representation," in which a person or thing stands for others "by being sufficiently like them."[82] The sense in which a map or a picture represents is not primarily an activity; that is why it can be predicated of inanimate objects. And when human beings represent in this sense, what matters is not their actions (though we have seen, and will shortly review one significant exception) but what they are, or are like. This is a plausible view of representation, based on important uses of the concept—representational art, representative samples, representativeness—yet it is as incomplete as the formalistic view. This kind of representing is only one aspect of the concept, and a general definition based on it alone will therefore be incorrect.

If we ask in what sort of context this view is most appropriate and relevant, the answer would seem to be: in contexts where the purpose of representation is to supply information about something not actually present. If representation always means that something absent is made present in some sense, although not literally present, then, in the contexts we have been discussing here, the making present consists of the presence of something from which we can draw accurate conclusions about the represented, gather information about the represented, because it is in relevant ways like the represented. This is clearly true of the way in which a map or mirror represents, of a representative sample or example. In representational art the matter is more complex, since art is not primarily intended or used as a source of information (but rather, roughly speaking, for esthetic contemplation). Yet what makes a representational painting representational is a correspondence of features to something in the visible world, such that, where the representation is accurate, "those who understand the notation will derive no false information" from the painting. It need not, of course, be accurate in fact. Like the painter who represents the Crucifixion in a certain way, like the man who represents himself to be starving, the painting asserts or alleges something; its truth or accuracy is another matter.

When this view of representation is applied to the political realm, the implication is that in politics, too, the function of representative institutions is to supply information, in this case about the people or the nation. Actually, we must distinguish three somewhat different but related ways of bringing this view to bear on political life. The view may suggest that a legislature is like a map or mirror, essentially a passive object so put together that from it a spectator can gather information about the people—that it reflects or resembles the nation by its composition. It may, second, suggest that a representative legislature is like a painter or a "maker of representations to someone else," representing by its activity rather than its composition, but an activity of a very special kind. Or, third, the suggestion may be that if the representative legislature is a sufficiently accurate copy, a perfect replica, then it may safely and justifiably be allowed to substitute for the whole people, to act in place of the nation. Here the purpose is action by the representative, but that activity is not itself representation. Representation is, rather, a matter of accurate resemblance or correspondence, and a precondition for justifying governmental action.

The dividing line between the first and second possibilities is not very sharp. Probably few theorists who write at length about political representation are content to stay at the metaphorical level and insist that the legislature is simply to be "read" like a map for information about the people at large. Indeed, while it is still relatively easy to separate painting and painter, map and map-maker, the metaphor of the mirror rather combines the two; a mirror seems to be the maker of its own image, of the image it presents. If representatives are to reflect their constituents as a mirror does, we are left in doubt as to just how active or passive this "reflecting" might be. Certainly some writers seem to assume that the essential function of a representative body is to vote yes or no on proposals put before it, and that the measure of its representativeness is essentially whether it votes as the whole nation would if the question were put to a plebiscite. The representatives must simply vote as their constituents would; and the same result could be achieved by local plebiscites, with the representative merely delivering the result of the local vote to a central agency. Such writers often speak of the individual representative as if he were an inanimate object by means of which the people act: a "speaking trumpet," a "mouthpiece," a "communications device."[83] The picture is a very static one; it is not so much that the representative should decide in the way that the people would decide, as that he should have the opinions and feelings they have. These writers sometimes sound as though everyone has opinions ready on every possible question, and hence the only political problem is to get accurate information about a national opinion which already exists.

But much more subtle and important versions are possible

as one moves toward a more active "presenting" of information. John Stuart Mill coupled his advocacy of proportional representation with a view that made the ideal representative body "an arena in which not only the general opinion of the nation, but that of every section of it, and as far as possible of every eminent individual whom it contains, can produce itself in full light."[84]

Griffiths has suggested that we may well regard legislatures

as primarily the places where discussion or debate occurs: discussion or debate, on the whole, about what social or political action, if any, is to be taken. . . . Then we shall want to be sure that [the assembly's] composition permits that on any given topic every opinion, or every worthwhile opinion, in the country finds its spokesman. Now it is this latter demand that is peculiarly bound up with descriptive representation. For if our concern is that a country's assembly should be the forum for every given opinion that the country contains, it is natural and reasonable to suggest that the assembly should be composed of descriptive representatives drawn from every opinion-holding group.[85]

Downs, approaching representative government from economic theory, has formulated a similar view.[86] Representatives, he suggests, are agents of their political party; their job is to tell the party what the people want (and occasionally to tell the people about their party). They are "specialists in discovering, transmitting and analyzing popular opinion." The government (and each party) "wants to enact policies which fit the desires of its constituents, but it does not know what these desires are. Therefore it employs, as part of its own institutional structure, a group of men whose function is to scatter into the corners of the nation and discover the will of the people."[87] Hence, Downs argues quite consistently, on the many issues on which people have no will, or do not know what they want, "there is nothing for representatives to represent."

Representing means giving information about the represented; being a good representative means giving accurate information; where there is no information to give, no representation can take place. Given such a formulation, although there must be a representative for "every worthwhile opinion," the number of representatives from each particular opinion is essentially irrelevant. If representing means presenting a point

of view, one spokesman is as good as ten. Here the metaphors
of artist or map-maker have triumphed over the metaphors of
portrait or map. It is no longer correspondence of characteristics
that matters so much as the presenting of accurate information.
Representatives should be articulate rather than just typical.

Here representing is no longer merely a "standing for" something absent by virtue of resemblance, but a kind of activity.
But it is activity very different from the general acting in the
name of another that formalistic theorists discuss; it is not a
matter of agency, of being authorized to commit others, of acting
with a later accounting to others. It is not an "acting for" but a
giving of information about, a making of representations about;
hence it entails neither authorization nor accountability. That is
why theorists of descriptive representation so often argue that
the function of a representative assembly is talking rather than
acting, deliberating rather than governing.

Finally, descriptive representation may be applied to the political realm in a third way. Some writers, while agreeing that
the legislature is an active, governing, decision-making agency
in the fullest sense, argue that its activities are not representation.
Representation is accurate correspondence to the nation, being
a perfect replica, so as to justify the actions of the legislature as
"what the nation would have done." Representing may be seen
as an accurate correspondence between legislature and nation,
not for purposes of information, but to ensure that the legislature does what the people themselves would have done if they
had acted directly. Thus accurate representation becomes a way
of justifying government of the many by the few, a rationale for
representative democracy. Whatever the legislature does will be
what the whole nation would have done in its place; so no one
will have right or reason to complain. A copy sufficiently like an
original can be substituted for the original without making any
difference.

This kind of justification of substituting representatives for
the whole people is linked with radical democratic ideology, according to which direct democracy is the ideal system of government and representation a mere second-best approximation.[88]
Ideally, it is argued, every man has the right to govern himself,
or at least to participate in decisions which affect his interests.

In a small community this ideal can be achieved through direct democratic action; political decisions can be reached in an assembly of all the people. But the size and extent of modern states make this ideal impossible, and so representation is introduced as the best approximation to it, a way of allowing each man to participate by proxy.

The notion that parliamentary representatives are substitutes for the rest of the people is actually much older than radical democratic theory, and need not be connected with it. The concept apparently began in the thirteenth century in England, where it was linked with the idea of Parliament as a court finding the law in particular cases, rather than a legislature making law. Recent historians have traced the rise in the thirteenth century of the Roman law doctrine that parties who have legal rights at stake in a judicial case are entitled to be present or be consulted in its decision.[89] This doctrine of *quod omnes tangit ab omnibus approbatur est* apparently fostered the requirement, in both church and secular government, that extraordinary taxes must have the consent of those taxed. It was never strictly applied, but it played a major role in promoting the summoning of knights and burgesses to meet with the king's council in England. Consent did not mean democratic consent; the knights and burgesses were not elected at first, much less democratically elected. Probably the earliest sense in which they acted "for" their boroughs and shires was in performing a duty for which the whole shire or borough was responsible. The idea of men being sent to Parliament "for" their communities, and consenting on their behalf, received a further application in the fourteenth century, when judges began to argue that, since everyone was presumed to know the actions of Parliament, ignorance was no excuse for disobedience. Everyone was taken to know the law because everyone was considered ("intended") to be present there, either personally or "by procuration."[90]

From these beginnings arose the doctrine that the meeting of Parliament is a substitute for the meeting of everyone in the realm, which would be physically impossible. That doctrine, which developed as early as the fifteenth century, was not then a democratic doctrine. "Being present," while it was vaguely associated with the attendance of knights and burgesses at the

Parliament, had nothing to do with any demand for accuracy of correspondence between legislature and nation, nor with the democratic idea that each man has a right to be present and participate in his government, so that representation is a substitute for direct democracy.[91] By the time of the American and French Revolutions, the argument was commonly expressed in these terms, and it is still common today.[92] This view of representative government is intimately linked with the idea of representation as resemblance or reflection. If representative government is a substitute for direct democracy, if the legislature is a substitute for the assemblage of the whole people, it should approximate the original as closely as possible. If we cannot have the ideal, at least we want something as near to it as can be achieved.

Thus it is no surprise that this doctrine is often conjoined with the metaphors of descriptive representation. Those who, in the American Revolution, likened a good legislature to an accurate portrait did so because they saw the legislature as a substitute for the democratic assemblage of the whole people. "Representation is made necessary," they said, "only because it is impossible for the people to act collectively."[93] Or again, "in a community consisting of large numbers, inhabiting an extensive country, it is not possible that the whole should assemble"; so a representative body must serve as "the most natural substitute for an assembly of the whole."[94] In the French Revolution, when Mirabeau compared a legislature to a map of the nation, he added that representation is necessary whenever "a nation is too numerous to meet in a single assembly."[95] Similarly, proportionalists have held representative government to be "the modern form of democracy, . . . a machinery necessitated by modern civilisation and requirements of life to make democratic government possible."[96] The machinery is more perfect in proportion as it accurately duplicates the working of the people as a whole.

Behind all the applications of the descriptive view to political life hovers the recurrent ideal of the perfect replica, the flawless image, the map which contains everything, including "the map of the map; the map of the map, of the map, and so on endlessly." But that ideal may well be chimerical, and therefore dangerous.

Perfect accuracy of correspondence is impossible. This is true not only of political representation but also of representational art, maps, mirror images, samples, and miniatures. Paintings, however visually accurate, always have a style which can mislead unless it is understood. Maps and blueprints, too, need to be "read." Furthermore, maps vary not merely in accuracy but also, and more significantly, in kind: in the features or characteristics of a territory they are supposed to show. Even a mirror or photograph shows only visible features. The most perfect replica in miniature will not duplicate every characteristic of the original; or rather, we should distinguish between the kinds of objects that can be completely reproduced in miniature replica (like large and small porcelain figurines differing only in size) and those which cannot (like nations). (And would we call a perfect replica, a second object just like the first, a "representation" at all?) Even a representative random sample, although it allows us to state with precision the mathematical probability of any amount of inaccuracy of correspondence, can yield only certain kinds of information; specifically, it is limited to information about numbers of individuals in a population. So it is always a matter of our purpose: Is it information that we need, and, if so, what kind of information—what features are to be reproduced, what will be significant?

In politics, too, representation as "standing for" by resemblance, as being a copy of an original, is always a question of which characteristics are politically relevant for reproduction. In a general sense, we are very much aware that politically significant characteristics vary with time and place, and that the doctrines about them vary as well. Religious affiliation, which for many centuries was an issue suitable for warfare and revolution but has become relatively unimportant today, is perhaps the classic example. But the history of representative government and the expansion of the suffrage is one long record of changing demands for representation based on changing concepts of what are politically relevant features to be represented. The nation is not like a geographic area to be mapped—solidly there, more or less unchanging, certainly not changed by the map-making process.

Many descriptive theorists are willing to acknowledge that the ideal of a perfect condensation is unattainable; but they argue that it can nevertheless function as a goal to be approximated more or less closely, although always out of reach. So long as we think that the function of representation is to yield information about the represented, this suggestion is essentially correct: the more accurate the copy, the more accurate the information. Even here it tends to gloss over the problem of choosing what kind of information is relevant. But the real difficulties come if we are to use accuracy of correspondence not as a source of information, but as a justification for letting the representatives act for us. The argument is tempting, to be sure. If one could produce a perfect replica of the nation, like it in every conceivable respect, then surely it would produce the same policies, decisions, compromises, and actions as would the whole nation. Then no one could reasonably object to substituting the replica for the original. But if the perfect replica is an ideal that can never be achieved but only approximated, there is a problem. The degree of accuracy will no longer guarantee the degree of similarity of action, let alone the degree of justifiability of substituting replica for original. As soon as the correspondence is less than perfect, we must begin to question what sorts of features and characteristics are relevant to action, and how good the correspondence is with regard to just those features.[97]

A recent article has pointed out that much of the empirical research on the characteristics of legislators, especially in relation to the characteristics of their constituencies, assumes that these characteristics determine in large part what the representative will do. Legislative decisions are what really concern us:

the appropriate process for selecting public decision-makers has never been the really fundamental question for theories of representation. Behind every proposal for altering the method of selecting officials is some assumption, at least, about the effect of such changes on what decision-makers or decision-making institutions do, and how they do it. Proposals for reform must assume or show that the proposed change will bring it about that *what* representatives decide and *the way* they reach decisions is more nearly in accord with expectations and demands.[98]

In the same vein, Charles Hyneman has criticized empirical studies which simply examine legislators' characteristics at random, without showing their relevance to political action. Too often such empirical studies assume that a certain element in the population is inadequately represented simply because not many legislators themselves are of this element. "Facts about the men who enact statutes are, presumably, significant only if they bear some relation to legislative behavior—significant only if they affect the content or form of laws, or influence the procedure by which laws are enacted."[99]

We tend to assume that people's characteristics are a guide to the actions they will take, and we are concerned with the characteristics of our legislators for just this reason. But it is no simple correlation; the best descriptive representative is not necessarily the best representative for activity or government. Griffiths points out that a lunatic may be the best descriptive representative of lunatics, but one would not suggest that they be allowed to send some of their numbers to the legislature.[100] In the same way, "while we might well wish to complain that there are not enough representative members of the working class among Parliamentary representatives, we would not want to complain that the large class of stupid or maleficent people have too few representatives in Parliament: rather the contrary."[101] If we are interested in information about the public, the ideal of perfect reflection or resemblance does no harm, but if our concern is with political action by our representatives, the idea of accuracy is likely to mislead.

Descriptive representation is obviously relevant to political life, yet it is again only a partial view, and therefore deceptive in areas where it does not apply. We need only remind ourselves of some of the things it cannot do, aspects of political and other representation which it neglects. Obviously it cannot account for the kind of representing Hobbes was talking about—authoritative action that is binding on the represented. For the theorists we have been discussing in this chapter, it may be a good idea to insist that a man who can make commitments in your name should resemble you, but aside from that practical consideration his authority to make those commitments has nothing to do with representing. Representing means being like you, not acting for you. Similarly, the descriptive view has no room for representation as accountability. In a practical way, perhaps one can assure accurate correspondence between representative and constituents if the former is elected by the latter. But voters often prefer to elect men who are not representative (typical) of the district, and that may be a good thing. In any case, a man can only be held to account for what he has done, not for what he is; so at most a descriptive representative might be held to account for whether he has given accurate information about the constituents; and here selection by random sampling might well be more effective than elections.

Finally, the view of representation we have been discussing does not allow for an activity of representing, except in the special and restricted sense of "making representations," giving information. It has no room for any kind of representing as acting for, or on behalf of, others; which means that in the political realm it has no room for the creative activities of a representative legislature, the forging of consensus, the formulating of policy, the activity we roughly designate by "governing." It may be desirable to have such activity carried out by representatives, but carrying it out is not representing; representing here can at most mean being typical or resembling. If we are discussing the duties of a representative, or distinguishing good from bad representing, the descriptive view is not totally irrelevant, as formalistic views are. It is irrelevant insofar as representing involves no action at all but only characteristics; in that case representing is not something that any one man can do well or badly (though one man can be more typical than another). But if we speak of it as the activity of "representation making" or information giving, then a representative does seem to have a duty; he must reflect his constituents as truly and accurately as possible. Where they have no views or relevant characteristics to be displayed, representing is impossible. Either way, there is no room within such a concept of political representation for leadership, initiative, or creative action. The representative is not to give new opinions to his constituents, but to reflect those they already have; and whatever the legislature does with the nation's opinions once expressed is irrelevant to representation. If it leaves the activity of governing to the executive, then he cannot be said to represent. If we restrict representing to the descriptive view, to a giving of information, then we cannot account for the other, conflicting ways in which the concept is used, and we cannot explain how a governing executive represents. Yet descriptive representation *is* representation. The examples ring true and cannot be ignored; we do speak of representativeness, of representational art, of representative samples. And the descriptive view can serve as a healthy corrective for the formalistic view, pointing to some of what the latter omits. But neither view by itself, nor yet a combination of the two views, is the whole story about representation. We must look further.

5

"Standing For":
Symbolic Representation

Descriptive likeness is not the only basis on which one thing can
be substituted for another, can represent by "standing for." Symbols, too, are often said to represent something, to make it present
by their presence, although it is not really present in fact. This
kind of representing, too, can be taken as central and definitive,
and all other kinds, including political representation, can then
be interpreted in terms of it and approximated to it. We may
call this the "symbolic representation" or "symbolization" view,
and writers who adopt it, "symbolization theorists." For they see
all representation as a kind of symbolization, so that a political
representative is to be understood on the model of a flag representing the nation, or an emblem representing a cult. "Representation is a matter of existential fact; up to a certain point it just
'happens,' and is generally so accepted. Why should this be?
Repraesentare means to make present something that is *not* in
fact present. A piece of cloth may in that sense represent a vast
power complex, or the Stars and Stripes the United States of
America."[1]

But human beings, too, can be thought of as symbols, can
under the right circumstances stand for a nation just as the flag
does. The case probably most familiar from the literature of

political science is that of the king in a constitutional monarchy. A recent textbook on British government tells us that the monarch "stands for the majesty, the authority, the unity of the British nation, and in each of the units of the Commonwealth . . . he represents its statehood."[2] He is in this respect just like a flag or other inanimate symbol, except that "as a living symbol he is more interesting." The same kind of symbolic representation is often attributed to heads of state in general; they "represent or embody, that is, are symbols for the unity of the people of the state; as flags, coats of arms, national anthems are in a more material and functional way."[3]

Students of representation have attempted to fit such phenomena into a more general framework, relating the role of the political leader to personification, primitive magic, and religious rituals, all of which seem to involve a belief in hidden connections. Maude Clarke sees the beginnings of "the representative principle" wherever, "for a religious purpose, some creature or object is deemed to be the symbol or agent of hidden and unearthly power. In primitive society . . . the king or chief stood half-way between his people and the unseen world, typifying or representing both humanity and divinity."[4] Clarke then cites the case of the Jewish scapegoat, "upon whom the sins of the community were laid and thereby expiated," when it was driven out into the desert. Similarly, she refers to other substitute sacrifices, whether human or animal, as in *Maccabees*: "But I as my brethren, offer up my body and life for the laws of our fathers . . . that in me and my brethren the wrath of the Almighty which is justly brought upon all our nation, may cease."[5] To these instances a German commentator adds primitive magic thinking, as when a tribal doctor heals the sickness of others on parts of his own body, on the basis of a magic connection between the two.[6]

These all seem to be instances of representation, and to belong in the same general category as "symbolic." But to understand their significance for political thought, we must first examine the way in which symbols represent, and the differences between representing and symbolizing.[7] Since we have discussed representational art, it may be useful to distinguish symbolic art from it. We are told that a symbolist painter is one who "aims at symbolizing ideas *rather than* representing the form or aspect of actual objects."⁸ This is not to say that symbolist art must be nonrepresentational; but representation is not its major aim, and the things that are represented are not the ones that are symbolized. Simple representations are not said to "represent" but just to "be" a tree, a cat, and so on. Symbols, in contrast, are often said to represent their referent. The artist "represents" his subject *as* something, or as having certain characteristics when he depicts it, makes allegations about its appearance. When he represents something *by* a symbol, that symbol may well be a recognizable object, but it need not be and usually is not a representation of what it symbolizes.

Early Christian artists used the fish as a symbol of Christ, especially for secret reference, on the basis of an acrostic on the Greek word ἰχθύς. The fish was a symbol of Christ, but not a representation of him. The artist who painted a fish was not representing (showing) Christ as a fish; he was making no allegations about Christ's appearance. Unlike representations, symbols are not likenesses of their referents, and do not resemble them. They make no allegations about what they symbolize, but rather suggest or express it.⁹

Yet symbols do sometimes seem to share some characteristics with the things for which they stand. Thus the United States flag has fifty stars to correspond to the fifty states of the nation, and the fish could serve as a symbol of Christ because of the letters in its name. The dictionary defines a symbol as "something that stands for or denotes something else (not by exact resemblance, but by vague suggestion, or by some accidental or conventional relation)."¹⁰ But that way of putting it can be misleading. It suggests that the flag is a symbol of the nation because its "resemblance" to the nation is vague rather than exact; in reality the connection is simply not a matter of resemblance at all. It is not visible characteristics that the flag shares with the nation—neither exactly nor vaguely.

The term "symbol" derives from the Greek *symbolon*, "a sign by which one knows or infers a thing," which is compounded out of *sym*, "together" and *ballein*, "to throw." One of the earliest uses of the verb "to symbolize" in English was in sixteenth-century physics, where it referred to substances which would combine when put together, or to the transmutation of elements.

One may hazard a guess that the harmonious unification of elements was considered dependent on their having qualities in common. ("But Aire turne Water, Earth may Fierize, because in one part they do symbolize.") Here again there is a suggestion of hidden or inner qualities rather than of outward resemblance. Accordingly, we tend to expect a hidden connection or rationale for symbols; we expect an explanation why the ship should be an appropriate symbol of the church; the eagle, of America; the palm branch, of victory. Some writers argue on this basis that a symbol differs from a sign because the latter is arbitrary, whereas the former "is never wholly arbitrary; it is not empty, for there is the rudiment of a natural bond between the signifier and the signified. The symbol of justice, a pair of scales, could not be replaced by just any other symbol, such as a chariot."[11] One could conceive of another symbol of justice, but it would have to have some rationale or connection. Our flag might have looked very different if Betsy Ross had had a different inspiration, but, whatever its features or colors, some of them might have been "explained" in terms of features of the United States.

There is, however, a certain kind of symbol that is completely arbitrary, that does not share even hidden characteristics with its referent. These, often called "conventional" symbols, occur, for example, in mathematics. We speak of the "signs and symbols of algebra," meaning, by the former, indicators of operations to be performed ($+$, $-$, $\div$, etc.), and, by the latter, letters that stand for unknown quantities (x, y, etc.). These symbols of algebra have no connection, neither resemblance nor hidden common qualities, with the unknown quantity for which they stand in the solution of algebraic problems. We assign them new meanings quite arbitrarily at the outset of each problem. Another example is that of map-makers' symbols, the various geometric figures used on a map or chart to indicate camping places, enemy gun emplacements, growths of new timber, and so on. These symbols may be iconographically representational, as when a small treelike shape is used to indicate timber; but often they are totally arbitrary, and one must look at the key or legend to understand them. This kind of conventional symbol is a mere neutral token of what it stands for.

Some writers contend that, at the other end of the scale from arbitrary conventional symbols, there is a different class of symbols having no element of arbitrariness. Their symbolic reference is so clear and so universal that anyone who encounters them understands it. These are sometimes called "natural" symbols. The basic dream symbols of psychoanalytic theory are often postulated to function in this universal way, in everyone's unconscious.[12] There is considerable disagreement over whether natural symbols exist at all, and, if so, how many there are, and which ones. One writer might call the rose a natural symbol: "The image of a rose symbolizes feminine beauty so readily that it is actually harder to associate roses with vegetables than with girls."[13] But another writer could suggest a dozen different meanings for roses depending on times and contexts."[14]

But even the way in which a plausible natural symbol represents is very different from representational art or other kinds of descriptive representation. Symbolic representation, although it is a "standing for," is not the same as descriptive representation. Consider the distinction in meaning between the two things symbols are most frequently said to do: symbolizing and representing. For this purpose, conventional symbols, like the algebraic, are particularly useful, because, although we call them symbols, they do not (are not normally said to) symbolize.

In preparing to do a problem in algebra, we may say any one of a number of things, such as: Let x be the number of apples John has. Let x stand for the number of apples John has. Let x represent the number of apples John has. But we would not naturally and spontaneously say: Let x symbolize the number of apples John has.

Why not? To say that something symbolizes something else is to say that it calls to mind, and even beyond that evokes emotions or attitudes appropriate to the absent thing. This is not true of the algebraic x. Indeed, one of the great advantages of algebra for problem solving is that it lets us put aside for a time the cumbersome facts of apples and dollars and square feet, and deal only with the x, without thinking of what it stands for. That is why the beginning student often needs to be reminded to "reduce his answer" to the appropriate units when the problem has been solved. Arbitrarily assigned symbols have no inner characteristics that correspond to the characteristics of their referent, nor do they suggest or evoke it; they do not symbolize. They merely refer. In the same way, the symbols on a map do not ordinarily symbolize trees or gun emplacements.

When we speak of something as symbolizing, we are calling attention to just those features of the situation which are missing with algebraic or map-making symbols. We are calling attention to someone's reacting (or being supposed to react) to the symbol in a manner appropriate to its referent (kissing the Cross, saluting the flag). We are emphasizing the symbol's power to evoke feelings or attitudes. And we are calling attention to a vagueness, looseness, and partial quality of the reference. More precisely, symbolizing is "an exact reference to something indefinite."[15] We can never exhaust, never quite capture in words, the totality of what a symbol symbolizes: suggests, evokes, implies. It is the only possible embodiment of what it symbolizes, and therefore both exact and of undefinable meaning. This quality of most symbols, that they can symbolize, is taken as definitive by almost all writers on the subject. Many of them vaguely recognize that there are also conventional symbols, which do not symbolize; but either disregard them as trivial or define them away as signs.[16] This is understandable and not particularly harmful in works on literary symbolism or symbolist art; but for our purposes it disguises an important distinction. For by noticing that some symbols cannot (are not normally said to) symbolize, but only represent or stand for, we can learn about the way in which symbols represent.

When we speak of a symbol (any symbol) as "representing," we are assimilating it to a conventional symbol, to the kind of symbol that can *only* represent. We are, for example, about to specify the symbol's referent explicitly in words. What a symbol symbolizes (if it does) can never be exhaustively stated in words. When we identify the meaning of a symbol, especially when we do so briefly and simplistically, we tend to say that this is what it "represents." Thus we suggest that the symbol is, roughly, a substitute for what it represents; but a symbol is not a substitute for what it symbolizes. "Symbols are not proxy for their objects, but are vehicles for the conception of" what they symbolize.[17] As William York Tindall has put it, symbolizing does not mean being there "like a sign to point to something else, to take the place of something else, or even to stand for it"; rather, the symbol "display[s] itself with all it has created and welcome home." A symbol cannot simply be "exchanged with what it symbolizes, as if the halves of the equation were of equal importance. This may be true of certain signs or of symbols that only convenience recommends," but it is not true when a symbol symbolizes.[18]

We seem particularly inclined to say "represents" when we are not merely identifying the referent of a single symbol, but giving a brief explanation of a whole group of symbols, as in explaining a particular poem or painting. Then we say, "This represents this, and that represents that," and so on, giving a sort of explanation of the "code" used by the artist. This corresponds to the key or legend of a map; it is another instance of representation that is not a single relationship between two isolated things, but a repeated relationship of point-by-point correspondence between two groups of things, an isomorphism. What Tindall says about the sign applies equally to the symbol that represents: it "means a one-to-one correspondence."[19]

A particular symbol in a particular situation may both represent and symbolize; but that does not mean that we are saying the same thing about it if we say the one or the other. To say that a symbol represents is to suggest a precise correspondence, a simple reference or substitution, and perhaps the existence of a whole series of further correspondences of which this one is but a single instance. To say that a symbol symbolizes is to suggest the vagueness or diffuseness of what it stands for, the impossibility of exchanging the one for the other, expression rather than reference. Of course, a symbol's representing is often causally related to its capacity to symbolize. Thus the flag can represent (substitute for, refer to) the United States for certain purposes just because it symbolizes (suggests, evokes, arouses feelings appropriate to) the honor and majesty of the United States. Conversely, one of the ways in which we learn to react in the appropriate manner toward the flag is through its being used and presented as a "stand-in" for the United States.

This distinction between symbolizing and representing should help us to distinguish between symbolic representation and other kinds of representation. If we start from the symbols, and define representation on that basis, the entire concept becomes skewed or distorted in the direction of symbolizing. The very suggestions or implications found in "symbolize" by contrast with "represent" may be expected to show up in a theoretical treatment of representation that is built, for instance, on the way the flag stands for the nation.

Even when a symbol represents rather than symbolizes, it does so in a somewhat different way from an artistic representation or other instances of descriptive representing. The purpose, the context, the point of its representing is different. A symbol is not a source of information about what it represents; it does not allege anything about what it represents. True, the number of stripes in the flag corresponds to the original number of American colonies; so we could say of the flag what was said in the last chapter about representational art: if the correspondence is accurate, those who understand the style will gather no misinformation about what it represents. But we do not ordinarily use the flag as a source of information; and if we did so use it, it would not then be functioning as a symbol. We do not use symbols as sources of information, as bases for drawing conclusions, about what they stand for. That is why there is no such concept in our language as "missymbolizing," to correspond to "misrepresenting." Nor are there accurate and inaccurate symbols. Accuracy of correspondence is not an issue in symbolic representation, even where there is some connection, some correspondence of (hidden) characteristics between symbol and referent.

But then, what do we use symbols for? Rather than a source of information, the symbol seems to be the recipient or object of feelings, expressions of feeling, or actions intended for what it represents. It is "the focus of attitudes thought appropriate" to something else; or it has done to it what we would do to its referent.[20] Thus there are specific appropriate ways to treat the flag, and other things that must not be done to it. If you "let the old flag touch the ground," you are insulting not just a piece of cloth but "the Republic for which it stands." In the same way, you rise for the playing of the national anthem, kneel before the Cross, and so on. In literature, too, the symbol is supposed to evoke or express feelings appropriate to what it stands for, and what happens to a symbolic figure must be considered as happening to its referent as well.

Because of the element of arbitrariness in most if not all symbols, because their connection with what they represent is not based on resemblance of outward characteristics, the only criterion of what constitutes a symbol is in people's attitudes and beliefs. If we ask what it is that "*makes* symbols out of anything— out of marks on paper, the little squeaks and grunts we interpret as 'words,' or bended knees," the answer is clearly: the beliefs, attitudes, assumptions of people.[21] With conventional symbols this is obvious; unless you refer to a "key" or are told what x stands for in a particular algebra problem, you have no way of knowing. Such symbols stand for whatever they are currently taken or defined to stand for. But even with other kinds of symbols, you need to know whether the thing suggests or expresses something beyond itself to some people, or is supposed to, or has at some time in the historic past. You need not yourself believe in everything that you call a symbol; it is possible to discuss Christian symbolism without being a believer. But for such a thing as Christian symbolism to exist, somebody must believe (or have believed) in the symbolic significance of the Cross, the ship, the fish, and so on. A symbol is considered to have a meaning beyond itself, not because of its actual resemblance to the referent, not because of any real connection, but just because it is so considered. In this sense, symbolic representation either exists or does not exist in any particular case. If someone believes (or believed), it exists; if no one believes, it does not exist. That is why the flag can be said to be an example of "existential" representation, "a matter of existential fact," that "just happens."[22] And a number of writers, starting from symbolic representing as a model, derive the same conception of all representation: it is "existential," present or absent in people's beliefs.[23] It is a "condition," "primarily a frame of mind."[24]

Two further aspects of symbolic representation naturally follow. Since the connection between symbol and referent seems arbitrary and exists only where it is believed in, symbolic representation seems to rest on emotional, affective, irrational psychological responses rather than on rationally justifiable criteria. There can be no logical justification, no reason for believing in a connection that is purely conventional or arbitrary. The thrill of pride at the sight of the flag is not based on its accurate resemblance to the United States. The response depends more on training and habit than on learning or understanding. Accordingly, writers who emphasize symbolic representation as central usually stress the role of irrational psychological responses in bringing about the condition of representation.

As a result, in the second place, such writers take a great interest in the creating of symbols. Just as in descriptive representation the sense in which a picture or map represents is closely related to the way in which a painter or map-maker represents, so too with symbols. The theorist is soon led beyond the flag or the Cross that stands for nation or church, to the process by which these symbols become capable of doing so, and then to the human activity that can set the process in motion. We have already encountered the contrast between "representing *as*" and "representing *by*." The former is the activity of the artist or other maker of a descriptive representation; the latter is not. Thus a painter might represent Christ *as* a tall man, but not as a fish, although he might well represent Christ *by* a fish. This kind of symbol-making activity clearly has to do with conventional symbols; the map-maker or mathematician turns a formerly meaningless mark into a (conventional) symbol by defining it, entering it in the map key. (Or, of course, he may simply use a familiar and accepted conventional symbol.)

The creation and use of symbols that can symbolize, however, is not just a "representing by"; it is not just an arbitrary stipulation, which anyone who wants to consult the map will not hesitate to accept. To get people to believe in, accept, respond appropriately to a nonconventional symbol, one must arouse certain responses in them, form certain habits in them, invite certain attitudes on their part. Unlike making a descriptive representation, creating a symbol is apt to be a matter of working on the minds of the people who are to accept it rather than of working on the symbol itself. And since there is no rational justification for the symbolic connection, for accepting this symbol rather than that one, symbol-making is not a process of rational persuasion, but of manipulating affective responses and forming habits.

When symbolic representation is taken as definitive, and all other kinds of representing are seen in terms of it, these characteristic features of the way symbols represent become generalized and projected, for example, into political life.[25] The political representative will then seem to have only arbitrary, conventional, or hidden connections with those he represents. Representing people will seem no different from symbolizing an abstraction like the nation. The crucial test of political representation will be the existential one: Is the representative believed in? And the basis of such belief will seem irrational and affective because no rational justification of it is possible. Hence, political representation will be not an activity but a state of affairs, not an acting for others but a "standing for"; so long as people accept or believe, the political leader represents them, by definition. Insofar as activity will seem at all relevant, it will be neither the activity of acting for others nor the activity of making a representation or giving information about the represented. It will be the activity of making people believe in the symbol, accept the political leader as their symbolic representative.

The essentially static "standing for" kind of application of symbolic representation to political life emerges most clearly in regard to the head of state in his symbolic, ceremonial functions. We distinguish practical activity rationally directed toward bringing about "real" goals, on the one hand, from expressive, symbolic actions, on the other. It is precisely insofar as the actions of the head of state are merely ceremonial that we consider him a symbol. Thus the President of the United States is a symbol of the nation just when, and insofar as, he performs functions which are almost purely ceremonial and symbolic, like receiving ambassadors. We say that he is functioning "as figurehead *rather than* working head of our government."[26] Such a leader may endanger his status as symbol and embodiment of the whole people if he becomes involved in active, partisan politics.[27] And an ambassador can serve particularly well as a symbol of his state abroad, be honored at ceremonial functions, just because everyone knows it is not he who makes policy decisions.[28] He is not the real active force behind policy but a mere agent; so he can easily serve as symbol.

Perhaps the most frequent expression of this correlation is in the literature concerning the modern British monarch, which emphasizes the contrast between the "rational activity" of Parliament and prime minister, and the "inactivity" of the king.[29]

One commentator says that the king is "the symbol of the community and the formal representative of the state," but that this means, "He ceases to be a living and acting person, and becomes a magnificent cipher," who "has nowhere the power of decision."[30] Another points out that when the monarch does act in times of crisis, it is by "representative acts of expression" like visiting the wounded.[31] The king can retain and fill his position as symbol, the textbooks tell us, only at the price of abstaining from "real" (that is, causal rather than expressive) political activity. The position of the royal family "is largely due to the fact that it takes no part in politics, wields no open political power, takes sides publicly in no political controversy, and therefore makes no political enemies."[32] The king "can do no wrong" because "politically, he can do nothing at all."[33] He is a symbol, like a flag, and hence the object of feelings and actions, not an actor.

But what shall we say of cases where the head of state is also the working head of government, at once a static, "standing for" symbol and an active leader of the nation? This seems to indicate that a symbol can be rationally, causally active after all. But again, the fact that we can truly predicate two different things of the same person does not prove that those two things are (or mean) the same. Although we may sometimes speak of the United States President as both symbol of the nation and its active political leader, we are not saying the same thing about him in the two characterizations. Insofar as he is a symbol, qua symbol, he is not the nation's agent authorized to act for it; he exists as an expression of it.

To be sure, where the symbol is a human being or group of human beings, symbolic representation may be much enhanced by, may even require, a certain amount of ritual activity. But it is precisely ritual, expressive, symbolic activity that might be required. Surely if the queen skipped down the aisle at her coronation instead of marching slowly and regally, the symbolic illusion would be destroyed. But we distinguish that sort of expressive activity from her "rational," "causally relevant," "nonceremonial" duties in, say, selecting a prime minister on those (rare) occasions when the choice is not completely dictated by parliamentary politics.

In speaking of the ritual activities that may be required of a human being representing symbolically, however, we approach the more general category of symbol-making, which plays a major role in the symbolization view of political representation. For a political leader to represent symbolically, like any symbol he must be believed in, and such belief can be fostered or created. Who must believe in him, who creates the belief, and how? The only requirement for symbols in general is for someone to believe in the symbolic connection, but writers who apply this view to politics inevitably require that the belief exist in the minds of the governed. A ruler represents to the extent that those subject to his rule accept him, believe in him as a symbol. Most frequently this idea is conceptualized as meaning that the represented must believe in the symbol. A ruler is a representative to the extent that those he rules and represents believe in him; representing means being-believed-in or accepted-as a symbol of the nation by the represented, the people who make up the nation. It is all in the mind of the governed. In this sense, as one commentator says, all political rulers and leaders are representatives "on the assumption that they are acceptable to those under authority."[34] Another writer equates "the representative quality of a board or commission" with whether it is acceptable to, and has the confidence of, the groups it regulates.[35]

This view is taken as definitive and made fully explicit by De Grazia and Gosnell.

Representation of an individual in a society is a condition which exists when the characteristics and acts of a person in a position of power in the society are in accord with the desires, expressed and unexpressed, of the individual.
Representation is a condition that exists when the characteristics and acts of one vested with public functions are in accord with the desires of one or more persons to whom the functions have objective or subjective importance.[36]

For both writers, representation is a condition characterized by the represented's being satisfied, "primarily a frame of mind."[37] It can exist or fail to exist for as many people as are in the society, subject to power; it exists or fails to exist for each individual separately. De Grazia encounters some difficulties when he tries to generalize this definition for a whole society, to define representative government: "In the opinion of many, democracy is a society in which the public functionaries give a maximum of representation to a majority of the population. By contrast, a despotism has often been viewed as a society in which only the despot, or his family, or the nobility, has possessed the maximum of representation."[38] But that would be to define democracy as a government in which most people are satisfied with the rulers, and despotism as one where only the ruler is satisfied. There could be no such thing as a nondemocratic government welcomed or accepted by the mass of the people; and even a regularly elected government would lose its democraticness whenever its policies or characteristics ceased to please the majority.

Looking only to the beliefs and attitudes of the represented to establish the presence of representation fails when the symbol represents an abstraction or idea or inanimate object. Then whether something is a symbol may depend on the states of mind of some people, but not on the mind of the represented, the thing symbolized. Rather, we would be inclined to speak of an audience, or a group which either believes or does not believe in the symbolic representation enacted before it. "In a non-rational sense, representation may be based upon any system of values which a certain community shares. Thus the Pope is said 'to represent Christ on earth.' Evidently he does so only for a believing Catholic."[39] The Pope is a member of the community of Catholics, but it is not that community that he here represents. He is said to represent Christ, and the community is a sort of audience or third party, which either believes or does not believe in the representation. And presumably if no one believes that the Pope represents Christ, he does not. The example does not require (and logically could not really require) that the represented, Christ, must believe in the representation for it to exist. We must look to the beliefs of people outside the representative relation itself, to observers or audience.

Some writers have argued that representation can exist only where there is a third party or audience of this kind, what German theorists call an *Addressat*, before whom representation can take place. They argue that representation "presupposes three factors: first, the one who is represented; second, the representative; third, the one before whom representation takes place. . . . The representative of a business, for instance, has to represent his firm before another firm, which constitutes the third factor; if that were not the case there would be no need for his services. Or consider the diplomat, who represents his country before a foreign government."[40] They further maintain that parliamentary representation was once representation in this "true" sense, before a king as *Addressat*, but that it is no longer so.[41] Others argue that there is no logical reason why the same people cannot be both represented and *Addressat*; today, they say, Parliament represents the People before the People.[42] But still other writers deny that an *Addressat* or third party is necessary to representation at all.[43]

The existence of representation is to be measured by the state of mind, the condition of satisfaction or belief, of certain people, be they the represented or the audience. This makes representation a kind of two-way correspondence; it "concerns the agreement prevailing between ruler and ruled."[44] What matters is whether this agreement exists; since it is a two-way relationship, it can obviously be achieved as well by adjustments at the ruler's as at the subject's end. For representation to exist, it does not really matter how the constituent is kept satisfied, whether by something the representative does, or how he looks, or because he succeeds in stimulating the constituent to identify with him. As Gosnell puts it, we must be able, *within* the definition of representation, to ask with equal freedom, "What do the representatives do to the people?" And "What do the people do to their representatives?"[45] But in that case, a monarch or dictator may be a more successful and dramatic leader, and therefore a better representative, than an elected member of Parliament.[46] Such a leader calls forth emotional loyalties and identification in his followers, the same irrational and affective elements produced by flags and hymns and marching bands. And, of course, representation seen in this light need have little or nothing to do with accurate reflection of the popular will, or with enacting laws desired by the people.

This doctrine is often associated with stress on the integrative function of government in general, and representation in particular. If the main goal to be achieved is the welding of the nation into a unified whole, the creation of a nation, then it is tempting to conclude that a single dramatic symbol can achieve this much more effectively than a whole legislature of representatives.[47] Nor is this view confined to totalitarian theorists; as one recent historian explains,

> The history of despotism, from the Renaissance to the present day, naturally inclines us to consider the personification of a people or a country by a monarch or dictator as deadly to political growth, but we must not on that account ignore the great part that has been played by kingship as a symbol of national unity. It is, in fact, hard to see how men, who dwelt in any but the smallest geographic areas, could have acquired the coherence necessary for political development, if they had not, for a long period of time, personified their common habits and business under the figure of a king.[48]

Similarly it has been argued that in politically underdeveloped communities a "despotic government" may "provide a more real representation . . . than could be afforded by electoral machinery."[49] Real representation is charisma.

The concept of the political leader as essentially passive, standing for others symbolically, must thus be supplemented by the view that he is a symbol-maker, making himself into an accepted leader through his activity. But this activity is not what we would ordinarily call the activity of representing, and it is certainly not "acting for" one's constituents. Nor is it merely ritual activity. Rather, it is a kind of activity to foster belief, loyalty, satisfaction with their leaders, among the people. Representation becomes identified with "effective leadership."[50] Since there can be no rational justification of the symbolic representative's position as leader, the emphasis (as with symbols) must fall on the nonrational or emotive elements in belief, and on leadership techniques which exploit such elements.

At the extreme, this point of view becomes the fascist theory of representation (not the theory of the corporate state, but that of representation by a *Führer*). The approach from symbolic representation suggests that it makes no difference which end of the representative relation is altered to maintain the accord or agreement between ruler and subject. But in fascist theory, this balance is definitely shifted to the other side: the leader must force his followers to adjust themselves to what he does. "Representation is not a process of extracting consensus by molding the state in the image of the subjects; rather, the state molds the individuals into a cohesive body."[51] The leader creates the unity of wills among his followers out of his own inner resources, and aligns them to himself.[52] Whatever means are effective for this purpose are to be used, so long as the end product is the requisite alignment: "By fraud, violence, noble words, shrewdly planned moves, etc., that creative person called representative gets the support of others and *makes them want what he wants*."[53] Thereafter, the fascists tell us, "the will of the free man coincides with the will of the state."[54]

Representation is a power relation, that of the leader's power over his followers; Hitler claimed that he had greater right to say that he represented his people than did any other statesman.[55] Representation may be a matter of consent, but this consent is created by the leader's energy, intelligence, and masterful personality.[56] For the fascist, no other conception is possible, because the people are amorphous and incapable of action or will. They can only accept the impact of a leader's action. Hence the people "are the instrument on which the political leader must play. If he elicits the right tones from this instrument, that is, if the People has confidence in his leadership, he receives thereby the indispensable foundation for his activity of political leadership."[57]

From this point of view, elections become merely one of many possible devices for keeping alive popular acceptance and belief; and elections are not nearly so effective for this purpose as parades and uniforms.[58] Elections serve only as one rather ineffective means for creating or sustaining representation. Even some democratic theorists share this view, seeing elections as a process which "enables the whole or a majority of the people to identify themselves, as the ruled, with their representatives, as the rulers."[59] Again, whatever facilitates identification or acceptance brings about representation. What matters is always the alignment of wills between ruler and ruled; representation *is* that alignment, no matter how it is brought about.

But the extremeness of the fascist theories reveals that something has gone wrong here. In fact, the difference between changing the subjects to suit their ruler, and changing the ruler to suit his subjects, is very great indeed. The difficulty can be perceived in the way in which nonfascist commentators struggle to explicate the fascist view. Ernest Barker, for example, after trying hard, is forced to the conclusion that in fascist thought "the term 'representation' is . . . being used in a new and strained sense." It may be true, he concedes, that the fascist dictator has a large and willing body of followers; but "The fundamental fact is the fact that this following represents or reflects the will of the leader, and not that the leader represents or reflects the will of the following. If there is representation, it is inverse representation, proceeding downwards from the leader. The party represents the leader: the people, so far as it takes its colour from the party, equally represents and reflects the direction of the leader."[60] In a passage like this, the other aspects of representation, other than symbolic representing, seem to rise up to reclaim their rightful share of the concept. Perhaps symbolic representation can be brought about by propaganda or coercion, but the resulting picture offends against the implications of descriptive representing. If the people "reflect" the leader, Barker says, then *they* represent *him*; clearly Barker is no longer thinking (merely) of symbolic representation.

Again we have set out from a grain of truth, certain valid examples of representation, generalized into a definition that is false because it is blind to other, different, equally valid examples. Symbols do (are said to) represent; symbolic representation is an instance of representation. That much is true. But it is not the only kind of representation; so, if it is taken as definitive, its peculiarities distort our understanding of other kinds. To say, as the symbolization theorists do, that representing is coextensive with satisfying, being-accepted-by the constituent, is to let the example of symbols lead us astray.

It is true that representation is a human concept, which would not exist if human beings had not conceived it. And so there is a tempting plausibility to the argument that in each instance, representation exists only where someone believes that it exists—sees the painting as a portrait, uses the map for information, responds to the flag as to the nation, authorizes an agent and later acknowledges the contracts he has made. But although plausible, this way of talking is a mistake. For, if a picture is representational, it is representational whether or not any particular individual sees that it is; if a map contains information about a territory, the information is there whether or not it is used. Even the question of whether you have been authorized to act for me is to a very great extent independent of whether I think you have; I may be bound by your action even though I do not believe that I made you my agent. Only symbolic representation, because it involves no rational, objective, justifiable connection between what represents and what is represented, seems to rest entirely on people's belief or acceptance, however engendered. (But even there, a Christian symbol is a Christian symbol whether or not any particular individual recognizes it as such.) Belief in or acceptance of any particular symbol is not something that can be justified, that depends on accuracy of correspondence or on services performed. It makes no sense to ask whether a symbol represents well, for there is no such thing as mis-symbolizing.

But these things are not true of other kinds of representation, and if they are extended to the political representative, serious problems result. Political representation does have something to do with people's irrational beliefs and affective responses, and it is important to ask when people are satisfied by their representatives, and under what circumstances they feel they are not being represented. But that is not the whole story, and to make it into the whole story one would have to gloss over some important distinctions. For one thing, accepting a leader and following him is not the same as accepting him as a symbol of the nation; seeing him as symbol is at most one basis for accepting his leadership, but not the only one. Or again, although the activity of making descriptive representations is sometimes called representing, and the using of conventional symbols (as on a map) is called representing, the activity of creating belief in, acceptance of, a nonconventional symbol is *not* (called) representing. Adjusting what is to represent until it is aligned with what is to be represented may be a part of the activity of representing, but the converse adjustment is not. The leader who molds his followers to suit his aims and interests is, if anything, making them represent him.

Although representation may be a condition in the minds of men, and it is important to inquire into the causes of that condition, we must not confuse the causes with representation itself.

It is important to ask what makes people believe in a symbol or accept a leader, but it is equally important to ask when they ought to accept, have good reason for accepting a leader. Only if we narrow our view of representation exclusively to the example of symbols are we tempted to overlook the latter question. For concerning symbols it makes no sense to ask for reasons for belief, or when men ought to believe. But concerning political leadership such questions do make sense. As one political scientist expressed it, "Representation concerns not the mere fact" that the represented do accept the representative's decisions, "but rather the reasons they have for doing so"; and reasons are different from causes.[61]

Both descriptive and symbolic representation, then, enlarge our view of the concept, but do not complete it. They make it possible to speak of representing by inanimate objects, although each of them introduces a special kind of activity as well, the activity of making something represent. For descriptive representation, this is an activity working on the thing that is to represent, making it into a likeness, map, random sample, or whatever. But symbol-making need not be a matter of working on the symbol; it seems rather to involve working on the minds of those who are to be represented or who are to be the audience accepting the symbolization. In neither case is the activity an acting for the represented, on behalf of, instead of, in the interest of them; it is in no sense a matter of agency. Both descriptive and symbolic representation supplement the formalistic views we examined earlier, and thus enlarge our understanding of the concept. Descriptive representation introduces the idea of correspondence or likeness and the importance of resembling one's constituents; symbolic representation suggests the role of irrational belief, which is neglected by the formalistic view, and the importance of pleasing one's constituents. Yet all these views put together still do not exhaust the concept of representation. We need to find an equivalent in the realm of action for the descriptive and symbolic "standing for" views—not the activities of making representations or symbols, but the "acting for" equivalent of the connection between image and original or symbol and referent. In the next chapter we shall try to find such an equivalent.

6

Representing As "Acting For": The Analogies

The view of representation centered on the activity of representing, the role of a representative, has not, to my knowledge, been articulated as an explicit definition by any writer on representation. I know of no representation theorist who says, in so many words, "Representation is a certain characteristic activity, defined by certain behavioral norms or certain things a representative is expected to do." The greater part of the literature on political representation takes such an assumption for granted, and is concerned with specifying what may be expected of a representative, how he ought to act, what his obligations are, how his role is defined. But to understand that literature and master its controversies, we need to be clear about what is entailed in viewing representation as activity, and how such a view differs from what has gone before.

In each of the views discussed so far, a theorist attempts to draw conclusions about the proper conduct for a representative, or the proper way of institutionalizing representative government. Yet the definitions we have examined do not lend themselves to the drawing of such conclusions; they are not suitable for telling a representative what to do, or for telling us how to judge his performance.

Authorization theorists like Hobbes are relatively consistent in recognizing this problem, and often argue that the representative has no special obligations, no special activity, no special role to perform as representative, that he is free to do as he pleases with binding consequences for others. But even Hobbes' own text contains ambiguities on this score, and examples of representation that suggest the contrary—limits on what the representative may do, or obligations that hedge in his activity.

Accountability theorists are even more vulnerable in this respect. Their aim is to show that true representation entails responsiveness to the represented, attention to his wishes or needs. And they see accountability as essential for achieving this purpose, hence as the essence of representation. Yet by defining representation in terms of accountability they defeat their own aims. By defining a representative as anyone who will eventually have to account to another for his actions, they make it impossible for the idea of representation to serve as a guide or standard for his actions. His conduct remains irrelevant to representation.

Where the representative is likened to a descriptive representation or a symbol, he is usually seen as an inanimate object and not in terms of any activity; he represents by what he is or how he is regarded. He does not represent by doing anything at all; so it makes no sense to talk about his role or his duties and whether he has performed them. On the other hand, this conception of representing as "standing for" brings with it another notion— the making or creation of representations or symbols; and that *is* a kind of activity. In the creating of symbols, the analogy is of doubtful validity, since we do not seem to call symbol-making "representing." But if the analogy is nevertheless accepted, it would seem to imply a single rather broad criterion for representative activity: that it be successful in getting accepted, in convincing. In descriptive representation-making, on the other hand, the activity is a matter of truthfulness, of accurate rendering of information about something absent.

What neither of these activities can give us, however, is representation as an acting for others, an activity in behalf of, in the interest of, as the agent of, someone else. Neither giving information about someone nor stimulating belief or acceptance in him could generally be characterized in such terms. Yet representation does sometimes mean such activity. The acting for others discussed in this chapter, differs from the representation- or symbol-making and the standing for others of the last two chapters. It differs also from the formalistic views; for, while they would see the representative as active, even as acting for others, his status as representative would be defined in terms of formal arrangements that initiate or terminate the activity, not in terms of the nature of that activity itself. We are now interested in the nature of the activity itself, what goes on during representing, the substance or content of acting for others, as distinct from its external and formal trappings.

The formalistic theorists allowed of no limits on, or standards for, the conduct of a representative qua representative; yet in various ways (including the very conflict between authorization and accountability views) they hinted at the existence of such limits or standards. The views of representation as "standing for" suggested what those standards or limits might be like: descriptive accuracy of correspondence or anything fostering belief or acceptance (in the represented or in the audience). But both suggestions, while expanding our view of representation, are also misleading. And neither one nor both of them together can account for the substance of the activity of representing as acting for others. What is needed here is some kind of activity or way of acting that is the equivalent of the way in which pictures or maps or symbols correspond to or embody what they represent. Any number of writers tell us that there must be some connection or relationship or tie between a representative and those for whom he acts; the difficulty lies in specifying what that tie is, in trying to characterize it. It is spoken of in the literature again and again as a "connection," a "contact," a "correspondence," a "chain of communication."[1] We are variously told that his actions, or his opinions, or both must correspond to or be in accord with the wishes, or needs, or interests, of those for whom he acts, that he must put himself in their place, take their part, act as they would act. But which, if any, of these formulations is the right one, and what does it really mean in practice? To answer that question we need an articulated view of representing as a (substantive) activity. We may call this view "the activity of representing," although that might be confused with the artist's activity in making a representation; or "acting for" others, although that might be confused with the formalistic view; or perhaps most clearly, "substantive acting for" others.

Only such a view will allow us to discuss the obligations of the representative as agent or actor-for-others, to judge his actions. And only such a view can account for certain ordinary ways of speaking about representation where activity for others is involved, but activity without the formal arrangements of authorization or accountability.

Political science literature contains many discussions on whether a particular legislature represents the people, the nation, or whether it "really" represents special interests. And the same question is frequently raised about an individual representative and his district. If someone in the visitors' gallery in Congress points to a certain Congressman on the floor and asks his neighbor whom that man represents, he may be expecting any one of several rather different kinds of answers. Which question he is asking, which answer he expects, must be determined from context. He may be asking whose representative the Congressman is "officially," so that an appropriate answer would be, "New Jersey's sixth district." He may be asking party affiliation. If he is a tourist, he probably has one or both of these questions in mind. But if the questioner and his neighbor are political scientists or journalists on the track of a pressure-group scandal, the appropriate answer may be, "Oh, he represents the natural-gas boys." This does not mean that he is their official or authorized representative nor that he stands for them as symbol or source of data; it apparently refers to the interests he looks after and the persons from whom he takes orders.

For a time California liberals amused themselves by referring to one of their state's senators as "the Senator from Formosa." Apart from the merits of the charge implied, what was the point of the joke? They knew perfectly well that the man was not "really" the Senator from Formosa; he was the Senator from California, and Formosa has no senator. But the point was, of course, that they considered him overly concerned with the welfare of the Kuomintang government, overly friendly with the China lobby, overly active in its interest. ("He's so active and concerned, why, you'd think he was their senator, representing them.") In this sense a man represents what (or whom) he looks after or concerns himself with, the interest that he furthers. We are all familiar with the journalistic literature investigating whether a certain official represents the nation or whether he "really" represents some special interest.[2] And when a political scientist writes that in all governments "what is represented is opinion organized as force," we know fairly well what he is trying to say.[3] He is not talking about the formalities—the geographic districts or other groupings that are officially represented; he is saying something about who gets his way, or what forces can be thought of as acting by or through the government.

This sense of representation is frequently involved, also, in dealing with appointed rather than elective representatives. When an appointed administrative board is to consist of a representative of labor, one of management, and one of the consumer interest, in what sense do these men represent? They are not authorized by labor, management, or consumers, nor must they account to these groups. Their actions and decisions do not commit or bind their respective groups (although orders issued by the board as a whole may be binding law). They are, of course, formal representatives in the sense that they do hold an official position: "Labor Representative on the X Commission." But if we ask what they are to do, in what sense they might correctly be called representatives, it is not a matter of rights or obligations, or of being a symbol or a descriptive sample. Their role, the reason for labeling their job as "representing," is to speak for, act for, look after the interests of their respective groups. Here again the substance of representing is activity. This is what a political scientist means when he says that the test of representation is not whether the leader is elected, but how well he acts to further the objectives of those he represents.[4]

This sense of representing may be illustrated by considering the question of whether judges are representatives. Where judges are elected, an additional complexity is introduced; but even appointed judges have been called representatives, and that is the argument most relevant here. It can take various forms, depending on the view of representation a writer adopts. From a formalistic standpoint, a judge is an agent of the state like all government officials. His pronouncements are not private expressions of opinion, but official utterances of the state. Hence he represents the state.[5] In a democracy where all agencies of the government are servants of the sovereign people, the judge might be said to represent the people. From the "standing for" interpretation, he may represent by embodying the values of a society; he may be a symbol representing the society. From the doctrine that anyone whose commands are obeyed and whose leadership is accepted is a representative, a judge certainly represents.[6] In this sense it can even be argued that the judge may be "less representative" if elected than if appointed.[7]

But all of these notions we have met and criticized before. What we are interested in now, is still another sense, in which judges are sometimes said to represent. A number of theorists, of whom Bentley is the foremost example, consider judges to be representatives because they are responsive to pressures and popular demands: "so far from being a sort of legal machine, they are a functioning part of this government, responsive to the group pressures within it, representative of all sorts of pressures, and using their representative judgement to bring these pressures to balance, not indeed in just the same way, but on just the same basis, that any other agency of government does."[8] This kind of argument can be made only if we ascribe to the courts, as Bentley does, a good deal of freedom to act and to choose. If we adhere to the older jurisprudential doctrine, that the judge merely discovers and expounds the law, we cannot regard him as the representative of group pressures. From this point of view we might oppose elective judgeships, for fear that judges might then represent group pressures instead of interpreting the law impartially.[9] In the same way it has been argued that a judge cannot ordinarily be said to "represent justice" because he is not free to act according to abstract justice.[10] He is bound to apply the law; hence it is the law he represents. Only in exceptional situations, for instance on a Supreme Court or an international tribunal, might a judge have sufficient freedom so that one could say he represents justice.

In these instances, again, one represents whatever guides one's actions. A judge who represents group pressures is a judge conceived as responding to group pressures, through whom such pressures act. A judge who represents justice is one whose actions are governed by or in accord with justice (which requires that he be free from other restraints). This is not a matter of who authorizes the judge or who is bound by his pronouncements. Nor is it a matter of whom (or what) the judge symbolizes or stands for. There is no reason why even a judge whose discretion is narrowly defined could not be a symbol of justice. What we have here is representation as the substance, or content, or guiding principle of action.

This view of representation is by far the most difficult of any of the views yet discussed. On a practical, common-sense level it is easy to see that acting for others involves special behavior and obligations; the theoretical formulation is what is difficult to find. People do behave differently, reach decisions differently, when they are acting on behalf of others. And we have certain expectations of someone who acts for us that we would not have if he were entirely on his own. As Machiavelli pointed out, the virtue of generosity in private persons can become a great vice in the Prince.[11] We ought not to be as ready to give away the property of others as our own. We ought not, in general, to be so willing to sacrifice someone else for whom we are acting, as to sacrifice ourselves. Similarly, we are expected to be more cautious when we act for others, less willing to take risks.[12] What is courage or daring on our own behalf becomes irresponsibility when committed on behalf of another. These seemingly more stringent limitations on the actions of a representative can sometimes have the reverse effect, giving him a kind of freedom to do things for his principal that the principal could not properly do for himself. The representative may be free to push his principal's claims and interest to the very limit, to drive a hard bargain, where the principal acting in person would be expected to show much greater modesty and unselfishness. The divorce of action from certain personal virtues can cut both ways. The representative should not be too generous with his principal's possessions, but then he need not be generous with them either. He should not take excessive risk, but then he need not make self-sacrificial (principal-sacrificial) gestures either.

Another feature of acting for others that is fairly easy to recognize on a practical level is that it should be deliberate action.

When we act for someone else we may not act on impulse; we may not risk what others have at stake "just because we happened to feel like it." We are expected to act as if we would eventually have to account for our actions. Thus we ought to have reasons for what we do, and be prepared to justify our actions to those we act for, even if this accounting or justification never actually takes place. This is what the formalistic accountability theorists try to express, but it is a matter of acting *as if* we would be held to account rather than of institutionalized accountability. But by what criteria will we be judged in this hypothetical holding to account? By what criteria is the role of representative defined? What is needed here is a consistent theoretical formulation in terms of the meaning of representation, not merely practical *ad hoc* observations.

For this purpose the literature makes available material of two kinds. First, it supplies a number of adverbial expressions purporting to summarize the representative's role, the way he must act. We have been using the basic expression "acting for" another, but besides that writers have used acting "in" or "on behalf" of others, acting "in their place" or "stead" or "instead of" them, "supplying their place," acting "in their name," "on their authority," "for their sake," "in their interest," "in accord with their desires" or "wishes" or "wants," pursuing their "welfare" or "needs," so as to "please" or "satisfy" them, or acting "as they would have acted themselves."

Second, and often in combination with these, the literature supplies a vast array of analogies, also intended to illuminate the activity of representing. The representative has been variously likened to or defined as an actor, an agent, an ambassador, an attorney, a commissioner, a delegate, a deputy, an emissary, an envoy, a factor, a guardian, a lieutenant, a proctor, a procurator, a proxy, a steward, a substitute, a trustee, a tutor, and a vicar. One writer may use analogical terms to define representation; another will only liken the representative to them; still another may take some of the analogies as definitive and others as merely similar in meaning. At least one writer argues that "at one time or another, and wholly or in part, representative government . . . has passed through all these phases."[13] Some writers want to make sharp distinctions within the list of analogies, asserting that a representative is like some of the items listed but unlike others. And in drawing these distinctions they disagree with each other. One theorist argues that a representative is no "mere agent," another that he is a "free agent." One says that he is no "mere delegate," another that he is free and independent precisely because he acts "on delegated authority." Occasionally confusion is piled upon confusion:

> Perhaps "deputy" comes nearest to conveying accurately one of the contrasted ideas; "representative," the other. The lawyer may see in "deputy" the notion of agency; in "representative" the notion of trusteeship. The expounder of political science may prefer to think of a "deputy" as an ambassador; of a "representative" as a plenipotentiary. The man in the street may feel that the postman is a "deputy" or may think priest or pastor to be his "representative."[14]

Well, this is not wrong, exactly. We get some notion of the distinction the writer is trying to draw, but is the postman a deputy? Is a minister your representative? The combination form "ambassador plenipotentiary" is common in the literature of government. Is an agent the deputy of his principal?

One source of difficulty is that the verb "to represent" has a much wider use than the corresponding substitutes. "Representing" is not confined to representatives and representations; all kinds of things may stand for something absent; all kinds of social roles may involve representing in one of that word's many diverse uses. So, if we look for analogies to "representative" by scanning all that can (be said to) represent, we may be led farther and farther afield. If a trustee can represent, and a guardian his ward, then parents "really" represent their children, and anyone in charge of another or making decisions that affect him is his representative. Or again, if a substitute or deputy represents, then a physician represents his patients and an engineer his clients, and indeed "*any* specialization of function involves the idea of representation."[15]

It is an embarrassment of riches. There are too many rival terms, all plausible, all suspect, with no clear way to proceed among them. Although each of the suggested analogies is in some contexts or in certain ways like a representative, none of them is synonymous in meaning with "representative." Thus each, if taken as definitive, distorts the meaning of representation in a slightly different way. Presumably the differences in meaning and the resulting distortions could be laid bare by sufficient linguistic analysis, but with so large a number of terms the work involved would far exceed the value of the results.

We shall confine ourselves to classifying the rival terms in a few major groups on the basis of similarity of meanings, and examining the implications of terms in each group when they are applied to representation. We shall begin with terms which most directly emphasize the element of action in representing: "actor," "factor," and particularly "agent," together with the expression "acting for." Second, we shall consider terms centering on the idea of taking care of another or acting in his interest: "trustee," "guardian," and the various words deriving from "procurator." Third, we shall turn to the notion of substitution and acting in another's stead or place, together with terms like "deputy," "attorney," "lieutenant," and "vicar." A fourth group of terms involves the idea of being sent, especially being sent with a message or instructions, as in "delegate," "ambassador," and "commissioner." And, finally, we shall look at the idea of the specialist as representer, before summarizing what can be learned from all these terms.

Of the various analogies to representation, the three which place the most stress on activity are "actor" (especially in a sense now obsolete), "factor," and "agent." Of these, "actor" came first into English, as a translation of the Latin *actor*, to mean "a manager, overseer, agent, or factor," from *agere*, "to act, do."[16] It meant first what we now call an agent, and somewhat later one who brings a legal action, a plaintiff or pleader. In its modern uses the word has dropped these early suggestions of agency; while a stage actor does represent, this is not a matter of his acting *for* anyone. "Factor," with its roots in the Latin action-verb *facere*, "to do, make," first came into English meaning something very like our modern "agent," someone who acts for another. Thus one could speak, for instance, of "the Emperor's factor at Alexandria," meaning his agent or representative. But this meaning is now rare. The word early developed a more specific use in commercial dealings, where it means a particular kind of agent who buys or sells for someone else, particularly an agent to whom goods are consigned for sale.

Thus, both these terms would have been synonyms for our modern "agent" in their early uses, but at that time "agent" was not yet an English word. It apparently took over these functions when it made its appearance late in the sixteenth century. Like "actor," it derives originally from *agere*. In its earliest English meanings it was simply one who acts or does, without the notion of acting *for* someone else. Actually it began as an impersonal, scientific notion: the material cause by which an effect is produced. This use is still retained in modern speech, along with the later meaning which always implies that there is a "principal" behind the agent, *for* whom he acts. Like "actor" and "factor," "agent" is apparently related to representation, insofar as it can refer to one who acts not merely autonomously but for, instead of, on behalf of, someone else; hence, representing. The term is handled in two seemingly contradictory ways by students of representation: some say that a representative is, or is like, an agent; others say that a representative is not, or should not be. The contradiction results from an ambivalence in the meaning of "agent" itself. On the one hand, the stress on action seems to imply freedom to act, strength, initiative. In this sense, putting something into the hands of an agent seems to be turning it over to him to do, the action being his. In this sense we speak of someone's being a "free agent," or of agents and reagents in chemistry. On the other hand, "agent" can also mean someone acting *for* someone else, hence not autonomously, not on his own initiative, but in some way dependent on his principal. It is in this sense that we say "a mere agent," one who does the actual work, but only at the behest of another.

This duality between "free" and "mere" agency parallels an important duality in the concept of representation, as we shall see. But there are also differences between an agent and a representative, although they are not easy to specify. Is there, for instance, any difference between calling a man the agent of a corporation and calling him its representative? One's first impulse, perhaps, is to say that representative sounds more prestigeful, more dignified or authoritative. But perhaps there is also a difference in meaning to account for this different "feeling" about the two words. Although legal terminology makes no formal distinction between "agent" and "representative," and the two are supposed to be equivalent, legal situations can nevertheless be of some help in separating the two terms.[17] Courts do distinguish an agent-representative from certain other legal roles, particularly from a "servant" and an "independent contractor." And the way in which these distinctions are drawn yields, by analogy, some insights about agents and representatives. In general, an independent contractor is too distant from, unrelated to, or independent of his employer to be considered the employer's representative.[18] He has merely been hired to do a job, and has no other connection with the man (or corporation) that hired him.

The distinction between an agent-representative and a servant has given the courts more trouble. It has been variously alleged that agency "relates to commercial or business transactions," the establishing of contractual relations, and that it implies a certain amount of discretion on the part of the agent. Service, in contrast, deals with "matters of manual or mechanical execution," and "has reference to actions upon or about things."[19] The servant does not negotiate contracts; he operates "under the direction and control of the master," and "renders service *to* rather than *for* the master." Thus the distinction seems to be based on the degree of discretion as well as the nature of the services performed.

The need to draw these distinctions arises in various cases involving employees of companies or corporations. In some states the law provides that a corporation may be sued only in a county where it has an agent-representative, on whom the legal papers can be served. The question then is: What must be the relationship between a person and a corporation to make him its agent-representative, so that it can be sued in the county where he is? Courts have rendered such rulings as: "an employee who adjusts claims and solicits and fills orders" for a corporation is its representative for the service of process.[20] On the other hand, the corporation's attorney is not; he is an independent contractor. This is an interesting finding from our point of view, for in other situations an attorney is a prime example of an individual's representative, and the courts frequently say that a man's attor-

ney *is* his agent-representative. At the same time, the court's
holding that he is not a corporation's representative for purposes
of suit has a certain logical appeal; an attorney does, in this context, seem more of an independent contractor, not "really" connected with the corporation. The court explained that here agent
or representative meant "someone employed in forwarding the
particular business for which the corporation was organized,"
which also does not quite succeed in expressing the distinction one
feels. Somehow an attorney's connection with the corporation is
too remote.

A servant or an employee may, however, be in a sense too
much a part of the corporation to be its agent-representative.
Thus a court has held that employees who operate oil wells for
a corporation are its servants, and not agents; hence the corporation may not be sued in a county where it merely has some employees operating wells. Here there can be no question that the
men are connected with the corporation; but it is not their job to
deal with the outside world. They are not important enough, do
not have sufficient discretion, to be held equivalent to, and taken
as a substitute for, the corporation for which they work.

The same sort of question comes up in a group of cases arising
under workmen's compensation laws. Such laws often provide
that a corporation is liable only for injuries of which it is informed within a given period of time. The question then becomes: Who must be informed for the corporation to be informed? Courts have held, for example, that informing a foreman
is the same as informing the corporation, because the foreman
here is the corporation's representative. In a different context, a
court has held that "one superintending the stringing of wires of
a Telegraph Company is its representative in that his knowledge
is the knowledge of the Company." On the other hand, a court
has ruled that a man may not recover damages from the company for which he works for an injury sustained as a result of
the company's negligence, when in fact he was himself the employee who had been negligent (as it were, on behalf of the company).

There are also questions of ascription and imputation. Whether
a corporation for which a person works is to be considered as
doing or knowing or being present through him is a question of

representation. If yes, it is because he represents the corporation in that context. If no, it is because he does not. To assert that he represents is to assert that his action or knowledge should be ascribed or imputed to the corporation. This kind of ascription or imputation we dealt with in the section on formalistic theories of representation. But in these cases no clear-cut authorization to represent is given at the outset. The courts must decide, from the circumstances and from the actual nature of the employee's relationship to the employer, whether ascription is justified. The criteria which the court uses to make this decision concern the substantive content of acting for someone else. If the employee's situation and activity were such that his actions ought to be attributed to the corporation, then he is its agent-representative.

The criteria which the courts seemed to use in these cases had to do with the nature of the connection between employee and corporation. When a foreman is notified of an injury to a worker, the corporation has been notified; if the janitor had been notified, perhaps the court would have ruled otherwise.[21] Why? It seems to depend on the responsible nature of a foreman's job; he is "closer to the heart of" the corporation, more genuinely a part of its management. His job normally requires a fairly high degree of discretion to make decisions for the corporation. Conversely, an employee who merely operated oil wells is not equivalent to the corporation.

Leaving strictly legal terminology aside, I think this sort of estimate of a relationship is helpful in distinguishing the meaning of "agent" from that of "representative." An agent is someone who "does the actual work," from Latin *agere*. When we call a man someone's agent we are saying that he is the tool or instrument by which the other acts. He is a corporation's information-receiving tool (agent, organ), its money-dispensing tool (agent, organ), and so on. When we call him a representative, on the other hand, we are saying not so much that he is a part or tool of the corporation as that the entire corporation is present in him. He is not so much a part through which corporate action flows, as a miniature or embodiment of the whole acting corporation. Thus, although one can act "by agency of" another as well as "by deputy," "by attorney," or "by proxy," and experience things vicariously, one cannot act "by representative."[22] (We do not normally speak of someone as acting by representative; such a locution sounds odd.) It is the representative who acts; and although we must in some sense also conceive of the action as being another's, the representative is no mere instrument in another's hands. In many cases we shall be able to say with equal truth that a man is an agent or that he is a representative, but that does not mean that we are saying quite the same thing about him each time. The two terms are confusingly close, but they are not identical.

The main adverbial expression stressing the representative's activity is acting "for" itself. But that phrase has developed two rather distinct senses. On the one hand, it can mean acting instead of; on the other hand, it can mean acting to the benefit of; or it can mean both at once. The former notion, of substitution, appears in contexts where "acting for" is set off against just "acting," where the stress falls (as it were) on the second word in the phrase: "acting *for* him." Thus, if we are both gambling in a casino, betting from a common fund we have established by sharing our gambling money, and I grow weary of the tension of constant decisions, I may say, "This time you decide." But if I am gambling with my own money only and you are merely kibitzing, and I grow weary of decisions, I may turn to you and say, "This time you decide *for* me." To say that someone acts for another in this sense is to imply that normally the other would act for himself directly; the new decider is a substitute acting in his stead.

But in a different context, "acting for" may mean acting for the sake of. Thus a mother fussing over her daughter's graduation dress may encounter an outburst of adolescent impatience: "Don't fuss so much! You keep ripping out seams and putting them back." Whereupon the mother may respond in genuine surprise, "But I'm doing it for you!" Here she means not that she is sewing instead of her daughter, but for her benefit. That we do, indeed, have two senses of "acting for" here, is indicated by the fact that in many contexts we would simultaneously mean both and be unable to choose between them if asked which we meant.[23]

Much the same distinction, incidentally, is reflected in our use of the term "behalf," separating "*on* behalf of" from "*in* behalf of." The *Oxford English Dictionary* tells us that "on behalf" means "on the part of (another), in the name of, as agent or representative of, on account of, for, instead of," while "in behalf" is said to mean "in the interest of, as a friend or defender of, for the benefit of (with the notion of interposition: 'speak in my behalf' equals in my interest, say a good word for me)." But the *Dictionary* adds wistfully that "on behalf" is coming to be used in the sense of "in behalf," "to the loss of an important distinction."

We seem to emerge with two elements or aspects of one man's acting for another, and we might suppose that they are elements in representing as well. Yet neither taking care of another nor replacing him is by itself equivalent to representing. To see this, we must turn to the groups of analogies and adverbial expressions that center on these two ideas: those of trusteeship and those of substitution.

It is often argued that a representative is more like a trustee or guardian than like an agent. Representative government, we are told, "by its essential nature . . . is a trusteeship."[24] A representative parliament is "the trustee which the nation has authorized to act on its behalf; and it exercises sovereign power, under the terms of its trust, for the nation."[25] And the individual representative, too, is said to hold "a trust" which he must "fulfill."[26]

A trust is a legal arrangement whereby someone is given title (ownership) of a piece of property, subject to the proviso that he is to use it for the benefit of another. In England it apparently came into use in the early fifteenth century, as a convenient way to escape the feudal equivalents of an inheritance tax—the payments due a lord when one of his tenants died and his property passed to someone else. By transferred meaning, a trustee is now anyone held responsible for the preservation or administration of anything; but typically he owns what he administers, yet must administer it for the benefit or use of someone other than himself. This beneficiary need not be a person or group of persons, but may be a "charitable purpose."

Maitland, in his splendid historical essay on trusts, shows how widely the concept comes to be applied and how it passes into the political realm in English thought: "So when new organs of local government are being developed, at first sporadically and afterwards by general laws, it is natural not only that any property they acquire, lands or money, should be thought of as 'trust property,' but that their governmental powers should be regarded as being held in trust. Those powers are, we say, 'intrusted to them' or they are 'intrusted with' those powers."[27] What is implied about representative government by calling it a trusteeship? First, that its powers are, in Burke's words, not "given for the sake of the holder." Representation certainly is, as many writers have pointed out, a fiduciary relationship, involving trust and obligation on both sides.[28] If a representative is not just a person doing whatever he pleases or acting just for himself, calling him a trustee can underline his obligations to others.

Second, the analogy suggests that the powers of government may be thought of as property, to which the representatives have title, but which they must administer for the benefit of others. Thus it might be their duty to preserve the national wealth, employ the income from it in certain ways, or divide it among the beneficiaries. And if the representatives have "title" to this "property," their connection with the beneficiaries is remote. They are under no obligation to consult their beneficiaries or obey their wishes. They are to do whatever they think best in the light of the trust obligation. The notion of a trust does not even require persons as beneficiaries; the "beneficiary" may be a charitable purpose. Thus the representative's duties might not even be to those who elect him, but perhaps to the national interest or to generations yet unborn. Again the implication is one of freeing the representative from the wishes or opinions of his constituents, while yet regarding him as having an obligation to their welfare.

Often the notion of trusteeship is linked with the idea that the beneficiary is incapable of acting for himself, or at least that the trustee is far more competent than he. One aspect of the stress on taking care of property is that it seems more a matter of skill than of relative values or wishes. It should be easy to judge whether property has been well managed or has been dissipated and allowed to decline in value; and surely one cannot object to letting the able man take care of one's property. One writer has criticized the notion of resemblance and reflection in a representative legislature as being

as vain and impossible in politics as it is recognized to be in every other kind of business. No one would regard it as a correct principle in the organization of a joint stock company that the management should be such as would fairly reflect such knowledge as the shareholders might have about the business the company is to carry on. The principle universally relied on there is a grant of power to men of special knowledge and capacity, subject to responsibility for results.[29]

In this respect it is significant that a number of the writers about whom we are sometimes told that they liken representative government to a trusteeship, in fact apply this analogy to *all* government. Thus for them it evidently has no necessary implications about accountability to the governed or responsiveness to their wishes, although it obviously has implications about looking after their welfare. This may well be true of Locke, as it certainly is of Burke. For Burke says, "The king is the representative of the people; so are the lords; so are the judges. They are all trustees for the people."[30] It is thus a mistake to argue, as several commentators have, that Burke meant the trustee to be held accountable to the people, the beneficiaries of the trust.[31] Burke regards hereditary monarchies as trusteeships just as much as elected governments; and he never says that the trustee is accountable to the beneficiary, for that would be false in any case. What Burke does say is that "it is of the very essence of every trust *to be rendered accountable*; and even totally to cease, when it substantially varies from the purposes for which alone it could have a lawful existence."[32] But this is in reference to the East India Company's rule in India; and he is talking about the Company's accountability to the English Parliament, not to the people of India.[33] Accountability may be an important part of trusteeship, but accountability to the beneficiary of the trust is no part of it. That is why Burke could regard all government as trusteeship; no democratic implication need be involved, nor are elections necessary.

It is easy to become confused here about trusteeship specifically as distinguished from various notions of trust in general. It is true that all public office requires trustworthiness, that representation is a relationship of mutual trust and obligation. But this is true of many human institutions, which may or may not involve accountability, and may or may not resemble trusteeship in the specific sense. Between trusteeship and representation there are also some important differences. As a matter of fact, a trustee is not normally (said to be) the representative of the beneficiary of his trust.[34] He must act for the latter's benefit, but the property is in the trustee's own name; when he administers it he is not acting in someone else's name. He does not take orders from or consult with the beneficiary. Nor does he legally bind the beneficiary; a contract made by a trustee binds him, not the beneficiary. We do not ordinarily attribute his actions to the beneficiary; hence we have no occasion to call him a representative. The implications of calling government a trusteeship are thus by no means democratic ones. It is implied that the government must then act for the benefit of the people, but it is equally implied that this does not require consultation or responsiveness to their wishes.[35]

This distinction can be seen even more clearly in other terms that mean looking after property for someone else and are sometimes equated with representation. A steward manages the affairs of an estate or household, or any property on behalf of its owner or lord. The word derives from Old English terms meaning the keeper of a house; in an early sense now obsolete, it meant literally an official who controls the domestic affairs of a household. Is a steward a representative of the owner of the household or estate? He may sometimes act as the owner's agent or representative as part of his job, as when he accepts goods on consignment in the owner's name. Then indeed, he represents the owner. But a steward qua steward is not a representative; he is simply an employee who runs an establishment for someone else. A mere acting for the benefit of another, again, does not suffice to create representation.

Another case is that of a tutor or guardian, who is in charge of the estate or the person of a minor, a lunatic, or other legally incapable person.[36] Like the trustee, the guardian is not under any obligation to consult his ward or obey the ward's wishes. Unlike the trustee, he does not hold the ward's property in his own name; he acts in the ward's name, and can bind the ward by contract.[37] Thus he can be said to represent the ward with regard to his property. But it is interesting to contrast the situation regarding property with that regarding person. Insofar as a guardian is simply in charge of, and responsible for, his ward's person (leaving the matter of property aside for a moment), we would not call him a representative. He is obligated to look after the ward's welfare, and he may make decisions about the ward's future, but we have no occasion to attribute his actions to the ward himself. He no more represents the ward by taking care of him than the headmaster of a boarding school represents his pupils during the ordinary course of his activities. This sort of analogy can be quite misleading, as when it influences some writers to argue that parents represent their children. Parents may, on occasion, represent their children in court; but ordinarily parents decide the fate of their children, issue instructions to them, and are obligated to take care of them without ever being their representatives.

If A hires B to act for him as an agent, A can sometimes be said to have done the action "by agency of" B; but if B is A's representative, there is no corresponding phrase; A cannot act "by representation of" B. We have suggested that this is because of the need for a certain distance or difference between representative and represented. If the latter is conceived as acting, the former is a "mere agent" and not a representative. Now we can add that A cannot act "by guardianship of," "by tutorship of," or "by trusteeship of" B. When a guardian or trustee acts, we do not ordinarily conceive of the ward or beneficiary as involved in the action—even less so than a principal is involved in the action of his representative. Accordingly, a guardian or trustee has an obligation to attend to the welfare of another, but this is not equivalent to representing him.

A third group of analogies centers on the idea of substitution, seeing a representative as one who acts instead of those he represents. The word "stead" originally meant quite literally place or room; acting in someone's stead means appearing in his place, where he might otherwise be expected to appear. He is re-placed by his substitute; indeed, "substitute" derives from the Latin *substatuere*, to set up in place of. Similarly, "attorney" (by way of Old French from the Latin *attornare*, to turn to, assign, attribute, appoint) once had a very broad use for almost any kind of substitute action. Early English members of Parliament sent from shires and boroughs were called attorneys long before they were called representatives. The idea of substitution or replacement is found also in "deputy," which comes by way of Old French from the Latin *deputare*, "to consider as, destine, or allot," from *putare*, "to think," and thus suggests someone thought of, considered as another for whom he acts. So, too, a lieutenant is one who holds the place of another, in lieu of him; and "vicar" derives from the Latin *vicarius*, or substitute.

Given such an array of suggestive synonyms for "representative," it is no wonder that some writers come to regard representation as essentially a matter of substitution. Indeed, some representatives do substitute for those they represent. But it is by no means true that all substitutes represent or are representatives. Hans J. Wolff suggests that, while both substitute and representative replace another, in substitution the one replaced is not held responsible for the conduct of his substitute.[38] Wolff's example here is a substitute sitting in for a player in a card game. What the player who is replaced *is* responsible for, Wolff says, is choosing his substitute wisely—what in legal terminology would be a *diligentia in eligendo*. But other common examples of substitution show that even this need not be the case. A substitute teacher or a football substitute is in no sense a representative and does not represent the one he replaces (which is not to say that he could not represent the latter under special circumstances). The substitute teacher or football player is not selected by the one he replaces, nor responsible to him, nor is the latter responsible for what he does. The substitute's actions are not attributed to the other, nor is he expected to consult the other, act in his interest, act as he would, or anything of the kind.

A deputy is sometimes said to "represent his principals" or to act "on behalf of his principal."[39] A familiar scene in a Western film is the deputizing of a posse to help hunt down the killers. Strictly speaking, the volunteers are made deputy sheriffs or deputy marshalls; yet they do not thereby become representatives, nor do they thereby represent the sheriff or the marshall. A deputy may serve as a substitute for the sheriff, if the latter is unable to act, perhaps because he has been shot. But deputy sheriffs can work along with a very active sheriff. And in either case they are not his representatives; they do not act for him, but as enforcers of the law. They have duties, not to him but to the law. They have a certain authority, which the sheriff conferred, but it is not his authority they have. It is not his rights they exercise. And he is not responsible for their actions, but at most for whether he selected them wisely for the job. They do not act in the sheriff's name, but say, "Surrender in the name of the Law!"[40]

The deputy is a public official holding an office, and that office is a kind of replacement for a higher office, as the vice-presidency is for the presidency. But that does not make the vice-president the representative of the president. Much the same thing may be said of lieutenants and vicars. The crucial distinction between substitution and representation, following a suggestion by Wolff, would seem to be this: in many instances of substitution, the substitute totally eclipses and replaces the other. There is no kind of ascription of anything about him or his action to the other. In other cases, the replaced person is somehow present in his replacement or in the latter's action, and then representation may be involved. Wolff says that representing is a standing *for* rather than *in place of* another.[41] And an American philosopher has recently put it this way: "Most commonly a substitute takes another's place in such a way as to exclude the other, at least temporarily; the job is now the substitute's job, not the regular's job. A representative, on the other hand, if he is not a representative in name only, acts in place of another without excluding him; although he is not the principal, he 'stands for' the principal; the principal is 'present through him'."[42]

A fourth group of analogies expresses the notion of being sent from one place or another on orders, or in an official capacity, by a superior. The term most frequently invoked by representation theorists in this group is "delegate," from the Latin *legare*, "to send with a commission." But there is also "ambassador," from the Latin *ambactiare*, "to go on a mission," as well as "envoy," "emissary," and "commissioner," all of whom are persons officially sent: an emissary is sent *out*; a commissioner is sent *with* a message or other commissioners.

When applied to political representation, these terms suggest that the representative is sent from his locality to the central government, which is often true. They suggest further that he is sent in an official capacity, by an organized and official group.

This is particularly evident in the term "delegate." We speak of delegated powers as those which were first officially in one body or office and then were passed on to a subordinate body or group. Thus there are constitutional questions about the extent to which Congress may delegate its powers. One is not ordinarily said to "delegate" tasks which are not "rights" or official "powers" but merely everyday activities. There is something odd or strained about George Cornwall Lewis' statement that "a man delegates to a tutor the education of his children."[43] It implies a formality and officiality that the task does not in fact have, as if the duty of education had first been assigned to the parents (say, by the state) and then devolved upon the tutor. Thus the term has somewhat the same effect as "deputy" when applied to political representation. It, too, suggests that the electorate originally held an office or had certain official functions, and that these functions or this office were then given to their representatives.

Both "delegate" and "commissioner" (unlike "deputy") suggest that the representative is sent to the central government with explicit instructions, or to do a particular thing. He is sent with a commission; he is sent on a mission. And it is suggested that those sending him are a unified and official body; "delegate" particularly means someone sent by an association to attend the meeting of some other association in their name. The implication that those who send the representative are an organized or official association makes it likely that they gave specific instructions and may give further instructions from time to time. There is no doubt that delegates, commissioners, and ambassadors are subordinates of those who send them.[44]

In another analogy, representation is likened, in a general way, to every action that one person performs for others in ordinary life. This suggestion seems typically to be reached by a kind of extrapolation or logical extension from one of the other analogies, particularly from substitution or from trusteeship. The approach from substitution runs something like this: people often need to ask others to perform some task for them which ordinarily they would perform for themselves. This replacement is a kind of representation, and "representation itself is a matter of daily occurrence, and common necessity."[45] As the "vicarious performance" of tasks that "cannot be personally exercised," it "intervenes in commerce, in jurisprudence, in education, and in a thousand other forms. In a multitude of circumstances people are compelled to place themselves or their interests in the hands of others."[46]

Persons do have representatives because they cannot "be present" themselves, in a particular role, to do a job, or exercise the rights and obligations of the role. . . . One person cannot be wise in all matters, and he cannot be in all places at once. And since the pursuit of his goals in a complex society requires him to be in many "places" at once, he has to have help. Representation provides one form of this help.[47]

It is thus essentially a matter of the division of labor in society, and the more advanced and complex society becomes, the more need exists for representation.[48] "An engineer represents his clients in his work, as does a doctor his patients."[49] And the busy man's need for assistance is as true of political life as of other matters. Being "too much engrossed by their private pursuits," people choose political representatives to take care of politics for them, "just as they select a physician to attend to their health, and a lawyer to draw their conveyances or to conduct their lawsuits."[50]

Thus, it is argued, whenever we seek professional help or services, we are asking to be represented. But this introduces the idea of the professional or expert, and shifts the emphasis from mere substitution (where the representative is, if anything, the subordinate of the man who employs him) toward trusteeship (where the representative must be given a free hand to exercise his superior wisdom or skill). "Any specialization of function involves the idea of representation. . . . A specialist is someone who takes better care of certain of the people's interests than they could if they assumed the task themselves."[51] The implications for political representation are clear: if you have turned the job over to an expert, leave it to him.

In particular, the analogy of the political representative to a physician is used by commentators of widely varying persuasion, and so deserves careful attention. We are told that "the doctor is an agent of the patient," and "represents" him.[52] But the reason why the patient goes to a doctor instead of trying to cure him-

self is to benefit from the doctor's superior knowledge and skill.
Many authors utilize this fact in a political analogy: "The true
representative obeys the people by doing the things he knows
they would want done if they possessed his knowledge, insight
and experience—as a physician, when he prescribes things
disliked and opposed by his patient, nevertheless represents the
patient's real will to get well."[53] The presumption of a specialized knowledge or skill in the representative suggests that he
need not take orders from his constituents. He may know better
than they how to achieve what they really want, and if he follows
his own knowledge he is representing them even "when he prescribes things disliked and opposed by them." Some writers make
the suggestion very explicit:

As the physician, whose time and attention and faculties are
chiefly devoted to the art of healing, cannot without injury be
restricted in his treatment of disease by the views and desires of
the patient who requires his assistance, although they may very
properly be taken into consideration; so to the political representative, unshackled by instructions, must be left the discretion of
acting according to his own view of the public welfare. . . .[54]

The suggestion that the political ruler is exercising a specialized knowledge or skill not possessed by his subjects is at least
as old as Plato's *Republic*, but Plato did not argue that the
specialist in ruling is thereby a representative. For Plato, the
assumption that politics is a matter of expert knowledge and
wisdom meant that it should be placed in the hands of the wise
and expert man and left there. For theorists of representation
the implications are slightly different. The act of placing one's
affairs in the hands of the expert assumes a greater importance,
and is to be reconsidered and repeated at intervals. In the
meantime, however, the representative is to proceed according
to his own expert knowledge rather than the wishes of his constituents. This view is frequently coupled with the argument that
the average man lacks the skill and knowledge to govern, but
knows enough to evaluate how well he is being governed.

The business of the voters is not . . . to determine what regulations affecting their own welfare shall be passed, but merely to
appoint persons to determine for them. . . . They are not required to pass on the merits of complicated political questions,

but on the fitness of individuals for the duties of legislation. . . .
There are similar grounds for judging in this case, as there are
in choosing a lawyer to plead a cause, or a physician to treat a
case.[55]

The average man should be confined to what is within his capacities: the selection of experts. Any voter, it seems, could say,
"I don't know much about government but I know what I like."
This has been presented as a description of modern democracy:
"Essentially the freedom permitted to the patient is that of choosing his doctor, and of terminating the relation at will—if he can!
. . . under modern conditions freedom is largely that of choosing
agents, of deputizing actual decision-making."[56]

Of the writers who equate representation with the services of
a specialist like a physician, Gosnell is the only one who attempts
to draw any distinctions from political representing. At first he
argues that political representatives differ from other specialists
only in that they hold power, but later he notes a further difference: there is disagreement over the solution of political problems. The politician cannot always know what his "clients" want:
"An engineer knows specifically his clients' desires. A doctor
knows his patient wants health . . . The political situation establishes different attitudes . . . A brief can frequently be made for the
theory that the public knows not what it wants. . . . Wants are
indefinable, unascertainable; means are debatable and numerous."[57] Similarly, the politician's "client" cannot judge him as
easily as a patient can his doctor: "It is relatively easy to find out
whether a doctor is a good practitioner, but it is much harder
to tell whether a representative is a good legislator." Thus in
politics there are "more problems of representation" than in
other fields where specialists operate, simply because political
questions are the ones on which we lack knowledge, or on which
the experts disagree. In articulating this last idea, Gosnell makes
a curious comment: "Significant it is, that whenever a problem
of the specialized sciences is debatable among its practitioners
and likewise important to the public, it is hurled into the political
sphere, there to become a problem in the solution of which
people desire representation."[58] But we have just been told that
every specialist gives his clients representation. Surely Gosnell

is not saying merely that people demand from their political experts what they would be getting from any other expert, or indeed, from anyone who performs a specialized function in society? Perhaps it is now time to reëxamine the basic assumption of this whole group of writers: Do specialists and experts "represent" their clients?

An attorney really would seem to be a specialist who acts for others, and who is indeed said to represent them. We talk of his representing someone in court; we can imagine him saying to a client, "Well, if you want me to represent you, the fee will be . . ." Or to a fellow attorney, "I hear you're representing the wife in the Williamson case," and so on.[59] Is the same true of a physician or an engineer? Clearly not. We cannot imagine a physician saying such things to one of his patients or to a fellow doctor. He does not talk about how many patients he has represented during the past year, nor does an engineer or architect speak in this way about people who hire his services. And we do not speak about their functions as "representing."[60] Would the physician who is prescribing "things disliked and opposed by his patient" say to him, "I am representing you in doing this, and therefore I insist," or anything of that sort? Certainly not. He might say to a child, "I am doing this for your own good," but to an adult patient even this would have to be more moderately put: "I recommend this for your own good," "I must insist for your own good." But even the passage cited above (note 53) does not say literally that the physician, prescribing something disliked by the patient, represents his patient; it says "he represents the patient's real will to get well." Representing someone is not the same as "representing his real will"; and while the latter could conceivably be said of the doctor, the former cannot. (Nor is it because the patient is recalcitrant that we are having difficulties; the physician no more represents a willing patient than an unwilling one.)

There are, however, special situations of doctor and patient in which it could be said that the one represents the other. The doctor might have to do something for the patient's welfare while the patient was in a coma—something which could ordinarily be done only by the patient or with his permission: for example, open his safe-deposit box (to discover what kind of poison he has just taken). Then perhaps the doctor might, in exasperation, say to the bank official who is holding to the letter of the law, "But, damn it, I represent Mr. Jones. I'm his physician!" He would be invoking the authority of the patient for his own action, acting in the patient's name, and also for his sake. He would in a sense be answering the bank official's unvoiced protest, "Only Mr. Jones can open this safe-deposit box. You're not Mr. Jones, so you cannot," with the unspoken reply: "Consider me as if I were Mr. Jones because of the circumstances." This is the familiar ascription of actions in order to exercise another's right.

But it is, indeed, a special situation; and generally specialists and professional people (other than lawyers) do not represent their clients. Their actions are not to be attributed to the client. Theorists may tell us a physician "is the agent of his patient," but do we ever have cause to say, "The patient cured himself by the agency of Dr. Smith"? It seems fairly evident that this is not our usual account of medical services. No more do employees who perform functions or services for others represent those they serve. A janitor or a postman or a riveter, in the ordinary performance of his job, does not represent anyone.

From the chaos of the many analogies and adverbial expressions, and the many implications of each, three major ideas emerge: the idea of substitution or acting instead of, the idea of taking care of or acting in the interest of, and the idea of acting as a subordinate, on instructions, in accord with the wishes of another. None of the three, by itself, turns out to be a satisfactory equivalent of the idea of representing.

Although some representatives may be substitutes for those they represent, most substitutes are not representatives and do not represent those whom they replace. As with the formalistic authorization view, so here also, it seems to be a matter of the ascription of actions. We begin to speak of representation only when the substitute's actions are, in some way or for some reason, to be ascribed to another. And, again, such ascription may occur for essentially formal reasons: to invoke another's right to act, to assign to him normative consequences of the action which would normally fall on the actor himself, or on the basis of a prior formal agreement. But we are now concerned with other reasons for ascribing a substitute's actions to the ones he replaces—reasons which seem by comparison more substantive than rights or normative consequences and which do not rest on prior formal agreement.

It is tempting to look for those reasons in the other sense of "acting for," the idea of taking care of or looking after the interest or welfare of another. This, too, is not by itself equivalent to representing. The trustee, the guardian, the teacher or parent who takes care of a child, the doctor who looks after a patient—these are not normally said to represent those they care for. They are not representatives. In the first place, merely performing a service for another, without further reason for ascribing the action to him, is not yet representation. The connection is too remote, like that between a corporation and an independent contractor hired to do a job. And, in the second place, looking after another as an expert or specialist or superior, the way in which adults look after small children, falls short of being representation in still another way. It is not so much the remoteness of the connection between actor and looked-after as the helplessness and subordination of the latter. The actor has an obligation, but the one who is taken care of has nothing to say about it, is not conceived as being capable of saying anything about it or acting for himself. It is as if the idea of representation required a relative equivalence between the representative and the represented, so that the latter could conceivably have acted for himself instead, and the representative is in that sense a substitute. As the "re" in "representation" seems to suggest, and as I have argued in rejecting the fascist theory of representation, the represented must be somehow logically prior; the representative must be responsive to him rather than the other way around.

In the third conception, the actor is seen as subordinate, the ones for whom he acts as dominant. Either he is seen as receiving explicit instructions from them and carrying out those instructions, as suggested in the analogies of "being sent"; or he is seen as responding to their wants or wishes, as essentially acting to please them. But this conception, too, is inadequate by itself to account for representing. For if the agent is seen as too subordinate, as a mere tool in the hands of others with no independence, he is like the subordinate employee of a corporation—too subordinate to serve (or be thought of) as a substitute for the corporation itself. He does not act for it; it acts through him, or by means of him.

Griffiths has expressed this idea by distinguishing between an agent who has a certain measure of discretion, of freedom to act in one way or another, and an agent who has none.[61] Thus someone serving as a stand-in in a proxy marriage is in a rather different position from a business agent; there is little that can go wrong with what the former is supposed to do, and even if something did go wrong it probably would not be ascribed to the man for whom he is proxy. Now, one cannot say simply that such a case is not one of representation. It could very well be one of representation in the formal sense or in the sense of "standing for"; we ascribe the marriage to the absent man, not to his proxy. But it is not a case of representation in the sense that interests us here—the substantive activity of representing another. That can enter the picture only where substantive activity is going on, as distinct from mere presence—where, as Griffiths puts it, "judgment, which is normally involved in action, is alienated."[62] For only then is it meaningful to ask how the representative is supposed to act; only then does it make sense to say that his role imposes obligations that he could fail to fulfill.

If, instead of seeing the representative as a mere tool in the hands of others, we say that his role is to please those others, to do what they want, we encounter other difficulties. If we say that the political representative's duty is simply to please those for whom he acts, then short-term palliatives are likely to become preferable to genuine cures, and dramatic symbols to intelligent statesmanship. As we have seen in discussing fascist theory, it then becomes irrelevant whether the represented are mistaken or misled in their judgment; they alone have the right to evaluate the representative's performance.

Like the other views we have discussed, representing as a substantive acting for others has its foundation in familiar examples of ordinary usage; but, like the other views, it has limitations. It is not the whole of the concept of representation. Obviously it cannot account for any kind of representation, any context, in which the represener is an inanimate object that cannot engage in activity. It cannot explain representative art, the representative sample, symbolic representation. Nor can it account for the way in which an artist represents, or someone making representations about something. Like the formalistic view, it is of use to us, is relevant, where human representatives and their actions are involved, where one man's actions are to be ascribed to others (or to an abstraction or organization). But it deals with substantive rather than formal reasons for ascribing action. This view, therefore, is the one we invoke wherever we see representing without any formalities—without the exercise of another's rights or the ascription of normative consequences, without an "official" represener. We turn to this view also when we question the basis of formal ascription, when we want to ask, "Yes, but does he *really* represent?" Only this concept can be applied to what Tussman has called the "perspective of the actor," the representative's own concern with what is required of him by his role.[63] Accordingly, only this concept supplies us with standards for judging the representative's action, for deciding whether he has represented well or ill (as distinct from whether he is a good likeness, a typical man).

This substantive concept is the "something" that was missing from the authorization view—something having to do with limits on the representative, or standards to which he must conform. In descriptive and symbolic representation we saw hints of what that something might be, but we saw also that those views could not be directly applied in the realm of actions. The fact that a man or an assembly is a very good descriptive representation does not automatically guarantee that they will be good representatives in the sense of acting for, that their activity will really be representing. In the realm of action, the representative's characteristics are relevant only insofar as they affect what he does. Thus, for the activity of representing, the ideal of a perfect copy or likeness is chimerical. In the same way, a good symbol need by no means be a good representative when we want activity on our behalf. No matter how enthusiastic we might be about Miss California, few of us would want to elect her to Congress. And while there is a relationship between representing well and pleasing the represented, the relationship is not as simple as the symbolization theorists would have us think.

The activity of representing as acting for others must be defined in terms of what the representative does and how he does it, or in some combination of these two considerations; but the analogies and adverbial expressions found in the literature are of limited usefulness in defining it further. Since none of the analogies is an exact synonym of "representative," simple substitution is never in order. Any of them can sometimes (be said to) represent, but so can almost anything. The study of groups of analogies seems to yield only negative results: we reach some conclusions about what substantive acting for others is not, rather than what it is. We need a more positive definition of the activity, and its specific relation to political life.

7

The Mandate–Independence Controversy

Representation means the making present of something which is nevertheless not literally present. What I should like to say about substantive acting for others is that the represented thing or person is present in the action rather than in the characteristics of the actor, or how he is regarded, or the formal arrangements which precede or follow the action. But this locution is far from clear, and we still have the task of specifying what kind or manner of action is required here.

The suggestion probably most familiar from the literature on representation is that the representative must do what his principal would do, must act as if the principal himself were acting.[1] This is a very tempting account because of its obvious proximity to the idea of making-the-represented-present, the idea of resemblance and reflection found in the descriptive view, and the idea of democratic consent associated with modern representative government. But on closer examination it entails problems. If we think of a representative acting not merely for a single principal but for an entire constituency, an unorganized set of people, then "Act as if your constituents were acting themselves" becomes a questionable slogan. If the contemplated action is voting, then presumably (but not obviously) it means that the representative must vote as a majority of his constituents would. But any activities other than voting are less easy to deal with. Is he really literally to deliberate as if he were several hundred thousand people? To bargain that way? To speak that way? And if not that way, then how?

The slogan is not even right for a representative acting for a single principal; even representing one man is not a matter of imitation. For example, I am attending a business conference as Jones's representative, chosen to act for him there because it is a financial conference and he has no head for figures. The time comes to make a decision. I ask myself, "What would Jones do?" But the answer is clear: he would throw up his hands in horrified defeat at the sight of all those figures, and would probably make the wrong decision. Surely it is not my obligation or role to do that for him. Imitation is not what is called for here; acting for another is not acting on the stage. But the only alternatives seem to be either that I do what Jones would want, or that I do what seems best for him, in terms of his interest.

So, again, the two familiar elements of wishes and welfare seem to be the only available choices. But these two elements form two opposed sides in a long-standing debate, undoubtedly the central classic controversy in the literature of political representation. The question at issue may be summarized as: Should (must) a representative do what his constituents want, and be bound by mandates or instructions from them; or should (must) he be free to act as seems best to him in pursuit of their welfare? This mandate-independence controversy has become encrusted with a number of other issues, partly related but partly irrelevant. It occurs mostly in contexts where political representation is at stake; so the basic question is soon entangled with such issues as the relative priority of local versus national interest, the role of political parties, and the nature of political questions. It tends to be complicated also by the differences between representing a single principal and representing a diverse political constituency. Still, the underlying conceptual problem is worth isolating and examining in its own right. What I shall argue about this conceptual dispute is, first, that the way in which it is usually formulated makes a consistent answer impossible; second, that the meaning of representation nevertheless supplies a consistent position about a representative's duties; and, third, that this consistent position only sets outer limits, within which there remains room for a wide range of views on how a political representative should act or what distinguishes good from bad representing. A writer's position in this range of views is correlated with his conception of political life in the broadest sense: his ideas on the nature of political issues, the relative capacities of rulers and ruled, the nature of man and society— in short, what we might call his metapolitics.

A number of positions have at one time or another been defended, between the two poles of mandate and independence. A highly restrictive mandate theorist might maintain that true representation occurs only when the representative acts on explicit instructions from his constituents, that any exercise of discretion is a deviation from this ideal. A more moderate position might be that he may exercise some discretion, but must consult his constituents before doing anything new or controversial, and then do as they wish or resign his post. A still less extreme position might be that the representative may act as he thinks his constituents would want, unless or until he receives instructions from them, and then he must obey. Very close to the independence position would be the argument that the representative must do as he thinks best, except insofar as he is bound by campaign promises or an election platform. At the other extreme is the idea of complete independence, that constituents have no right even to exact campaign promises; once a man is elected he must be completely free to use his own judgment.

But whatever his precise position, a theorist is likely to invoke the appropriate analogies and adverbial expressions to defend it. A mandate theorist will see the representative as a "mere" agent, a servant, a delegate, a subordinate substitute for those who sent him. The representative, he will say, is "sent as a servant," not "chosen with dictatorial powers," and so the purpose which sent him must have been the constituents' purpose and not his own.[2] They sent him to do something for them which they might have chosen to do for themselves, which they are perfectly capable of doing and understanding.[3] Hence the representative was sent to pursue his constituents' will and not his own. Other mandate theorists invoke the metaphors of descriptive representation, seeing the representative as a mechanical device through which his constituents act—a mirror or megaphone. As to the national interest, the mandate theorist is likely to argue that the sum of local constituencies is the nation, and the sum of constituency interests is the national interest. Besides, if each representative was not intended to act as an agent of his locality, why was he locally elected?[4]

Independence theorists, too, have appropriate analogies at their disposal; they see the representative as a free agent, a trustee, an expert who is best left alone to do his work. They thus tend to see political questions as difficult and complex, beyond the capacities of ordinary men. In any case, they argue, a constituency is not a single unit with a ready-made will or opinion on every topic; a representative cannot simply reflect what is not there to be reflected.[5] Further, if each representative were pledged to and instructed by his constituency, political compromise would become impossible. It is necessary to leave room for the crucial activities of the legislature itself—the formulating of issues, the deliberation and compromise on which decisions should be based. And, as Burke asked, what sort of a system is it "in which the determination precedes the discussion; in which one set of men deliberate, and another decides; and where those who form the conclusion are perhaps three hundred miles distant from those who hear the arguments?"[6]

Further, the independence theorist argues that the representative, although locally elected, must pursue the national interest, which will by no means emerge automatically from the sum of local constituency desires. He must be left free of instructions so that he can pursue it.[7] Moreover, to allow a representative to act only on instructions is to rob him of all dignity and thus to undermine respect for the government.[8]

These are the two sides of the controversy in primitive form. Frequently they are complicated, however, by arguments about political parties. One argument is that in the modern state the legislator is neither bound by the wishes of his constituency nor free to act in the national interest as he sees it, but that he is bound to act in accord with the program of his political party. Sometimes this view is expressed by saying he is the representative of his party.[9] A second possibility is to regard parties as a

link between local wishes and national interests. The party presumably has a program on national issues; by electing the member of a certain party, the voters in each constituency express
their wishes on this program. The legislator is then bound to
this program because of his duty to party and his duty to his
constituents' wishes, and (presumably) because it accords with
his view of the national interest (why else is he in that party?).[10]
Third, it has been argued on the independence side, particularly
by continental writers, that the interests of party are partial and
special and not equivalent to the national interest; so the representative must be left free of party obligations to act in the national interest as he sees it.[11]

Various compromise positions have been taken. Some writers
argue that both extremes are true: the representative has an
obligation both to the wishes of his constituents and to the best
policy as he sees it; but they do not tell us how to reconcile the
two.[12] Some maintain that the representative's duty to his constituency is to plead their cause, to speak for them; but that
he must then vote in accord with his own judgment.[13] Many
writers have argued that time is the crucial factor; that the representative is not bound by every temporary whim or wish of his
constituents, but must obey their long-range, deliberate desires.
Some seem to take the curious position that a representative must
ignore his constituents except just at election time, and that at
election time they must remove him if they are not pleased.

What is most striking about the mandate-independence controversy is how long it has continued without coming any nearer
to a solution, despite the participation of many astute thinkers.
Each in turn takes a position—pro mandate or pro independence
—but the dispute is never settled. The two sides seem to talk
past each other; their arguments do not meet. Each seems convincing when read in isolation. Nor do the compromise solutions seem satisfactory. This state of affairs has led some commentators to reject further (as they put it) normative speculation,
and to call for empirical investigation of what representatives in
fact do.[14] Such investigation leads them either into a survey of
historical examples, or into studies of legislative behavior and
public opinion in the contemporary world.

The historical examples these writers adduce range over every possible degree from mandate to independence. In many political bodies the members have had power to vote or act only insofar as they had explicit instructions from those who sent them. The Imperial German Bundesrat, the modern American electoral college, the United Nations Assembly are examples.[15] In other bodies the members were bound by instructions given at the outset of their term of office or even during their term. The practice of instructing one's representative was explicitly recognized in a number of early American state constitutions. At other times and in other places, legislators have considered themselves almost completely independent of those who elected them. The same variety is found with regard to parties: historical experience ranges from the bound members of the Australian Labor Party to the great freedom enjoyed by American politicians today, or even to the absence of parties in earlier periods. The writers who make such surveys can conclude only that the range of acceptable relationships between representative and constituents is very wide.

Similarly, commentators who turn to empirical study of the contemporary American political scene find great diversity. Some legislators pronounce themselves as most responsive to the demands of constituency, and some to those of party, while others maintain that they act on their own independent judgment of the national interest.[16] Study of their voting behavior also shows considerable variety.[17] Public opinion polls to determine what the people expect from their representatives show a fairly even division of opinion.[18] The legislators tend to incline toward independence, the people toward mandate, but in each division there is a substantial minority. Empirical investigation is no less ambiguous in its results than the traditional "normative" controversy.

Now, a dispute as persistent as the mandate-independence controversy has been, may indicate the presence of a philosophical paradox, a conceptual difficulty at its root. The dispute itself may be formulated in such a way as to make settlement impossible. In that case it will not help to turn to historical or empirical evidence, for whatever conceptual ambiguity is at fault will be built into the questions we ask of history or of the population we interview. Our researches will simply perpetuate the initial difficulty on a new level. If such a conceptual difficulty is involved in the controversy, neither a blind choosing of sides nor a new method of amassing more relevant facts will settle it. What is needed is clarification, a demonstration of what is right and what is wrong with each side, and of why they talk past each other. I am not suggesting that the mandate-independence controversy is merely a conceptual paradox that could be settled by philosophical analysis, but rather that it is complicated and made insoluble by such a paradox, that the nonconceptual, political issues cannot be consistently dealt with until the conceptual problem is clarified.

We shall therefore turn aside, for a time, from these political arguments to concentrate on another kind of appeal that has been made by both sides—an appeal to the meaning of representation itself. In addition to all the arguments we have examined, both mandate and independence writers insist that the concept itself supports their views. "It just isn't really *representation*," the mandate theorist will say, "if the man doesn't do what his constituents want." "It just isn't really *representation*," the independence theorist responds, "if the man isn't free to decide on the basis of his own independent judgment." But, rather than putting words into their mouths, let us examine how such views are in fact expressed. For the mandate theorists, we may take a passage from Hillaire Belloc and G. K. Chesterton's early joint book on political parties: "Either the representative must vote as his constituents would vote if consulted, or he must vote in the opposite sense. In the latter case, he is not a representative at all, but merely an oligarch; for it is surely ridiculous to say that a man represents Bethnal Green if he is in the habit of saying 'Aye' when the people of Bethnal Green would say 'No.' "[19] A typical articulation of the same appeal to the meaning of representation by an independence theorist might be Lord Brougham's:

The essence of Representation is that the power of the people should be parted with, and given over, for limited period, to the deputy chosen by the people, and that he should perform that part in the government which, but for this transfer, would have been performed by the people themselves. It is not Representation if the constituents so far retain a control as to act for themselves. They may communicate with their delegate . . . but he is

to act—not they; he is to act for them—not they for themselves.[20]

Confronted by two such arguments, does one not want to say
that both are right? One can see the logic of each position in turn.
It is true that a man is not a representative—or at most is a representative "in name only"—if he habitually does the opposite of
what his constituents would do. But it is also true that the man
is not a representative—or at most is a representative in name
only—if he himself does nothing, if his constituents act directly.
But can both views be right when they seem to support opposite
and incompatible conclusions about the role of a representative?
Perhaps they can if each holds part of the meaning of representation, but extrapolates incorrectly from that part.

Imagine a situation in which representing would genuinely be
reduced to the extreme of the mandate position, to a mere mechanical reflection or delivery of the wishes of the constituents.
Imagine a body somewhat like our modern electoral college, but
with any ambiguities removed for purposes of our illustration.[21]
The members come simply to deliver and announce a decision
made in their home districts by the voters. Is this representation?
Are these members representatives? The independence theorists
say no. But one might speak of them as representing; we would
understand at once what was meant. A visitor to the meeting of
this body might point to one of the members and ask, "Whom
does he represent?" or "What state does he represent?" But this
would be representation purely in the sense of "standing for." The
members would represent in much the same way as a group of
fifty little girls in a pageant, each labeled to represent a state in
the Union. One can tick them off: this one represents Arkansas,
that one Oregon. But this is not representing conceived as activity.

Approaching the same example with representation as activity
in mind, we would have to deny that the body is representative
or that its members represent anyone. "You can *say* that he's
representing Arkansas, but of course he's really not doing anything. The real decision was made long ago and not by him. This
is just a formality." The real action was taken directly by the
state's voters; no one was acting for them. If they had mailed in

their decision, surely one would not say that the envelope that brought it represented them?

If we start from the idea of representation as acting for others, then the more we think of the member of this body as a mechanical thing, as a tool or limb or extension of those who act through him, the more inclined we are to say that they acted themselves and that no representation took place. I do not say that my hand "represents" me when I pick up a pen with it; *I* picked up the pen. This seems to be what happens in the thinking of the independence theorists when they consider whether a representative must obey the wishes and instructions of his constituents. They are thinking of representing as activity, and activity implies a certain minimum of autonomy, of animation. That is why Lord Brougham argues that it is not representation if the constituents have so much control over their representative that they act for themselves. "He is to act—not they; he is to act for them—not they for themselves." Thus there is a good deal to be said for the logic of the independence position, if we are thinking of representing as activity.

But there is something to be said for the mandate position as well—not the version of the mandate position that likens a representative to a mechanical device, but a different aspect of the argument. Consider the case of a member of a ruling body who not only fails to follow the instructions of his constituency, but also persists in doing the opposite of what the constituency desires. He may nevertheless be their formal representative, the official holder of the office. But would anyone maintain that he really represented that constituency? Would we not feel that there was something very wrong in such a case? Belloc and Chesterton's formulation of this issue is compelling: "it is surely ridiculous to say that a man represents Bethnal Green if he is in the habit of saying 'Aye' when the people of Bethnal Green would say 'No.' "[22] Only a fool or a hypocrite would try to tell Bethnal Green that such a man was truly, substantively representing them. This does not prove that a representative must obey or even consult his constituents before he acts; at most it proves that he may not act counter to their wishes habitually over a long period of time. If he does, he may still be their representative in name, formally, but is not really substantively so. On this score the case of the mandate theorists is indisputable.

The concept of representation itself is what accounts for the truth in each of the two conflicting positions. Being represented means being made present in some sense, while not really being present literally or fully in fact. This paradoxical requirement imposed by the meaning of the concept is precisely what is mirrored in the two sides of the mandate-independence controversy. The mandate theorist says: if the situation is such that we can no longer see the constituents as present then there is no representation, and if the man habitually votes the opposite of their wishes we can no longer see them as present in his voting. At most it might be a formal representation; they will be bound by his vote. The independence theorist says: if the situation is such that we can no longer see the representative acting, but rather we see the constituents acting directly for themselves, then there is no representation; and where he merely carries out their orders they seem to be acting directly for themselves. At most he might be said to stand for them descriptively or symbolically, but not to represent them in his activity.

In distinguishing between an agent and a representative, we noted that the agent of a corporation is more like its part or limb, while in the representative the corporation is (conceived as) present in its entirety. If, similarly, we are to think of the entire constituency as present in the action of its representative, two consequences seem to follow. First, if it is present in its entirety, why can it not change its mind here and now? Second, if it is present in its entirety, how can the action it takes here be in conflict with its express wishes? From the first consequence derives what is valid in the independence theory. The representative must have some freedom, some discretion to act, or it is difficult to imagine his constituency wholly present in him. If he is totally bound and instructed, we tend to think of him more as a tool or limb or puppet whose motivating or deciding power is elsewhere. From the other consequence derives what is valid in the mandate theory. The representative cannot be persistently at odds with the desires of his constituency, or else it is again too difficult to conceive the constituency as present in him. When they are at odds, we tend to think of him as a separate being acting on his own to pursue his own goals.

So, insofar as the mandate-independence controversy contains a conceptual dispute based on the meaning of representation, both sides are right. The seemingly paradoxical meaning of representation is perpetuated in our requirements for the activity of representing: the represented must be both present and not present.[23] The representative must really act, be independent; yet the represented must be in some sense acting through him. Hence there must be no serious persistent conflict between them. Thus one might suppose that the best examples of representing as activity would be found where absolutely no conflict could occur between representative and represented, because the latter is a child or otherwise incapable of judging for himself. But that is far from true. The represented must himself be capable of action, have a will and judgment of his own; otherwise the idea of representation as substantive activity is not applicable. Taking care of someone or something helpless or totally incompetent is not representing.

To be sure, representing need not necessarily be of a person or persons; abstractions, too, can be represented in the substantive sense of acting for them. Again it is difficult to distinguish such cases from standing for an abstraction symbolically or descriptively, or acting for it in the formalistic sense (as in *Organschaft*). Griffiths points out that although there are many Labor Party members in the British Parliament, and even some members of the working class, one might still want to deny that there is anyone in Parliament "who fully represent[s] the spirit and traditions of the working class movement. Perhaps only Keir Hardie ever really did."[24] Now, the "spirit and traditions" are not a person, nor are they an organization of which someone can be an official. Further, what the hypothetical speaker is saying of Mr. Hardie and denying of other members is not a symbolic presenting of the "spirit and traditions." He is not suggesting that Keir Hardie represented that spirit and tradition in the way in which the flag represents a nation or Uncle Sam represents America. What is being discussed here is representation through activity, speaking and voting in Parliament. Similarly, a political speaker may assert that he represents world peace, meaning not that he embodies its qualities by being very calm, but that he speaks and acts to further it. On other occasions we may variously say that someone represents (through his actions) union solidarity, justice, truth, the Christian point of view, the World Spirit, and so on.

Such abstractions cannot literally act for themselves and do not have wishes that could be consulted. Yet they can be represented, and we do not feel that their alleged representative is merely taking care of them, as a guardian takes care of a child. What distinguishes the abstraction from the helpless child being taken care of is apparently a matter of how we conceive the situation. If we think of the abstraction as acting through its representative, present in his activity, animating and directing what he does, then we will speak of representation.[25] Even a helpless child could be spoken of as being represented in this way; but if we *think* of him (or of an abstraction) as helpless and incapable of action, as being taken care of, then we will *not* speak of representation. An abstraction does not have wishes and cannot suddenly rise up and object to what a representative is doing in its name. With people, however, that is likely to happen from time to time; thus the puzzle of mandate versus independence arises only when we think of the representing of people, since they may have their own views of what is in their interest and those views may clash with their representative's decision.

The substance of the activity of representing seems to consist in promoting the interest of the represented, in a context where the latter is conceived as capable of action and judgment, but in such a way that he does not object to what is done in his name. *What* the representative does must be in his principal's interest, but *the way* he does it must be responsive to the principal's wishes. He need not actually and literally act in response to the principal's wishes, but the principal's wishes must be potentially there and potentially relevant. Responsiveness seems to have a kind of negative criterion: conflict must be possible and yet nevertheless not occur. But now representing begins to sound like an extraordinarily fragile and demanding human institution. Insufficient independence in the representative destroys the "illusion"; insufficient independence in the represented destroys the "illusion"; conflict between the two independent judgments also destroys the "illusion." But perhaps these requirements are not, after all, as extraordinary as they seem. I believe that they do rest on a fundamental assumption about human beings and human action, but an assumption which is not confined to the concept of representation, but pervades our entire vocabulary of action. To put it bluntly: we assume that normally a man's wishes and what is good for him will coincide. Thus if a representative in fact succeeds in doing what is good for his constituents, normally he should not then find himself in conflict with their wishes.

This duality can be most fruitfully studied in the concept of interest, which is ubiquitous in representation theory. For, in the first place, the concept of interest forms a kind of link between the representing of abstractions (which do not have wishes) and the representing of people (which do). An interest is itself an abstraction. And just as one can represent world peace or Justice, one can represent the interest of world peace or justice. But one can also represent the interest of certain people, of an individual or a group. Sometimes interests are the interests *of* someone. Thus the interest of consumers, though an abstraction, is an abstraction of a special kind in that it is linked with, referred to, a particular set of people whose interest it is—consumers. Representing the interests of consumers could conceivably require attention to their wishes, whereas representing the interest of world peace could not require such attention because there is no correspondingly relevant group to consult. The concept of interest thus occurs sometimes as attached to a certain group of people and sometimes in unattached form. In this respect it is unlike certain other abstractions—wishes, feelings, opinions—which are always attached, always the wishes, feelings, or opinions *of* some*body*.

In the second place, the concept of interest is dualistic in its meaning and in its etymological history, having become bifurcated into two separate senses, the one more or less equivalent to welfare ("Is it to your interest to see him?"), the other more or less equivalent to attention or concern ("Are you interested in him?").[26] The former has to do with what is "*to* someone's interest" or "*in* his interest." "To his interest" is strictly an adjectival form; an action, a law, a measure taken can be described as to someone's interest. "In his interest" is primarily but not exclusively adverbial; one can act in someone's interest. One cannot act to someone's interest. When a court speaks of "interested parties" it does not mean those whose curiosity has been aroused by a case, but those who have legal rights at stake. Similarly, when the eighteenth century condemned the "interested member" of Parliament, it meant not the one who took an interest in his work, but the one who had something personal to gain or lose by his decisions, and therefore could not act with detachment. And we still speak of "vested interests," and require some government officials to divest themselves of stockholdings to avoid "conflicts of interest." The converse of being interested in this sense of having something at stake is being "*dis*interested" or impartial.

The other sense of interest, equivalent to attention or concern, has to do with what we "take an interest in," what we find "interesting." The converse of being interested in this sense is being "*un*interested," indifferent, unconcerned.[27]

Etymologically, the word derives by way of French from the Latin *interesse*, "to be between," "to differ," "to make a difference"; and apparently it already had its dual significance in the Latin, meaning "to make a difference" both objectively and subjectively.[28] In English the objective sense is much earlier; the word first appears in the fifteenth century, in a legal sense meaning to be objectively concerned in a law suit, to have a legal claim, right, or title at stake. Similarly, the early meanings of "to interest" had this objective reference of having something at stake rather than any psychological one. Even "interesting" meant, quite literally, "important." Only later were these words applied to a psychological attitude that would be appropriate *if* one were objectively involved or had something at stake.[29] The adjective "interested" was first to be used in this psychological sense; the earliest examples in the *Oxford English Dictionary* are from the latter half of the seventeenth century; the noun and verb were not so used until late in the eighteenth century.

Only the sense of having something objectively at stake can occur as unattached interest. In that case it can be a cause or other abstraction that has something to gain or lose, rather than a person or group. But only animate beings can "take an interest" in something, "become interested" in it, or "find it interesting." The psychological sense is always attached to a person or persons. The psychological concept of what one finds interesting has been the almost exclusive concern of a tradition of thought in educational psychology. There are any number of studies on what people find interesting, how to arouse students' interest in their work, vocational guidance through "interest inventory" tests, and so on.[30] These studies usually ignore the fact that there is another sense of "interest"; for them (understandably) the word has only a psychological, subjective import.[31] In this sense, a person's interests depend on him as subject, on his reactions. Either the thing interests him or it does not. (Yet even within this sense of the word, some writers distinguish between subjective ways of defining what is interesting, like asking the person himself, and objective ways, like watching his behavior.)[32]

For the other major sense of "interest," having something objectively at stake, interpretations range from objective to subjective in various senses. At the most objective end of the scale are unattached interests, where there is no particular person or group whose interest it is (and who could, therefore, claim a right to define it). Not only is the interest of world peace not a psychological state, but there is no particular person or group in whom it might be measured. Someone is acting in the interest of world peace if he furthers world peace; that is all.

Even attached interests can be conceived as independent of anyone's feelings or thoughts. In Marxist theory the interest of a class is objectively determinable whether members of the class know it or not. What benefits a class is to its interest; with the passage of time the members of the class will become aware of their interest. But even before they become "class-conscious," various events may in fact be (or not be) in their class interest; they just do not know it yet. This kind of idea of interests independent of wishes or opinion seems to have flourished in economics, perhaps because profit and loss provide a standard that seems temptingly objective, whether or not somebody wants the profit. In any case, the idea has recently been applied to the sociopolitical world by a political scientist, who argues that

people have objective interests—things that are good for them—
quite apart from what they happen to want. He even attempts
to list some of these interests.[33] ─ C. Bay,

Thus even attached interest in the sense of what one has at
stake can be treated as totally objective and independent of
anyone's thoughts or wishes. But more often complications set
in at this point. Once we are dealing with attached interests, the
interests of labor, or Jones's interest, it is difficult to avoid the
question whether laboring people or Jones do not or should not
have something to say about what their interests are. It can be
maintained that their wishes and opinions are relevant in a
special way. We are individualists and democrats and relativists
in our thinking, not quite content to tell a man what is in his
interest without any regard to his wishes. We tend to think that,
in the last analysis, each man has the right to define his own
good, and, if he rejects something, no one has the right to insist
that it is good for him.

So most of our modern theories of interest, although they deal
with its objective sense of having something at stake, introduce
a subjective element. Who but the person involved has the right
to say whether he has anything at stake or not, we ask? Who is
to tell him he stands to gain or lose in a transaction if he insists
that he feels no gain or loss? Thus it is possible to equate interest
with having something at stake, but to leave to the individual
concerned the final determination of whether he has something
at stake.

This view originates with Utilitarianism, and it certainly
forms a central strand in Utilitarian theory. In much of Utilitarian
thought, each person is the only reliable measure of his own
interest; no one else can know what it is as well as he does.
Hence no representative can ever act in your interest contrary
to your wishes. In any event, he probably would not, because he
himself is motivated by his own interest. But even if he were
acting altruistically, he could never know your interest as well
as you know it, so he could only act in it by following your
express directions. Nothing forcibly imposed against your will
can ever be in your interest.

Among contemporary political scientists, this view is quite

common. A man's interest is equivalent to what the man wants, and the common interest of society is what the members of society want.

> The ultimate test of my interest is the satisfaction I experience when once it is attained. No condition barely imposed upon me by an external agency . . . can be in my interest, unless I come ultimately to recognize and accept it as such. . . . The common interest of society, therefore, must be what its members feel and accept as their own, and it can be served by no action merely forced or imposed upon them without their consent and concurrence.[34]

Similarly, interest is defined as "a pattern of demands and its supporting expectations."[35] Or we are told that it is "the settled and avowed aspirations of a man or group of men," which they consider "realizable"; and hence that "conflicts of interest" exist only as long as the parties involved feel dissatisfied.[36] Or again, another writer sees an interest as "any fairly persistent attitude toward the environment, expressing itself variously as a purpose, claim or expectation, whose satisfaction the possessor regards as a 'good' or 'utility' and whose frustration by another produces a feeling of disappointment or resentment."[37] We are thus directed to the psychological states of those concerned as the ultimate test of what their interest is.

This leads some commentators to confuse this sense of interest with the psychological "finding something interesting." They write as if what one finds interesting were exactly equivalent to what one considers to be to one's interest. They define the interest of an individual as that which "seriously enlists his attention," but when they turn to group interests this leads to confusion.[38] For a group as such has no psychological attention that can be enlisted or aroused. As a group, it can only engage in certain activities or pursue certain goals. So the interest of a group becomes "the object which it chiefly seeks."[39] Nor does such a writer seem to feel any inconsistency in the transition. But while it may be true that the objects we seek enlist our attention, it is certainly not always true that whatever enlists our attention is an object we seek. Not everything that interests us is something we consider to be to our interest.[40]

There are still two possibilities within the idea that interest is what one has at stake, in one's own judgment. Just as psychological "being interested" could be measured by asking the individual or by observing him; so also, what someone thinks he has at stake can be measured in two ways. One can ask an individual or group what they are after; or one can observe their behavior and draw one's own conclusions.[41] These two techniques have again been termed "subjective" and "objective." In the subjective camp, "the ultimate test" of interest is the "satisfaction" felt by the one whose interest it is, when it is attained."[42] The interests of a group, then, are the *attitudes* which its members share, "towards what is needed or wanted in a given situation"; so a group interest can exist even before the group is formed and organized.[43] But it can be maintained that these attitudes are to be observed empirically and objectively from behavior.[44] For other writers, the interest of a group is not an attitude of its members or any shared "psychological feeling or desire," but consists entirely in group activity. Interest "is the equivalent of a group. . . . The group and the interest are not separate. There exists only the one thing, that is, so many men bound together in or along the path of certain activity."[45]

The concept of interest, then, profoundly embodies the duality of our thinking about who is to say what is good for people. At the one extreme are unattached interests, where there are no relevant wishes to consult; at the other extreme, what a person finds interesting, which is surely up to him. And in between is a wide range in which interest *means* what a person has in fact, objectively at stake; yet we also feel that he must eventually have some say in defining what that is. Nor is the duality confined to this term, although it shows up with particular sharpness here. It runs through all our ideas about action, responsibility, and social life, and all our terms in this area are equivocal, some more, some less. Consider welfare. Surely sometimes we can promote a person's welfare even against his wishes; yet we would not want to say in general that people's wishes are irrelevant to a definition of their welfare. Or, at the other extreme, consider attached abstractions like wants or wishes. Even here we sometimes tell a child (or someone whom we are teaching,

say, how to play chess), "You don't really want to do that."
Such ways of talking can be abused, to be sure, but they are not
always without point.

We assume—and our language embodies the assumption—
that normally wishes and welfare will coincide, and a person will
want that which is objectively in his interest. This may not be
true with the insane or with small children, but it is our expectation about normal adults. Men are not children to be coerced
indefinitely for their own good.[46] That is why our complex
expectations about the activity of representing are not as extraordinary as they may seem. We assume that normally if a man
acts in the interest of another, the latter will have no objection
to what he does. Children and the insane cannot be relied on in
this respect, but then they are taken care of rather than represented. Representation enters the picture precisely where the
person acted for is conceived as capable of acting and judging
for himself; and of such a person we assume that he will want
what is in his interest.

It might be said that to act in someone's interest is to do
what he ought to want. There is nothing tricky about that
"ought"; it simply expresses our assumption about the normal
case. And to speak here of a normal case is not to assert that
the contrary never happens. Of course men sometimes want something that is not in their interest, nor to their real benefit. When
this happens, we assume that there must be an explanation, a
reason for the discrepancy. If we are told, "This would be best
for X, but he doesn't want it," we assume that there must be an
explanation. Perhaps he does not know all the facts; perhaps he
is not quite right in the head; perhaps it is not really best for
him in every respect. The representative's obligation is to the
constituent's interest, but the constituent's wishes are relevant
to that interest. Consequently, the representative also has an
obligation to be responsive to those wishes. He need not always
obey them, but he must consider them, particularly when they
conflict with what he sees as the constituent's interest, because
a reason for the discrepancy must be found.

It follows that representation does not require the principal
to have formulated "a will" on issues before the representative,
or even to know about them. One can represent others on matters

they neither care nor know about. What the representative must do is act in his constituents' interests, but this implies that he must not normally come into conflict with their will when they have an express will. But this prohibition is not equivalent to saying that he represents only when he acts in accord with their actual, conscious wishes. Quite the contrary: leadership, emergency action, action on issues of which the people know nothing are among the important realities of representative government. They are not deviations from true representation, but its very essence. It is often for that very purpose that people choose representatives.

Nor is it very helpful to say, as some writers do, that the constituents have a "latent" or "unconscious" or "unexpressed" will on everything, and that a representative must anticipate this will.[47] Such statements attempt to express the ideas I am setting forth here, but they are misleading. The fact is that, at least in political representation, the represented have no will on most issues, and the duty of the representative is to do what is best for them, not what they latently want.[48] We assume that if the representative acts in the interest of his constituents, they will want what is in their interest and consequently will approve what the representative has done. That is why the most telling and persuasive arguments of the mandate school are couched in negative terms: surely it cannot be called genuine representation if the man habitually does the opposite of what his constituents want! Why? Because surely it cannot be to their interest, if it is always the opposite of what they want. We just cannot believe that there could be good reasons for habitually reaching the opposite conclusions from one's constituents. Indeed, the word "habitually" strongly suggests that the representative is not acting on the basis of reasons.

The deceptive factor here is that the only *sure guarantee* of not being in conflict with someone's wishes is to act on his express orders. But a guarantee is not required in representation. It is a commonplace of political life that representatives not only act without knowledge of their constituents' wishes, but often act contrary to those wishes when they are known. I am arguing merely that the latter case calls for an explanation, not that it does not occur. Thus, when a representative finds himself in conflict with his constituents' wishes, this fact must give him pause. It calls for a consideration of the reasons for the discrepancy; it may call for a reconsideration of his own views. It is not sufficient for him to choose; it is necessary that the choice be justifiable. Canning, the nineteenth-century British statesman, expressed this idea when he told his constituents, "It may happen that your own judgement may occasionally come in conflict with my own. . . . In all such cases, I promise you not indeed wholly to submit my judgement to yours; . . . but I promise you that any difference of opinion between us will always lead me to distrust my own views, carefully to examine, and, if erroneous, frankly to correct them."[49] But if the representative has reconsidered, and his judgment remains the same, what then? Then he probably will have in mind some explanation of the discrepancy. He is likely to think, and to say, if challenged, that "the people don't understand the significance of this issue," or "they would agree with me if they knew all the facts."

If a representative acts contrary to the known wishes of his constituents, some such rationale is necessary. Acting contrary to their wishes is not necessarily wrong, not necessarily bad representation or a violation of a representative's duty. It may, indeed, be required of him in certain situations. But it is abnormal in the sense that it calls for explanation or justification. And not just anything the representative says will be satisfactory. To say that the constituents would approve what he is doing if they knew all that he knows, may be satisfactory, but other justifications may not be. Thus it will not do for a representative to assert that he did what he did for his own private interest; after all, he is not there for himself.

As a matter of political fact, legislators often pattern their actions not on what their constituents ought to want but on what they anticipate their constituents will want (in all their ignorance). This is natural; the legislators want to be reëlected. But the representative's duty, his role as representative, is generally not to get reëlected, but to do what is best for those he represents. In a democracy, the voters pass the final judgment (or at least a fairly final one) on their representative by reëlecting him or refusing to do so. But it does not follow that whatever will get him reëlected is what he is obligated to do, or is equivalent to "true" representation. His reëlection is not absolute proof that he is a good representative; it proves at most that the voters think so.[50] And again the voters' opinions, although highly relevant, need not be ultimately decisive. A representative may be unjustly voted out of office, defeated in spite of the fact that he has been an excellent representative.

If all this is a correct formulation of what representing as an activity means, if the representative must act independently in his constituents' interest and yet not normally conflict with their wishes, it follows that the basic question of the mandate-independence controversy is wrongly put. It poses a logically insoluble puzzle, asking us to choose between two elements that are both involved in the concept of representation. In that case, it is not enough to choose between the representative's judgment and the constituents' wishes; and there is no rational basis for choosing between them *tout court*. Representation as an idea implies that normally they will coincide, and that when they fail to coincide there is a reason. Which should prevail depends in each case on why they disagree and which is right. Nor does it help to ask whether the representative ought to act in his constituents' interest as he sees it or as they see it.[51] Both formulations distort; he must act in their interest, period. Their view of their interest may or may not be definitive, depending on the issue and the situation; but if he follows it, it should be because the action really accords with their interest, not because they merely think it does. That is why public opinion surveys get equivocal results when they ask: "Ought a representative to do what he thinks best, or what his constituents want?" To ask this question is to present people with a puzzling situation which requires more data for a satisfactory answer. One needs to know who is right—he or his constituents? And why do they disagree? Normally, the conflict between what he thinks best (for them) and what they want (as best for themselves) simply should not arise. When it does arise, it will not do to choose blindly between "his side" or "their side." No wonder the pollsters found responses fairly evenly divided.[52]

But what is the use in insisting that the representative's obligation is neither to follow his constituents' wishes nor to do what he thinks is in their interest, but to do what is, in fact, objectively in their interest? For in any real situation where a decision is to be made, he will have to rely on what he thinks and (possibly) what they think. He needs to know which to follow, but, as we have seen, there is no universal, safe principle to guide one in that dilemma. Neither "follow their wishes" nor "ignore their wishes" will do; the decision must depend on why they disagree, and in a practical case that means his judgment on why they disagree. But the standard by which he will be judged as a representative is whether he has promoted the objective interest of those he represents. Within the framework of his basic obligation there is room for a wide range of alternatives.

We have seen that, as traditionally formulated, the mandate-independence controversy cannot be consistently solved, but that one can nevertheless say something consistent about the activity of representing as acting for others. The representative must act in such a way that, although he is independent, and his constituents are capable of action and judgment, no conflict arises between them. He must act in their interest, and this means that he must not normally come into conflict with their wishes. But that is not all that needs to be said about the mandate-independence controversy; it does not "settle" that controversy. The conceptual puzzle embodied in the controversy is by no means the whole of it; even if the puzzle is solved, there is still a great deal of leeway for a variety of views. The conceptual principle sets the limits of representation, of what we are willing to recognize as representing (or a representative) and what no longer qualifies. If a state of affairs deviates too much in one direction or another, we shall say that it is no longer representation at all (he is simply an oligarch; he is simply a tool). But within the limits of what is no longer representation at all, there is room for a variety of views on what a good representative should and should not do.

The view that a political theorist develops within that range tends to be correlated with his image of politics, with his position on all the political issues in the mandate-independence controversy, which we set aside at the beginning of this chapter in order to get at the conceptual problem in isolation. His view will depend on whether his model is the representing of abstractions like unattached interests, or of attached interests, or of people. It will depend on what he considers the relative intelligence and ability of rulers and ruled, what importance he attaches to national versus local welfare, how he thinks about political parties, and so on. In the broadest terms, the position a writer adopts within the limits set by the concept of representation will depend on his metapolitics—his broad conception of human nature, human society, and political life. His views on representation will not be arbitrarily chosen, but embedded in and dependent on the pattern of his political thought. To see how this is so, we turn next to a few examples: to Burke, who deals with the representing of unattached interests; to Liberal political theory, which deals with the representing of people who have attached interests; and to a more extreme view in which interests become so subjective that representation is impossible. In each case, the view of representation is correlative with the viewer's conception of interest and with the theory as a whole.

8

Representing Unattached
Interests: Burke

What happens to the idea of representation when a writer concentrates on the representing of unattached abstractions is nowhere shown more clearly than in the thought of Edmund Burke.
For Burke, political representation is the representation of interest, and interest has an objective, impersonal, unattached
reality. The implications of such a view must be extracted from
his writings with some care, for he is seldom systematic and not
always even consistent. This, no doubt, is why he has been the
subject of so many conflicting interpretations, and has so often
been charged with opportunism and theoretical variability. To
some, Burke has seemed "the last and greatest champion of Parliamentary oligarchy . . . protesting against the notion of a democratic franchise."[1] Others maintain that "in practice as well
as in theory he defended the rights of the people."[2] Still others
find that a writer so inconsistent may be "a splendid rhetorician
and advocate. But he is not a seeker after truth; he is not a
philosopher."[3]

Since Burke seems to present no consistent doctrine of representation, we must begin by identifying several separate and
seemingly inconsistent views of the concept. The first and perhaps most familiar view is elitist, ratiocinative in character, and

national in scope. It appears particularly when Burke is speaking of the representing of the whole nation by Parliament, or
derivatively by each member of Parliament. These members are
an elite group, discovering and enacting what is best for the nation; that activity is what representation means. Burke holds that
inequalities are natural and unavoidable in any society, that some
"description of citizens" must always be uppermost.[4] In well-
ordered society, however, this ruling group is a genuine elite,
what he calls a "natural aristocracy."[5] Such an elite "is an essential integral part of any large body rightly constituted," because the mass of the people are incapable of governing themselves, were not made "to think or act without guidance and
direction."[6] Power "in the hands of the multitude . . . admits of
no control, no regulation, no steady direction whatsoever."[7]

A well-appointed state, then, is one which breeds and trains
a true natural aristocracy and allows it to rule, recognizing that
it can perform this function best. Representatives should be superior men of wisdom and ability, not average or typical or even
popular men.[8] What matters is their capacity for practical reasoning, for Burke conceives of their function as essentially ratiocinative. Only, in Burke's view, reasoning is not a purely intellectual matter, but is intimately bound up with morality and
what is right.[9] The function of political reason is to discover the
laws of God and nature, not in the abstract, a priori, intellec-
tualized manner of the French *philosophes*, which he vehemently
rejects, but with practical wisdom. Thus the superiority of the
natural elite and the desirable qualities of a representative lie
less in intellect or knowledge than in judgment, virtue, and wisdom derived from experience.[10] That is what "reason" means,
properly understood. There are morally right answers in politics,
and they can be found through the exercise of reason and judgment.

Hence for Burke government should rest on wisdom and not on
will; the good of the nation emerges not from a general will but
from "the general reason of the whole."[11] Accordingly, a representative is not to consult the wishes of his constituents; government is not to be conducted according to anyone's wishes. As
Burke told his Bristol constituency, "If government were a matter of will upon any side, yours without question ought to be

superior. But government and legislation are matters of reason and judgment."[12] This, in turn, is because government has to do with duty and morality, and "neither the few nor the many have a right to act merely by their will, in any matter connected with duty, trust, engagement or obligation." Indeed, "duty and will are ever contradictory terms."[13] Will can never be "the standard of right and wrong," and right and wrong are what matter in politics.[14]

Furthermore, since they depend on reason and not will, right political decisions emerge only from rational parliamentary deliberation. The process of debate in a representative assembly is an essential element in the discovery of right answers to political questions. Consequently it would make no sense for a representative to consult his constituents about what to do, since he is present at the parliamentary deliberations and they are not. "What sort of reason is that in which the determination precedes the discussion, in which one set of men deliberate and another decide, and where those who form the conclusion are perhaps three hundred miles distant from those who hear the arguments?"[15]

Thus for a number of reasons the first Burkean concept of representation seems to preclude democratic responsiveness to the electorate. It makes no sense for wise, superior men to take counsel with stupid, inferior ones. It makes no sense for those present at deliberations on a question to consult with those who were not present. And, above all, governing is not an exercise of will; so the will of the people can have no special status. They owe their representative complete freedom to act as he sees fit; and they owe it "as an act of homage and just deference to a reason, which the necessity of government has made superior to their own."[16] He in turn owes them the full exercise of his superior ability, not obedience or servility. If he "sacrifices" his judgment to their opinion "he betrays, instead of serving" them.[17] Representation has nothing to do with obeying popular wishes, but means the enactment of the national good by a select elite.

This first concept of representation found in Burke's work is a national one, seeing representation as something Parliament does for the nation as a whole.[18] The duty of each member is to reason and judge about the good of the whole; the selfish wishes

of parts of the nation, the wills of individual voters have nothing
to do with it. He must discover and enact the national interest.
If he is truly a member of the natural aristocracy he will be able
to do so, both because he will have the necessary wisdom and
rationality, and because "a true natural aristocracy is not a separate interest in the state, or separate from it."[19] A truly elite group
of representatives has no interest other than the national interest. Probably the single most famous passage in Burke's writings
is the one in which he sets forth this view to the electors of
Bristol:

Parliament is not a congress of ambassadors from different
and hostile interests, which interests each must maintain, as an
agent and advocate, against other agents and advocates; but Parliament is a deliberative assembly of one nation, with one interest, that of the whole—where not local prejudices ought to guide,
but the general good, resulting from the general reason of the
whole. You choose a member, indeed; but when you have chosen
him he is not a member of Bristol, but he is a member of Parliament.[20]

Since relationship of each member is to the nation as a whole,
he stands in no special relation to his constituency; he represents
the nation, not those who elected him. Elections are merely a
means of finding the members of a natural aristocracy, and presumably any other method of selection would be as acceptable
if it were equally efficient at picking them out.[21] Burke himself
at times suggests that some other process of selecting the elite
might be superior. He favors a very restricted suffrage, since it
takes an elite group of voters to select the most elite rulers. At
one point, late in life, Burke estimates at 400,000 the number of
persons in England and Scotland whose characteristics qualify
them to vote. These he calls "the British publick," sometimes
equating them with "the people" in a political sense, at other
times calling them "the virtual representatives of the people."[22]
In one early and extreme formulation, Burke actually says that
decreasing the number of voters would increase representation
because it would add to the voter's "weight and independency."[23]
This is perfectly consistent if representation means government
by a true elite, and elections are a means for finding that elite.
Representation here becomes a synonym for good government,
which is why Burke can maintain that "the king is the representa-

tive of the people; so are the lords; so are the judges. They are all trustees for the people."[24] Representing is trusteeship, an elite caring for others.

The first concept of representation encountered in Burke's thought is thus an aristocracy of virtue and wisdom governing for the good of the entire nation. A number of interpreters of Burke have taken this concept as the only one he held, and have consequently taken other aspects of his thought (notably the distinction between virtual and actual representation) as instances or applications of the same elitist, ratiocinative, national idea. One commentator says that Burke defended rotten boroughs and other (what we would consider) inequities of representation in his time "because they could provide seats [in Parliament] for those who might not please the ordinary elector, but who had high qualities of mind and character."[25] Another suggests that it was this elitist doctrine "that *led him to formulate* the theory of virtual as distinguishable from an actual or elective representation. From the standpoint of election the precise point of the theory is that *those elected by a few are presumed to represent all*."[26] And this commentator further equates virtual representation with the "assumption that Parliament is likely to be most effectively representative when its members are selected from the ranks of the privileged few by the voters of an insignificant minority of the people."[27] Thus virtual representation is seen as an instance of Burkean elitism: even localities and people who do not vote are represented if Parliament is truly elite, for being represented merely means being governed by the elite. Hence, "if virtual representation should fail to produce at a given time and place a ruling class of proven ability which rules in the interest of all, the case for it collapses as a matter of fact."[28]

In all fairness, some passages in Burke's writings seem to support this interpretation. For example, he argues that localities without a member in Parliament nevertheless "have an equal representation, *because you have men equally interested in the prosperity of the whole*, who are involved in the general interest and the general sympathy. . . ."[29] Nevertheless, if we examine Burke's doctrine of virtual representation with care, we see that it expresses a different concept of representing. If representation is equivalent to being-governed-by-an-elite, then at any given time it is equally good or bad for all parts of the kingdom. So long as the elite is sufficiently able, no part of the kingdom could ever justifiably ask that it be given actual representation, be allowed to send a member to Parliament. But Burke denies the effectiveness of virtual representation in two famous instances: that of the disfranchised Catholics with regard to the Irish Parliament, and that of the American colonists. Unless a different concept of representation is involved here, one can only conclude that Burke is highly inconsistent.

N.B.

Representation in this sense might exist without elections; all representation might be virtual. As one commentator quite reasonably concludes: "the doctrine proves too much. If a citizen does not need a vote to be well represented, why should any citizens have votes? If it would be bad for Manchester to send a member to Parliament, how can it be good for Bristol to send two? . . . Why, in short, should the House of Commons exist? . . . Virtual representation makes a case for eliminating actual representation. It even makes a case for absolute monarchy."[30] But Burke says that virtual representation "must have a basis in the actual," that elections are apparently necessary after all.[31] In the absence of different interpretations of his concept of representation, this must be taken as another instance of Burkean inconsistency, in which, curiously enough, "it does not seem to have occurred to him" that the rules of logic were being violated.[32]

What Burke, in fact, says is that some parts of the nation are represented "actually" or "literally," that is, they elect one or more members to Parliament; but a town or region that is not actually represented may nevertheless be represented "virtually"— virtual representation being a relationship in which "there is a communion of interest and sympathy in feelings and desires between those who act in the name of any description of people and the people in whose name they act, though the trustees are not actually chosen by them."[33] But communion of interest and sympathy of feelings are very different notions from those of natural aristocracy; they are factors of relation between representative and constituents, not elite characteristics of the representative. When Burke talks about virtual representation he is not talking about the representation of the whole nation by every member of Parliament; he is talking about particular disfranchised groups or localities. They do not send a member to Parliament, yet they are represented by some member from some other constituency. Thus some disfranchised groups are virtually represented and others are not. Here the first Burkean concept of representation, that of rule of the whole nation by a rational elite, is no longer sufficient; there is representation of particular constituencies by particular members of Parliament.

This is the second concept encountered in Burke's thought: the representation of interests. Although the city of Birmingham elects no members to Parliament, it can still be virtually represented there because Bristol sends members; and these are really representatives of the trading interest, of which Birmingham, too, is a part.[34] Although a member may be called the Representative of Bristol since he is elected there, he really represents Bristol's interest, which may also be the interest of many other cities like Bristol.

Burke conceives of broad, relatively fixed interests, few in number and clearly defined, of which any group or locality has just one. These interests are largely economic, and are associated with particular localities whose livelihood they characterize, and whose over-all prosperity they involve. He speaks of a mercantile interest, an agricultural interest, a professional interest. To a very great extent, these interests are conceived as "unattached"; it is not the interest of farmers but the agricultural interest—an objective reality for Burke apart from any individuals it might affect. A locality "partakes of" or "participates in" such an interest; the locality does not "have" the interest, nor is the interest Bristol's any more than it is the farmers'. Burke almost never speaks of an individual's interest, or of the interest of a group, or of one group or locality as having more than one interest. His concept is thus very different from the subjective, personal interests of Utilitarian thought, and from the modern idea of a multiplicity of self-defined, changing interests at all levels of society. "The legitimate interests were not shifting groups of individuals who happened to share similar opinions and wishes, as was the case with the great pressure groups, formed as voluntary associations in the nineteenth century. They were more like the 'fixed interests' of modern pluralistic theory."[35] It is only in terms of such broad, fixed interests that Burke *can* argue as he does, that the representative of Bristol, because he represents *the* trading interest, also virtually represents all other "out-ports and centers of shipping and commerce."[36] Sometimes Burke singles out certain interests that no longer quite seem to fit this pattern—the interest of Irish Catholics, for example. But even this interest he treats as though it conformed perfectly to his basic concept of broad, lasting, easily identifiable, and (as we shall see) objective interest.

Virtual representation, being a communion of interest and sympathy in feelings and desires, will presumably bear fruit in action. Burke points out that Bristol's representative may look out for Birmingham's interest very well. We know, however, that an elected representative does not always do a good job for his own actual constituents, and it follows that virtual representation may sometimes be better and more reliable than actual:

> Such a representation I think to be in many cases even better than the actual. It possesses most of its advantages, and is free from many of its inconveniences; it corrects the irregularities in the literal representation, when the shifting current of human affairs or the acting of public interest in different ways carry it obliquely from its first line of direction. The people may err in their choice; but common interest and common sentiment are rarely mistaken.[37]

This assertion, which has shocked many democratic commentators, is, in effect, tautological. If the actual representative from Bristol fails to look after the interest of Birmingham, he is not a bad virtual representative: he simply is not a virtual representative at all. Where one finds virtual representation at all, it is good virtual representation. And since actual representation varies in quality, it must follow that virtual representation is "in many cases even better than the actual."[38]

To be "virtually" so is to be so "in essence or effect, although not formally or actually; admitting of being called by the name so far as the effect or result is concerned."[39] Burke uses the term in just this way in speaking of virtual representation. He conceives that representation has a substantive content, an effect which its formal institutionalization is supposed to produce. Election of members to Parliament is intended to supply this content and bring about this effect. If it fails to do so it becomes an empty *how aggreg' into nat. interest?*

formality. Virtual representation exists where the substantive content and effect occur without election. Thus virtual representation always has the substantive content, by definition, whereas actual representation may or may not have. In each case, the content of representation, the substance, is a "looking after the interest" of the constituency. This view of the content of representation accounts for Burke's treatment of the proper relationship between a member of Parliament and his actual constituency. Just as virtual representation is based on common interest, so the duty of a member toward his actual constituency is to pursue the interest in which the constituency participates.[40]

in resp. to what?

The member is to pursue the interest of his constituency rather than do its bidding; the characteristic feature of the Burkean approach is that such a contrast is possible and even highly meaningful. This contrast is expressed in Burke's distinction between interest and opinion.[41] The objective, fixed "interest" of a constituency is quite different from the opinions of some or even all of the people that compose it. The true interest of any group, or for that matter of the entire nation, has an objective reality about which one may be right or wrong, about which one may have an opinion. The intelligent, well-informed, rational man, who has studied and deliberated and discussed the matter, is the man most likely to know the true interest of any group. Conversely, particular individuals or groups may be mistaken about what is to their interest. Thus the representative's duty toward his constituents is "a devotion to their interests *rather than* to their opinions."[42] And, accordingly, Burke frankly tells his Bristol constituency that, instead of obeying their instructions, he "conformed to the instructions of truth and nature," and "maintained your interest even against your opinions."[43] Since interest is objective, and rationally discoverable, and since people's wishes are usually based on their opinions, which are often wrong, the representative may have to pursue the interest of his constituency even against their will. For "the will of the many and their interest must very often differ"; and the representative owes the people "devotion to their interest" rather than "submission to their will."[44] This does not hold in a long-range sense, but, on any immediate issue, will and opinion can be expected to diverge from rationally discernible interest.[45]

But at this point we are again confronted by the question why elections are necessary at all. If it is the representative's job to look after the interest of a certain locale or group, and if there is no reason to suppose that its people know that interest, why should they choose the representative? If they ought not to instruct him, need they elect him? Since the substantive content of actual and virtual representation is the same, why not rely exclusively on the latter? Here again, as the commentators charge, the doctrine of virtual representation seems to lend itself "to the elimination of election altogether."[46]

But Burke rejects that position both in theory and in practical cases. On the theoretical level he tells us that "virtual representation cannot have a long or sure existence if it has not a substratum in the actual. The member must have some relation to the constituent."[47] To understand how such a passage can be consistent with the doctrine of virtual representation developed so far, we must consider the practical cases where Burke himself rejects virtual representation and favors an extension of the suffrage. Burke approves of past extensions to Wales, Chester, and Durham; and, more importantly, when members of Parliament try to argue that the American colonists are virtually represented, Burke mocks them: "What! does the electric force of virtual representation more easily pass over the Atlantic than pervade Wales, which lies in your neighborhood? or than Chester and Durham, surrounded by abundance of representation that is actual and palpable?"[48]

The assertion that virtual representation must have a substratum in the actual occurs in a discussion of Ireland, the clearest statement of Burke's aims. He argues that the franchise should be extended to (at least some) Irish Catholics, since they, not being allowed to vote, are not represented even virtually: "As things stand, the Catholic, as a Catholic, and belonging to a description, has no virtual relation to the representative—but the contrary."[49] In the Irish Parliament, the sentiments and interests of all the members correspond to those of their non-Catholic, and indeed anti-Catholic, constituents.[50] No member looks after the interest or shares the sentiments of the Catholics; so no member represents them virtually. The trouble is, of course, that none of the constituencies that *do* elect members shares the interest of the excluded group. Birmingham is virtually represented in the English Parliament because both it and Bristol are of the trading interest. Bristol sees to it that a representative of the trading interest is sent to Parliament, and Birmingham thus has its spokesman. The Irish Catholics, on the contrary, are not represented because none of the enfranchised constituencies in Ireland shares their interest, and hence no representative of their interest is sent to Parliament. Indeed, it is more likely that all the representatives are hostile to the Catholic interest rather than neutral. Similarly, the American colonists are not represented even virtually, because no constituency that does send members shares in the interest of the colonies.

This naturally raises the question how one is to determine whether a disfranchised group is or is not being virtually represented, whether any spokesmen for its interest have been sent to Parliament by some other constituency. Burke never explicitly answers this question, but I think the answer is evident from his writings. In the first place, we must keep in mind his peculiar concept of interest. Since interests are broad, unified, and easily identifiable, it is perfectly possible for an intelligent, impartial observer to determine the interest of a locality and see whether anyone in Parliament is defending that interest. But this is only the underlying rationale. Burke's actual criterion for deciding when an extension of the suffrage is justified is simply the existence of serious substantive grievances. Although he never sets forth the criterion in so many words, this is the basis on which he evaluates claims to an extension of the suffrage. If a group has serious, substantive grievances which are not being met in Parliament, this is taken as evidence that its interest is not being protected there, and hence that it has a unique interest not shared by any of the places that do send members. To win Burke's sympathies, a group must display "real" rather than merely "speculative" grievances. Thus he writes of the Irish Catholics that they

ask a share in the privilege of election; not as a matter of speculative right, not upon general principles of liberty, or as a conclusion from any given premises, either of natural or even of constitutional right. . . . *They ask it from a practical sense of the evils they feel* by being excluded from it. It is necessary for the free enjoyment of their industry and property, to secure a fair dispensation of justice both criminal and civil; and to secure them that just estimation and importance, without which, in human tribunals, they cannot obtain it.[51]

But Burke rejects and ridicules the claims of some disfranchised places in England, because it seems to him they have no real grievances. Of such claims, Burke asks: "Are the local interests of Cornwall and Wiltshire, for instance, their roads, canals, their prisons, their police, better than Yorkshire, Earwickshire, or Staffordshire? Warwick has members: is Warwick or Stafford more opulent, happy, or free than Newcastle or than Birmingham? Is Wiltshire the pampered favorite, whilst Yorkshire, like the child of the bondwoman, is turned out to the desert?"[52] Since they have no genuine complaints, Burke assumes that their interests are being looked after; hence they are virtually represented.

Burke's position on this question is in accord with, and undoubtedly animated by, his general hostility to political proposals based on abstract reasoning, or the claims of natural rights and natural law.[53] Although Burke sometimes opposes an extension of the franchise even though it is not claimed on the grounds of natural rights, still he says that "nine tenths of the reformers argue . . . on the natural right."[54] His "Speech on the State of the Representation" is almost exclusively a combat with the natural rights doctrine. Of those demanding reform without having substantive grievances he says impatiently: "This is like the unhappy persons who live, if they can be said to live, in the statical chair—who are ever feeling their pulse, and who do not judge of health by the aptitude of the body to perform its functions, but by their ideas of what ought to be the true balance between the several secretions."[55] As always, for Burke, we must look to the substance and effect of political institutions rather than to their form.[56] Needless to say, Burke himself decides who has substantive grievances and who does not, but he undoubtedly thinks that he is making an objective evaluation of the facts. We may consider him mistaken in his judgment that the disfranchised in England have no substantive grievances; but the point is that where he *sees* substantive grievances, Burke is willing to extend the franchise, and only there.[57]

This is why virtual representation, although sometimes better than actual representation, must have a substratum in the actual in order to ensure its permanence. It can happen at any time that some member of Parliament is spokesman for the interest of a disfranchised place. But the only long-range guarantee of the presence of such a spokesman in Parliament, is for some constituency that actually sends a member, to share that interest. But this involves the crucial assumption that the representative will protect the interest of his own constituency, and thereby all others like it. Except in cases where Bristol "errs in its choice," Bristol's member can be expected to further the trading interest. Again, this is the substantive content of representation that the formalities of election are supposed to ensure. But now we can see that Burke assumes that these formalities will ensure the substance most of the time; otherwise they could not serve as a substratum for virtual representation. Actual representation is no guarantee of the substance or "virtue" in any particular case, but it is their best assurance in the long run.[58]

And here one again must ask how Burke, with his elitist suspicion of popular capacities, can expect elections—actual representation—to produce even a fair degree of alignment between constituency interest and member activity. He clearly does not expect this to be brought about by the member's obedience to constituency opinion or wishes. Only at elections is the representative subject to their over-all judgment of his performance in office. Beyond that, Burke relies partly on restricting the suffrage to a fairly elite group. Partly he counts on the people's ability at least to determine whether things are going well or ill with them. But, above all, Burke here builds upon his unstated assumptions about the nature of interest. He sees interest very much as we today see scientific fact: it is completely independent of wishes or opinion, of whether we like it or not; it just is so.[59] This means, on the one hand, that an intelligent, honest representative can find it; and, on the other hand, that his constituents eventually will accept it. Given enough time and thought, any reasonably intelligent and unprejudiced person will find it to be so, just because it is. Long-range disagreement between representative and constituents can occur only if the representative is corrupt or incompetent. When Burke does speak of the people replacing a representative, it is almost always in terms of corruption or lack of ability, never in terms of an ordinary conflict on policy.

The key ingredients for an eventual concurrence on interest are time and deliberation. Opinion tends to be hasty, passionate, prejudiced, subject to violent but short-lived fluctuations; the passage of time will correct many of these aberrations. Thus Burke tells his constituency: "I aim to look, indeed, to your opinions; but such opinions as you and I must have five years hence. I was not to look to the flash of a day."[60] The people are at a disadvantage in discovering their true interest because they cannot participate in parliamentary deliberations. This is more difficult to overcome, but here, too, the passage of time is of assistance. Burke makes explicit the parallel between rational deliberation in Parliament and the more slow and irrational, but equally wise sifting of opinions through society over time. He says, "mind must conspire with mind. Time is required to produce that union of minds which alone can produce all the good we aim at."[61] In this respect Parliament "imitates in the sphere of government the natural character of society as a whole" and, through rational deliberation and wise judgment, reaches conclusions which the society could arrive at only indirectly and more slowly.[62] Thus Burke often distinguishes between hasty opinions and the "deliberate sense" of the people; even the famous passage in which he asserts that the multitude is foolish but the species is wise actually begins: "the multitude, *for the moment,* is foolish, *when they act without deliberation.*"[63]

And when Burke says that the deliberate wishes of the people must prevail, he is not turning pseudodemocrat with a sudden inconsistency. He is not saying that the people's will shall prevail over the representatives' will if the former are persistent enough. He is saying that if the people persistently see their interest differently from the members of Parliament, there must be something wrong in Parliament. If Parliament is doing its job well, if it discovers interest accurately, the people will in general, and in the long run, concur. Burke essentially makes the negative assertion that a lasting discrepancy between the member and the people is *in*consistent with true representation. A Parliament cannot indefinitely stand in the people's way and still be considered representative. The argument is negative in its formulation, as when Burke says it would be a dreadful situation if any power were strong enough to oppose effectively the general, deliberate wishes of the people.[64] "Where 'the deliberate sense of the kingdom' on a great subject was known, Burke said that 'it must be prevalent.' . . . when the people as a body . . . expressed their wishes 'strongly, decidedly, and upon long deliberation,' then their 'general sense' was to be taken for wisdom."[65]

But Burke's expectation that voters will eventually concur in wise parliamentary decisions, at least sufficiently to reëlect wise members, should not mislead us on his basic short-run attitude. On any particular current issue, popular opinion is unreliable and the representative's duty is to ignore it and pursue constituency interest. The whole electoral machinery is only the formal trappings of representation for Burke; its substance or "virtue" is the promotion of interest.

However, these statements apply only to the representation of interests, and this is not the only kind of representing known to Burke. He also recognizes the representation of *persons* as a different thing, which would have different consequences. Burke attacks the reformers who want to introduce manhood suffrage and equal electoral districts. Such a rearrangement of the constitution, he argues, would introduce "personal representation," and would make the member of Parliament represent the people of his district.[66] He would then function as their agent and be subservient to their will. The reformers, says Burke, "lay it down that every man ought to govern, himself, and that where he cannot go, himself, he must send his representative."[67]

But so long as the constitution remained unchanged, the members of Parliament represented interests rather than people. The House of Commons "is not, and never has been, representative of the people as a collection of individuals."[68] One commentator goes so far as to assert that Burke thinks of England as "a collection not of individuals, but of associations or interests."[69] This may be too strong, but it is certainly interests that are to be politically represented. Since he represents an interest, and since there is good reason to suppose that the people in his constituency have mistaken opinions about that interest, the member of Parliament is under no obligation to do what they tell him, as he would be if he were representing them as persons. As Burke told his own constituency in defending himself against the charge that he never came to Bristol to have contact with the people, "I canvassed you through your affairs, and not your persons."[70]

Yet even in talking about representation as he actually finds it in England, the representation of interests, Burke sometimes sounds as if he were an adherent of the descriptive representation view. We must distinguish these passages as still another component of representation in his work. Burke says, for example,

It was hoped that [the House of Commons] would feel with a more tender and nearer interest everything that concerned the people than the other remoter and more permanent parts of the legislature. Whatever alterations time and the necessary accommodation of business may have introduced, this character can never be sustained unless the House of Commons shall be made to bear some stamp of the actual disposition of the people at large. . . . *The virtue, spirit and essence of a House of Commons consists in its being the express image of the feelings of the nation.*[71]

It is always "sentiment" or popular "feelings" that are to be reproduced or reflected accurately in representation. We have marked the difference between "interest" and "opinion," between "reason" and "will." But Burke recognizes still another concept relevant here: the expression of needs or suffering or symptoms, which he refers to as "feelings," "sentiments," or "desires." "Feelings" are a simple expression of something that is wrong, a complaint. "Opinions" may grow out of these, but they go beyond them into the realm of more abstract speculation, suggesting what may be the cause of the trouble, and what may be an appropriate remedy in the light of interest. Unlike opinions, feelings are reliable; and people are seldom mistaken when they perceive a pain or symptom, be it physical or political. It is only when they attempt to speculate abstractly on the basis of what they feel that they go astray into opinion. "The most poor, illiterate, and uninformed creatures upon earth are the judges of a practical oppression. It is a matter of feeling; and as such persons generally have felt most of it, and are not of an over-lively sensibility, they are the best judges of it. But for the real cause, or the appropriate remedy, they ought never to be called into council about one or the other."[72]

Feelings, unlike interest or scientific fact, are essentially personal, and the only reliable authority on what someone feels is the person himself. Hence it becomes important for the people's feelings to be transmitted accurately to the government. This is why the House of Commons must be "the express image of the *feelings* of the nation." For the role of the representative is to find, through rational deliberations, the interest of the people, and to do so he needs to know their feelings. "The people are the masters. They have only to express their wants at large and in gross. We are the expert artists; we are the skillful workmen, to shape their desires into perfect form, and to fit the utensil to the use. . . . They are the sufferers, to tell the symptoms of the complaint; but we know the exact seat of the disease, and how to apply the remedy."[73]

Here, then, is a further reason why virtual representation must have "a basis in the actual," another way in which elections ensure the substantive content of representation. They help to promote the necessary reflection of popular feelings. Thus when Burke says that the House of Commons must mirror the nation he is not talking about numerical accuracy of correspondence. He only wants to make sure that the complaints of the people are accurately expressed before Parliament.[74] Quite consistently, Burke does not insist that this be done only through the representatives; Beer has called attention to the role played also by petitions submitted through the channels of various "official outlets," like municipal corporations, universities, cathedral chapters, and the like.[75] But the primary responsibility for the transmission of popular feelings lies with the representative. That is why Burke defines virtual representation, the substantive content of representation, as "a communion of interest *and* sympathy in feelings and desires." Both are necessary elements.[76]

This accurate reflection of popular feelings does not constitute representation for Burke so much as it is a prerequisite for representation. But it is nevertheless interesting, in the light of our earlier discussion of descriptive representation, to note the context in which these passages appear. It is just when Burke is concerned with accurate information about the nation that he falls back upon terms like "image" and "reflection."

But how is this "reflection" or "image" concept related to

Burke's other notions of representation? Is his thought hopelessly fragmented? I think not, and we now have at hand all the necessary materials for a reconstruction of the relationships among them and their underlying consistency. The distinction between representation of interests and of persons must remain. These are two different kinds of representing-as-an-activity for Burke: he who represents a person must act in accord with that person's wishes; he who represents an interest must act in accord with that interest. It is the latter kind of representation that concerns Burke, since it is the kind he finds and wants to preserve in British politics.

There remain the elitist, ratiocinative representation of the whole nation, the actual and virtual representation of constituencies, and the accurate reflection of popular feelings. The first two are instances of the representation of interests. To represent the nation means to represent the national interest. To say that a man represents a certain constituency is a formal way of saying that he represents the interest of which it is a part. Still, is there not a conflict between these two kinds of interest representation? In the former concept, the representative is to look to the national interest rather than to local ones; in the latter, he represents only insofar as he looks after some local or functional interest. In the former, the natural aristocracy "is not a separate interest in the state"; in the latter, a good representative must have a "communion of interest" with his constituency. In the former, the representative is part of an elite, and is to be judged on whether he has the elite characteristics of wisdom, rationality, and judgment; in the latter, he is to be judged on service to the interest he represents. The former emphasizes reason and deliberation resulting in a decision; the latter seems to call for support of an interest to which one is committed from the outset. And what of the reflection of feelings?

The juxtaposition of interest and personal representation also calls attention to other puzzling features of Burke's thought. In neither concept of interest representation—the particular or the national—does it seem important to him how many representatives any particular place or interest sends to Parliament. Where Burke is speaking of an elite discovering and acting on the general good, this is obvious: so long as they are an elite, it does not matter how they got there or how many come from any one place. But it seems equally true of the representation of particular interests. How else could a place be virtually represented by a member from some other place, unless his mere presence in Parliament were all that mattered? Apparently one member is just as good as a dozen. And yet virtual representation is not just an empty formula for Burke: it is to be judged by its results. How could he expect a single man to outweigh the votes of all the other members and protect the interest not only of Bristol, which elected him, but also of Birmingham?

The first key to these puzzles lies, again, in the nature of interest. We are accustomed to think of special or local interests as hostile, almost by definition, to the "interest of the whole." And on a few occasions Burke slips into this way of speaking too. But most of the time, in his fundamental thought, interests are not only broad and objective but additive. The interests of the realm, added together, compose the interest of the realm. All the different localities and functional groupings in the nation are part of the nation, and consequently have an interest in the welfare of the whole. It cannot really be to the interest of Wiltshire to improve its roads if that can be done only at the cost of inadequate national defense. And, conversely, it is to the interest of the whole nation that each of its parts should prosper and be well administered.[77] The national interest is the sum of the objective interests that compose the nation, when these are correctly determined through rational deliberation. "Expedience" in politics is "that which is good for the community, and good for every individual in it."[78] Hence "all policy is very suspicious that sacrifices any part to the ideal good of the whole."[79]

Burke is no lighthearted optimist arguing that the truth will always out, or that men do not really disagree. Nor is he a Hegelian proponent of a "real will" as distinct from what men apparently want. But beneath the surface of his arguments runs a strong presumption that, insofar as solutions can be found, the way to find them is through rational consideration of the issues by wise men. The widespread interests that compose the nation and the Empire "must be considered—must be compared—must be reconciled if possible."[80] Burke says "if possible," implying that it is not always possible. But the fact that he makes this the task of the legislature and the essence of representation implies that it will be possible most of the time. Burke is not always consistent and not always clear, but fundamentally he conceives of "interest" as something objective and discoverable that can be fitted into an orderly schema, the interest of the whole.

Some passages seem to imply the opposite, seem to contrast local, necessarily hostile interests with the national interest, as when Burke says that Parliament "is not a congress of ambassadors from different and hostile interests . . . [but] a deliberative assembly of one nation with one interest."[81] But such passages are deceptive and do not give us the whole of Burke's view. They are as much a rejection of an incorrect concept of interest as of an incorrect doctrine of representation. Burke is not so much saying that, although there are local, hostile interests the representative must ignore them, as he is saying that interests are not merely local and hostile. The manufacturing interest is part of the interest of the whole; and, indeed, the process of deliberation to discover the national interest requires presentation of the various interests that compose it. But of course, this presentation must not be an unshakable, unthinking commitment to a position, beyond all reasoning; Parliament is not a congress of committed ambassadors. True interest must be discovered by deliberation, and the discovery of the national interest and of the other fixed and permanent interests of the kingdom are simultaneous processes.

Thus there is no real contradiction for Burke in thinking of a member of Parliament as representing, say, the trading interest, and yet of every member of Parliament as representing the national interest. The two are part of the same process: both the parts and the whole emerge from rational deliberation, and neither requires that the member convey the will or opinions of any group outside Parliament. The interests are only discovered in Parliament, through debate. But their discovery presupposes the participation of representatives of every interest so that all considerations will be brought to light in the debate. For Burke this has nothing to do with compromise among the wishes of conflicting groups; government is a matter of reason and not of will. But reason needs able deliberators from every relevant point of view.

not bargaining (Barry)

Furthermore, it needs information. Before it has reason to act or to deliberate, Parliament needs to know that something is wrong, and what. The rational deliberations on interest are not conducted in a vacuum; they require data on which to work. These data are the feelings, the needs, the symptoms of the people; this is why the legislature needs to have accurate information on them, must indeed be an image of the feelings of the nation. Only when the symptoms are known can the physician go to work; only when the needs are known can the skillful workman begin. The accurate transmission of popular feelings thus is a prerequisite to representation. It is not, to Burke, in itself representation; it is the material on which representation works.[82] Thus the source of Parliament's information about feelings does not matter, so long as it is accurate.

On the basis of this information, with at least one able representative of every interest participating, rational deliberation discloses the national interest. Burke thinks of this deliberation as resulting in consensus and agreement, not in a divided vote where the majority prevails. Parliament is to deliberate until it finds the answer, and Burke assumes that an answer can be found. This is why the number of representatives from any particular place or interest does not matter. Voting, the counting of noses in Parliament, is of no importance; what is required is that all the facts and arguments be accurately and wisely set forth. This is why, also, a group's having legitimate grievances is evidence that it is not being represented. If its interest has even a single competent member in Parliament, it will be looked after, because it is not his vote but his arguments that matter. The assumption that Parliament will arrive at consensus parallels the assumption that in the long run people can be expected to concur in what an able representative has done in their interest; both rest on the same base.

This entire complex of ideas—elite representation of the nation, actual and virtual representation of constituencies, parliamentary deliberation, accurate reflection of popular feelings—together makes up Burke's theory of political representation. It is misleading to say, as one recent commentator does, that Burke emphasizes the deliberative function of the legislature "in contrast to the representative function."[83] Deliberation is the heart of "the representative function" for Burke; his concept of representation is, like much of his thought, highly complex.

For Burke, then, the representative has no obligation to consult his constituents, except in the very restricted sense that the legislature needs an accurate reflection of popular "feelings." Even this is not so much a part as a prerequisite of representation, and can be accomplished by any number of agencies. Burke's position on this issue is related to other strands in his thought, all of which are mutually supporting. It is related to his antidemocratic, elitist hostility to unnecessary extensions of the franchise. It is related to his concentration on the representation of interests rather than of people. It is related to his conceiving of interests as objective and unattached. And it is related to his view of government and politics as matters of knowledge and reason, not of opinion or will; to the idea that political questions have right answers which can be found.

It is because the modern world shares so few of these attitudes or assumptions, that no one today takes a Burkean view of representation, although as late as 1857 George Harris fought a last-ditch defensive action against the rising tide of democracy by arguing that "the interest of numbers" was only one of the several interests composing a state, that ought to be represented.[84] But for most representation theorists since Burke's time, political questions are inevitably controversial ones without a right answer, interests are the interests *of* someone who has a right to help define them, and no reliable elite group exists in society. For most of them, people, not interests, are represented in politics. Some continue to speak of the representation of interests, but the distinction loses much of its importance when all the other assumptions are gone.

9

Representing People Who Have Interests: Liberalism

A view more familiar to us than Burke's was already being articulated in his time by the theorists of Liberalism on both sides of the Atlantic. In America, representation was clearly to be of persons, and interests became an inevitable evil, to be tamed by a well-constructed government. In England, Utilitarianism not only favored the representation of persons, but made interest an increasingly personal concept. The theorists of Liberalism generally thought of representation as being "of individuals rather than corporate bodies, 'interests' or classes. In harmony with the individualism of their economic outlook, they also thought of representation as based upon rational, independent, individual persons."[1]

In America, this is reflected in the notion of equal electoral districts or "representation by population" established for the House of Representatives. A number of speakers at the constitutional convention defended the Senate as a safeguard for "property" as opposed to "numbers," and many of our founding fathers were far from being democrats; the representation of people does not necessarily mean the representation of all people. But when the Liberals favor property qualifications for the suffrage, they usually justify them on the basis that property is the best rough index of capacity, stability, and good will in the individual. "The true reason of requiring any qualification with regard to property, of voters, is to exclude such persons as are in so mean a situation that they are esteemed to have no will of their own."[2] Accordingly, there is no discussion, either within English Liberalism or in the American version, of anything like virtual representation.[3]

For Alexander Hamilton, John Jay, and particularly James Madison in the *Federalist Papers*, representative government is a device adopted instead of direct democracy, because of the impossibility of assembling large numbers of people in a single place, "a substitute for the meeting of the citizens in person."[4] As we have seen, this doctrine has a lengthy English tradition, and need not be linked with any preference for direct democracy. Certainly, in the *Federalist*, representation is, though a substitute for direct participation, a far preferable substitute. Still, theirs is a far cry from the Burkean view, and much more compatible with a notion of representing persons than of representing interests. With the revolutionary slogan "Taxation without representation is tyranny" only a decade behind them, it was almost inevitable that the authors of the *Federalist* should treat participation in government as a personal right; since they feared and opposed democracy, representation seemed a desirable way to allow such participation in safety. It meant, as Madison says, "the delegation of the government . . . to a small number of citizens elected by the rest," instead of the conducting of public affairs by all citizens "in person."[5]

But if representation has become representation of persons, it does not follow that interests disappear from the scene. Interests play a central role in Liberal psychology and politics, but they are conceived very differently from the Burkean sense. The concept of interests in the *Federalist* is much more pluralistic than it ever was for Burke, and it is essentially pejorative. Interests are identified with "factions," and are evil. In the tenth *Federalist* paper, Madison argues that the diversity of human faculties leads to property and hence to the variety of interests in society. No longer are interests the clearly defined, broad, objective groupings that compose the nation; no longer do people or places "belong to" or "partake of" an interest. An interest is something men "feel."[6] For Madison, interests are multiple, shifting alignments, largely subjective, and likely to conflict with the welfare of the nation.

While there is still a "landed interest" and a "manufacturing interest," "These classes may again be subdivided according to the different production of different situations and soils, and according to different branches of commerce and manufactures."[7] These economic groupings are supplemented and crosscut by others "founded on accidental differences in political, religious, or other opinions, or an attachment to the persons of leading individuals."[8] Societies are divided into various interests "as they happen to consist of rich and poor, debtors and creditors, the landed, the manufacturing, the commercial interests, the inhabitants of this district, or that district, the followers of this political leader or that political leader, the disciples of this religious sect or that religious sect."[9]

Madison almost always speaks of interests in the plural, whereas Burke most often speaks of this or that interest.[10] Madison does not conceive of groups, or even the whole nation, as having one interest which dictates a particular course of action on particular issues. Rather, each has many interests in respect of various needs and situations at various times. In Madison's thought, the term "interest" becomes almost interchangeable with Burke's "opinion" and "will," or even "feeling" and "sentiment." None of these is considered objective or impersonal, nor are Madisonian interests ever "unattached." A man's interest is what he thinks it is, just as his opinion is what he thinks. Indeed, interests have for Madison just those qualities that Burke assigned to "opinion"; they are subjective, personal, shifting, unreliable, and usually antagonistic to the real welfare of the nation.

There still is such a thing as "the real welfare of the nation" for Madison; there is still an objective good, but "interests" have crossed over from resembling this "real welfare" to resembling "opinion." Actually, even this is not quite true, for the *Federalist* does occasionally distinguish between two kinds of interests: "true interests" or one's "enlarged and permanent interest" on the one hand, and "momentary passions and immediate interests," or "an impatient avidity for immediate and immoderate gain," on the other hand.[11] The latter conception is the central sense of "interest" in the *Federalist*; the former appears only in contrast with it, never in isolation. Nevertheless, there is supposed to be such a thing as objective welfare or benefit, in the enlarged and long-range sense, even though the term "interest" is not usually applied to it.[12]

The pluralistic, shifting interests of the people play an important role in Madisonian representation, even if it is representation of persons. For people are motivated by their interests, and it is assumed that the representatives of people will seek to further those plural, shifting interests. This is never made explicit, since the Federalist never takes up the duties of a representative as such. But only on this assumption can representation offer a cure for faction in the way in which Madison says it does. We must therefore examine the theory of faction, and the cures for faction—a part of Madisonian doctrine that has sometimes been misunderstood.

A faction, defined in the tenth *Federalist* paper, is more or less equivalent to an interest group; it is "a number of citizens, whether amounting to a majority or a minority of the whole, who are united and actuated by some common impulse of passion, or of interest, adverse to the rights of other citizens, or to the permanent and aggregate interest of the community."[13] This adverse effect, the disruptive element in faction, must somehow be rendered harmless by a well-ordered government. And Madison argues that the new Constitution is a well-ordered government in this respect, particularly because it is a representative government: "A republic, by which I mean a government in which the scheme of representation takes place, opens a different prospect, and promises the cure [for the evils of faction] for which we are seeking."[14]

Just how does representation render factions harmless? At this point some commentators on Madison argue that Madison's answer is essentially parallel to Burke's elitism: the representatives will be superior, dispassionate men, calmly debating in the light of reason, and so will refuse to give way to the factious desires of their constituents. They will deliberate on "the common good" instead of merely reflecting "the will of the people."[15] And commentators cite the famous passage in the tenth *Federalist Paper*, likening representation to a filter that will "refine and enlarge the public views, by passing them through the medium of a chosen body of citizens, whose wisdom may best discern the true interests of their country, and whose patriotism and love of justice, will be least likely to sacrifice it to temporary or partial considerations."[16] But this passage must be read in context for its proper significance to be understood. Madison says that a republic differs from a democracy in two important ways. First, in a republic there is representation: government is delegated to a few men by the rest. Second, as a result, a republic can include a greater geographic area and a larger number of citizens than a democracy. The effect of the first difference, as regards the evils of faction, is the filtering effect we have just discussed. But Madison goes on to say that, under representation,

it *may well happen* that the public voice, pronounced by the representatives of the people, will be more consonant to the public good than if pronounced by the people themselves, convened for that purpose.

On the other hand, the effect may be inverted. Men of factious tempers, of local prejudices, or of sinister designs, may, by intrigue, by corruption, or by other means, first obtain the suffrages, and then betray the interests of the people.[17]

The filter is thus likely to turn into a distorting mechanism, to "filter out" desirable instead of undesirable materials. Madison does not really rely on any filtering by superior wisdom, for only one page earlier he argues:

It is vain to say that enlightened statesmen will be able to adjust these clashing interests, and render them all subservient to the public good. Enlightened statesmen will not always be at the helm. Nor, in many cases, can such an adjustment be made at all, without taking into view indirect and remote considerations, which will rarely prevail over the immediate interest which one party may find in disregarding the rights of another or the good of the whole.[18]

Since the filtering effect of wise representatives is no safeguard against the evils of faction, what Madison really relies on is the second characteristic of a republic: that it can be large and consequently diverse. In a large and diverse state there is a greater possibility of finding wise and public-spirited representatives, but again this is not dependable, and is not Madison's real hope. The crucial hope is that in a large state there will be more separate interests, and therefore less likelihood that they can combine for effective factious action.

Extend the sphere, and you take in a greater variety of parties and interests; you make it less probable that a majority of the whole will have a common motive to invade the rights of other citizens; or if such a common motive exists, it will be more difficult for all who feel it to discover their own strength and to act in unison with each other. . . .

The influence of factious leaders may kindle a flame within their particular States, but will be unable to spread a general conflagration through the other States.[19]

In the system that Madison envisages, the danger is action and the safeguard is stalemate, or, as he would have it, balance. Factious interests are to be "broken," "controlled," and "balanced" against each other to produce "stability."[20] How strange this would seem to Burke! For Burke, the national welfare emerges from the discovery of interests by wise and rational representatives, deliberating in Parliament with a minimum of interference from the people. The authors of the *Federalist* can conceive of such a situation, but they can as readily conceive of congressional leaders intentionally betraying the popular interest, which is something the people themselves could never intentionally do.[21]

For Madison, the welfare of the nation is achieved by inaction and stability. On the rare occasions when positive action is required, he assumes that there will be no difficulty in securing a substantial majority to support it. His concern is to prevent action based on factious interests, and it is this end that representation serves. Representation makes possible a large republic, which makes it more difficult for any faction to become a majority. But in a wider sense, Madison envisages representation as a way of bringing dangerous social conflict into a single central forum, where it can be controlled by balancing and stalemating.[22]

The task of representative government is thus, in a sense, to bring the major social forces into the legislature and keep them there until time passes. Here we come to the significance of Madison's references to a more rational, objective, and long-range interest than the interests of factions—what he calls "true" or "enlarged and permanent" interest. For Madison does have hope that time will correct passion and prejudice, and allow "the mild voice of reason" to prevail over immediate, selfish gain; consequently the task of representative government is to preserve the status quo until the mild voice can do its job.[23] Although "interested men" may mislead the people at times to pursue "some irregular passion, or some illicit advantage," the people "themselves will afterwards be most ready to lament and condemn" those measures.[24] That is why "the cool and deliberate sense of the community ought, in all governments, and actually will, in all free governments, ultimately prevail over the views of its rulers."[25] Like Burke, Madison thinks that even ordinary men can be expected to see the light given enough time and information. But Burke considers representation as a device for arriving at the right solution in Parliament and enacting it, with hopes that the people will eventually accept the action. Madison, by contrast, sees representation as a way of stalemating action in the legislature, and thus in society, until wisdom prevails among the people.[26]

Consequently, although he deals with the representation of persons rather than interests, Madison sees this activity as a pursuit of their interests in accord with their wishes. Only if each representative pursues the factious interests of his constituency can the various factious interests in the nation balance each other off in the government; only if the dangerous forces in society are brought into the legislature to be balanced and held there can they be rendered harmless. This leads one commentator to say that the authors of the *Federalist* saw the represented "less as unique individuals than as repositories of types of interests and motives."[27] This may be too strong; men are seen as individuals, but all individuals are motivated mainly by interest. Saying that interests and motives become correlative is another way of stressing the subjectivity of Madison's concept of interest. But it is important also that men, being individuals, often change their interests, and so interest groupings are shifting and temporary. This important truth is disguised if we say that men are merely "repositories of types of interests." But it is true that the *Federalist* treats government as "the restraining, balancing, and accommodating machinery for processing interests," and that this is what it means by representation.[28]

There is a potential difficulty in the assumptions made by the *Federalist* about interest and representation. On the one hand, for representative government to do what the authors expect of it, representatives must pursue the interest of their constituents. On the other hand, these interests are subjective, shifting, and unstable. Can a representative really know such interests well enough to pursue. them? The problem is not discussed in the *Federalist*. A rather pessimistic answer may be inferred from a statement of Madison's at the Constitutional Convention:

if the opinions of the people were to be our guide, it would be difficult to say what course we ought to take. No member of the convention could say what the opinions of his constituents were at this time; much less could he say what they would think if possessed of the information and lights possessed by the members here; and still less what would be their way of thinking six or twelve months hence.[29]

But are interest and opinion identical? Can a representative know his constituents' interests better than he can know their opinions? The difficulties posed by a subjective view of interest for representation theory are foreshadowed here. The *Federalist* as a whole seems to assume that the representative can know constituent interests well enough to pursue them.

Unlike the Burkean representative, however, Madison's representative does not know his constituents' interests better than they do themselves; if anything, he is in this respect roughly their equal. His furtherance of their interests is conceived as fairly responsive; and when, in time, an enlarged and rational view prevails, it prevails both in the legislature and in the minds of the people. Politics is not a realm of knowledge and reason for Madison as it is for Burke. It is much more a realm of pressures and opinion. The legislators are "advocates and parties to the causes" which they have to decide, and it is to be expected that interest "would certainly bias [their] judgment and not improbably, corrupt [their] integrity."[30] There is a link between Burke's view of interest and politics as matters of reason and wisdom, and his conviction that forms of government are not very important so long as they are operated by the right kind of men. In the same way, Madison's view of politics and interests is linked with his unwillingness to rely on the right kind of men ("enlightened statesmen will not always be at the helm") and his insistence on the forms of government.[31]

A further step in the direction of subjectivity is taken by the English Utilitarians. They argue variously that all men are always, or most men are usually, motivated by their own interests.[32] At the very minimum, most men almost always prefer their own interest to that of anyone else. With this Madison would undoubtedly agree, but when he speaks of interest he is still thinking of something that groups of men have in common. The groups are smaller, more multiple, less permanent than those partaking of Burkean interests, but they are groups. The Utilitarian concept of interest is even more subjective, and basically it is personal to each individual. This, at least, is the concept of interest for which the Utilitarians are best known, and which is developed in their philosophical and economic studies. We shall see that their political theories are something else again. But when the Utilitarian looks at man as an economic creature, he sees individual self-interest at work.

Further, each man is the best judge, if not the only reliable one, of his own interest. As Bentham puts it, "There is no one who knows what is for your interest, so well as yourself."[33] It follows that each individual is the only reliable guardian of his own interest, either because other men are too selfish to guard it, or because they do not know it well enough to guard it, or both. Thus it would seem to follow that no government can really act for the best interests of its subjects, or at least not as well as they could if left to themselves.[34] In Adam Smith's thought this conclusion results in the famous "invisible hand": each man pursuing his own interest produces a social good, often better than any public authority could.[35] And at least in his earlier writings on economics, a Utilitarian like Bentham is very much in agreement with this doctrine: "Each individual bestowing more time and attention upon the means of preserving and increasing his portion of wealth, than is or can be bestowed by government, is likely to take a more effectual course than what, in his instance and on his behalf would be taken by government."[36] Hence the proper guiding precept for government is "be quiet."

It is easy to see what sort of theory of representation follows from such a subjective view of interest. If no one can act in the interest of anyone else, then the motto for representatives is the same as that for governments: be quiet. Representing as a substantive activity becomes impossible. The representative (being a man) can act only in his own interest. But some men do get pleasure from altruism, and some institutions can make it personally advantageous for a representative to further the interest of others if he can. But he cannot, for he cannot know what is to the interest of another. The most a representative can do is to act on orders from his principal; if he asks his principal often enough what to do, then it is possible for him to further the principal's interest. But at the extreme this becomes direct action by the principal, and the representative becomes a mere puppet in the other's hands. Thus there may be formalistic representation, or representation as "standing for," but acting for someone else independently and with discretion is not possible.

Yet, strangely enough, this is not the theory of representation that the Utilitarians in fact develop. They are saved from it by writing on topics other than economics, where a different notion of interest emerges.[37] All the Utilitarian writers recognize the existence of a "common" or "general" interest, the good of the whole society.[38] Bentham maintains that there is a "universal interest" in every society, which is simply the "aggregate" or "sum of the interests of the various members who compose" the society. This sounds like Smith's invisible hand, and we have seen that in economics Bentham sometimes accepts that doctrine. But Bentham is also a legislative reformer; he knows very well that the common good does not always emerge automatically from private pursuits.[39]

In the context of legislation, then, he tells us that each person has both a public and a private interest, both a social and a self-regarding interest.[40] His public, social interest is that which is compatible with the "Universal interest." The good of the whole is the aggregate of the public or social interest of each of the members. But most men prefer their private, self-regarding interest. "In every human breast, rare and short-lived ebullitions, the result of some extraordinary strong stimulus or incitement excepted, self-regarding interest is predominant over social interest: each person's own individual interest, over the interests of all other persons taken together."[41] The exceptions are so rare, Bentham tells us in a revealing comparison, that they "cannot reasonably be regarded as being so frequently exemplified as insanity."[42]

The job of the legislator is to attach punishments to people's self-regarding actions, and rewards to their social actions, so that the latter become more desirable. The law must make it unattractive for men to act contrary to the common good, and attractive to act for it. Then men can act for their own selfish interest (to avoid punishment or gain rewards) and thereby further that of the whole. Outside the realm of economics, the invisible hand is that of the legislator.

But this presupposes that the legislator, at least, must be able to know what is in the public interest, and to have sufficient motivation in terms of his own private interest to enact the appropriate legislation. And although we might expect the opposite, the Utilitarians do think that this is possible. Bentham, obviously still thinking of the single, great master-legislator, relies on his altruism; he will be one of the rare men who derive pleasure from helping others to be happy.[43] But as soon as *the* legislator is replaced by an institutionalized legislature, simple altruism no longer seems a persuasive argument; it must be replaced by institutional safeguards which make it to the government's private interest to pursue the public interest. Here the Utilitarians would agree with the authors of the *Federalist*: "The interest of the man must be connected with the constitutional rights of the place . . . that the private interest of every individual may be sentinel over the public rights."[44] As Bentham puts it:

At present, the cause of the misrule is this: viz. the rule is completely in the hands of those whose interest it is—their interest, and thence of necessity their desire, and as far as depends upon them, their determination—that the misrule should continue: the thing required is . . . so to order matters, that the controlling part of the government shall be in the hands of those whose interest it is that good government shall take the place of misrule.[45]

The legislature "will be the better . . . in proportion as its interest is similar to that of the community."[46]

How is this congruence of interest between government and

the community to be brought about? Mainly by means of representation. The specific way in which it is interpreted and applied varies, but on this the Utilitarians are agreed. One possibility is the fairly simplistic solution offered by James Mill. Since the "community cannot have any interest opposite to its interests," all that is required is for "the interests of the representatives to be identified with those of the community."[47] The way to do this, Mill argues, is simply to make them part of the public they serve. The terms of office must be short, and there must be rotation in office, so that each representative has to live as a subject under the laws he has made. Thus it is to his interest to make good laws. Mill, then, treats government and the community on analogy with an individual. Only each individual can know and further his own interest, but the community has an interest which it knows and furthers. And if the rulers are sufficiently part of the community, they will share this interest. The transition from individual to society is taken for granted.[48]

Bentham does not rely simply on making the rulers part of the subject population. He introduces a "principle of dislocability," which is the familiar notion that officeholders want to be reëlected, and hence will do what the voters want; elections make it to their interest to further the voters' interest.[49] But Bentham often writes as if he agreed with James Mill, that this is simply a matter of making the rulers further a single, unified interest— that of the whole people. "The people? What interest have they in being governed badly?—in having their universal interest sacrificed to any separate and adverse interest?"[50] Give the people control over their rulers through elections, and the collective interest of that entity, the people, will be enacted. What is needed is "a form of government, in which the interest of the whole is the only interest provided for," and this is achieved by letting "the whole" vote.[51]

But the community is composed of individuals, each of whom (as Bentham has pointed out) has both "public" and "private" interests. One cannot give control over the government to the people without giving it to all the separate individuals that are the people; and they will use their power as they see fit. If people usually prefer their separate, selfish interests, how is the public welfare to be attained by giving them control of the government?

Sometimes the Utilitarians simply ignore this difficulty, speaking of the people only as a unified whole with one interest. That is James Mill's solution, and one sometimes used by Bentham. A second possibility is simply, when the problem comes up, to reject the basic axiom that people usually prefer their own selfish interests. To justify universal suffrage, Bentham argues: "According to a . . . supposition, the truth of which has, it is presumed, been proved,—on the part of the electors—at any rate, on the part of the majority of them—there *does* exist the disposition to contribute towards the advancement of the universal interest, whatsoever can be contributed by their votes."[52] He does not mean that he has proved it earlier in the essay, but that experience has proved it to be true; Bentham was particularly impressed with the American example.[53] But this is the same Bentham who thought insanity more frequent than willingness to sacrifice selfish for public interest!

John Stuart Mill wrestles with much the same dilemma. He, too, acknowledges man's fundamental selfishness. It is a "universally observable fact" that a man will prefer his "selfish interests to those which he shares with other people, and his immediate and direct interests to those which are indirect and remote."[54] For this very reason, Mill is a strong advocate of representative government, universal suffrage, and proportional representation: "It is important that everyone of the governed have a voice in the government, because it can hardly be expected that those who have no voice will not be unjustly postponed to those who have."[55] But given this view of human nature, can representative government perform what Mill expects of it? He argues that a representative government must fail; it "cannot permanently exist" under conditions where "nobody, or only some small fraction, feels the degree of interest in the general affairs of the State necessary to the formation of a public opinion, [where] the electors will seldom make any use of the right of suffrage but to serve their private interest, or the interest of their locality."[56]

Sometimes Mill tries to cope with this dilemma by arguing that it is not necessary for most people to act in the public interest so long as some do. For the selfish interests will cancel each other out. This is remarkably like the *Federalist*'s hope that the selfish factions will balance each other, allowing the common good to emerge. Mill defines the term "class" almost exactly as Madison does "faction": "If we consider as a class, politically speaking, any number of persons who have the same sinister interest— that is, whose direct and apparent interest points towards the same description of bad measures; the desirable object would be that no class, and no combination of classes likely to combine, should be able to exercise a preponderant influence on the government."[57] To avoid the danger of majority factions the representative system must be so organized that the contending classes are equally balanced in Parliament. Then, *deadlock ?*

assuming that the majority of each class, in any difference between them, would be mainly governed by their class interests, there would be a minority of each in whom that consideration would be subordinate to reason, justice, and the good of the whole; and this minority of either, joining with the whole of the other, would turn the scale against any demands of their own majority which were not such as ought to prevail.[58]

Madison, in a sense, performs an act of faith when he assumes that a large republic will produce so many factions that they balance each other to a stalemate. John Stuart Mill does not have a large republic at his disposal, and so is forced to an even greater act of faith: "The reason why, in any tolerable constituted society, justice and the general interest mostly in the end carry their point, is that the separate and selfish interests of mankind are almost always divided."[59] Unlike Madison's, John Stuart Mill's argument requires not only that the selfish interests balance, but also that there be a minority who act on the basis of "reason, justice, and the good of the whole."

This brings us to still another thread in the Utilitarian justification of representative government: the role of facts, knowledge, and reason. Granted that people have two kinds of interests— selfish private interests and shared public ones—which ought they to pursue? The Utilitarians sometimes say that people will pursue their selfish private interests, and, at other times, that a fair proportion of men will act according to their shared public interests. I think that this seeming contradiction must be understood in the light of the Utilitarians' underlying conviction that shared public interests are *better* than selfish private ones.[60] Hence if people pursue selfish interests it is through ignorance;

they do not know where their real interest lies. (This, of course, is a direct contradiction of the original axiom that each man is the best judge of his own interest.)

In Bentham's thought the matter is not quite clear. Some people, like the aristocracy and the king, apparently have "genuine" sinister interests.[61] When they pursue what seems in their own interest, which conflicts with the common good of the whole society, they are not misguided. They really have interests contrary to those of the whole. But for ordinary people, Bentham does not think this is true; when the ordinary voter acts contrary to the good of the whole (when he pursues his selfish interest rather than his shared public interest), he is misguided.[62]

In John Stuart Mill there is no longer much equivocation on this point. Any man's true interest is his share in the public interest; when he pursues his selfish interest he is misguided.[63] Accordingly, Mill calls a man's share in the common good his "real" as distinct from his "apparent" interest. His real interest is often long-range, remote, and hard to discern; he does not know what would be best for him. Hence it behooves the voters to bow to the superior wisdom of their representatives.[64]

But what happens to the original axiomatic assumption that each man knows his own true interest better than anyone else can? Ayer suggests that to make Utilitarianism consistent we must reinterpret this precept in a more limited way.[65] He argues that what the Utilitarians had in mind was not really that each knows his own interest best. They meant that each is the final judge of his own interest, because the person who is having an experience is the only sure authority on whether it gives him pain or pleasure.[66] Only the wearer can tell if the shoe pinches. But this does not mean that the wearer knows in advance which shoe will pinch him; in fact, it is much more likely that a shoe specialist will know this better than he.

A man's true interest, then, is what gives him pleasure (in the largest sense) when he experiences it. The assumption of the Utilitarians is that this true interest of each is part of the common good of the whole, is each man's "share in the universal interest." The invisible hand is transformed from an assertion about what men will actually do, to an assertion about their best interests. But most men do not know how to get what will really give them pleasure (at least in politics), because they are distracted by immediate gain. Hence a representative can often promote their true interest (separate and common) by disobeying their wishes.

We now see how the Utilitarians are saved from the conclusion that no one can act for, or represent, another. There is such a thing as objective interest after all. The fact that the individual is the final judge of whether something is in his interest is not equivalent to saying that no one but he can know what is likely to be in his interest. Men can know this about others, and the more intelligent, informed, rational man is likely to know it best.

The wonderful theoretical advantage of representation as Liberalism sees it, then, is this: representation makes it possible for each to participate in government as the final judge of whether his particular shoe pinches; yet it allows the rulers to use their wisdom and information to further people's true interests, where direct action would be misguided by short-range, hasty decisions. And, at the same time, representation makes it to the interest of the ruler to act in the interest of the subjects—not to give in to their passing whims, but to act in their true interest. For if he gives in to their passing whims, they will not really be pleased; the shoe that looked so attractive in the store will turn out to pinch. Only if he uses his wisdom to promote their true, long-range interests will they be truly pleased, and support him at the polls.

On this point, Bentham and John Stuart Mill end up in a position remarkably like Burke's. What Burke called popular "opinion" corresponds to people's misguided short-range interests in Utilitarianism; the representative must ignore it. And all agree that if the representative promotes the people's true interests, the people cannot fail to support him, for they can tell whether they are feeling pleasure or pain. Still, the parallel can be pushed too far, and we must notice some major differences between Burkean representation and that of Bentham and Mill. Because of differences over whether people or interests are to be represented, differences over whether interests are attached or unattached and differences over the nature of political knowledge, the Utilitarian representative is not really in the role of an expert. Burke was sure that interests could be known—so sure that even opinions seemed irrelevant. But for Bentham and Mill the representation of opinions is extremely important. They are no longer sure there is such a thing as reliable political knowledge, or that any group of men have certain access to it. The representative may be in a better position to know than his constituents, but he may still not be in a very good position to know. The fact that there is a best answer is no longer a guarantee that that answer can be found. Perhaps after all the most we can have on many political questions is an educated opinion. That is why the Utilitarians are so concerned about the number of representatives any particular group has, although Burke was not.

Finally, there remains a fundamental difference in the attitude taken toward the people. For Burke, what is right is right, and the fact that the masses can be expected to accept it once they experience it is a sort of minor convenience. For Liberalism, even if people are often misguided ahead of time, the final definition of what is right comes from each individual. At times, also, Bentham and Mill go a long way toward the doctrine that even ordinary people can be shown their true interest, although they may mistake it if they are not told. Hence the suffrage may be limited, after all, to those with sufficient intellectual capacity. Hence, also, the representative not only must do what is right, but he must tell his constituents why it is right. Bentham says that the legislator "must enlighten the people, he must address himself to the public reason; he must give time for error to be unmasked. Sound reasons, clearly set forth, are of necessity stronger than false ones."[67] And in the same vein John Stuart Mill defends the deliberative function of Parliament on the grounds that "those whose opinion is overruled, feel satisfied that it is heard, and set aside not by a mere act of will, but for what are thought superior reasons, and commend themselves as such to the representatives of the majority of the nation."[68]

The change from Burkean thought has, in a sense, been twofold. As the certainty of the knowledge possessed by legislators becomes more doubtful on the one hand, the opinions of the people (though often mistaken) become more valuable, on the other. The relative superiority of the one over the other diminishes, and the role of the representative changes as a result. A far greater contrast with the Burkean view would result if the

Utilitarians consistently maintained only their more extreme view of interests as entirely personal and subjective. Their own writings on economics suggest what happens to representation on such a basis; but there are a few political theorists whose writings give even more explicit examples.

Rousseau is the obvious case. He does not discuss interest, but the grounds on which he rejects representation are exactly the same as those on which one would have to reject it (at least as a substantive activity) if one accepted a completely subjective theory of interest. The more subjective interest is, the more it resembles the things a man can only define for himself—his opinion, his wants, his will. Rousseau argues that legislative representation is impossible, because it means "willing for others," and no man can will for another.[69] He can will instead of another, of course; this corresponds to what we have called formalistic representation. But there is no reason to suppose that the representative's will is going to coincide with the will of his principal. The principal continues to want things whether he is being represented or not. Hence to have someone else's will substituted for his means simply to be ruled by another.[70] In the same way, if one's interest is definable only subjectively, to have anyone else allegedly acting in one's interest can only be an empty formality.

Among modern writers, this sort of difficulty is encountered in a more moderate form by some pluralists. G. D. H. Cole argues that no man can represent another, "because no man's will can be treated as a substitute for, or representative of, the wills of others."[71] But Cole allows that men can represent the common purposes or goals of an association, and thus can act for a group. This is because every association "has a specific object or objects" which the members have previously determined as desirable.[72] In order to represent the association, one acts to further its objects. This men can do, apparently because they can know the objective interests of an association, whereas they cannot know the subjective interests of individuals.

Occasionally even contemporary political scientists despair of the possibility of representation—not in response to any new empirical findings, it seems, but simply from pursuing the logic of what they have persuaded themselves representation must really mean. "Seldom, if ever," one writer concludes, "can any person completely represent even another single person unless bound by definite instructions."[73] And a second writer judges that the representation of individual persons, as distinct from groups, "posits the impossible—the representation of one man's interests and opinions by another who himself has his own interests or opinions."[74] The problem is clear enough. If "to represent" as an activity is to have a substantive meaning, it must be "to act in the interest of" or "to act according to the wishes of," or some such phrase. But if the key word of the phrase is defined as entirely a subjective matter, then by definition no one can really act for another. Consequently, to the degree that interests, will, welfare, or whatever is supposed to be involved in representing as activity is regarded as something each man can only define for himself, representing as activity becomes impossible. Only the formalistic, descriptive, and symbolic senses remain.

10

Political Representation

Burkean and Liberal theories can be useful in more than one way for our view of representation as a substantive acting for others. Not only should they enrich and illustrate what has been said about the representative's role; but, since these writers are explicitly concerned with political representation, their ideas can serve to bring a rather abstract discussion into more direct confrontation with the realities of political life. Thus we should now be in a position to summarize what has been learned about the last view of representation, then to measure it against and relate it to what we know about the workings of politics. The formulation of the view we have arrived at runs roughly like this: representing here means acting in the interest of the represented, in a manner responsive to them. The representative must act independently; his action must involve discretion and judgment; he must be the one who acts. The represented must also be (conceived as) capable of independent action and judgment, not merely being taken care of. And, despite the resulting potential for conflict between representative and represented about what is to be done, that conflict must not normally take place. The representative must act in such a way that there is no conflict, or if it occurs an explanation is called for. He must not be found persistently at odds with the wishes of the represented without good reason in terms of their interest, without a good explanation of why their wishes are not in accord with their interest.

This rather complex view only sets the outer limits of what will be acceptable as representing in the substantive sense. Within those limits a wide range of positions is possible, depending on the writer's views about what is represented; about the nature of interests, welfare, or wishes; about the relative capacities of representative and constituents; and about the nature of the issues with which the representative must deal. The first of these criteria is also the simplest. Where representation is conceived as being of unattached abstractions, the consultation of anyone's wishes or opinions is least likely to seem a significant part of representing. Burke did not think that representing had much to do with consulting the represented or doing what they wanted; that is because he was talking about the representation of un-attached interests—interests to which no particular persons were so specially related that they could claim to be privileged to define the interest. But when people are being represented, their claim to have a say in their interest becomes relevant. At that point, the writer's conception of interest—or welfare, or wishes, or whatever terms of this kind he is working with—also becomes relevant to his position. The more he sees interests (or welfare or whatever) as objective, as determinable by people other than the one whose interest it is, the more possible it becomes for a representative to further the interest of his constituents without consulting their wishes. If they have a "true" interest about which they know very little, then the representative is justified in pursuing it even against their wishes. Burke's theory is the most extreme in this respect. But if such a view is pushed too far we leave the realm of representation altogether, and end up with an expert deciding technical questions and taking care of the ignorant masses as a parent takes care of a child.

In contrast, the more a writer sees interest, wants, and the like as definable only by the person who feels or has them, the more likely he is to require that a representative consult his con-stituents and act in response to what they ask of him. At the extreme, again, substantive acting for others becomes impos-sible, and a theorist must either fall back on other views of rep-resentation or declare the concept an illusion.

This range of possibilities is closely related to conceptions of the relative abilities and capacities of representative and represented. The more a theorist sees the representative as member of a superior elite of wisdom and reason, as Burke did, the less it makes sense for him to require the representative to consult the opinions or even the wishes of those for whom he acts. If superior wisdom and ability reside in the representative, then he must not subordinate them to the opinions of his ignorant, inferior constituents. Conversely, to the extent that a theorist sees representative and constituents as relatively equal in capacity and wisdom and information, he is likely to require that the views of the constituents be taken into account. If the representative is an ordinary, fallible man with no special knowledge or abilities, it seems highhanded and unjustifiable for him to ignore his constituents. Again the extremes are outside the concept altogether: a true expert taking care of a helpless child is no representative, and a man who merely consults and reflects without acting is not representing in the sense of substantively acting for others. But the intermediate range is broad.

These considerations, in turn, are related to the way in which theorists think of the representative's work—the kinds of issues and problems with which he has to deal. The more a theorist sees political issues as questions of knowledge, to which it is possible to find correct, objectively valid answers, the more inclined he will be to regard the representative as an expert and to find the opinion of the constituency irrelevant. If political issues are like scientific or even mathematical problems, it is foolish to try to solve them by counting noses in the constituency. On the other hand, the more a theorist takes political issues to be arbitrary and irrational choices, matters of whim or taste, the less it makes sense for a representative to barge ahead on his own, ignoring the tastes of those for whom he is supposed to be acting. If political choices are like the choice between, say, two kinds of food, the representative can only please either his own taste or theirs, and the latter seems the only justifiable choice. At the extremes, again, representation disappears. The expert scientist solving a technical problem is not representative at all, is not deciding anything, is not pursuing anybody's interest. The man choosing for others in matters of arbitrary taste is not acting for them in the substantive sense either; he can only substitute his will for theirs or else consult them and act as they wish. He cannot decide independently in their interest, for, where choice is a matter of taste, no interest is involved.

Political issues, by and large, are found in the intermediate range, where the idea of representing as a substantive acting for others does apply. Political questions are not likely to be as arbitrary as a choice between two foods; nor are they likely to be questions of knowledge to which an expert can supply the one correct answer. They are questions about action, about what should be done; consequently they involve both facts and value commitments, both ends and means. And, characteristically, the factual judgments, the value commitments, the ends and the means, are inextricably intertwined in political life. Often commitments to political values are deep and significant, unlike the trivial preferences of taste. Politics abounds with issues on which men are committed in a way that is not easily accessible to rational argument, that shapes the perception of arguments, that may be unchanged throughout a lifetime. It is a field where rationality is no guarantee of agreement. Yet, at the same time, rational arguments are sometimes relevant, and agreement can sometimes be reached. Political life is not merely the making of arbitrary choices, nor merely the resultant of bargaining between separate, private wants. It is always a combination of bargaining and compromise where there are irresolute and conflicting commitments, and common deliberation about public policy, to which facts and rational arguments are relevant.

But this is precisely the kind of context in which representation as a substantive activity is relevant. For representation is not needed where we expect scientifically true answers, where no value commitments, no decisions, no judgment are involved. And representation is impossible (except in a formalistic or symbolic or descriptive sense) where a totally arbitrary choice is called for, where deliberation and reason are irrelevant. We need representation precisely where we are not content to leave matters to the expert; we can have substantive representation only where interest is involved, that is, where decisions are not merely arbitrary choices.

And yet, if political issues involve partly irrational, deep, lasting value commitments, can our conception of representing as a substantive activity apply to them at all? We have said that the representative must pursue his constituents' interest, in a manner at least potentially responsive to their wishes, and that conflict between them must be justifiable in terms of that interest. But what becomes of terms like "interest" and "justifiable" if there can be lifelong, profound disagreement among men as to what their interest is—disagreement that remains despite deliberation and justification and argument? To the extent that this is so, the possibility of a substantive acting for others breaks down, and that view of the concept becomes irrelevant to politics. To the extent that this happens in practical political life, we seem then to fall back on descriptive representation; we choose a representative who shares our values and commitments and prevent the irresoluble conflict. Failing that, we can retreat to symbolic representation; we can let ourselves be influenced by emotional ties in spite of our doubts about whether our interests are being served. Or, failing even that, we can cling to our formal and institutional representative arrangements even when they seem devoid of substantive content. We can continue to obey, although we feel abused, or continue to remove a series of accountable representatives from office, although none of them serves our interest.

But if a theorist stays with the substantive activity of representing, he is likely to see that activity in relation to his conception of politics and political life. Indeed, there is some basis for arguing that the kinds of correlations we have been tracing here have significance not only conceptually but for empirical understanding of political systems as well. It may be that the more egalitarian a nation is in its general outlook, the more it feels that it is just as good as its rulers are, and perfectly capable of judging them, the less inclined it is to give them a wide range of discretion. Similarly, if there is sharp, deep-seated cleavage on important value commitments in the society, there will presumably be an increasing number of questions on which agreement cannot be reached by rational debate. Consequently we might expect an increasing desire in such a society for representativeness in its legislators, a desire to pick them from a particular group as the only safe guarantee of action in the interest of that group. Then more and more questions seem as arbitrary as a choice of candy, though they are by no means as trivial. Friedrich has pointed out that it is often the very countries for which proportional representation is most dangerous that insist on having it.[1] Even though it introduces into the legislature the irreconcilable antagonisms that pervade the society, they insist on it because they feel that only a member chosen from the particular group can act in its interest. And they may sometimes be right.

Within any functioning representative system, the same considerations apply to the personality of the legislator and to the particular issue before him. A representative who characteristically feels sure of his own knowledge and convictions is more likely to act on them; one who tends to feel skeptical and cautious about his own views is more likely to want to know what his constituents think. Some issues are more easily seen as having a right and a wrong side; others seem arbitrary, confusing, or a matter of opinion. Again, the more uncertain a representative feels about what he ought to do, the more likely he is to conceive of the issue as relevant to constituent feelings or opinion.[2] On such issues and to such men, politics seems more a matter of will than of right and wrong. This accounts for one of the difficulties in studying representation empirically. It will not do to examine voting on only a single issue; in the more extensive studies the issue sooner or later emerges as a relevant variable.[3] Again we can see why a simple choice: "Should he do what he thinks right or what you want?" is bound to produce equivocal answers.

All these elements—what is to be represented, whether it is objectively determinable, what the relative capacities of representative and constituents are, the nature of the issues to be decided, and so on—contribute to defining a theorist's position on the continuum between a "taking care of" so complete that it is no longer representation, and a "delivering their vote" so passive that it is at most a descriptive "standing for." But besides illustrating this observation, our examination of Burkean and Liberal theory has precipitated us into another dimension of substantive acting for others—the special features and problems of political representation: the distinction between private and public representing, between acting for a single principal or organization and acting for a constituency. It is now time to return to those political complications in the mandate–independence controversy which we earlier set aside, if only to show that our conceptual argument is even relevant to politics, and how it is relevant.

Representing as a substantive activity may often have seemed remote from the realities of political life. A political representative—at least the typical member of an elected legislature—has a constituency rather than a single principal; and that raises problems about whether such an unorganized group can even have an interest for him to pursue, let alone a will to which he could be responsive, or an opinion before which he could attempt to justify what he has done. These problems are further heightened when we consider what political science teaches about the members of such a constituency, at least in a modern mass democracy—their apathy, their ignorance, their malleability. Furthermore, the representative who is an elected legislator does not represent his constituents on just any business, and by himself in isolation. He works with other representatives in an institutionalized context at a specific task—the governing of a nation or a state. This reintroduces the familiar problem of local or partial interests versus the national interest, and the question of the political representative's role with respect to them.

Political representation need not raise any problems about the national interest; a symbolic head-of-state can stand for the nation without such a question even seeming relevant. Or the institutional context may be such that one person or body may act for the nation, while another body is composed of local representatives who do not govern or act for the whole nation.[4] The problem of the national interest arises only in the context of a representative legislature, a body composed of persons representing (as we say) various constituencies, and, at the same time, supposed to govern the nation and pursue the national interest. That context has often led theorists to formulate the classical dilemma: If a man represents a particular constituency in the legislature, is his duty to pursue its interest or the interest of the nation as a whole?

As with the mandate–independence controversy, theorists seem far too ready to accept this as a true dilemma, with mutually exclusive alternatives. But, as with the mandate–independence controversy, there is something to be said for both sides. If a man represents a certain constituency, then, according to the argument in the last four chapters, his obligation is to that constituency's interest. And in a practical sense, it is politically and socially important that local and partial interests should not be ruthlessly overridden and sacrificed in the name of the nation. On the other hand, someone has to govern and the national government must pursue the national interest. If the representatives as a group are given this task, they are thereby also given the national interest to look after. And, in a practical sense, it is politically and socially important that local and partial interests not be allowed to outweigh the needs and interests of the nation as a whole.

It is possible to avoid one horn of this dilemma by shifting ground on who or what is represented. If the legislator represents his constituency, the substantive "acting for" view of representation suggests that he must pursue its interest. So, if we want to show that his obligation is to the national interest, we say that it is really the nation he represents. A number of European constitutions can be cited as illustrations:

The members of the Reichstag are the representatives of the people as a whole, and shall not be bound by orders or instructions.
The members of Congress are representatives of the nation and not of the colleges which elect them.
The members of the two Houses shall represent the nation, and not the province alone, nor the subdivision of the province which elects them.
Deputies shall represent the nation as a whole, and not the several provinces from which they are chosen.[5]

But such formulations are no solution to our theoretical dilemma; they simply reject one of the alternatives, opting for the national interest instead of constituency interest. Such representatives might as well be elected at large, nation-wide.[6] This position is the obverse of the diehard defense of constituency interest; both tend to obscure the relationship between constituency and nation, between part and whole. They take the choice to be genuinely either-or, as if constituency and nation were mutually exclusive and unrelated units. They suggest that for a representative elected in California to have the duty of "representing" the interest of the whole nation is the same as if he had a duty to "represent" the interest of New York. But of course this is not so; California is part of the nation. If we assume that a nation and its parts confront each other like two hostile nations, the problem is indeed insoluble. For then to admit that the national welfare is paramount would preclude representation of the locality. And, conversely, the locality could not be blamed for objecting to the emphasis on the national interest if that interest were necessarily hostile to its own.[7] But in fact, one of the most important features of representative government is its capacity for resolving the conflicting claims of the parts, on the basis of their common interest in the welfare of the whole.

A slightly more ambitious argument that frequently appears in the literature overcomes this weakness by postulating an automatic harmony between local and national interest. A sort of political "invisible hand" is supposed to prevent any real conflict. The nation is made up of its parts; so the national interest must be the sum of local or partial interests. The trouble with this argument is that it is false. We all know of cases in which the interest of some locality is in conflict with the national welfare. Moreover, this argument will not accomplish what its proponents expect from it, for it cuts both ways. A Congressman may say, "I'm here to represent my district. What is good for the majority of districts is good for the country,"[8] and take that to sanction his pursuit of his district's interest. But Burke can equally well maintain that every locality, being part of the whole, has a share in the national interest; and he can take that to sanction the representative's devotion to national welfare rather than constituency claims.

What is difficult here is the correct verbal formulation of the obvious facts: in a sense the nation is the sum of its parts, but in another sense the nation must sometimes ask some parts to sacrifice their welfare for its welfare. For a community to exist and persist, its members and subdivisions must benefit from its existence, have an interest in its perpetuation. In that sense each district is part of the whole, and the national interest is not a separate interest, hostile to its own. However, the national interest cannot just ignore or override the welfare of parts of the nation or even of individuals. In representative assemblies the national interest is often formulated out of the rival claims of interests and localities within the state. Yet sometimes a simple addition of these claims will not suffice; sometimes a direct, public-spirited attention to national welfare itself is required.

It would be useful to distinguish between what we might call initial-interest-claim, on the one hand, and final-objective-interest, on the other. The initial-interest-claim of a locality or group can be and often is opposed to the initial-interest-claim of the nation. But the nation also has an interest in the welfare of its parts and members, and they have an interest in its welfare. So, in theory, for each case there should exist an ideal final-objective-interest settlement (whether or not we can find it or agree on it), giving just the right weight to all considerations. A minor benefit to the whole nation purchased at the price of severe hardship to a part may not be justified. A minor benefit to a part purchased at the price of serious damage to the nation probably is not justified. About final-objective-interest one could say that the interest of the parts adds up to the interest of the whole, but such an optimistic formula must not be allowed to obscure the obvious conflicts in initial-interest-claim. Politics entails the reconciliation of conflicting claims, each usually with some justice on its side; the harmony of final-objective-interests must be *created*.[9]

The national unity that gives localities an interest in the welfare of the whole is not merely presupposed by representation; it is also continually re-created by the representatives' activities. As Charles E. Merriam has put it, "The generality of special interests must be woven into a picture" that is the national good.[10] There may be institutional systems in which this task is not performed by a representative body, where representatives plead their districts' cause before a monarch or other executive or national judge, who makes the final decisions. But this is not the typical situation in modern representative government.

The representative is, typically, both special pleader and judge, an agent of his locality as well as a governor of the nation. His duty is to pursue both local and national interest, the one because he is a representative, the other because his job as representative is governing the nation. That dual task is difficult, but it is neither practically nor theoretically impossible.

But there are other political realities to be considered, in addition to the problem of the national interest. The constituent, the voter who is to be represented, is not, of course, the rational, informed, interested, politically active citizen our formula seems to require.[11] Most people are apathetic about politics, and many do not bother to vote at all. Of those who do vote, the majority vote on the basis of a traditional party loyalty; sometimes personal characteristics of the candidate also play a role. But generally both personal characteristics and policy commitments are used to justify a pre-formed preference rather than as the basis for making a choice. The voters tend to ascribe to the candidate whatever policy they favor; few of them know anything about the Congressman's voting record. Decisions seem to be motivated mainly through contact with primary groups; people vote as their family, friends, and associates do. Thus voting decisions depend largely on habit, sentiment, and disposition rather than on rational, informed consideration of the candidate's or the party's stand on issues.

It would seem farfetched to imagine such voters in rational dialogue with their representative: "Why did you vote this way when we asked you to vote the opposite way?" "Ah, but I know certain facts of which you are ignorant, had you considered that . . . ?" "Well, yes, that does change matters. . . ." Surely nothing could be farther from what actually goes on in an election.

Similar problems exist when we turn to the representative and the realities of legislative behavior. Does the representative frequently consult his constituents' wishes, or, if not, does he apply his expert knowledge to a dispassionate, rational evaluation of what is best for them and the nation? Again, if these are one's assumptions, the facts would seem very disillusioning. For the legislator's position is far more complex than such a model would suggest. The modern representative acts within an elaborate network of pressures, demands, and obligations; and there is considerable disagreement among legislators about the proper way to perform their role.[12]

In the first place, the political representative has a constituency and constituents, not a principal. He is chosen by a great number of people; and, while it may be difficult to determine the interests or wishes of a single individual, it is infinitely more difficult to do so for a constituency of thousands. On many issues a constituency may not have any interest, or its members may have several conflicting interests.[13] And the representative knows of the voters' ignorance and apathy and irrationality, the diversity of their views and interests. Further, he seldom has access to accurate information about what views and interests they do have.[14]

In the second place, he is a professional politician in a framework of political institutions,[15] a member of a political party who wants to get reëlected, and a member of legislature along with other representatives. He must be sensitive to his political party (both local and national) and to various public and private groups and interests. As a member of the legislature, he occupies an office to which certain obligations and expectations are attached.[16] He must comply with its traditions and work within the framework of the rules and mores of the legislative body. He must get along with his colleagues, especially certain important ones among them.[17] To act effectively he must keep in mind not only the formal and informal rules of his legislative body but also its place in the whole structure of government.

In the third place, he will also have views and opinions, at least on some issues. He will feel that some measures are intrinsically unsound, immoral, or undesirable. At the same time, his opinions may, in turn, be shaped by those around him and his sources of information. His own opinion on a measure may be shaped by party leaders or other colleagues, by friends or effective lobbyists, or even by the mail. He himself may not be a reliable source of information as to just what shapes his opinion on some issue or even what determines his vote.[18] And issues do not come before him in isolation; issues are interrelated, and he may wish to compromise on some in order to gain on others.[19] A particular measure may have many parts, to which he responds in varying ways.[20] He also may see measures as having a significance beyond their immediate content, for example as part of an over-all party program.[21]

Thus in legislative behavior a great complexity and plurality of determinants are at work, any number of which may enter into a legislative decision. The legislator represents neither by a simple response to constituency desires nor by detached, Olympian judgment on the merits of a proposal. None of the analogies of acting for others on the individual level seems satisfactory for explaining the relationship between a political representative and his constituents. He is neither agent nor trustee nor deputy nor commissioner; he acts for a group of people without a single interest, most of whom seem incapable of forming an explicit will on political questions.

Must we then abandon the idea of political representation in its most common sense of "acting for"? This possibility has sometimes been suggested; perhaps representation in politics is only a fiction, a myth forming part of the folklore of our society. Or perhaps representation must be redefined to fit our politics; perhaps we must simply accept the fact that what we have been calling representative government is in reality just party competition for office. Yet, to "redefine" representation to equate it with the empirical reality of representative government, even if that reality displays no elements of what we would ordinarily call representation, seems pointless and misleading.

But perhaps it is a mistake to approach political representation too directly from the various individual-representation analogies—agent and trustee and deputy. Perhaps that approach, like descriptive or symbolic representation, leads us to expect or demand features in the representative relationship which are not there and need not be there. Perhaps when we conventionally speak of political representation, representative government, and the like, we do not mean or require that the representative stand in the kind of one-to-one, person-to-person relationship to his constituency or to each constituent in which a private representative stands to his principal.[22] Perhaps when we call a governmental body or system "representative," we are saying something broader and more general about the way in which it operates as an institutionalized arrangement. And perhaps even the representing done by an individual legislator must be seen in such a context, as embodied in a whole political system.

Political representation is primarily a public, institutionalized arrangement involving many people and groups, and operating in the complex ways of large-scale social arrangements. What makes it representation is not any single action by any one participant, but the over-all structure and functioning of the system, the patterns emerging from the multiple activities of many people. It is representation if the people (or a constituency) are present in governmental action, even though they do not literally act for themselves. Insofar as this is a matter of substantive acting for others, it requires independent action in the interest of the governed, in a manner at least potentially responsive to them, yet not normally in conflict with their wishes. And perhaps that can make sense and is possible even in politics, if we understand how and where to look for it.

Even if the representative does not examine his conscience as to the national interest on every issue, he may still be following a course of action designed to promote that interest. He may be playing his complicated role in the institutionalized political system in such a way that it strikes us as—that it *is*—representing. The mere fact that he is functioning within a representative system is, of course, no guarantee that he is truly representing; but it allows for more complex and long-range ways of representing than are possible for an isolated individual agent.

Similarly, although the political representative may ignore or even override constituency opinion, he may offer justifications, rationales, for doing so, in much the way that a substantive representative must be prepared to do. If we ask an American legislator whether he acts independently of constituents' wishes, and why, he is likely to answer in terms of his knowledge and their ignorance and true interest.

> The majority of my constituents occasionally lack knowledge of relevant facts and circumstances. For me not to take this into account would be a violation of my oath of office as a legislator, not to mention my obligation to my own conscience, judgment and sense of duty.

> I knew full well and without the slightest question that had the five thousand people who had written me been in the possession of the knowledge which was mine, at least a majority of them would have taken [my] position.

> Much sentiment is manufactured and the result of gross misinformation.

> . . . he replied that he knew but one way to ascertain the public opinion of Connecticut; that was to ascertain what was right. When he found that out, he was quite sure that it would meet the approval of Connecticut.

> . . . they do not really understand the matter.

... they don't even know what a tariff is. . . . Of course they don't know what they're talking about.

I understand the problems of that area. I know what is best for the farm section. . . . I vote my convictions and hope that the constituents will follow these. They expect this—unless a real organized group is excited about something. They generally expect that you have more information than they do. . . . I try to follow my constituents—to ignore them would be a breach of trust—but I use my judgment often because they are misinformed. I know that they would vote as I do if they had the facts that I have.. . . . I figure if they knew what I know . . . they would understand my vote.[23]

These statements are not evidence but illustration. Indeed, they could not serve as evidence, for legislators make any number of statements about why they vote as they do, and none of them need be accurate. But the statements suggest that the view of representing as substantive activity may not, after all, be too abstract and idealized for application to real political life.

It may even make sense to speak of the people—the ignorant, apathetic, nonpolitical citizens—as being capable of collective action and judgment, as having, on occasion, a will or an opinion with which to confront their representative. But we must not succumb to an overly simplified picture of public opinion and the popular will. Political scientists have long known that "voting is essentially a group experience."[24] We vote, indeed we perceive political reality, through the people with whom we are in contact. Most of us are reached by the mass media only in a two-step process, by way of other people's perceptions of and reactions to them. There can be a good deal of latent opinion in the behavior of individuals who may not be able to articulate their opinions at all. As one recent study has put it:

The relation of Congressman to voter is not a simple bilateral one but is complicated by the presence of all manner of intermediaries: the local party, economic interests, the news media, racial and national organizations, and so forth. . . . Very often the Representative reaches the mass public through these mediating agencies, and the information about himself and his record may be considerably transformed as it diffuses out to the electorate in two or more stages. As a result, the public—or parts of it—may get simple positive or negative cues about the Congressman which were provoked by legislative action *but which no longer have a recognizable issue content.*[25]

The readiness of citizen A to vote for a certain candidate, derived from a casual conversation with B, who got it from over-
hearing C discuss an article in publication D—this readiness
is, in a sense, a part of public opinion, even though A may not
be able to muster a single reason for his vote, and may not care
about the immediate issues. Perhaps it is to this kind of public
opinion that the representative must be responsive, and can be
responsible.

I am not suggesting an organic group mind. What the public
does or thinks must (in theory) be translatable into the behavior or attitudes of individuals. I am only suggesting that this
translation is not simple or obvious. The voting behavior of people in a representative democracy can respond to issues and
policies, even if many individual voters do not respond directly
to them. The process may be complex, involving an interaction
among organizations, news media, and personal relationships.
Even if most people vote in an irrational and uninformed response to primary group pressures, this does not preclude the
system as a whole from displaying a degree of "rational" response.

All this is only meant to sketch a framework on which one
could maintain what seems to me in fact the case: that political
representation is, in fact, representation, particularly in the sense
of "acting for," and that this must be understood at the public
level. The representative system must look after the public interest and be responsive to public opinion, except insofar as non-
responsiveness can be justified in terms of the public interest. At
both ends, the process is public and institutional. The individual
legislator does not act alone, but as a member of a representative
body. Hence his pursuit of the public interest and response to
public opinion need not always be conscious and deliberate, any
more than the individual voter's role. Representation may emerge
from a political system in which many individuals, both voters
and legislators, are pursuing quite other goals. I am not suggesting that it must emerge from any particular system; there is no
guarantee that it will. But it may emerge, and to the extent that
it does we consider that system as being a representative government.

We must be cautious, also, about the absence of rational pursuit
of the public interest by individuals. I do not wish to suggest

that it is totally expendable, for I doubt whether any institutional framework could produce representation without conscious, rational, creative effort by some individuals. But there is latitude in a political system for apathy, ignorance, and self-seeking. That the social institution can produce a "rationality" most individual members seem to lack is easier to believe at the level of the voter than at the level of the legislator. And this may well be because a higher degree of individual rationality, of conscious representing and pursuit of the public interest is required in the legislative system than in the public. Undoubtedly, creative leadership is needed in any political system, and such leadership does not just happen. But when we speak of political representation, we are almost always speaking of individuals acting in an institutionalized representative system, and it is against the background of that system as a whole that their actions constitute representation, if they do.

We are now in a position to look back over the various "views" about the meaning and nature of representation, each persistent and plausible because it is founded in the familiar, valid, ordinary, unproblematic uses of some word in the "represent-" family. Despite their foundation in truth, these views are mutually incompatible and ultimately wrong, because they generalize too readily and too widely from a few examples, ignoring other equally valid examples. A correct and complete view of representation (the thing, "out there in the world"), of what representation is, depends on a correct and complete understanding of "representation" (the word, together with the other words in this family), what "representation" means. While we can, of course, redefine and revise the concept, it behooves us first to be clear on what it already means. For we are English speakers, and what it means in English is very likely what it means to us, what it is for us, in our world.

Each of the various views of representation makes some sense when applied to political life, and certain aspects of political life lend themselves to interpretation by each of the views. Heads of state, or elected legislative representatives, or government agents are, for certain purposes and under certain circumstances, authorized representatives, with authority to bind those in whose *accountable.*

name they act. Elected political representatives, under certain circumstances, are "true" representatives only if they must eventually account for their actions to those for whom they act. It may be useful to think of an elected legislature as the image or reflection of the whole nation, or as a representative sample. When we deal with political ceremonial, or the role of political leaders in fostering loyalty and a sense of national unity through their own person, symbolic representation seems apropos, as it does for inanimate political symbols like the flag or the scales of justice. Under other conditions, in other contexts, representing as a substantive activity will seem the very essence of what is going on politically.

But although each of these views of representation has some relevance to political life, a mere recognition of that fact is not enough. It is not enough to say that representation means now one thing, now another; nor does it follow that each writer is entitled to his view and that all theories or representation are equally valid. For each view has its particular and peculiar assumptions and implications, deriving from examples of our ordinary use of words in the "represent-" family on which it is based. Think of the legislature as a pictorial representation or a representative sample of the nation, and you will almost inevitably concentrate on its composition rather than on its activities. Think of the same body as a symbol and you will almost inevitably be more concerned with its psychological impact on the minds of the people than with any accuracy of correspondence between it and the nation. Think of it, in turn, as an agent or collection of agents, and your interest will focus on other concerns. Thus it is necessary to know what each view implies and assumes, and which view is appropriate under the circumstances.

For to say that all the views are relevant to politics, and that all are related in the sense of being views of the same, single concept, is not to say that they are mutually interchangeable, or fit political life at the same point and in the same way. Something absent can be made present in many different ways, depending on what sort of thing it is; but not everything can be made present in every way. Although both descriptive and symbolic representation are representation, it does not follow that the best descriptive representative is the best symbolic representative, or that either will do the best job of representing as activity. Indeed, the perfection of one kind of representation, "making present," may preclude the perfection of other kinds in any particular case. And not every kind will even be possible in every context.

The aspects of political life that seem to embody representation are extremely various and diverse. A government as a whole may be said to represent its state, nation, country, or people. This assertion may be made concerning all governments, or it may be used to distinguish what we call "representative" government from other forms. Within a state, representation most commonly is ascribed to the legislature; but a theorist may find that each member represents the nation, or his own constituency, or his political party. In the case of proportional representation he may say that each member represents those who elected him; in the case of occupational representation, that he represents his profession; in the case of a geographic constituency, that he represents it or its residents or their interest. Nor is it necessary that a collegiate representative body be a legislature or have sovereign power; it can be an advisory body. But we can also speak of representation by the executive, whether he is a directly elected president or an indirectly chosen prime minister. We speak of representation by monarchs and titular heads of governments. Courts, judges, and juries have been discussed as representative organs of the state, and similarly we recognize administrative representation. Ambassadors represent a state abroad. Every government official or agent may sometimes be said to represent, in the sense that his actions are official state actions. We also recognize as political representation the activities of certain persons "before" government agencies. Thus we say that a lobbyist represents a certain group or interest before Congress, or before a Congressional committee. An agent or expert may represent an interest before an administrative tribunal. And a lawyer represents his client before the courts, although this is not usually regarded as political.

But these many persons and institutions do not all represent in the same sense or in the same way. Political representation is as wide and varied in range as representation itself will allow.

The most that we can hope to do when confronted by such multiplicity is to be clear on what view of representation a particular writer is using, and whether that view, its assumptions and implications, really fit the case to which he is trying to apply them. Consider one of the most significant expressions in the realm of political representation—"representative government." There are many ways in which a government may be said to represent, but not all of them correspond to the idea of a representative government. Any number of theorists have gone wrong in this respect, noticing only one sense in which a government may be said to represent, and immediately concluding that must be what "representative government" really means.

It is sometimes argued, particularly by authorization theorists, that every government represents its subjects in the sense that it has authority over them and makes laws for them.[26] Governments do have that authority; the authority to make laws seems part of the very meaning of government. Yet authority is not coextensive with representation; one need not represent in order to have authority to issue orders. But a government also acts in the name of its subjects. Thus a slightly modified position would be that all governments represent in the formalistic sense that their actions not only bind their subjects but are attributed *to* these subjects.[27] The government acts, and we say that the nation has acted. Yet this kind of representing will not enable us to distinguish representative government from other forms; it would make "representative government" a redundancy.

Other theorists supplement the *de jure* authority of a government to act in the name of its subjects as a nation, with its *de facto* capacity to win support and obedience from them.[28] They may then argue that a government represents only to the extent that its decrees are obeyed and it is accepted by its subjects. This doctrine is close to the views of De Grazia and Gosnell, that representing is a matter of pleasing the represented. A representative government could be distinguished from other forms, under such a notion, by the high degree of obedience or consent or support it received from its subjects. And, as with De Grazia and Gosnell, the way in which that consent or support is engineered and achieved seems totally irrelevant: one may adjust the ruler to the ruled, but one may equally adjust the ruled to what he wants of them. Representative governments defined by the degree of their popularity need not have elections or other democratic institutions.

The will on which a government rests may be democratic, even if oligarchic or plutocratic influences are powerful in creating it. It is quite possible that an interested minority may so control the avenues of information and suggestion that a majority will suffer persuasion contrary to their own interests. The decision of a leader may induce millions to support measures which they would have opposed if his prestige had been thrown to the other side.[29]

And all this seems perfectly compatible with representation and representative government.

Finally, some writers argue that a government is representative to the extent that it pursues the interest of its subjects and looks after their welfare, as distinct from merely being popular with them. "All government is somewhat representative," a writer tells us, "insofar as it identifies itself with the people's interests. . . ."[30] A representative government might, however, be distinguished, under such an approach, as one that pursues its subjects' interests to a very high degree.

But none of these senses in which one can say that (some) governments represent is what we mean when we speak of representative government. Whether governments have legitimate authority to bind their subjects, whether the subjects are obligated to obey, are largely philosopher's questions. For the ordinary layman or politician they simply are not problematical; laws are the kinds of things that ordinarily oblige and bind, just as promises are the kinds of things that one keeps. For anyone other than a speculative political philosopher, the right of government to bind its subjects is problematic only at times of resistance or revolution. Would-be revolutionaries might attempt to justify themselves by arguing that the government no longer represents them. And the international lawyer may have to decide which government is the legitimate spokesman for a nation, which in turn may depend on what government has effective control. Thus we may inquire whether the Peking government or that on

Formosa properly represents China, or which government's delegation should represent the Congo in the United Nations.

There are occasions, also, when we become concerned with
the "responsibility" of subjects for the actions of their government, meaning something different from the obligation to obey
its laws. At the end of the Second World War and during the
Nuremberg trials there was much speculation about the war
guilt of the German people. Were they guilty of the atrocities
committed in their name by the Hitler government? The kinds
of arguments considered relevant here are undoubtedly familiar:
How much popular support did Hitler have? How much resistance was there to him within Germany? How much did people
know about what was being done? Did they approve of what
they knew? But these questions are not coextensive with whether
Nazi Germany was a representative government. We may agree
that it was not. At most, the kind of information we want could
be approximated by asking whether the German people would
have supported a representative government that followed the
same policies. Many people might argue the responsibility of
the German people even though the Nazi government was not
representative. We might agree, however, that in the case of
a representative government the responsibility would be more
clear-cut.[31]

But these are not at all the kinds of arguments we would
normally consider relevant to deciding whether a particular government is or is not representative. By representative governments we mean to designate certain governments but not others.
The United States, Great Britain, and Switzerland are usually
regarded as representative governments. Dictatorships, true
monarchies, and imposed colonial administrations are not usually
so regarded. But is the Soviet Union a representative government? Is the Union of South Africa? Is Ghana? Is the United
States, "really"? We know, at least in a general way, what the
relevant arguments on such questions are. They probably begin
with whether or not the rulers are elected. But they soon range
beyond this. We want to know how genuine the elections are,
who has the right to vote, whether the elected officials have the
real governmental power, and how much opposition is permitted.

Note, first, what subjects these questions do not cover. To decide whether a government is representative, we do not ask whether it has the authority to make binding laws in the name of its citizens. Every legitimate government has this authority. Nor do we ask how effective this authority is; a country does not necessarily have a representative government because its crime rate is low and disobedience is infrequent. Could we show that a government is representative by demonstrating that its policies are beneficent and promote the welfare of its subjects? This criterion, at least, seems more tempting. But the actions of a benevolent dictatorship might be directed toward the welfare of the populace, and make no concessions to anything resembling democratic participation. Surely this would not be a representative government. We do expect a representative government to promote the popular welfare, and perhaps think it unlikely that other governments will do so. But the fact that a government looks after the interests of its subjects is at most a piece of evidence, a necessary but not a sufficient criterion for calling it representative.

How about a government which keeps its subjects happy, whose policies are widely accepted by them? Could we show that a government is representative by demonstrating its popularity among its subjects? Here I think the temptation is very great to say yes, but we must be cautious. Could we not imagine cases to the contrary? Suppose that a drowsy tropical island (before the Second World War, we had better say) is delightfully administered by a benevolent despot from the colonial office. The natives love him. But surely this is not a representative government. Or again, a dictator may perfect a new tranquilizing drug, and feed "happy-pills" to all his subjects so that they approve wholeheartedly of whatever he does. Surely not a representative government. Again, the contentment of the subjects is not sufficient to define representation.

Just as it is not enough to say that the individual representative who pleases his constituents represents them, so, at the level of government, it will not do to define representation by the acquiescence of the subjects. People may at times support a hereditary monarch; they may have nothing but good to say about a dictator (the critical members of the population having been removed). A dictatorship may have "active and preponderant" consent, but that does not make it a representative government.

If support for the regime is manufactured by way of a monopoly of control over the media of mass communication, supplemented by severe coercion against oppositional elements. . . . If a political regime relies heavily on a highly organized propaganda monopoly, . . . and ruthlessly suppresses all political dissent, one must conclude that no amount of evidence of public support to the regime can prove that the people's genuine interests are not being exploited in the interest of the ruling few.[32]

By the same token, no amount of public support can then prove that the government is a representative one. When a ruler manipulates an inert mass of followers to accord with his will, we hesitate to say that he represents them. In the same way, if an interest group engages in a vast propaganda campaign to persuade the public in favor of some measure, we do not regard this activity as representation of the public.

It seems to me that we show a government to be representative not by demonstrating its control over its subjects but just the reverse, by demonstrating that its subjects have control over what it does. Every government's actions are attributed to its subjects formally, legally. But in a representative government this attribution has substantive content: the people really do act through their government, and are not merely passive recipients of its actions. A representative government must not merely be in control. not merely promote the public interest, but must also be responsive to the people. The notion is closely related to the view of representing as a substantive activity. For in a representative government the governed must be capable of action and judgment, capable of initiating government activity, so that the government may be conceived as responding to them. As in nonpolitical representation, the principal need not express his wishes, or even have formulated any, but he must be capable of doing so; when he does, his wishes should be fulfilled unless there is good reason (in terms of his interest) to the contrary. Correspondingly, a representative government requires that there be machinery for the expression of the wishes of the represented, and that the government respond to these wishes unless there are good reasons to the contrary. There need not be a constant activity of responding, but there must be a constant condition of responsive*ness*, of potential readiness to respond. It is not that a government represents only when it is acting in response to an express popular wish; a representative government is one which is responsive to popular wishes when there are some. Hence there must be institutional arrangements for responsiveness to these wishes. Again, it is incompatible with the idea of representation for the government to frustrate or resist the people's will without good reason, to frustrate or resist it systematically or over a long period of time. We can conceive of the people as "acting through" the government even if most of the time they are unaware of what it is doing, so long as we feel that they could initiate action if they so desired.[33]

Because this kind of political representation requires only potential responsiveness, access to power rather than its actual exercise, it is perfectly compatible with leadership and with action to meet new or emergency situations. It is incompatible, on the other hand, with manipulation or coercion of the public. To be sure, the line between leadership and manipulation is a tenuous one, and may be difficult to draw. But there undoubtedly *is* a difference, and this difference makes leadership compatible with representation while manipulation is not.[34] This is because leadership is, in a sense, at the mercy of the led. It succeeds only so long as they are willing to follow. Thus it is not incompatible with our requirement that the represented be able to get their way when they have an explicit will. Manipulation by a ruler, on the other hand, is imposed on the ruled, and threatens their capacity to reject a policy or initiate a new one. A person can be led and yet go of his own free will; something that is manipulated does not move itself. An inanimate object can be manipulated, but it cannot be led. Again, these are not just verbal games, but the right terms for naming a distinction in reality: the difference between democratic and dictatorial relationships between ruler and ruled. Only if it seems right to attribute governmental action to the people in the substantive sense do we speak of representative government.[35]

But all this makes the notion of representative government seem far more impressionistic, intuitive, and temporary than it really is when we use it. Judging a government to be representative is not merely a matter of a sort of over-all esthetic impression one has formed; though there may be difficult borderline cases, not all cases are borderline. Nor does this kind of representativeness fade in and out periodically. We do not say that a government is representative today, because it happens to be responding to popular wishes, and stops being representative the next day because it is frustrating them. Representative government is not defined by particular actions at a particular moment, but by long-term systematic arrangements—by institutions and the way in which they function. No particular act of compliance with popular demands is proof of a representative government, although a few serious cases of the frustration of legitimate popular demands will serve as counterevidence. John Plamenatz points out that a dictator might choose to do what his subjects want and nevertheless not be a representative. Only if he institutionalizes this decision, so that there is not merely occasional response when he pleases, but regular, systematic responsiveness, does he become a representative. And we tend to feel that this is impossible without elections. Our concern with elections and electoral machinery, and particularly with whether elections are free and genuine, results from our conviction that such machinery is necessary to ensure systematic responsiveness. Our concern with the popularity of a regime is an attempt to find an operational measure for potential responsiveness. The fact that the people have no unfulfilled demands is an indication that they can get their demands fulfilled whenever they wish, but it is not conclusive proof. This is why a manipulated or coerced acquiescence does not satisfy us.

And here the formalistic accountability view, the descriptive view, and perhaps others as well become relevant to representative government. For only certain kinds of institutional arrangements will satisfy our requirement. An absolute monarch or dictator who chooses, for a reason of his own, to take public opinion polls and do whatever the people seem to want is not yet a representative government. We require functioning institutions that are designed to, and really do, secure a government responsive to public interest and opinion. Such a government may have a president, it may be headed by a prime minister, or it may be an assembly government. It may have geographic constituencies, proportional representation, or some other system of apportionment. It may have no political parties, weak ones, strong ones, many or few. All these forms may be representative governments; some are more successful than others.

For this purpose, our basic prerequisites seem very few. We would be reluctant to consider any system a representative government unless it held regular elections, which were "genuine" or "free."[36] We would be reluctant, further, to consider a government representative unless it included some sort of collegiate representative body in a more than advisory capacity.[37] We would not readily accept a system as representative in which the entire government was in the hands of a single ruler, even if he was subject to reëlection at regular intervals. Perhaps it is merely historical tradition that there should be a collegiate body composed of representatives of the various "parts" of the society. Perhaps it has to do with the persistent element of isomorphism or one-to-one correspondence in descriptive representation. Or perhaps it is simply that we cannot conceive that a political system could be truly responsive unless a number of minority or opposition viewpoints are officially active in its government.

Our notion of representative government thus seems to incorporate both a very general, abstract, almost metaphorical idea—that the people of a nation are present in the actions of its government in complex ways—and some fairly concrete, practical, and historically traditional institutions intended to secure such an outcome. The notion has both substantive and formal components. In this way, representative government is an excellent illustration of a phenomenon that seems to be very common in human practices and their corresponding concepts: the duality and tension between purpose and institutionalization.

The sequence of events may be somewhat like this: men have a purpose or goal in mind, the substance of which they want to achieve. In order to achieve it, particularly if it will take time and involve many people, perhaps several generations, they establish institutions—write laws, set up administrative bodies, arrange training programs, and so on. But institutions develop a momentum or an inertia of their own; they do not always work as intended, and they may not produce the result for which they were established. Thus men may find themselves torn between commitment to the original purpose and commitment to the agreed and established channels for achieving it. Or, alternatively, the causal sequence may run the other way around. For whatever reasons, and with no deliberate, common purpose, men may gradually develop fixed ways of doing something—institutionalized behavior which has become habitual. From this patterned behavior they may begin to abstract express ideas about what it is for, how it is to be done, what principles and purposes underlie it. And, in due time, those principles may themselves come to be used as new aims for revising the institution, as critical standards for assessing the way in which it functions and improving it. Again a tension between practice and principle can arise.

This kind of tension is often embodied in the associated concepts, with the result that their meaning seems to consist simultaneously of both formal, "outer" institutional aspects and substantive, "inner" purposive ones. Since this is rather vague, the two imaginary causal patterns may be illustrated more concretely. For the former pattern, consider a human practice or institution, for example, punishment.[38] Philosophers have long been troubled by the meaning of punishment. On the one hand, it seems to mean harm done to a person in retribution, because he has broken a law, has violated a norm. In that sense one cannot—logically cannot—punish a man unless he is guilty of wrongdoing. Not just any kind of harm under any circumstances will be punishment; it is punishment only if it is applied because of an offense committed. But, on the other hand, we set up official institutions for punishing criminals, and less formal social norms for punishing, say, our children. And then we call the normal operations of those institutions and the normal exercise of those behavior patterns "punishing" whether or not in that particular case the person being punished is guilty. Thus it makes perfect sense to say, after an unjust execution, "They have punished an innocent man!" So the concept of punishment seems to have a substantive side, making us want to say that one cannot punish the innocent, and a formal or institutional side making us want to say that, of course, one can, though one should not.

To illustrate the other causal pattern leading to the same kind

of tension, consider the idea of (fairness.) Piaget has suggested
that children develop much of their notion of fairness while playing games with their peers.[39] He has studied the way boys play
marbles in Switzerland, tracing their gradual initiation into the
game. They learn, more or less simultaneously (but, Piaget argues, in definite chronological stages), how to play the game,
what the rules are, what a game is, and what rules are, that rules
may not be broken, that rules can be changed, what are appropriate ways of changing rules, and so on. They also apparently
develop criteria for judging the rules themselves—notions of fairness, on the one hand, and of what Piaget calls "the spirit of the
game," on the other.[40] So, when they know the rules, and know
that rules are man-made (child-made in this case), and how they
can be changed, they are able to judge proposed innovations as
to their fairness and conformity to the game's spirit. Now it might
be supposed that people learning the meaning of "fair" in connection with a certain game and certain rules and ways of doing
things would be forever committed to that game, those rules and
ways; that would be what "fair" *meant* to them. But this mani-
festly is not so. From the old rules Piaget's children abstract
criteria and principles by which to judge innovations and hence
also to judge the old rules themselves (for they sometimes
modify the old rules and accept innovations). And, more generally, although we learn all our criteria of judgment in connection with existing social patterns, we can and do use them to
criticize and change those patterns. A practice which in one sense
seems to define the substance and meaning of "fairness" (or
"marbles") can nevertheless be found less than perfect in its institutionalized embodiment of fairness (or the spirit of marbles).

That this kind of duality or tension exists in the practice and
concept of representation should be clear, for it has been built
into the structure of our whole argument as it moved from formalistic views toward representing as a substantive acting for
others.[41] We encountered it also in Burke's distinction between
the virtue or essence of representation and its actualization. In
substance or virtue or essence, representation means the making
present of something that is nevertheless absent, and whenever a
set of circumstances strikes us that way we may speak of representation. Whenever circumstances seem otherwise, we may

deny that any representation is taking place. But there are also certain conventionalized and institutionalized ways of (say, political) representing. As with punishment, we apply the term "representation" to institutions because of their general structure and the original purpose they are supposed to embody, whether or not in a particular case they bring about the substance of representation.

Following Tussman, we may call these two aspects (form and substance) the "two great moods" of political and social life. Most theorists of society have stressed either the one or the other.[42] The hard-headed realist, the behavioral social scientist, the constitutionalist tends to stress institutions, behavior, and outward performance. Asked to define representation he will seek an operational definition and look to "what representatives actually do." Asked to reform it, he will construct institutions that lay down rules for the desired behavior. In terms of the views of representation we have discussed, he is likely to be a formalistic or a descriptive theorist. The idealist, the moral reformer, the educator, on the other hand, is likely to stress substance and purpose, intention, or even motive, the "real, inner essence" rather than the "mere outward semblance." Asked to define representation, he will look to the idealized role, the standard by which we judge representatives, what they ought to do rather than what they do in fact. Asked to reform it, he will teach men altruism and a concern for the interests of others or the public interest, to make them into good representatives. Among the views we have discussed he is likely to adopt representing as substantive acting for others.

We need these two great moods, and both together. To define representation institutionally, operationally, is to give up all hope of judging, assessing, improving, or reforming it, or even of instructing someone in the role of representative—or at least it is to give up all hope of doing these things in a rational, nonarbitrary way. Thus, if representation is "whatever representatives actually do when you watch them," nothing they do can fail to be representation. To define representation ideally, on the other hand, to concentrate on its virtue or essence to the exclusion of institutions, is likely to mean abandoning all hope of its practical implementation. It could lead us, as it led Burke, to accept gross inequities in an institutional system, because at any given time the system seems to be producing the essence of representation despite them. It might incline us to accept moment-to-moment, short-range performance as our criterion, which would make impossible any systematic, sustained implementation—in short, institutionalization—of our ideal purpose. What representatives, in fact, do would seem irrelevant to us, and thus our conception would remain forever impotently in the realm of Platonic forms.

No institutional system can guarantee the essence, the substance of representation. Nor should we be too optimistic about the capacity of institutions to produce the desired conduct; even the best of representative institutions cannot be expected to produce representation magically, mechanically, without or even in spite of the beliefs, attitudes, and intentions of the people operating the system.[43] Madison's dictum that "the interest of the man must be connected with the constitutional rights of the place" has merit, but there is merit also in Tussman's, that in his capacity as citizen a man must "be concerned with the public interest, not with his private goods," that he "is asked public, not private questions: 'Do we need more public schools?' not 'Would I like to pay more taxes?' "[44] For this reason, too, we need to retain the ideal of the substance of representation in addition to our institutionalization of it. Without reference to such an ideal, how could we teach those intended to operate the institutions what we require of them? How else, indeed, could we remember it ourselves?[45]

Without institutionalization, as Martin Drath has pointed out, the ideal of representation would remain an empty dream, or at most would occasionally recur as a fitful, inexplicable blessing, which we have no power to produce or to prolong.[46] The historically developed institutional forms, the culturally ingrained standards of conduct are what flesh out the abstract ideal, give it practical import and effective meaning.[47] Thus the development and improvement of representative institutions, the cultivation of persons capable of looking after the interests of others in a responsive manner, are essential if the fine vision that constitutes the idea of representation is to have any effect on our actual lives. At the same time, we can never allow institutions, habits of conduct, the behavior of representatives, to become our standard and ideal. Whether the governments we conventionally call "representative" involve genuine representation always remains open to question. Whether what we designate as representation in the world really is (what we mean by) representation will always depend on the way in which its structure and functioning work out in practice.[48]

The requisite institutions have been different at different times in history.[49] But men have always striven for institutions that will really produce what the ideal requires; and institutions or individuals claiming to represent have always been vulnerable to the charge that they do not really represent. Application of the label "representative" seems to invite a critical appraisal: Is this a fiction, an empty formula, or is it really the substance of representation? Thus it has been argued "that representative government is the ideally best form of government, for the very reason that it will not actually be representative in its character unless it is properly organized and conditioned. By its essential nature it is a system of trusteeship. . . . Institutions claiming to be representative can justify their character as such only to the extent that they establish and maintain such trusteeship."[50]

The concept of representation thus is a continuing tension between ideal and achievement. This tension should lead us neither to abandon the ideal, retreating to an operational definition that accepts whatever those usually designated as representatives do; nor to abandon its institutionalization and withdraw from political reality. Rather, it should present a continuing but not hopeless challenge: to construct institutions and train individuals in such a way that they engage in the pursuit of the public interest, the genuine representation of the public; and, at the same time, to remain critical of those institutions and that training, so that they are always open to further interpretation and reform.

Appendix
On Etymology

Although the ancient Greeks had a number of institutions and practices to which we would apply the word "representation," they had no corresponding word or concept. The term is of Latin origin, although in Latin, too, its original meaning had nothing to do with agency or government or any of the institutions of Roman life which we might consider instances of representation. The Latin *repraesentare* means "to make present or manifest or to present again," and in classical Latin its use is confined almost entirely to inanimate objects.[1] It can mean to make them literally present, bring them into someone's presence; accordingly it also comes to mean appearing in court in answer to a summons, literally making oneself present. It can also mean the making present of an abstraction through or in an object, as when a virtue seems embodied in the image of a certain face. And it can mean the substitution of one object for another, instead of the other, or the hastening of an event, bringing it into the present. Thus it can mean "to perform immediately" and even "to pay in cash." It has nothing to do with people representing other people or even the Roman state.

In the Middle Ages the word is extended in the literature of Christianity to a kind of mystical embodiment, "applied to the Christian community in its most incorporeal aspects."[2] But its real expansion begins in the thirteenth and early fourteenth centuries, when the Pope and the cardinals are often said to represent the persons of Christ and the Apostles.[3] The connotation is still neither of delegation nor of agency; the church leaders are seen as the embodiment and image of Christ and the Apostles, and occupy their place *per successionem*. At the same time, medieval jurists begin to use the term for the personification of collective life. A community, although not a human being, is to be regarded as a person (*persona repraesentata, repraesentat unam personam, unium personae repraesentat vicem*). The stress is on the fictive nature of the connection: not a real person but a person by representation only (*persona non vera sed repraesentata*).

Meanwhile there is current among glossators the notion, derived from Roman law, that the prince or emperor acts for the Roman people, stands in their place, looks after their welfare. In the thirteenth century the canonists begin to adopt this idea, to sharpen and develop it and apply it to religious communal life. Neither the glossators nor the canonists yet use the word "representation" in developing these Roman law ideas; but the parallel with allegorical church thought is close enough so that, by the middle of the thirteenth century, a writer familiar with both disciplines can argue that the magistrate represents the image of the whole state.[4] Here representation of an allegorical or imagic kind is applied to a secular magistrate.

Georges de Lagarde has discovered a very interesting passage in the writings of a late-thirteenth-century jurist, in which the sense of imagic representation of a community meets, as it were, head on with a notion of legal agency. The jurist Albert de Gaudino inquires whether a community can plead through an attorney (*par procureur*) in a criminal case. In a sense, he says, one is tempted to answer no, since every private person must appear in person, and a collectivity (*universitas*) is to be regarded as a person. But, in another sense, the attorney represents just the fictive person of the community. Therefore, if he appears, it is as though the community appeared in person. Here we have not only the collectivity that is taken to be one person by a fiction (*unius personae repraesentat vicem*) but also the attorney who appears in the place of this person (*qui repraesentet vicem universitatis*). The ordinary activities of an attorney in court are not yet called "representing" at this time; Gaudino uses *intervenire* and *respondere* for that.[5] But, from the end of the thirteenth century, jurists and then other writers begin using *repraesentare* for the way in which a magistrate or attorney stands and acts for the community.

To be sure, the new usage is not immediately adopted by everyone. Occam, for example, continues to attribute a metaphysical or mystical quality to the notion of representation, and hence rejects the term. Even where he talks about what we would call representation, he does not apply it. Thus Occam argues that all Christians have a right to be consulted in the general council of the church on matters which concern them. Those who do not attend in person may send delegates, whom Occam calls *personas habentes auctoritates et vices* of those who sent them, but not "representatives." But the new usage is never entirely lost; it becomes a regular and recognized sense of the word in late Latin.

A similar development seems to have taken place in French. According to the *Littré*, at least, *représenter* was used for images an inanimate objects embodying abstractions long before it came to mean anything like one person acting for others.[6] But by the thirteenth century a bailiff can be spoken of representing the person of his lord.

The same sequence of development reoccurs in English, after the word "represent" appears, probably late in the fourteenth century. At that point, according to the *Oxford English Dictionary*, it is used to mean "to bring oneself or another into the presence of someone," "to symbolize or embody concretely," "to bring before the mind." The adjective "representative" means "serving to represent, figure, portray or symbolize." During the fifteenth century, representing expands to mean also "to portray, depict, or delineate." It comes to be applied to inanimate objects which "stand in the place of or correspond to" something or someone. And it means "to produce a play," apparently a sort of depicting on the stage. At the same time, the noun "representation" appears, meaning "image, likeness, or picture." Now human beings are not entirely absent from these early uses; they appear in two ways. First, representation can be an inanimate object or image standing for a human being; but this is a minor case from our point of view. Second, representing is a human activity, but not an acting for others; it is the activity of presenting, of depicting, of painting a picture or staging a play. Not until the sixteenth century do we find an example of "represent" meaning "to take or fill the place of another (person), substitute for"; and not until 1595 is there an example of representing as "acting for someone as his authorized agent or deputy."

Did the development in the meaning of "represent" that took place in Latin in the thirteenth and early fourteenth century, and that was at least under way in French in the thirteenth century, really not take place in English until the sixteenth century? Or does the *Oxford English Dictionary* simply lack earlier examples though the change came earlier? It is possible that legal, juristic, and political works, in which representing in the sense of "acting for" would be most likely to occur, were not written in English until this later time, even in England. Such writings may rather have been formulated in Latin or French.[7] Despite a 1362 statute that English was to be used in the law courts, records of court decisions from as late as 1500 are still in French.[8] And the statutes were written in Latin throughout the fifteenth century.[9] The earliest known petition in English dates from 1414.[10]

To understand how the concept of representation moved into the realms of agency and political activity, we must keep in mind the historical development of institutions, the corresponding development in interpretive thought about those institutions, and the etymological development of the family of words we are concerned with. It is now generally accepted that the summoning of knights and burgesses to meet with the king and Lords in Parliament began as a matter of administrative and political convenience to the king.[11] The knights and burgesses came to assent to taxes, give information, "bring up the record" from the local court in disputed cases, and carry information back to their communities.[12] At first the crucial thing was that they come with authority to bind their communities to the taxes to be imposed. Somewhat later they began to be used by the communities as a way of presenting grievances to the king, and there were attempts to insist on redress of grievances before consenting to taxes. With this development began a gradual recognition that the member could further the interests of his community, in addition to committing it to taxation.[13] Knights and burgesses who went to Parliament began to be thought of as servants or agents of their communities. They were paid by the communities and, when they returned, might be required to give an account of what they had done in Parliament.[14] They came to Parliament with authority to commit their communities, but often there were specific limits on this authority or instructions that came with it. And some members had to consult with their communities before consenting to an unusual tax.[15]

From the fourteenth to the seventeenth century there was a gradual development of unified action by the knights and burgesses in Parliament.[16] They found that they had common grievances, and began to present common petitions instead of only separate ones. They came to be called "members" of Parliament.

This joint action went hand in hand with an increasing awareness of themselves as a single body. Parliaments lasted longer,
and members were reëlected, and so came to know each other
and work together. Their joint action was often in opposition to
the king, and they found strength to oppose him by acting as
a corporate group. This development culminated in the period of
the Civil War and the Protectorate and Commonwealth, when
there was no king to oppose or consent to. Suddenly there was
only Párliament to govern the nation and even to pass judgment
on the ruler in the name of the nation.

The development of political theory, of interpretations of
what Parliament was doing, paralleled these developments in fact.
In the early period the knights and burgesses were regarded as
the servants or attorneys or procurators of their communities.[17]
They were not called representatives because the word did not
yet have that meaning; legal attorneys in court were not said to
represent either. By the fifteenth century, as the Commons came
to act as a unified body, the members were occasionally spoken
of as being. jointly, "procurators and attorneys of all the counties
. . . and of all the people of the realm."[18] They began to think
of themselves, and be thought of, as those who "were commen
for the Communalte of the Londe."[19] This idea is still compatible
with the view that each member speaks for his particular district; the group thus adds up to the equivalent of the whole
nation. Still later came the further elaboration that each member
acts for the entire nation. This principle was recognized by the
early seventeenth century, when Coke wrote in the *Institutes*:
"it is to be observed though one be chosen for one particular
county, or borough, yet when he is returned, and sits in parlament, he serveth for the whole realm, for the end of his coming
thither as in the writ of his election appeareth, is generall."[20]

These changing views of the function of parliamentary members became linked with two other traditions of thought: the
idea that all men are present in Parliament, and the idea that
the ruler symbolizes or embodies the whole realm. The former
is essentially a legal fiction, probably originating in the medieval
quod omnes tangit doctrine from Roman law, that parties who
have legal rights at stake in a judicial action are entitled to be
present or at least consulted in its decision.[21] Thus the presumption was that Parliament, being considered a court rather than a
legislative agency, had the consent and participation of all tax-
payers. By the fourteenth century a judge could argue that igno-

rance of the law is no excuse, since everyone is taken to be present when Parliament acts.[22] This is not, of course, a democratic doctrine at the time.

The other idea that comes to enrich the tradition of thought about Parliament is that the whole nation is somehow embodied in its ruler, as the church is in Christ or in the Pope after him. It is a medieval and mystical conception: the king is not merely the head of the national body, not merely the owner of the entire realm, but he *is* the crown, the realm, the nation.[23] The idea goes beyond either representation or symbolization as we now conceive them, and involves a mystic unity which "theoretical analysis can scarcely divide."[24] The Latin word *repraesentare* comes gradually to be used in connection with this cluster of ideas. Then, as the authority of Parliament grows, and its role in pronouncing the law is more widely recognized, this symbolic position is ascribed to the king-in-Parliament jointly, as a single body or corporation.[25] Thus the king-in-Parliament that governs the realm is also seen as its mystic equivalent or embodiment.

These various ideas and doctrines converge quite naturally. The king-in-Parliament is the mystic equivalent or embodiment of the whole realm, and everyone in the realm is to be considered present in it. The lords and bishops and the king himself are present in person; the Commons as a whole (as an estate, for a time) are present through their procurators as a group.[26] Finally, each separate knight or burgess is thought of as acting for all the common people, for the entire realm.

A neat summary of the state to which these ideas had developed by 1583 can be found in Sir Thomas Smith's *De Republica Anglorum*, of that year.[27] Smith's work is also one of the earliest known applications of the English word "represent" to Parliament. Smith uses the word only once, but in a crucial position, writing of "the Parliament of Englande, which representeth and hath the power of the whole realme, both the head and the bodie. For everie Englishman is entended to be there present, either in person or by procuration and attornies. . . . And the consent of the Parliament is taken to be everie man's consent."[28] Smith says that Parliament represents the whole realm (or is it that it represent the power of the whole realm?), but he does not apply the word to the members of Parliament or to those particular members who are there as procurators and attorneys for the Commons. This seems to be the pattern in all the early applications of the word to parliamentary institutions in England; it is the Parliament as a whole (often including the king) that represents the whole realm.

What did "represent" mean, just before Smith applied it in this way? It already had some application to human beings and groups of human beings, in two rather distinct senses. It meant the activity of creating an image, producing a play, making something appear (or even be) present. But it had also been applied to human beings themselves functioning as the image, embodiment, or symbol of something, standing for something absent. Thus from 1509 the *Oxford English Dictionary* gives an example from a funeral sermon which praises the charitable deeds of the deceased lady. She gave lodgings to poor strangers: "Albeit she dyd not receyue in her house our sauyour in his owne persone . . . she neuertheles receyued them that dothe represent his persone." This is symbolic standing for; the representers are acted upon rather than active; the represented is a religious and historical figure, almost more an abstraction than a human being. The first instance in the *Oxford English Dictionary* of an application of "represent" to anything remotely resembling acting for others is not until 1595, twelve years after Smith's work.

It thus seems likely that Smith was either saying that Parliament depicted or made manifest the whole realm as a painter does his subject matter or a theatrical troupe its play; or else he was saying that Parliament symbolized or mystically embodied the whole realm, as one might say it of a flag or emblem, as the Middle Ages had said it of the king. Possibly he was expressing both ideas by employing this word. Besides its actual meaning at the time, the term would have been further enriched by its context—by the composition of Parliament and the doctrine that all men were present there. In any case, Smith was not talking about democratic responsibility to the people, or about acting for the people as an attorney represents his client.

Almost half a century passes after Smith's work before Parliament is again said to "represent," but then the term undergoes a sudden renaissance and widening of meaning. In the second quarter of the seventeenth century, spurred by the pamphleteering and political debate that preceded and accompanied the Civil War, "represent" and the various related words become political terms. The development is confusing because it is complex.

By the 1620's the noun "representation" and the adjective "representative" have widened from their original applications in art, religion, and the theater, to refer to any substituted presence, including people standing for other people. And they are applied to Parliament, as when that body is told, in 1628, "an indelible dishonor it will be to you, the State representative."[29] (The word is here an adjective; the noun appears later.) The terms come readily to hand soon thereafter when Sir Edward Coke wants to expound his constitutional theories. In the *Institutes* he writes that the knights and burgesses who sit in Parliament "represent all the commons of the whole realm": "And whosoever is not a lord of parliament and of the lords house, is of the house of commons either in person, or *by representation*."[30] And he adds that "the parliament represents the body of the whole realm."[31] In 1641 the Commons refer to themselves as "the Representative Body of the whole Kingdom," as distinct from the Lords, who are only "particular Persons."[32] Similarly in a political pamphlet of the time it is argued that Parliament is the "representative, elected, instructed councill" of the kingdom; or again: "the whole community in its underived Majesty shall convene to doe justice. . . . and that the vastness of its owne bulke may not breed confusion, by virtue of election and *representation*: a few shall act for the many."[33] In 1643 no less a conservative than Charles I refers to the Parliament as the "representative body of the people."[34]

In the 1640's, apparently, some new terms enter the political arena. The noun "representative" makes its first appearance in English, occurring in two separate senses. It means a specimen or sample (from 1647 we have: "All which drew eyes toward him, as the Image and Representative of the Primitive Nobility"). It also means (in a sense now obsolete) Parliament as a whole, or assemblies like it. In 1648 the act abolishing the office of king after the death of Charles I reads: "And whereas by the abolition of the kingly office provided for in this Act, a most happy way for this nation (if God see it good) to return to its just and ancient right of being governed by its own Representatives or national meetings in council . . . and that they will carefully provide for the certain choosing, meeting and sitting of the next and future Representatives."[35] This usage continues into the eighteenth century, and only then does it become obsolete.

The whole family of terms, thus, seems first to be applied to Parliament as a whole, or to the Commons as a group.[36] And the meanings are obviously in transition from the earlier "standing for" by way of substitution and substituted presence, to something like "acting for." The terms seem first to be used as an expression of, and as a claim to, authority, power, prestige. Let the Lords take heed: the Commons represent the whole kingdom. Let the king take heed: the Parliament represents the realm. At no time during this period are these words used to express the relation of an individual member of the Commons to his particular constituency, his duty to obey the wishes of those he represents, his power to commit them, or anything of the sort. The idea that members of Parliament are attorneys or agents of their communities exists, of course, but it is not expressed by the term "representation."

Not until the 1640's are any of the terms in the "represent" family applied to individual members of Parliament, and only much later to ordinary attorneys or agents. There is a curious flowering of names for the members of Parliament in this period. While a "representative" is still a body of men like Parliament, the separate members begin to be referred to as "representers," "representors," "representants," and "representees."[37] Thus the *Oxford English Dictionary* gives us, from 1643, "Their consents . . . should oblige the Commonalty as consenting in their Representors"; from 1644, the members of the House of Commons referred to as "Representees of the Commons"; and from 1648, "The Parliament, that is, of the Peers and Commons, representees of the people met in a lawful and free Parliament."

Of these various terms, "representer" is of special interest because its history precedes the Civil War period. From the late fifteenth century it is applied specifically to one who engages in the activity of painting, producing a play, creating representations. And this is its only meaning until it is applied to members of Parliament. We may perhaps take this as a further hint that the Parliament as a whole was thought of more as a symbol or embodiment of the nation than as the portrayer or presenter of the nation. At least such an assumption would explain why it was not called a "representer" but rather a "representative," a word which had no such active background. Clear examples of the contrast are found in the *Clarke Papers*, both from the Putney debates of 1647 and from as late as 1653.[38] The whole legislature is always called "the Representative," while its members are always "representors."

The earliest application I have come across of the noun "representative" to a *member* of Parliament occurs in 1651, when Isaac Pennington, the younger, writes: "The fundamental right, safety and liberty of the People; which is radically in themselves, derivately in *the* Parliament, their substitutes or representatives."[39] It is applied in this way with increasing frequency in the Protectorate Parliaments, until eventually this becomes the noun's major meaning, and various rival terms become obsolete.[40]

But 1651 is also the year in which Hobbes published the *Leviathan*, in the midst of this etymological development. His entire application of representation rests on identifying it with the formal aspects of legal agency: authorization, and the ascription of normative consequences. Hobbes has made the transition in thought and seen its value to his argument. A sovereign legislature, called a "Representative," is to be considered like all other representers—agents, attorneys, and so on: namely, as someone whose actions are formally attributed to another. Aside from this theory, Hobbes' use of the terms was consistent with that of his time. In the early part of the *Leviathan* he speaks only of individuals who represent, and calls them "Representers."[41] Then comes one transitional passage in which "Representative" appears, and banishes its rival. In this passage the multitude are called "authors, of every thing their Representative saith, or doth in their name; every man giving their common Representer, Authority from himselfe in particular; and owning all the actions the Representer doth."[42] Thereafter Hobbes uses only "Representative," even when referring to a single ruler or a private corporation.

Was Hobbes making a brilliant application, or merely expressing what the current conception of the terms had already become? We do not know, and for present purposes it does not matter. The point is that both the formalistic sense of representation and its substantive correlate, "acting for," emerged during this period, apparently by way of the idea that Parliament rep-. resented the whole realm, which in turn began in the notion of a mystic or symbolic "standing for."

The etymological development in this period is confused, and the available evidence is not conclusive, but it suggests that terms like "represent" were first applied to the Parliament as an image of the whole nation, at a time when they were not yet applied to agents, attorneys, or individual members.[43] Once the Parliament was regarded as the representative body of the whole kingdom, the application to individual members followed easily: if the whole Commons is to be regarded as all the people of the realm, what is each knight or burgess? Surely he is the substitute for equivalent to his particular county or borough, in the part-by-part isomorphism frequently involved in representation. And once this step had been taken, the doctrine of members of Parliament as limited, responsible attorneys or agents was ready and waiting to become linked with the term "representative."

This entire development took place when the individual member of Parliament was becoming less and less of an agent of his constituency. The individual member is said to "represent" only after he has come to be thought of as acting for the whole realm, and only after the body of Parliament of which he is a member has come to be thought of as representing the whole nation.

There are thus some striking parallels between the development of the concept of representation in English during the period preceding the Civil Wars, and that in Latin during the early fourteenth century traced by Lagarde. In both there is a sudden increase in the use of a familiar term; in both, increased usage is accompanied by a considerable expansion in meaning; and in both we witness the emergence of the "acting for" as well as the formalistic senses of representation. Prior to these periods of development, "represent" was a word for artistic images, for literary reproduction, for religious or mystic embodiment. In these very restricted senses it came to be applied to political authority—the Pope, the king, the king-in-Parliament. And only after and through this application did it come to refer to agency, to legal representation of individuals, to the activity of representing.

Lagarde calls attention to the effect of the composition of thirteenth-century church councils.[44] As the thirteenth-century popes enlarged the council to include not only bishops but also delegates from various chapters, religious orders, and even secular princes, people came increasingly to regard it as *une image fidèle* of all Christendom. Thus, when Marsilius of Padua asked himself who really represented the body of all Christians, the Pope or the council, it seemed clear to him that the council was a better, more representative image. This tendency in thought was further stimulated by the practical difficulties resulting from the Great Schism. Who but a council could determine the true pope when the papacy itself was in dispute?

Here, too, are some striking parallels with the English experience. At first it is the king who is head of the realm, its symbolic embodiment. Then, increasingly, Parliament comes to partake of and share in this role, and the symbolic representative of the kingdom is the king-in-Parliament, a corporate body. But when it becomes a matter of removing, replacing, possibly judging and beheading a king, a further development takes place. If Parliament embodies the whole realm, what other group could act to depose a king in the name of the realm? The claim of Parliament to represent all the people had long been used as a weapon to challenge the king; in the Civil War it becomes a justification for overthrowing him. Conversely, the king sought to keep the members of Parliament in their place by arguing that each spoke only for his own separate community; they did not collectively "represent" the realm.[45]

The history of the period suggests that the formalistic, authorization sense of representing may have emerged a little earlier than substantive "acting for." Embodiment or symbolization of the realm is succeeded by a claim to authority *from* the realm, and this in turn is linked with limitations on those in authority. First, the king-in-Parliament represent the realm in the sense of "standing for" as an image. They may be said to represent by virtue of the fact that they govern. Then, in seeking to assert its authority in opposition to the king, the Parliament claims to represent more truly than he: it "corresponds to" the parts of the realm, it is sent by the people, and so on. Because it represents the whole people it has the right to make binding laws. Thus, the Parliament has authority to govern by virtue of the fact that it represents; and the argument has come full circle. But the meaning of representation has been enlarged in the process: the authority of Parliament to govern has become connected with and dependent on its being truly representative. Because its individual members have been designated as representatives, the word has been associated with all the written and unwritten rules of agency, with the ancient obligations of knights and burgesses toward the communities that send them. As Richard Overton wrote in 1647, "no more than the people are the King's, no more are the people the Parliament's, (they) having no such propriety in the people as the people have in their goods, to do with them as they list."[46] And he maintained that the natural body may cut off diseased members from "the body representative," may even renounce and dissolve it, "upon total forfeiture of, and real apostasy from, the true representative capacity of Parliament."[47]

Notes

NOTES TO CHAPTER 1
(Pp. 1–13)

[1] *Baker vs. Carr* (1962), 369 U.S. 186. For a survey of subsequent cases and developments, see Howard D. Hamilton, *Legislative Apportionment, Key to Power* (New York, 1964).

[2] See J. A. O. Larsen, *Representative Government in Greek and Roman History* (Berkeley and Los Angeles, 1955). For a more extended discussion of the etymology of "representation" and the development of representative government, see the Appendix, below.

[3] For the development in Latin, see Georges de Lagarde, "L'Idée de Représentation dans les Oeuvres de Guillaume d'Ockham," International Committee of the Historical Sciences, *Bulletin*, IX (December, 1937), 425–451; Albert Hauck, "Die Rezeption und Umbildung der allgemeinen Synode im Mittelalter," *Historische Vierteljahrschrift*, X (1907), 465–482; Otto Hintze, "Typologie der ständischen Verfassungen des Abendlandes," *Historische Zeitschrift*, CXLI (1929–1930), 229–248.

[4] For a review of rival theories on origins of English parliamentary representation, see C. H. MacIlwain, "Medieval Estates," *Cambridge Medieval History*, VII: *The Decline of Empire and Papacy* (Cambridge, England, 1932), 664–715; Helen M. Cam, *Liberties and Communities in Medieval England* (London, 1944), chap. 15.

[5] A. F. Pollard, *The Evolution of Parliament* (London, 1926), pp. 109, 158–159; Charles A. Beard and John D. Lewis, "Representative Government in Evolution," *American Political Science Review*, XXVI (April, 1932), 230–233; Henry J. Ford, *Representative Government* (New York, 1924), p. 101n; James Hogan, *Election and Representation* (1945), pp. 142–143.

[6] Colonel Rainborow at the Putney debates of October 29, 1647: ". . . really I thinke that the poorest hee that is in England hath a life to live as the greatest hee; and therefore truly, Sir, I thinke itt's cleare, that every man that is to live under a Governement ought first by his owne consent to putt himself under that Governement; and I doe thinke that the poorest man in England is nott att all bound in a stricte sense

to that Governement that hee hath not had a voice to putt himself under . . ." Cited in Charles Firth, ed., *The Clarke Papers* (Camden Society, 1891), I, 301.

⁷ While the idea has medieval roots, the slogan was apparently popularized in the American colonies by Daniel Gookin (1612–1687), an Irish settler in Virginia who moved to Boston, where he became Speaker of the Massachusetts legislature and an agitator for popular rights. Hugh Chisholm, "Representation," *Encyclopaedia Britannica*, XXIII, (1910–1911), 109. On the various interpretations of the slogan during the revolutionary period and its role as a rallying cry, see Randolph G. Adams, *Political Ideas of the American Revolution* (New York, 1958), pp. 86–106; and Arthur M. Schlesinger, *New Viewpoints in American History* (New York, 1948), pp. 160–183.

⁸ See for example, Samuel Bailey, *The Rationale of Political Representation* (London, 1835), p. 6; Gerhard Leibholz, *Das Wesen der Repräsentation* (Berlin, 1929), p. 66; Cecil S. Emden, *The People and the Constitution* (Oxford, 1956), p. 2; Martin Drath, *Die Entwicklung der Volksrepräsentation* (Bad Homburg v.d.H., 1954), pp. 7, 27.

⁹ John Stuart Mill, *Considerations on Representative Government*, first published in 1861. Cited hereafter as *Representative Government*. I use the Everyman's edition throughout: *Utilitarianism, Liberty, and Representative Government* (London, 1947), pp. 175–393. Mill defines representative government (chap. 5, p. 228) but not representation; nor does he connect his definition of the former with the meaning of the latter.

¹⁰ Stanley Cavell, "Must We Mean What We Say?" *Inquiry*, I (1958), 200–202. On "representation" specifically, compare Leibholz, *Das Wesen der Repräsentation*, pp. 105–106.

¹¹ Pollard, *op. cit.*, p. 151; Robert Luce, *Legislative Principles* (Boston, 1930), p. 199; Chisholm, *op. cit.*, p. 108; Francis Luepp, "Do Our Representatives Represent?" *Atlantic Monthly*, CXIV (October, 1914), 434–435. Compare Heinz Eulau *et al.*, "The Role of the Representative: Some Empirical Observations on the Theory of Edmund Burke," *American Political Science Review*, LIII (September, 1959), 742–743; and Joseph Tussman, *Obligation and the Body Politic* (New York, 1960), p. 61.

¹² For example, Beard and Lewis, *op. cit.*; Alfred De Grazia, *Public and Republic* (New York, 1951); John A. Fairlie, "The Nature of Political Representation," *American Political Science Review*, XXXIV (April, June, 1940), 236–248, 456–466; Harold Foote Gosnell, *Democracy, the Threshold of Freedom* (New York, 1948), esp. chap. 8; Luce, *op. cit.*, esp. chaps. 9 and 21; Luepp, *op. cit.*

¹³ Henry B. Mayo, *An Introduction to Democratic Theory* (New York, 1960), pp. 95, 103.

¹⁴ See esp. Austin's *Philosophical Papers* (Oxford, 1961). My dissertation was essentially completed before I encountered Paul Ziff's *Semantic Analysis* (Ithaca, 1960) and the writings of Ludwig Wittgenstein. From the former I have borrowed what fitted into my text, and learned much. The latter has so much altered my thinking about language and philosophy that (except for a few footnotes) I have made no effort to incorporate Wittgensteinian ideas into my text in the process of revision. Thus this book is primarily Austinian and not Wittgensteinian in its orientation; if

I were to write it over again now, it would be a different book. From Stanley Cavell I have learned far more about language philosophy than can be gathered from his articles, which are nevertheless very useful.

[15] Charles William Cassinelli, Jr., "The Concept of Representative Government" (unpubl. thesis, 1950), p. 12; and "Representative Government: The Concept and Its Implications" (unpubl. diss., 1953); F. A. Hermens, *Democracy or Anarchy?* (Notre Dame, Ind., 1941), pp. 4–5; Gosnell, *op. cit.*, p. 148. The significance of analogies and nonpolitical usage seems to have been recognized only by Hans J. Wolff, *Organschaft und juristische Person* (Berlin, 1934), p. 22, although many commentators use one or another analogy.

[16] Stanley Bertram Chrimes, *English Constitutional Ideas in the Fifteenth Century* (Cambridge, England, 1936), pp. 85–86. Chrimes is speaking about the term "estates," but what he says has general validity.

[17] Carl J. Friedrich, *Constitutional Government and Democracy* (Boston, 1950), p. 267; and "Representation," *Encyclopaedia Britannica*, XIX (1960), 163–167. Fairlie, *op. cit.*, p. 236; Friedrich Glum, *Der deutsche und der französische Reichswirtschaftsrat* (Berlin, 1929), p. 27; Leibholz, *Das Wesen der Repräsentation*, p. 26; Wolff, *op. cit.*, pp. 18–29.

[18] See esp. Carl Schmitt, *The Necessity of Politics* (London, 1931), p. 69; also Glum, *op. cit.*, pp. 25–36; and Leibholz, *Das Wesen der Repräsentation*, pp. 26–35, 46, 166–175.

[19] *Op. cit.*, p. 29; translation mine.

[20] The metaphor developed in my thinking quite independently of the similar one I later discovered in Ziff's work. *Op. cit.*, p. 181: "An element m_1 can have associated with it a set of sets of conditions Cm_1. Think of m_1 as a jewel, of each member of Cm_1 as one facet. Then which facet catches the light depends on contextual and linguistic environmental features, thus on its setting. So one says 'He's my brother.' or 'He's been a brother to me.' or 'He's a brother of the order.' " in each case, if it is a standard case, a different facet of the word is turned to catch the light."

My idea may have germinated from Sheldon Wolin's suggestion that "political philosophy constitutes a form of 'seeing' political phenomena and that the way in which the phenomena will be visualized depends in large measure on where the viewer 'stands,' " his particular "perspective" or "angle of vision." *Politics and Vision* (Boston, 1960), p. 17. I now believe, on the basis of reading Wittgenstein, that the metaphor is in some respects profoundly misleading about concepts and language. But on the concept of representation it happens to work fairly well. Since it is central to the structure of this book I have let it stand.

[21] *The Literary Symbol* (New York, 1955), p. vii.

NOTES TO CHAPTER 2
(Pp. 14–37)

[1] *English Works*, ed. Sir William Molesworth (London, 1839–1845), cited hereafter as *E. W.* Karl Loewenstein goes so far as to call the principle of representation incompatible with the Hobbesian doctrine: *Volk und Parlament* (Munich, 1922), p. 35. Among commentators on Hobbes, the importance of representation seems to have been noticed only by

Ferdinand Tönnies in *Thomas Hobbes* (Stuttgart, 1925), p. 238, and by
Joseph Tussman in "The Political Theory of Thomas Hobbes" (unpubl.
diss., 1947), pp. 89–119. The related concept of the "person" does get
some attention in the French literature. See Raymond Polin, *Politique et
Philosophie chez Thomas Hobbes* (Paris, 1953), chap. 10; René Gadave,
Thomas Hobbes (Toulouse, 1907), pp. 93–101; B. Landry, *Hobbes*
(Paris, 1930), chap. 10.

2 *The Elements of Law*, completed in 1640, was not published until
1650. *De Cive*, completed in 1642, appeared first in Latin and was not
published in English until 1651, the same year that the *Leviathan* appeared.

3 A similar stress on the connection with "person" is found in Carl
Schmitt, *The Necessity of Politics* (London, 1931), p. 60: "Only a person
can represent. . . ." Compare Harold Foote Gosnell, *Democracy* (New
York, 1948), p. 132; and De Grazia, *Public and Republic* (New York,
1951), p. 7.

The concept of "person" has a fascinating history in theology, psy-
chology, and law. See Gordon W. Allport, *Personality* (New York, 1937),
pp. 24–50; F. Max Müller, *Biographies of Words* (London, 1888), pp.
32–47; Siegmund Schlossmann, *Persona und πρόσωπον im Recht und im
Christlichen Dogma* (Kiel, 1906); Trendlenburg, "Zur Geschichte des
Wortes 'Person,'" *Kantstudien*, XIII (1908), 1; H. Rheinfelder, "Das
Wort 'Persona,'" *Beihefte zur Zeitschrift für Romanische Philologie*,
LXXVII (1928).

4 *E. W.*, III, 147.

5 Tönnies, *op. cit.*, pp. 238–239; Gadave, *op. cit.*, p. 139.

6 *E. W.*, III, 148.

7 *Ibid.*, 538.

8 *Ibid.*, 148.

9 *Ibid.*, 149.

10 *Ibid.*, 152.

11 Hobbes' ambivalence on this point no doubt is related to his peculiar
conception of rights, which depends on the idea of the state of nature.
See my "Hobbes' Concept of Representation—II," *American Political
Science Review*, LVIII (December, 1964), 902–918.

12 *E. W.*, III, 148.

13 *Ibid.*, 151.

14 *Ibid.*, 148.

15 *Ibid.*, 149–150.

16 Howard Warrender, *The Political Philosophy of Hobbes* (Oxford,
1957), p. 23.

17 *E. W.*, III, 150.

18 *Ibid.*, 149.

19 *Ibid.*, 147.

20 *Ibid.*; italics mine.

21 The concept of the self as an assumed role that we play, while evidently not entirely right, is most suggestive. Cf. Erving Goffman's extraordinary study, *The Presentation of Self in Everyday Life* (1958). But
of course we do not ordinarily play or represent ourselves; as Goffman's
title suggests, it is at most a matter of *pre*sentation; and even then the
self is neither totally distinct from its masks nor entirely exhausted in
them.

[22] *E. W.*, III, 148. Although no citation is given in the *Leviathan*, Hobbes uses the same quotation in his "Letter to Bishop Bramhall" (*E. W.*, IV, 310), where he attributes it to one of Cicero's letters to Atticus. I finally found the passage in II *de Oratore* 102.

[23] *E. W.*, IV, 310.

[24] My argument here holds only if, in writing of the vulgar expression "he's not his own person," Hobbes really had in mind "he's not his own man." Otherwise there might have been a seventeenth-century expression "he's not his own person," which *was* defined by acting on someone else's authority, as Hobbes suggests. I have not found any evidence of such a usage. It is not listed in the *Oxford English Dictionary*, which does, however, list "he's not his own man." The earliest example of this expression dates from the fourteenth century, and it has been in use since then. Its meaning corresponds to the one I suggest, not that given by Hobbes. It seems very likely that Hobbes had in mind "he's not his own man," and was misled by his authorization definition.

[25] "Author" derives from the Latin *augere*, "to make (something) grow." The connection is noted by Harvey Pinney, "Government—by Whose Consent?" *Social Science*, XIII (October, 1938), 297. It has recently been treated more fully by Hannah Arendt, "What Is Authority?" *Between Past and Future* (Cleveland, 1963).

[26] For a more detailed discussion see my article cited in note 11, above.

[27] The best discussion of obligation in the *Leviathan* is found in Warrender, *op. cit.*

[28] *E. W.*, III, 159–160.

[29] *Ibid.*, 151.

[30] *Ibid.*, 158; italics mine.

[31] *Ibid.*, 158–159, 207–210.

[32] *Ibid.*, 322.

[33] See Warrender, *op. cit.*, pp. 125–134. As he points out, this argument is much weakened in the case of sovereignty by acquisition, where the sovereign *is* party to the covenant. However, it can be argued that in the establishment of a commonwealth by acquisition, the sovereign merely promises to spare the lives of the conquered people *at the time the covenant is made*; so that afterward, he has already performed his obligation and owes no further obligation to his subjects. See *E. W.*, III, 190.

[34] *E. W.*, III, 163.

[35] *Ibid.*, 137.

[36] To my account of the significance of the authorization of the sovereign, Warrender offers an alternative but (I think) mistaken interpretation; *op. cit.*, pp. 109–110, 129–131, 178. He says that the authorization of the sovereign means only "that the conduct of the sovereign cannot be a moral affront of which the citizens may take note, and authorization serves to indemnify the sovereign from accountability to the citizen on such grounds." *Ibid.*, p. 110.

It seems to me that the reason the subject cannot have a valid claim against the sovereign is not that he has released the sovereign from accountability, but that the sovereign is incapable of violating any obligation to him. This is a result of authorization, but it is very different from resignation of accountability. The passage cited by Warrender (p. 131) shows that it is absence of obligation and not absence of accountability that is crucial. See *E. W.*, III, 200.

But, more important, to say that authorization signifies only that the sovereign is not accountable to his subjects, is to miss its most significant function. Authorization is a source of obligation *to* the sovereign. Through it, the sovereign is empowered to commit his subjects as if his will were theirs.

Warrender misses this point because he thinks that all the subject's obligations arise from contract alone. Hence he concludes that authorization merely means that the subject cannot judge the sovereign or hold him to account. Warrender says that this is what "makes the sovereign an authority" for the subject (p. 130). But an authority is not just someone whom we do not presume to judge; it is someone whose judgment we accept. Similarly, the subjects have not merely agreed to refrain from judging the sovereign; they have agreed to let him judge for them.

According to Warrender, the subject is not morally responsible for the sovereign's commands, because "one person cannot take moral responsibility for another person's action" (p. 110). But this is exactly backward. Hobbes says that the sovereign, not the subject, is responsible if the sovereign commands something contrary to the law of God and the subject does it. *E. W.*, II, 152; IV, 140–141, 185. And surely this is possible only if one man *can* be morally responsible for the actions of another. One is morally responsible only for one's own "natural and very will," and not for what the sovereign wills in one's name.

[37] "Under such circumstances representative government would obviously be such *only in name,* for a permanent mandate in a representative system is a contradiction in terms." James Wilford Garner, *Political Science and Government* (New York, 1928), p. 642; italics mine.

"All do not authorize the sovereign to act as a representative in any *literal* meaning of the term." Morton Kaplan, "How Sovereign Is Hobbes' Sovereign?" *Western Political Quarterly*, IX (June, 1956), 395; italics mine.

[38] Kaplan, *op. cit.,* p. 400.

[39] De Grazia, *Public and Republic,* p. 9.

[40] The phrase is from Charles L. Stevenson, *Ethics and Language* (New Haven, 1944), chap. 9. As the rest of this paragraph indicates, however, I have certain quarrels with Stevenson's concept.

[41] In my experience, undergraduates are often misled in just this way. Once it has been brought to their attention that Hobbes uses the concept of representation, they frequently jump to the conclusion that the sovereign is, indeed, required to consult his subjects' wishes and pursue their interest.

[42] This leads De Grazia to say that "Hobbes, in building up a monarchial system, strove so hard to take advantage of the positive coloration of the word 'representative' that he deprived it of much meaning." *Public and Republic,* p. 25. But Hobbes could take advantage of the word's "positive coloration" only insofar as it *preserved* its usual meaning. (This passage from De Grazia seems in conflict with the one cited above, at note 39.)

[43] "A main cause of philosophical disease—a one-sided diet: one nourishes one's thinking with only one kind of example." Ludwig Wittgenstein, *Philosophical Investigations,* trans. G. E. M. Anscombe (New York, 1953), p. 155.

Notes to Chapter 3
(Pp. 38–59)

[1] "Unter Repräsentation wird primär der . . . erörterte Tatbestand verstanden: dass das Handeln bestimmter Verbandszugehöriger (Vertreter) den übrigen zugerechnet wird oder von ihnen gegen sich als 'legitim' geschehen und für sie verbindlich gelten gelassen werden soll und tatsächlich wird." Max Weber, *Wirtschaft und Gesellschaft* (Tübingen, 1956), I, 171. This work was written between 1911 and 1913. The translation in this and all other passages from Weber is my own. An English translation is available: *The Theory of Social and Economic Organization,* trans. A. M. Henderson and Talcott Parsons (Glencoe, Ill., 1947); but the passages I am concerned with are translated too loosely by Henderson and Parsons for my specialized interest. Where Weber implies only the ascription of actions, the translation often implies the ascription of normative consequences. (These terms are explained below.)

[2] "Eine soziale Beziehung kann für die Beteiligten nach traditionaler oder gesatzter Ordnung die Folge haben: dass bestimmte Arten des Handelns a) jedes an der Beziehung Beteiligten allen Beteiligten ('Solidaritätsgenossen') oder b) das Handeln bestimmter Beteiligten ('Vertreter') den anderen Beteiligten ('Vertretenen') zugerechnet wird, dass also sowohl die Chancen wie die Konsequenzen ihnen zugute kommen bzw. ihnen zur Last fallen." Weber, *Wirtschaft,* I, 25. See also I, 171–176; II, 438–440.

[3] The reference to blood feud and collective responsibility is common among this group of theorists: Georg Jellinek, *Allgemeine Staatslehre* (Berlin, 1905), p. 553; Hans J. Wolff, *Organschaft und juristische Person* (Berlin, 1934), pp. 37–41.

[4] *Wirtschaft,* pp. 17–18.

[5] Robert Redslob, *Die Staatstheorien der französischen Nationalversammlung von 1789* (Leipzig, 1912), p. 119; J. C. Bluntschli, *Die Lehre vom modernen Staat,* Vol. II: *Allgemeines Staatsrecht* (Stuttgart, 1876), 49–56.

[6] Otto von Gierke, *Johannes Althusius* (Breslau, 1913), pp. 224–225; Jellinek, *op. cit.,* pp. 552–579; Redslob, *op. cit.,* p. 129; Karl Loewenstein, *Volk und Parlament* (Munich, 1922), p. 201; Conrad Bornhak, *Allgemeine Staatslehre* (Berlin, 1909), pp. 113–115.

[7] John A. Fairlie, "The Nature of Political Representation," *American Political Science Review* XXXIV (April, 1940), p. 237. Cf. Harold Foote Gosnell, *Democracy* (New York, 1948), p. 146; John Dewey, *The Public and Its Problems* (New York, 1927), pp. 18, 67, 75–77; James Hogan, *Election and Representation* (1945), pp. 120–121, 141.

[8] Dewey, *The Public,* p. 75. Cf. Bluntschli, *op. cit.,* p. 50; Jellinek, *op. cit.,* pp. 569–575; Joseph Tussman, *Obligation and the Body Politic* (New York, 1960), p. 21 *et passim.*

[9] Hogan, *op. cit.,* p. 120.

[10] Jellinek, *op. cit.,* p. 552.

[11] As when he stresses the continuing power of the people over their legislators (*ibid.,* pp. 569–571), uses the term *Repräsentativverfassung* to designate only those governments with elected legislatures (p. 571), or says that calling an absolute monarch a representative is devoid of content (pp. 576–577).

[12] *Ibid.*, p. 552; also pp. 565–566, 568, 573, 576–578.

[13] This idea, too, was already being debated at the time of the French Revolution; Redslob, *op. cit.*, p. 119; Loewenstein, *Volk und Parlament,* p. 202. Compare also Redslob, *op. cit.*, p. 129; Jellinek, *op. cit.*, p. 552; and Bornhak, *op. cit.*, p. 115. For a slightly different treatment, cf. Hans Kelsen, *The Pure Theory of Law* (Berkeley and Los Angeles, 1967), pp. 299–302.

[14] For an exception, see Francis X. Sutton, "Representation and the Nature of Political Systems," *Comparative Studies in Society and History,* II (October, 1959), 1–10. Sutton adopts Weber's definition for his anthropological work.

[15] Edward McChesney Sait, *Political Institutions* (New York, 1938), p. 476; Avery Leiserson, "Problems of Representation in the Government of Private Groups," *Journal of Politics,* XI (August, 1949), 566; Sir Ernest Barker, *Greek Political Theory,* p. 35, cited in Fairlie, *op. cit.,* p. 459.

[16] Karl Loewenstein, *Political Power and the Governmental Process* (Chicago, 1957), p. 38. Loewenstein actually says "the legal essence," but the context makes it clear that he means this as a general definition, that without authority to bind others there is no real representation.

[17] Harvey Pinney, "Government—by Whose Consent?" *Social Science,* XIII (October, 1938), p. 298. Cf. George Cornwall Lewis, *Remarks on the Use and Abuse of Some Political Terms* (Oxford, 1877), p. 98. Lewis develops what is in most respects an authorization view, but rejects the term "authorization" as making the representative subordinate to those who authorize him.

[18] Joseph Tussman, "The Political Theory of Thomas Hobbes" (unpubl. diss., 1947), pp. 117–118.

[19] John P. Plamenatz, *Consent, Freedom and Political Obligation* (London, 1938), pp. 4, 12.

[20] *Ibid.*, pp. 15 ff.

[21] *Ibid.*, pp. 16–17.

[22] Eric Voegelin, *The New Science of Politics* (Chicago, 1952), pp. 31, 1.

[23] *Ibid.*, p. 33.

[24] *Ibid.*, pp. 32, 30.

[25] *Ibid.*, p. 50.

[26] *Ibid.*, p. 36.

[27] *Ibid.*, p. 37.

[28] *Ibid.*, p. 40; cf. pp. 38–39, 45, 47. It is not easy to say whether Voegelin considers such expanded articulation desirable. He admires Athenian democracy (p. 71), but opposes the facile exportation of representative institutions to societies not ready for them, and the corresponding assumption that representative government is desirable for all peoples (pp. 50–51). Probably the articulation must grow organically from the society's own history rather than be imposed or borrowed from the outside.

[29] *Ibid.*, p. 47; cf. pp. 41–49.

[30] *Ibid.*, pp. 54, 75.

[31] *Ibid.*, pp. 53, 70, 73.

[32] *Ibid.*, p. 54; italics mine.

[33] *Ibid.*, pp. 28–31.

[34] *Ibid.*, p. 75.

[35] A. Phillips Griffiths and Richard Wollheim, "How Can One Person Represent Another?" *Aristotelian Society Suppl. Vol.* XXXIV (1960), 187–224.

[36] *Ibid.,* p. 189.

[37] *Ibid.,* p. 192.

[38] *Ibid.* This interesting distinction explains the compelling impact of an ultrademocratic passage cited by Alfred De Grazia, *Public and Republic* (New York, 1951), pp. 46–47. The passage is an attack on the doctrine of virtual representation, that the disfranchised are nevertheless represented in Parliament, and so have no grounds for complaint: they are represented "virtually," not "actually." Mocking this idea, the editor of a work of Jeremy Bentham's comments: "Why do not the oligarchs form themselves into a Grand Eating Club, to eat for the whole nation, and then tell the starving people they are virtually fed?" As an attack on the restricted franchise, the argument is striking and compelling; yet it is based on a fallacy that Griffiths here exposes. No man can genuinely eat for another, no matter how democratically he has been elected or how anxious he is to please the other.

[39] *Ibid.,* pp. 192–193.

[40] *Ibid.,* p. 193.

[41] *Ibid.,* p. 192.

[42] *Ibid.*

[43] Cf. Gerhard Leibholz, *Das Wesen der Repräsentation* (Berlin, 1929), p. 37; and Kelsen, *Pure Theory of Law,* pp. 158–163, 299–302.

[44] Cf. Harold D. Lasswell and Abraham Kaplan, *Power and Society* (New Haven, 1950), p. 164: "Agency, in short, is not identical with authority but is one form of it, depending for its power on a preexisting authority."

[45] Robert M. Hutchins, "The Theory of Oligarchy: Edmund Burke," *The Thomist,* V (January, 1943), 64.

[46] *Constitutional Government and Democracy* (Boston, 1950), pp. 263–264.

[47] Consider Howard Warrender's view, in *The Political Philosophy of Hobbes* (Oxford, 1957), pp. 109–110, that to Hobbes authorizing a representative simply means freeing him from any accountability; or Joseph Tussman's argument, in "Political Theory," p. 118, that the recurrence of elections at the end of a term of office cannot "alter the fact that an act of subordination has occurred" in the earlier election.

[48] Henry J. Ford, *Representative Government* (New York, 1924), p. 157.

[49] Terry Hoy, "Theories of the Exercise of Suffrage in the United States" (unpubl. diss., 1956), pp. 92, 97.

[50] F. H. Knight, *Intelligence and Democratic Action* (Cambridge, 1960), p. 27; cf. p. 127; and his argument in "Political Responsibility in a Democracy," *Responsibility* (Nomos III), ed. Carl J. Friedrich (New York, 1960), pp. 179–180.

[51] Arthur W. Bromage, "Political Representation in Metropolitan Areas," *American Political Science Review,* LII (June, 1958), 407; italics mine.

[52] *Ibid.,* p. 412. Cf. Bromage, *Political Representation in Metropolitan Agencies* (Ann Arbor, 1962), p. 4.

[53] Ford, *op. cit.,* p. 158, for example.

[54] Hutchins, *op. cit.*, p. 64, for example.

[55] Dewey and Tufts, *Ethics*, pp. 338–339, cited in Friedrich, *Responsibility*, p. 73. Cf. Friedrich's Introduction to F. A. Hermens, *Democracy or Anarchy?* (Notre Dame, Ind., 1941), p. xxi.

[56] Attention is called to the German terminology by Friedrich Glum, *Der deutsche und der französische Reichswirtschaftsrat* (Berlin, 1929), p. 27; and Albert Hauck, "Die Rezeption und Umbildung der allgemeinen Synode im Mittelalter," *Historische Vierteljahrschrift*, X (1907), 479. The distinction in meaning is noted also by Tussman, "Political Theory," pp. 98–99, and more recently by Griffiths and Wollheim, *op. cit.*, pp. 188–189.

NOTES TO CHAPTER 4
(Pp. 60–91)

[1] John Adams, "Letter to John Penn," *Works* (Boston, 1852–1865), IV, 205; cf. p. 195.

[2] John Adams, "Defense of the Constitution of Government of the United States of America," *ibid.*, p. 284. However, he also maintained in the "Defense" that a monarch or a hereditary aristocracy could represent a nation just as well as an elective assembly. For this inconsistency he was taken to task by John Taylor of Caroline, in a rather pedantic critique of the "Defense": *An Inquiry into the Principles and Policy of the Government of the United States* (Fredricksburg, 1814), pp. 109–111, 146, 431, 483, 527. Adams defended himself in a letter to Taylor: "What shall I say of the 'resemblance of our house of representatives to a leglislating nation'? It is perhaps a miniature which resembles the original as much as a larger picture would or could. But, sir, let me say, once and for all, that as no picture, great or small, no statue, no bust in brass or marble, gold or silver, ever yet perfectly represented or resembled the original, so no representative government ever perfectly represented or resembled the original nation or people." *Works*, VI, 462. The exchange displays both the advantages and the ambiguities of the metaphor.

[3] Cited in *The Records of the Federal Convention of 1787*, ed. Max Farrand (New Haven, 1927), I, 141–142, 132; James Wilson, *Works,* ed. James DeWitt Andrews (Chicago, 1896), I, 391.

[4] Edmund Burke, "Thoughts on the Cause of the Present Discontents" (1770), *Burke's Politics,* eds. Ross J. S. Hoffman and Paul Levack (New York, 1949), p. 28.

[5] Sir George Cave, speaking in the British House of Commons in 1918, cited in Cecil S. Emden, *The People and the Constitution* (Oxford, 1956), p. 4; cf. Robert Luce, *Legislative Principles* (Boston, 1930), p. 282; and Charles A. Beard, "Whom Does Congress Represent?" in *The People, Politics and the Politician,* eds. A. N. Christensen and E. M. Kirkpatrick (New York, 1941), p. 340. Robert H. Carr *et al., American Democracy in Theory and Practice* (New York, 1959), p. 302; Ernest Bruncken, "Some Neglected Factors in Law-Making," *American Political Science Review,* VIII (1919), 222, cited in Stuart Rice, *Quantitative Methods in Politics* (New York, 1928), p. 192; Charles A. Beard and John D. Lewis, "Representative Government in Evolution," *American Political Science Review,* XXVI (April, 1932), 225.

[6] Henry J. Ford, *Representative Government* (New York, 1924), p. 146; Herbert H. Asquith, speaking in the British House of Commons on July 4, 1917, cited in Clarence Gilbert Hoag and George Hervey Hallett, Jr., *Proportional Representation* (New York, 1926), p. 304; Sheldon S. Wolin, *Politics and Vision* (Boston, 1960), p. 278.

[7] William Seal Carpenter, *Democracy and Representation* (Princeton, 1925), pp. 40, 53.

[8] Cited in Carl J. Friedrich, *Constitutional Government and Democracy* (Boston, 1950), pp. 304–305.

[9] *Ibid.*, p. 286.

[10] Raymond Poincaré, addressing the French Senate on February 20, 1929; trans. and cited by Hoag and Hallett, *op. cit.*, p. 314.

[11] George Wharton Pepper, in the Pennsylvania Commission on Constitutional Amendment and Revision in May, 1920, cited *ibid.*, p. 311; *ibid.*, p. 3; Asquith, cited *ibid.*, p. 304.

[12] Honoré Gabriel Riquetti Mirabeau, *Oeuvres* (Paris, 1834), I, 7; translation mine.

[13] J. C. Bluntschli, *Die Lehre vom modernen Staat* (Stuttgart, 1876), p. 60; translation mine.

[14] This error probably resulted from the form in which Bluntschli presents the citation; it is part of a single paragraph with his own ideas, set off merely by a quotation mark. The error would seem to have been made first by Simon Sterne, *Representative Government and Personal Representation* (Philadelphia, 1871), p. 61; and perhaps after him by Emil Klöti, *Die Proportionwahl in der Schweitz* (Bern, 1901), p. 178. They are taken to task by Esmein, who points out that Mirabeau was far from being an advocate of proportional representation: A. Esmein and H. Nézard, *Éléments de Droit Constitutionel Français et Comparé* (Paris, 1927), I, 347–348. The same criticism is made by F. A. Hermens, *Democracy or Anarchy?* (Notre Dame, Ind., 1941), p. 13.

[15] Sterne, *op. cit.*, p. 61.

[16] Victor Considérant, "La Représentation Nationale Est un Mensonge," *La Phalange*, June 17, 1842, trans. and cited by F. A. Hermens, *Democracy and Proportional Representation* (Chicago, 1940), p. 2.

[17] Thomas Hare, *The Election of Representatives* (London, 1873), p. xxix.

[18] Hoag and Hallett, *op. cit.*, pp. xvii–xviii, 3, 117; John Roger Commons, *Proportional Representation* (New York, 1896), p. 8.

[19] John Stuart Mill, for example, advocates proportional representation not so much because it yields truer *representation* as because it yields truer *democracy*. Representation in proportion to numbers is advanced by him as "the first principle of democracy." He does not discuss the relationship of Parliament as a body to the nation as a whole, nor whether it is representative of the nation. *Representative Government*, chap. 7, p. 260, in *Utilitarianism, Liberty, and Representative Government* (London, 1947). But for a different interpretation cf. Carl J. Friedrich, Introduction to Hermens, *Democracy or Anarchy?* p. xxi.

[20] Mill, *Representative Government*, chap. 5, pp. 239–240.

[21] Sterne, *op. cit.*, p. 50. Cf. Harold Foote Gosnell, *Democracy* (New York, 1948), p. 126; Ford, *op. cit.*, p. 3.

[22] Friedrich, in Hermens, *Democracy or Anarchy?* p. xx.

23 Mill, *Representative Government*, chap. 5, p. 239; cf. p. 235.

24 Esmein and Nézard, *op. cit.*, p. 351.

25 Thomas Gilpin, *On the Representation of Minorities of Electors to Act with the Majority of Elected Assemblies* (1844), cited in Alfred De Grazia, *Public and Republic* (New York, 1951), p. 196.

26 Sterne, *op. cit.*, pp. 50–51; De Grazia, *Public and Republic*, p. 196. Cf. also Poincaré, cited in Hoag and Hallett, *op. cit.*, p. 314.

27 Walter Bagehot, *The English Constitution* (London, 1928), chap. 5. This work was first published in 1867. For criticism of proportional representation, see the works of F. A. Hermens; Friedrich, *Constitutional Government*, chap. 15; G. Horwill, *Proportional Representation, its Dangers and Defects* (London, 1925); James Hogan, *Election and Representation* (1945), pp. 108–113.

28 Albert V. Dicey, *Introduction to the Study of the Law of the Constitution* (London, 1924), p. lxix.

29 Hence it has "functions other than representative ones." ("nicht nur repräsentative Funktionen"). Gerhard Leibholz, *Strukturprobleme der modernen Demokratie* (Karlsruhe, 1958), p. 58.

30 Hogan, *op. cit.*, p. 89. Carl J. Friedrich cites this formulation with approval in his "Representation and Constitutional Reform in Europe," *Western Political Quarterly*, I (June, 1948), 128. See also his *Constitutional Government*, chaps. 15, 16.

31 *Democracy or Anarchy?* pp. 8, 4. Cf. Emden, *op. cit.*, pp. 310–312, who sees the choice as either "accurate representation or effective decision" (p. 310).

32 *Op. cit.*, pp. 130–133. This particular distinction is also sometimes drawn by men who are neither proportionalists nor critics of proportional representation. Cf. Heinz Eulau *et al.*, "The Role of the Representative," *American Political Science Review*, LIII (September, 1959), 744; Avery Leiserson, *Administrative Regulation* (Chicago, 1942), p. 9n; A. Phillips Griffiths and Richard Wollheim, "How Can One Person Represent Another?" Aristotelian Society Suppl. Vol. XXIV (1960), 212.

33 *English Works*, ed. Sir William Molesworth (London, 1839–1845), III, 151–152.

34 See esp. Ernst H. Gombrich, *Art and Illusion* (New York, 1960), the best discussion of representation in art that I know; but cf. Walter Abell, *Representation and Form* (New York, 1936); Richard Bernheimer *et al.*, *Art* (Bryn Mawr, 1940); Joyce Cary, *Art and Reality* (New York, 1958); John Dewey, *Art as Experience* (New York, 1934); J. Hospers, *Meaning and Truth in the Arts* (Chapel Hill, N. C., 1946); Arnold Isenberg, "Perception, Meaning and the Subject-Matter of Art," *Journal of Philosophy*, XLI (1944), 561–575; Susan Langer, *Philosophy in a New Key* (Mentor, 1942); Melvin Rader, ed., *A Modern Book of Esthetics* (New York, 1952).

35 Gombrich, *op. cit.*, pp. 370, 90.

36 Example from Langer, *op. cit.*, pp. 55–56.

37 Such a passage is cited in Funk and Wagnall's *New Standard Dictionary of English* (1960) from Rawlins' *Herodotus*.

38 Langer, *op. cit.*, pp. 56–57. She argues that this is because pictures are not pseudo-objects but symbols of what they depict. The former is surely true, but I do not believe that they are symbols either; a symbol

does not usually look like, is not a picture of, what it stands for. (See Chap. 5, below.)

[39] But cf. Isenberg, op. cit., p. 565, where representational art is defined as "works containing forms which are in certain respects like the forms of nature."

[40] Ibid.

[41] Examples from Oxford English Dictionary.

[42] William R. Anson, Principles of the English Law of Contract, and of Agency in Its Relation to Contract, ed. A. G. Guest (Oxford, 1959), p. 201.

[43] Words and Phrases (St. Paul, Minn., 1955), vol. 37, p. 35; italics mine.

[44] Anson, op. cit., p. 201.

[45] Words and Phrases, vol. 37, p. 36.

[46] Gombrich, op. cit., pp. 90, 299.

[47] Paul Ziff, Semantic Analysis (Ithaca, 1960), p. 88.

[48] Alfred Korzybski, Science and Sanity (New York, 1933), p. 58.

[49] Ibid.

[50] Karl Löwenstein, Volk und Parlament (Munich, 1922), p. 21; Otto von Gierke, Johannes Althusius (Breslau, 1913), p. 217.

[51] George Harris, The True Theory of Representation in a State (London, 1857), pp. 23–24; Carpenter, op. cit., p. 49.

[52] Harold J. Laski, Democracy in Crisis (Chapel Hill, N. C., 1933), p. 80.

[53] De Grazia, Public and Republic, p. 185.

[54] Luce, op. cit., pp. 199, 201.

[55] A. Lawrence Lowell, Public Opinion and Popular Government (New York, 1921), pp. 239–240; cf. Joseph Tussman, Obligation and the Body Politic (New York, 1960), p. 61.

[56] Marie Collins Swabey, Theory of the Democratic State (Cambridge, Mass., 1937), p. 25.

[57] Ibid.

[58] Ibid., pp. 25–26.

[59] Ibid., p. 28.

[60] It was used in courses on American government by the late Professor Peter Odegard, and may be found also in Robert A. Dahl and Charles E. Lindblom, Politics, Economics and Welfare (New York, 1953), p. 313: "Therefore the problem is not so much one of insuring that every citizen is politically active on every issue as it is one of insuring that all citizens have approximately equal opportunity to act, using 'opportunity' in the realistic rather than the legalistic sense. If all citizens have an approximately equal opportunity to act, there is a high probability that those who do act will be roughly representative of those who do not." Cf. Francis P. Canavan, The Political Reason of Edmund Burke (Durham, N. C., 1960), p. 160.

[61] Professor Ernst Haas has called my attention to a science-fiction story (to which I unfortunately do not have a reference) in which computers and sampling techniques are used to pick the most typical American to vote for all the rest. The results are, of course, disastrous.

[62] The suggestion that each representative should mirror or reflect his constituency was made, for example, by Henry Clay speaking in the

Senate in 1838, cited in Luce, *op. cit.*, p. 470; and by Francis Luepp, "Do Our Representatives Represent?" *Atlantic Monthly*, CXIV (October, 1944), 434. Ernest Barker suggests strangely that *each constituency* should be a "microcosm and mirror" of the whole nation. *Reflections on Government* (London, 1942), p. 42.

[63] Friedrich, *Constitutional Government*, p. 319.

[64] Rice, *op. cit.*, p. 189.

[65] *Ibid.*, p. 206. For a critical discussion of the Rice study, see Friedrich, *Constitutional Government*, p. 319. For other instances of the facile identification of representativeness with the essence of representation, see Avery Leiserson, "Problems of Representation," *Journal of Politics*, XI (August, 1949), 569 (but cf. his definition, p. 566); H. G. Nicholas, *The British General Election of 1950*, p. 64, cited in Bernard Mayo, *An Introduction to Democratic Theory* (Oxford, 1960), p. 102; Herman Finer, *The Theory and Practice of Modern Government* (New York, 1949), p. 219.

[66] Friedrich, *Constitutional Government*, p. 267.

[67] Rice, *op. cit.*, p. 194.

[68] Harvey Pinney, "Government—by Whose Consent?" *Social Science*, XIII (October, 1938), 299.

[69] Carr, *et al.*, *op. cit.*, p. 302. The section opens with the familiar ideas of sampling and reflection: "Congress is clearly not an accurate cross section of the American people. Nevertheless, the members of Congress probably mirror the American people pretty well."

[70] Reinsch, *American Legislatures*, p. 290, cited in Luce, *op. cit.*, pp. 279–280.

[71] Eulau, *op. cit.*, p. 743.

[72] De Grazia, *Public and Republic*, p. 3; Gosnell, *op. cit.*, p. 130. The two authors are discussed together here because the relevant sections of their arguments are closely parallel; De Grazia assisted Gosnell in the preparation of those chapters in the latter's book before he wrote his own work (see Gosnell, *op. cit.*, pp. 124n, 143n, 199n, 221n).

[73] Gosnell, *op. cit.*, p. 131.

[74] Gosnell makes a further attempt to connect representativeness with political representation by arguing that the traditional concept of agency involves the characteristics of the agent-representative. The acts of an agent "are supposed to be, and legally must be, based on the assumption of certain characteristics of the principal. The agent is supposed to look through the eyes of his principal" (pp. 131–132). To clarify this metaphor, Gosnell adds a footnote: "A appoints B as his agent to purchase Blackacre for him. B thinks Blackacre is a great bargain and buys it for himself. A can recover the land from B because B violated his agency. Thus the law prevents B from acting in his own interest when he should be acting as A would." No explanation is given as to how a "similarity of characteristics" is involved here; and it seems to me a mistaken notion. An agent need not in any way resemble his principal. To argue that he must, only clouds the relationship between "standing for" and "acting for."

Gosnell points out that one of the meanings of the Latin *impersonare* was "to represent," as in a corporate body, from which he concludes: "In other words, 'to possess the characteristics of' someone or something seems to have been all the time a connotation of the word 'representation.' " But to represent a corporation surely does not mean to possess its characteristics. Gosnell merely underestimates the variety in the word *persona*, which meant *both* a legal personality that could be exercised by an agent, and a psychological personality that had certain characteristics. Cf. Gordon W. Allport, *Personality* (New York, 1937), pp. 24–50.

De Grazia, on the other hand, asserts that an agent "must 'impersonate' his client to the best of his ability, and, indeed, the word 'impersonate' derives from the same root as the word 'representation.' " *Public and Republic*, p. 7. Both parts of this statement are false.

[75] *Public and Republic*, pp. 5, 8.

[76] *Ibid.*, pp. 5–6; italics mine.

[77] *Ibid.*, p. 6.

[78] Hans J. Wolff, *Organschaft und juristische Person* (Berlin, 1924), pp. 64–65.

[79] *Public and Republic*, p. 6.

[80] Rice, *op. cit.*, p. 193, Cf. Martin Drath, *Die Entwicklung der Volksrepräsentation* (Bad Homburg, 1954), p. 27.

[81] Ralph Waldo Emerson, *Representative Men* (Boston, 1952). My attention was called to Emerson's work by a reference in A. F. Pollard, *The Evolution of Parliament* (London, 1926), p. 151, although Pollard merely remarks that Emerson's representative men were not elected. Actually the significance of "representative" in the title seems to be multiple. Emerson maintains, first, that great men give the rest of mankind access to the moral or scientific truths they discover; hence they represent these truths to others (p. 14). Second, they have access to these truths because they themselves are a part of moral and physical nature; hence (oddly enough) they are representatives of it (p. 17). Third, such men are our proxies (hence, representatives) in the sense that we benefit from their work, see through their eyes, and so on. But a more fundamental idea, underlying the whole work, is that men are to be measured by the great ones among them, that they should and do take the great ones as models for mankind; hence it is the great, not the average, man who is representative (chap. 1, *passim*).

[82] Griffiths and Wollheim, *op. cit.*, p. 188.

[83] Francis Lieber, *Manual of Political Ethics* (Boston, 1839), II, 485–486; Parke Godwin, *Political Essays* (New York, 1856), pp. 40–42; Austin Ranney and Willmoore Kendall, *Democracy and the American Party System* (New York, 1956), p. 73. Cf. Gosnell, *op. cit.*, p. 148; Ernest Barker, *Greek Political Theory* (1913), p. 35, cited in John A. Fairlie, "The Nature of Political Representation," *American Political Science Review*, XXXIV (April, June, 1940), p. 459 ("A representative body must always be more of a filter than a phonograph . . ."); petition from the citizens of Paris cited in Loewenstein, *Volk und Parlament*, p. 21 (the representative's duty toward his constituents is "porte[r] leur voeu à l'Assemblée nationale").

[84] Mill, *Representative Government*, chap. 5, pp. 239–240.

[85] Griffiths and Wollheim, *op. cit.*, p. 212.

[86] Anthony Downs, *An Economic Theory of Democracy* (New York, 1957). For a fuller discussion of Downs' work, see Chap. 10, note 35, below.

[87] Downs, p. 89, and, more generally, pp. 88–91.

88 For an astute criticism of this point of view, see Hogan, *op. cit.*, pp. 108ff.

89 Gaines Post, "A Roman Legal Theory of Consent, *Quod Omnes Tangit* in Medieval Representation," *Wisconsin Law Review*, January, 1950, pp. 66–78; "*Plena Potestas* and Consent in Medieval Assemblies," *Traditio*, I (1943), 355–408; "Roman Law and Early Representation in Spain and Italy 1150–1250," *Speculum*, XVIII (1943), 211–232; Yves M.-J. Congar, "Quod Omnes Tangit ab Omnibus Tractari et Approbatur Debet," *Revue Historique de Droit Français et Etranger*, 4th ser., XXXVI (April–June, 1958), 210–259; J. G. Edward, "The *Plena Potestas* of English Parliamentary Representatives," *Oxford Essays in Medieval History Presented to H. E. Salter* (Oxford, 1934). For England cf. Helen M. Cam, "The Theory and Practice of Representation in Medieval England," *History*, XXXVIII (February, 1953), 11–26; and *Liberties and Communities in Medieval England* (Cambridge, England, 1944), esp. chap. 16. See also the Appendix, below.

90 In 1365, Thorpe, C. J., wrote in an opinion: "Though proclamation has not been made in the county, everyone is held to know a statute from the time it was made in parliament for as soon as parliament has decided anything, the law holds that everyone has knowledge of it, for parliament represents the body of all the realm. . . ." Y. B. 39 Edward III, Pas. pl. 3, fo. 7 (App. no. 8), cited in Stanley Bertram Chrimes, *English Constitutional Ideas* (Cambridge, England, 1936), p. 76. But, as Chrimes points out, this formulation "appears to be unique for many years." For one of its famous later statements, see Sir Thomas Smith, *De Republica Anglorum*, ed. L. Alston (Cambridge, 1906), Bk. II, chap. 1; this work was first published in 1583.

91 For a very early instance see Chrimes, *op. cit.*, p. 174: "I speke not to yowe that nowe represent the hele, but to them that ye come fro, whome for ther gret and confuse nombre and multitude nature can not wele suffre to assemble in oo place apt to the makynge of a lawe." Georg Jellinek shows that the same idea was known in Roman jurisprudence: *Allgemeine Staatslehre* (Berlin, 1905), pp. 555–556.

92 For American examples see Farrand, *op. cit.*, I, 132, 561. However, Carpenter exaggerates when he says, "in the Federal Convention representation was considered solely as a substitute for legislation by direct action of the people." *Op. cit.*, p. 39. Compare his view with that of Luepp; *op. cit.*, p. 435: "The Fathers of the Constitution had their own notion [of representation] . . . obviously the relation of guardian to ward." On the French Revolutionary period see Finer, *op. cit.*, p. 224; Loewenstein, *Volk und Parlament*, pp. 21, 184. For contemporary examples see Hogan, *op. cit.*, p. 108; Friedrich, Introduction to Hermens, *Democracy or Anarchy?*, p. xxii; Ernest Barker, *Essays on Government* (Oxford, 1951), p. 69; H. Belloc and G. K. Chesterton, *The Party System* (London, 1911), p. 16; George H. Sabine, "What Is the Matter with Representative Government?" in Christensen and Kirkpatrick, *op. cit.*, p. 406.

93 Farrand, *op. cit.*, I, 132; cf. Wilson, *op. cit.*, II, 14.

94 Adams, *op. cit.*, IV, 205; cf. 194–195.

95 *Op. cit.*, p. 6. Cf. a petition from the citizens of Paris of December 5, 1789, cited by Loewenstein, *Volk und Parlament*, p. 21: "Le grand nombre de citoyens ne permettant pas à chaque individu d'avoir son

représentant particulier aux États généraux, il est nécessaire que plusieurs citoyens aient un seul et même représentant, qui porte leur voeu à l'assemblée nationale." Note how the image is linked with the mechanical "carrying the vote."

96 Sterne, *op. cit.*, pp. 24–25, 50. For a linking of the view that representation is second best to democracy with the metaphor of the mirror, see Mayo, *An Introduction to Democratic Theory*, p. 101.

97 To some extent this difficulty is avoided by another metaphor, which I have found only in De Grazia, *Public and Republic*, p. 242: that representation may be considered "a simple matter of making government officials an exact *working model* of the mass of the people in action" (italics mine).

98 Eulau, *op. cit.*, p. 743.

99 Charles S. Hyneman, "Who Makes Our Laws?" *Political Science Quarterly*, LV (December, 1940), 556–581.

100 Griffiths and Wollheim, *op. cit.*, p. 190. Anyone who questions whether the insane man, the favorite example of political philosophers, has relevance to the realities of political life is referred to this item from the *San Francisco Chronicle*, November 10, 1960: "AROMA (France), Nov. 9 (UPI)—Mayor Pierre Echalon complained today that it is impossible to run this French village sensibly because mental cases outnumber sane citizens in the local electorate. Echalon told provincial authorities the population of Aroma consists of 148 normal villagers and 161 patients in a mental hospital, who through a quirk in the law enjoy full voting privileges. Provincial officials promised to 'look into the matter.' "

101 Griffiths and Wollheim, *op. cit.*, p. 190.

NOTES TO CHAPTER 5
(Pp. 92–111)

1 Carl J. Friedrich, *Constitutional Government and Democracy* (Boston, 1950), p. 267; cf. p. 357, and his "Representation and Constitutional Reform in Europe," *Western Political Quarterly*, I (June, 1948), 127.

2 Hiram Miller Stout, *British Government* (New York, 1953), p. 58; cf. A. Phillips Griffiths and Richard Wollheim, "How Can One Person Represent Another?" Aristotelian Society, Suppl. Vol. XXXIV (1960), 189; and notes 32 to 34, below.

3 Rudolf Smend, *Verfassung und Verfassungsrecht* (Munich, 1928), p. 28; my translation.

4 Maude V. Clarke, *Medieval Representation and Consent* (London, 1936), p. 278. She is explicitly followed by Alfred De Grazia, *Public and Republic* (New York, 1951), pp. 4–12; and Harold Foote Gosnell, *Democracy* (New York, 1948), pp. 145–147. Hans J. Wolff arrives at similar conclusions in *Organschaft und juristische Person* (Berlin, 1934), pp. 11–16.

5 Clarke, *op. cit.*, p. 279.

6 Wolff, *op. cit.*, pp. 12–13.

7 The series of distinctions is a difficult one, and I offer my own ideas with considerable hesitation. Other useful attempts are made by George Ferguson, *Signs and Symbols in Christian Art* (New York, 1954), p. xii;

Griffiths and Wollheim, *op. cit.*, pp. 188–189; Susan Langer, *Philosophy in a New Key* (1942), chap. 3 *et passim*; Gerhard Leibholz, *Das Wesen der Repräsentation* (Berlin, 1929), pp. 35–36; Ferdinand de Saussure, *Course in General Linguistics*, trans. Wade Baskin (New York, 1959), pp. 65–70; William York Tindall, *The Literary Symbol* (New York, 1955), pp. 15–21 *et passim*; Wolff, *op. cit.*, p. 21. I am indebted to all these discussions, although, I differ with them on some points. Tindall and Wolff are probably the most astute.

[8] *Oxford English Dictionary.*

[9] Wolff, *op. cit.*, p. 21.

[10] This and the following information is from the *Oxford English Dictionary*. Tindall's definition from Webster includes the phrase, "but not by intentional resemblance." *Op. cit.*, p. 5; cf. p. 12.

[11] Saussure, *op. cit.*, p. 68.

[12] Tindall discusses the difference in treatment accorded to dream symbols by Freud and by Jung. *Op. cit.*, pp. 65–66.

[13] Langer, *op. cit.*, p. 117.

[14] Tindall, *op. cit.*, pp. 41–43.

[15] *Ibid.*, p. 6.

[16] See for example *ibid.*, pp. 6, 11, 16–20, 31; Langer, *op. cit.*, chap. 3; Ferguson, *op. cit.*, p. xii; Saussure, *op. cit.*, p. 68. Leibholz, on the contrary, takes the arbitrary symbol as definitive, and hence finds symbols which embody value to be exceptional cases, approximating "true representation." *Das Wesen der Repräsentation*, pp. 35–36.

[17] Langer, *op. cit.*, p. 49.

[18] Tindall, *op. cit.*, pp. 19–20.

[19] *Ibid.*, p. 6. The distinction I am suggesting between symbolizing and representing is similar to that found by Barrows between symbolism and allegory: "while allegory establishes a definite and unmistakable connection between the abstract idea and its physical embodiment, symbolism makes no such point-to-point connection but merely suggests that such a relationship between seen and unseen, between abstract and concrete, is present, leaving it to our imagination to interpret the exact nature of the relationship." Herbert Barrows, *Reading the Short Story* (Boston, 1959), p. 14. Here again "symbol" is restricted to the sense of "symbolizing" and does not include arbitrary symbols.

[20] Griffiths and Wollheim, *op. cit.*, p. 189. The conventional symbol is not the focus of attitudes, but it *is* the object of actions, e.g., mathematical manipulations.

[21] Langer, *op. cit.*, p. 42; italics mine.

[22] Friedrich, *Constitutional Government*, p. 267.

[23] Wolff, *op. cit.*, p. 75; Friedrich Glum, *Der deutsche und der französische Reichswirtschaftsrat* (Berlin, 1929), p. 28; Carl Schmitt, *Verfassungslehre* (Berlin, 1954), p. 209.

[24] De Grazia, *Public and Republic*, p. 3.

[25] See for example, Friedrich, "Representation and Constitutional Reform," p. 127; De Grazia, *Public and Republic*, pp. 6–11; Gosnell, *op. cit.*, pp. 136–137; Tindall, *op. cit.*, pp. 12, 167; Clarke, *op. cit.*, p. 290.

[26] Clinton Rossiter, *The American Presidency* (1956), p. 11. Cf. Glum, *op. cit.*, p. 27.

[27] Smend, *Verfassung und Verfassungsrecht* (Munich, 1928), p. 28.

[28] Glum, *op. cit.*, p. 30. Accordingly (alas!) the embassy is a suitable place for window-breaking and demonstrations, if one strongly disapproves of a nation's policy.

[29] De Grazia, *Public and Republic*, p. 175.

[30] Ernest Barker, *Essays on Government* (Oxford, 1951), p. 4.

[31] De Grazia, *Public and Republic*, p. 175.

[32] John C. Ranney and Gwendolen M. Carter, *The Major Foreign Powers* (New York, 1949), p. 159.

[33] *Ibid.*, p. 162; cf. p. 166.

[34] John A. Fairlie, "The Nature of Political Representation," *American Political Science Review*, XXXIV (April, 1940), 237.

[35] Avery Leiserson, *Administrative Regulation* (Chicago, 1942), p. 100; in other parts of the book, however, he takes a different view. See also Glum, *op. cit.*, p. 28; Leibholz, *Das Wesen der Repräsentation*, pp. 140ff; John P. Plamenatz, *Consent, Freedom and Political Obligation* (London, 1938), p. 12; Schmitt, *Verfassungslehre*, p. 209; Wolff, *op. cit.*, p. 75 (but cf. p. 29); Martin Drath, *Die Entwicklung der Volksrepräsentation* (Bad Homburg, 1954), pp. 24–27.

[36] Gosnell, *op. cit.*, p. 130; De Grazia, *Public and Republic*, p. 4.

[37] *Public and Republic*, p. 3.

[38] *Ibid.*, p. 4.

[39] Friedrich, "Representation and Constitutional Reform," p. 127.

[40] F. A. Hermens, *Democracy or Anarchy?* (Notre Dame, Ind., 1941), p. 4. Cf. Bernard J. Diggs, "Practical Representation," *Representation* (Nomos X), eds. J. Roland Pennock and John Chapman (New York, in press); Josiah Royce, *War and Insurance* (New York, 1914).

[41] Hermens, *Democracy or Anarchy?* p. 4; James Hogan, *Election and Representation* (1945), pp. 181–182. See discussion in the Appendix, below.

[42] Wolff, *op. cit.*, pp. 84–85.

[43] Leibholz, *Das Wesen der Repräsentation*, p. 42.

[44] De Grazia, *Public and Republic*, p. 3.

[45] Gosnell, *op. cit.*, p. 133.

[46] For example in Wolff, *op. cit.*, p. 70; Leibholz, *Das Wesen de Repräsentation*, pp. 76, 145, 166–167, 171; Smend, *op. cit.*, pp. 25–27, 42, 94.

[47] Smend, *op. cit.*, p. 42.

[48] Clarke, *op. cit.*, p. 290.

[49] W. D. Handcock, "What Is Represented in Representative Government?" *Philosophy*, XXII (July, 1947), 107.

[50] René de Visme Williamson, "The Fascist Concept of Representation," *Journal of Politics*, III (February, 1941), 39.

[51] De Grazia, *Public and Republic*, p. 20.

[52] Frances Fergusson, *The Idea of a Theater* (Princeton, 1949), pp. 89–92.

[53] Williamson, *op. cit.*, p. 35.

[54] Gentile, *Che Cosa e il Fascismo?* (1925), p. 91, cited in De Grazia, *Public and Republic*, p. 20.

[55] Henry B. Mayo, *An Introduction to Democratic Theory* (New York, 1960), p. 97. See also Williamson, *op. cit.*, pp. 35ff.; Fergusson, *op. cit.*, pp. 89–92; Leibholz, *Das Wesen der Repräsentation*, pp. 145, 190 (where further references on fascist theory may also be found).

[56] Otto Koellreutter, *Grundriss der allgemeinen Staatslehre* (Tübingen, 1933), p. 113.

[57] *Ibid.*, p. 112; translation mine.

[58] Smend, *op. cit.*, pp. 32–33, 38–39.

[59] Hogan, *op. cit.*, p. 144; cf. Gerhard Leibholz, *Strukturprobleme der modernen Demokratie* (Karlsruhe, 1958), p. 10.

[60] Ernest Barker, *Reflections on Government* (1942), p. 377; cf. Francis W. Coker and Carlton C. Rodee, "Representation," *Encyclopaedia of the Social Sciences*, XIII (1935), 312, who say of the fascist system: "no attempt is made to secure any real popular representation."

[61] Heinz Eulau et al., "The Role of the Representative," *American Political Science Review*, LIII (September, 1959), 743.

NOTES TO CHAPTER 6
(Pp. 112–143)

[1] James Wilson, *Works* (Chicago, 1896), I, 389: "The chain may consist of one link, or of more links than one, but it should always be sufficiently strong and discernible," (cf. p. 533). See also Hans J. Wolff, *Organschaft und juristische Person* (Berlin, 1934), p. 37; James Hogan, *Election and Representation* (1945), pp. 116–118; Gerhard Leibholz, *Das Wesen der Repräsentation* (Berlin, 1929), p. 153; Léon Duguit, *Traité de Droit Constitutionel* (Paris, 1928), II, 549; Wilder W. Crane, Jr., "Do Representatives Represent?" *Journal of Politics*, XXII (May 1960), 295; Ben A. Arneson, "Do Representatives Represent?" *National Municipal Review*, XVI (December, 1927), 751.

[2] As in Charles E. Merriam, *Systematic Politics* (Chicago, 1945), p. 139.

[3] The phrase occurs in W. D. Handcock, "What is Represented in Representative Government?" *Philosophy*, XXII (July, 1947), 107. See also Elie Halévy, *The Growth of Philosophical Radicalism* (Boston, 1955), p. 122; Simon Sterne, *Representative Government* (Philadelphia, 1871), pp. 44–45; Gerhard Leibholz, *Das Wesen der Repräsentation* (Berlin, 1929), p. 104.

[4] Avery Leiserson, "Problems of Representation," *Journal of Politics*, XI (August, 1949), 570.

[5] Hogan, *op. cit.*, p. 121.

[6] For example, according to Simon Sterne, "Representation," *Lalor's Cyclopedia of Political Science*, III, 581, cited by Robert Luce, *Legislative Principles* (Boston, 1930), p. 199.

[7] "The Supreme Court of the United States would certainly seem to most people less representative if it were elected by the people. The reason for this is that all representation involves ideas; for only through an idea can the making present of one thing or person by another be conceived." Carl J. Friedrich, "Representation," *Encyclopaedia Britannica*, XIX (1960), 163; cf. his *Constitutional Government and Democracy* (Boston, 1950), pp. 260, 267.

[8] Arthur F. Bentley, *The Process of Government* (Evanston, Ill., 1949), p. 393.

[9] Robert M. MacIver, *The Modern State* (Oxford, 1926), pp. 372–373. MacIver sees the judge less as a focus of group pressures than as being guided "by the spirit of the code and of a great profession trained in its study."

[10] Leibholz, *Das Wesen der Repräsentation*, pp. 38–39. Cf. Carl Schmitt, *The Necessity of Politics* (London, 1931), p. 76.

[11] Niccolò Machiavelli, *The Prince*, chap. 16. I use the Max Lerner edition, *The Prince and the Discourses* (New York, 1940), pp. 57–60. Machiavelli's insight on this point must be understood in the light of his larger views on the "economy of violence"; see Sheldon S. Wolin, *Politics and Vision* (Boston, 1960), chap. 7, esp. pp. 220–228.

[12] Cf. Francis Lieber: "Every one feels his responsibility far more distinctly as a trustee than otherwise. Let a man in an excited crowd be suddenly singled out and made a member of a committee to reflect and resolve for the crowd, and he will feel the difference in an instant." *On Civil Liberty and Self-Government*, p. 167, cited in Luce, *op. cit.*, p. 494.

[13] Francis Luepp, "Do Our Representatives Represent?" *Atlantic Monthly*, CXIV (October, 1944), 435.

[14] Luce, *op. cit.*, p. 434.

[15] Harold Foote Gosnell, *Democracy* (New York, 1948), p. 146. Cf. Samuel Bailey, *The Rationale of Political Representation* (London, 1835), p. 122; Helen M. Cam, "Theory and Practice of Representation," *History*, XXXVIII (February, 1953), 18–19.

[16] The etymological information throughout this chapter is from the *Oxford English Dictionary* except where otherwise indicated.

[17] *Words and Phrases* (St. Paul, Minn., 1955), vol. 2A, pp. 453, 570; vol. 37, p. 63.

[18] *Ibid.*, vol. 2A, pp. 539–544.

[19] *Ibid.*, pp. 455, 578–582, for this entire paragraph.

[20] *Ibid.*, vol. 37, pp. 61–63, for this and the following paragraphs. Cf. vol. 2A, pp. 469, 488–489, 512–522, 578.

[21] *The New Yorker*, XXXVII (April 29, 1961), 152. "VIENNA, Apr. 10 (AP).—A United Nations conference on diplomatic law has decided that maids and chauffeurs must not represent foreign embassies in the absence of diplomatic personnel.—*The Herald Tribune*."

[22] But Ewart Lewis, *Medieval Political Ideas* (New York, 1954), p. 101, cites Blackstone to the effect that in England the people "debate . . . by representation."

[23] Paul Ziff, *Semantic Analysis* (Ithaca, 1960), p. 180.

[24] Henry J. Ford, *Representative Government* (New York, 1924), p. 148.

[25] Ernest Barker, *Essays on Government* (Oxford, 1951), p. 56.

[26] For example, John Stuart Mill, *Representative Government*, chap. 12, p. 318, in *Utilitarianism, Liberty and Representative Government* (London, 1947); Bailey, *op. cit.*, pp. 72, 143–145.

[27] Frederick William Maitland, "Trust and Corporation," *Selected Essays*, eds. H. D. Hazeltine *et al.* (Cambridge, England, 1936), p. 120.

[28] William R. Anson, *Principles of the English Law of Contract* (Oxford, 1959), p. 511; *Words and Phrases*, vol. 2A, pp. 456–457, 475; Wolff, *op. cit.*, p. 6.

[29] Ford, *op. cit.*, pp. 147–148; but cf. pp. 156–157.

[30] "Thoughts on the Cause of the Present Discontents" (1770), *Burke's Politics* (New York, 1949), pp. 27–28.

[31] For example see Robert M. Hutchins, "The Theory of Oligarchy," *The Thomist*, V (January, 1943), 64. Hogan, *op. cit.*, p. 161, apparently takes his cue from Hutchins' article.

[32] "Speech on Fox's East India Bill" (1783), *Burke's Politics*, p. 257; italics mine.

[33] "To whom, then would I make the East India Company accountable? Why to Parliament to be sure; to Parliament from whom their trust was derived. . . ." *Ibid.* Burke elsewhere makes it explicit that king, Lords, and Commons "in their several public capacities can never be called to an account for their conduct." "Reflections on the Revolution in France" (1790), *ibid.*, p. 293. He hints, however, at an accountability to God. *Ibid.*, pp. 314–315.

[34] *Words and Phrases*, vol. 2A, pp. 441, 456–457, 470, 590–593. The same for a guardian. *Ibid.*, pp. 485, 537.

[35] Thus it is misleading to argue that "what we want in legislation as in other trusts, are honest fiduciaries, men who will perform their duties according to our wishes." Parke Godwin, *Political Essays* (New York, 1856), pp. 41–42.

[36] See for example, Luepp, *op. cit.*, p. 434; John A Fairlie, "The Nature of Political Representation," *American Political Science Review*, XXXIV (April, 1940), 237.

[37] The legal situation is complex. There are some legal actions a guardian can take in his ward's name, and others he cannot. Sometimes a ward is liable for torts committed by the guardian, but generally he is not. In this respect a guardian is somewhere between a trustee (whose beneficiary is never liable) and an agent (whose principal very frequently is). *Words and Phrases*, vol. 2A, p. 537.

[38] *Op. cit.*, pp. 4, 7–10.

[39] Fairlie, *op. cit.*, p. 247; Harvey Walker, *The Legislative Process* (New York, 1948), p. 128.

[40] This distinction is pointed out by Georg Jellinek, in *Allgemeine Staatslehre* (Berlin, 1905), p. 568: "Der Stellvertreter des Reichskanzlers ist wegen der von ihm innerhalb seiner Stellvertretungsbefügnisse vollzogenen Akte nicht dem Reichskanzler, sondern dem Bundesrate und Reichstage verantwortlich. Dem Richter, der im Namen des Monarchen Recht spricht, kann der Monarch keinen auf die Rechtsprechung bezüglichen Dienstbefehl erteilen." See also Leibholz, *Das Wesen der Repräsentation*, p. 160; Harold D. Lasswell and Abraham Kaplan, *Power and Society* (New Haven, 1950), p. 162; *Words and Phrases*, vol. 2A, p. 525.

[41] *Op. cit.*, p. 4.

[42] Bernard J. Diggs, "Practical Representation," in *Representation* (Nomos X), eds. Roland Pennock and John Chapman (New York, in press).

[43] *Remarks on the Use and Abuse of Some Political Terms* (Oxford, 1877), p. 104.

[44] Discussions of the proper role for a representative often overlook the fact that he can take orders or instructions only if his constituents have "a voice"—are organized to instruct him. Accordingly, the historical instances of bound delegates usually occur where there is some sort of government or organization in the constituency that tries to get the representative to obey its wishes. This is very evident in the American Senate, where the practice of instructions was common until Senators became directly elected, and then largely disappeared. James Wilford Garner, *Political Science and Government* (New York, 1928), pp. 670–671; Francis

Lieber, *Manual of Political Ethics* (Boston, 1839), II, 481, 521; Luce, *op. cit.*, chap. 20; Alfred De Grazia, *Public and Republic* (New York, 1951), pp. 125–126.

[45] Thomas Hare, *The Election of Representatives* (London, 1873), pp. xxxv–xxxvi; cf. Hogan, *op. cit.*, p. 141.

[46] *Ibid.*

[47] Diggs, cited in note 42, above.

[48] See for example, Macaulay cited in Lieber, *op. cit.*, II, 555n; Hans Kelsen, *Vom Wesen und Wert der Demokratie* (Tübingen, 1929), p. 29.

[49] Gosnell, *op. cit.*, p. 146.

[50] Bailey, *op. cit.*, p. 122; cf. Cam, "Theory and Practice of Representation," pp. 18–19.

[51] Gosnell, *op. cit.*, p. 146. Cf. F. H. Knight, *Intelligence and Democratic Action* (Cambridge, 1960), pp. 185–186; Fairlie, *op. cit.*, p. 237; Luce, *op. cit.*, p. 434.

[52] Knight, *op. cit.*, pp. 185–186. Cf. Bailey, *op. cit.*, pp. 77–80; Francis W. Coker and Carlton C. Rodee, "Representation," *Encyclopaedia of the Social Sciences*, XIII (1935), 312; Gosnell, *op. cit.*, p. 146; Macaulay cited in Lieber, *op. cit.*, II, 555n; John A. Schumpeter, *Capitalism, Socialism and Democracy* (New York, 1947), pp. 250–251.

[53] Coker and Rodee, *op. cit.*, p. 312.

[54] Bailey, *op. cit.*, p. 124; cf. Macaulay cited in Lieber, *op. cit.*, II, 555n.

[55] Bailey, *op. cit.*, pp. 77–80.

[56] Knight, *op. cit.*, pp. 185–186.

[57] Gosnell, *op. cit.*, p. 146.

[58] *Ibid.*, pp. 146–147.

[59] Charles S. Hyneman has suggested that the lawyer so often becomes a member of the legislature just because he is (in both functions) our "professional representor." "Who Makes Our Laws?" *Political Science Quarterly*, LV (December, 1940), 564–569.

[60] With regard to private detectives, at least, I can submit expert testimony. In Rex Stout's "Method Three for Murder," in *Three at Wolfe's Door* (New York, 1960), p. 83, a young lady in the office of the famous sleuth accosts him thus: "Her head swung around. 'You're Nero Wolfe? You're even bigger.' She didn't say bigger than what. 'I'm Judy Bram. Are you representing my friend Mira Holt?' His eyes on her were half closed. ' "Representing" is not the word, Miss Bram. I'm a detective, not a lawyer. . . !' "

[61] A. Phillips Griffiths and Richard Wollheim, "How Can One Person Represent Another?" *Aristotelian Society*, Suppl. Vol. XXXIV (1960), 195–196.

[62] *Ibid.*, p. 196. Hence Griffiths argues (p. 191) that "ascriptive representation and representation of interests are exclusively *by* persons" because they imply "action on the part of the representative and of the principal." He thus fails to recognize that interests can also be symbolized, and that interests themselves cannot act. But he is quite right that where representing means substantive "acting for," the representative must be animate.

[63] Joseph Tussman, *Obligation and the Body Politic* (New York, 1960), pp. 12–13.

Notes to Chapter 7
(Pp. 144–167)

[1] Carl J. Friedrich, "Representation and Constitutional Reform," *Western Political Quarterly*, I (June, 1948), 127: "representation, and more particularly political representation, is associated with institutional arrangements which are intended to insure that the 'representative' participates in whatever authority he is wielding on behalf of those he represents in such a way as to permit one to say that he acted 'in their stead,' or 'as they would have acted, had they been able to participate themselves.' "

James Hogan, *Election and Representation* (1945), p. 141, says: "the representative acting as if the constituent himself were present." Talleyrand-Perigord in the French National Assembly of 1789, cited in Karl Loewenstein, *Volk und Parlament* (Munich, 1922), p. 193, said that the deputy is, "l'homme que le bailliage charge de vouloir en son nom, mais de vouloir comme il voudrait lui-même, s'il pouvait se transporter au rendez-vous général." And Senator William Maclay of Pennsylvania, cited in Robert Luce, *Legislative Principles* (Boston, 1930), p. 462: "Were my constituents here, what would they do?"

[2] For example, Senator Maclay cited in Luce, p. 462.

[3] For example, Richard Overton, "A Remonstrance of Many Thousand Citizens" (1646), *Leveller Manifestoes of the Puritan Revolution*, ed. Don M. Wolfe (New York, 1944), p. 113.

[4] See for example, Luce, *op. cit.*, p. 507; Lewis Anthony Dexter, "The Representative and His District," *Human Organization*, XVI (Spring, 1957), 3.

[5] Henry J. Ford, *Representative Government* (New York, 1924), pp. 147–148. Cf. Madison's views and those of James Wilson, cited in John A. Fairlie, "The Nature of Political Representation," *American Political Science Review*, XXXIV (April, 1940), 243–244. This argument is often linked with the view that political questions are too complex and difficult for public opinion to cope with. See for example Sir Henry Maine, *Popular Government*, pp. 89–92, cited in Luce, *op. cit.*, p. 492.

[6] "Speech to the Electors of Bristol" (1774), *Burke's Politics* (New York, 1949), p. 115; cf. Hogan, *op. cit.*, p. 109; T. D. Woolsey, *Political Science*, I, 296, cited in Luce, *op. cit.*, p. 479.

[7] This point is often made by Burke. See also Loewenstein, *Volk und Parlament*, pp. 193–194; James Wilford Garner, *Political Science and Government* (New York, 1928), p. 666.

[8] This argument is common among the German theorists: Gerhard Leibholz, *Das Wesen der Repräsentation* (Berlin, 1929), pp. 73, 92–93, 140, 166; Hans J. Wolff, *Organschaft und juristische Person* (Berlin, 1934), pp. 54–60.

[9] For instance, Howard Lee McBain, *The Living Constitution* (New York, 1948), p. 208; Anthony Downs, *An Economic Theory of Democracy* (New York, 1957), pp. 89–90; Garner, *op. cit.*, p. 665.

[10] Gerhard Leibholz, *Strukturprobleme der modernen Demokratie*

(Karlsruhe, 1958), pp. 75–76 *et passim*; Hans Kelsen, *Vom Wesen und Wert der Demokratie* (Tübingen, 1929), pp. 21–22. This view is linked with the modern doctrine of the mandate—the obligation of the majority party to abide by voter decisions on the issues in an election; see Cecil S. Emden, *The People and the Constitution* (Oxford, 1956).

[11] Leibholz, *Das Wesen der Repräsentation*, pp. 98–101, 104, 113–114; Simon Sterne, *Representative Government* (Philadelphia, 1871), pp. 51–61.

[12] For instance, Carl J. Friedrich, *Constitutional Government and Democracy* (Boston, 1950), p. 263; or William Howard Taft, *Popular Government*, p. 62, cited in Luce, *op. cit.*, p. 495.

[13] For instance, Jeremy Bentham, "Constitutional Code," p. 44, cited in Samuel Bailey, *The Rationale of Political Representation* (London, 1835), p. 142. Another compromise position was suggested by Abraham Lincoln as a candidate for the Illinois legislature in 1836: "If elected, I shall consider the whole people of Sangamon my constituents, as well those that oppose as those that support me. While acting as their representative I shall be governed by their will on all subjects upon which I have the means of knowing what their will is, and upon all others I shall do what my own judgment teaches me will best advance their interests." Cited in Luce, *op. cit.*, p. 471.

[14] For instance in Heinz Eulau *et al.*, "The Role of the Representative," *American Political Science Review*, LIII (September, 1959), 748; John C. Wahlke and Heinz Eulau, eds., *Legislative Behavior* (Glencoe, Ill., 1959), p. 6.

[15] The electoral college is not strictly a case in point, since the boundness of electors is a matter of state law, and a few states do not bind their electors.

[16] Wahlke and Eulau, *op. cit.*, pp. 179–189; Dexter, "The Representative"; Frank Bonilla, "When Is Petition 'Pressure'?" *Public Opinion Quarterly*, XX (Spring, 1956), 39–48; Eulau, *op. cit.*; L. E. Gleeck, "96 Congressmen Make Up Their Minds," *Public Opinion Quarterly*, IV (March, 1940), 3–24; George W. Hartmann, "Judgments of State Legislators Concerning Public Opinion," *Journal of Social Psychology*, XXI (February, 1945), 105–114; John C. Wahlke *et al.*, "American State Legislators' Role Orientation toward Pressure Groups," *Journal of Politics*, XXII (May, 1960), 203–227; Charles O. Jones, "Representation in Congress," *American Political Science Review*, LV (December, 1961), 358–367.

[17] Wahlke and Eulau, *op. cit.*, pp. 121–149, 197–217; Duncan MacRae, Jr., *Dimensions of Congressional Voting* (Berkeley and Los Angeles, 1958); Julius Turner, *Party and Constituency: Pressures on Congress* (Baltimore, 1951).

[18] Hadley Cantril, *Public Opinion 1935–46* (Princeton, 1951), p. 133. These questions were asked in the surveys Cantril reports: "Do you believe that a Congressman should vote on any question as the majority of his constituents desire or vote according to his own judgment?" "Should members of Congress vote according to their own best judgment or according to the way the people in their districts feel?" "In cases when a Congressman's opinion is different from that of the majority of

the people in his district, do you think he should usually vote according
to his own best judgment, or according to the way the majority of his
district feels?" Results ranged from two-thirds in favor of constituency
feelings to more than half in favor of the representative's judgment.

19 H. Belloc and G. K. Chesterton, *The Party System* (London, 1911),
p. 17.

20 Lord Brougham, *Works*, XI, 35–36, cited in Luce, *op. cit.*, p. 442.
Cf. Hogan, *op. cit.*, p. 112; Emden, *op. cit.*, p. 4; Leibholz, *Strukturprobleme*, pp. 21, 145.

21 The electoral college is an unusually popular example in this context, perhaps because it was originally intended to function very differently from the way it does, thus providing a seeming contrast in extremes of representation. See Tussman, "Political Theory," pp. 117–
118; Luce, *op. cit.*, p. 211; Arthur T. Hadley, *Standards of Public
Morality* (New York, 1907), p. 106; Guy C. Field, *Political Theory*
(London, 1956), pp. 151–152.

22 *Op. cit.*, p. 17.

23 Turner sees the paradoxical duality, but considers it characteristic
of American politics rather than of the concept of representation. *Op.
cit.*, p. 164.

24 A. Phillips Griffiths and Richard Wollheim, "How Can One Person
Represent Another?" Aristotelian Society, Suppl. Vol. XXXIV (1960),
188.

25 Cf. Wolff, *op. cit.*, pp. 46–47.

26 The main expression that is ambiguous as between these two senses
is "to have (or possess) an interest." Writers who attempt to use it as
a label for one of the two senses get into difficulties. For example, Harold D. Lasswell and Abraham Kaplan, *Power and Society* (New Haven,
1950), p. 24; Charles William Cassinelli, Jr., "Some Reflections on the
Concept of the Public Interest," *Ethics*, LXIX (October 1958), 48. I am
not sure whether the two senses are sufficiently distinct to be called two
meanings. See Paul Ziff, *Semantic Analysis* (Ithaca, 1960), pp. 176–180.

27 Etymologically, the original meanings of "disinterested" and "uninterested" have been almost exactly reversed. "Uninterested" at first
meant impartial, and "disinterested" meant either impartial or indifferent.
But by the end of the eighteenth century the latter meaning of "disinterested" had become obsolete, and that function had been taken over by
"uninterested." Perhaps this development accounts for our tendency to
confuse the two.

28 *Oxford English Dictionary*.

29 It is not uncommon for a word to mean both the substance and the
outward appearance of a state or condition; thus "deliberately" means
not only "with deliberation" but also "*as if* with deliberation." J. L. Austin,
Philosophical Papers (Oxford, 1960), p. 147.

30 See for example, John Dewey, *Interest as Related to Will* (Chicago,
1899); Douglas Fryer, *The Measurement of Interests in Relation to
Human Adjustment* (New York, 1931); Nathaniel L. Gage, *Judging Interests from Expressive Behavior* (Washington, D. C., 1952); J. P. Guilford *et al.*, "A Factor Analysis Study of Human Interests," *Psychological
Monographs: General and Applied*, LXVIII (1954), no. 4.

31 The only reference to the other sense of the word I have found in

the psychological literature is a footnote by Dewey rejecting the other sense as morally inferior: "It is true that the term interest is also used in a definitely disparaging sense. We speak of interest as opposed to principle, of self-interest as a motive to action with regards only one's personal advantage; but these are neither the only nor the controlling sense in which the term is used. It may fairly be questioned whether this is anything but a narrowing or degrading of the legitimate sense of the term." *Interest*, p. 13n.

[32] The distinction is drawn in this way by Fryer, *op. cit.* Other ways of distinguishing "subjective" from "objective" interests are suggested by Dewey in psychology and MacIver in sociology. Dewey says that what one finds interesting is both subjective (because being interested is an internal, psychological state) and objective (because one is interested in an object, something outside oneself). *Interest*, pp. 13–15. MacIver says that the objective interest of a group is the goal or object for which it strives, and that this must be distinguished from its attitude toward that object. Wealth might be a group's objective interest, cupidity its attitude. MacIver rejects subjective interests, which he apparently equates with attitudes in this sense. Robert M. MacIver, *Society* (New York, 1931), pp. 48–49; "Interests," *Encyclopaedia of the Social Sciences*, VIII (1935), 147. For a radically different treatment of "interest" and of the "objective"-"subjective" distinction, cf. Albion W. Small, *General Sociology* (Chicago, 1905), pp. 372–396, 425–442, esp. p. 435.

[33] Christian Bay, *The Structure of Freedom* (Stanford, 1958), p. 97. See also John P. Plamenatz, *Consent, Freedom and Political Obligation* (London, 1938), pp. 11, 159; but cf. his later views in "Interests," *Political Studies*, II (February, 1954), 1–8.

[34] Errol E. Harris, "Political Power," *Ethics*, LXVIII (October, 1957), 2.

[35] Lasswell and Kaplan, *op. cit.*, p. 23.

[36] Plamenatz, "Interests," pp. 1–2, 4, 6; but cf. his earlier views in *Consent*, pp. 11, 159.

[37] John Dickinson, "Social Order and Political Authority," *American Political Science Review*, XXIII (May, 1929), 295, cited in Frank J. Sorauf, "The Public Interest Reconsidered," *Journal of Politics*, XIX (November, 1957), 635.

[38] MacIver, *Society*, p. 49.

[39] *Ibid.*, p. 158; and more generally, pp. 152–171. The same difficulty in transition is found in Avery Leiserson, *Administrative Regulation* (Chicago, 1942), pp. 5–6.

[40] The potential for confusion here is remarkable, as in this passage: "It is because perception is so conditioned by involvement that we can dispense with a politics of disinterest as opposed to a politics of interest and can assume that every action a man takes in politics must be an interested action. All groups in which he participates are interest groups in the true sense that he is interested in them. . . . Some hold his interest more than others." Alfred De Grazia, "The Nature and Prospects of Political Interest Groups," American Academy of Political and Social Science, *Annals*, Vol. 319 (September, 1958), p. 115. See also Cassinelli, "Some Reflections," p. 48.

[41] Cassinelli, "Some Reflections," p. 51.

⁴² See note 34 above. The same is true of Dickinson and Plamenatz. Cf. John Dewey, *The Public and Its Problems* (New York, 1927), p. 27, where an interest is *"generated"* only when people become *aware* that some matter concerns them.

⁴³ David B. Truman, *The Governmental Process* (New York, 1959), p. 34.

⁴⁴ *Ibid.*; Lasswell and Kaplan, *op. cit.*, p. 23.

⁴⁵ Arthur F. Bentley, *The Process of Government* (Evanston, Ill., 1949), pp. 211, 214. Cf. Cassinelli, "The Concept of Representative Government," (unpubl. thesis, 1950), pp. 22–25; Leiserson, *Administrative Regulation*, pp. 5–6; MacIver, *Society*, pp. 49, 152–171.

⁴⁶ Cf. T. V. Smith, *The Promise of American Politics* (Chicago, 1936), p. 163; or consult Machiavelli, who tells us that "where men's lives and fortunes are at stake they are not all insane," cited in Lasswell and Kaplan, *op. cit.*, p. 24.

⁴⁷ Harold Foote Gosnell, *Democracy* (New York, 1948), pp. 134–135.

⁴⁸ Lewis Anthony Dexter makes a cogent criticism of some public opinion polls on this score, that they tend to elicit an "opinion" from people who might never otherwise utter one, or even think of themselves as having an opinion on the subject. "Candidates Must Make the Issues and Give Them Meaning," *Public Opinion Quarterly*, XIX (Winter, 1955–56), 408–414.

⁴⁹ In an address to his constituents in 1812, cited in Emden, *op. cit.*, p. 27.

⁵⁰ The modern relativistic reader may feel that there is no such thing as "being a good representative—period"; that there can only be "being a good representative in your own eyes," "being a good representative in your constituents' eyes," "being a good representative in Smith's eyes," and so on. This view seems to me incorrect. Each of these expressions means something different and is appropriate for use on slightly different occasions—the first no less than the rest. We do sometimes criticize a man for representing his constituency badly even though he has been reëlected and his constituency is pleased with him. And it makes sense to do so.

⁵¹ Austin Ranney and Willmoore Kendall, *Democracy and the American Party System* (New York, 1956), p. 74.

⁵² See note 18 above. Compare these questions with the more sophisticated ones asked by Hartmann of legislators, and the kinds of answers he got. Hartmann, *op. cit.* See also Jones, *op. cit.*, p. 365: "Some of the more detailed analyses of the process of representation were offered by senior members who replied that representation on policy was not a simple choice between independent judgment on the one hand and constituency wishes on the other."

NOTES TO CHAPTER 8
(Pp. 168–189)

¹ James Hogan, *Election and Representation* (1945), p. 157.

² Philip Arnold Gibbons, *Ideas of Political Representation in Parliament 1651–1832* (Oxford, 1914), p. 34.

³ Robert M. Hutchins, "The Theory of Oligarchy," *The Thomist*, V

(January, 1943), 63, 78; cf. Robert Luce, *Legislative Principles* (Boston, 1930), pp. 199, 313.

[4] "Reflections on the Revolution in France" (1790), *Burke's Politics* (New York, 1949), p. 301; cf. Francis P. Canavan, *The Political Reason of Edmund Burke* (Durham, N. C., 1960), pp. 98, 143.

[5] Without a natural aristocracy "there is no nation." Such an aristocracy is not merely hereditary; its elite quality rests on an unbringing for responsibility, perfected over generations. "Appeal from the New to the Old Whigs" (1791), *Burke's Politics*, pp. 397–398. Without a natural aristocracy, "every dominion must become a mere despotism." Cited in Canavan, *op. cit.*, p. 98.

[6] "Appeal," *Burke's Politics*, p. 397; Canavan, *op. cit.*, p. 143. Cf. "Reflections," *Burke's Politics*, p. 328; Hogan, *op. cit.*, p. 159; Ernest Barker, *Essays on Government* (Oxford, 1951), p. 199.

[7] "Appeal," *Burke's Politics*, p. 393.

[8] Samuel H. Beer, "The Representation of Interests in British Government: Historical Background," *American Political Science Review*, LI (September, 1957), 616.

[9] Barker, *Essays on Government*, p. 230. Cf. Charles Parkin, *The Moral Basis of Burke's Political Thought* (Cambridge, England, 1956), p. 38.

[10] "Reflections," *Burke's Politics*, pp. 305, 316; Canavan, *op. cit.*, p. 143.

[11] Beer, *op. cit.*, p. 616. Cf. Canavan, *op. cit.*, p. 148; "Speech to the Electors of Bristol" (1774), *Burke's Politics*, p. 116, and "Appeal," *ibid.*, p. 392.

[12] "Speech to the Electors," *ibid.*, p. 115; cf. Canavan, *op. cit.*, p. 94.

[13] "Appeal," *Burke's Politics*, p. 393.

[14] "Reflections," cited in Barker, *Essays on Government*, p. 230. See also "Appeal," *Burke's Politics*, p. 395: "Political problems do not primarily concern truth or falsehood. They relate to good or evil. What in the result is likely to produce evil is politically false; that which is productive of good, politically true." Besides, the reduction of government to a matter of will destroys political stability: "The moment will is set above reason and justice, in any community, a great question may arise in sober minds, in what part or portion of the community that dangerous domination of will may be the least mischievously placed." Cited in Barker, *Essays on Government*, p. 230.

[15] "Speech to the Electors," *Burke's Politics*, p. 115.

[16] Cited in Canavan, *op. cit.*, p. 156.

[17] "Speech to the Electors," *Burke's Politics*, p. 115.

[18] Canavan, *op. cit.*, p. 149; Barker, *Essays on Government*, p. 199.

[19] "Appeal," *Burke's Politics*, p. 397.

[20] "Speech to the Electors," *ibid.*, p. 116.

[21] For an example of this view, see Luce, *op. cit.*, p. 438.

[22] "First Letter on a Regicide Peace" (1796), cited in Canavan, *op. cit.*, p. 144. Regarding "virtual representatives," see below.

[23] Edmund Burke, "Observations on the State of the Nation" (1769), *Works* (New York, 1847), I, 135.

[24] "Thoughts on the Cause of the Present Discontents" (1770), *Burke's Politics*, pp. 27–28.

[25] Beer, *op. cit.*, p. 616. Cf. Hogan, *op. cit.*, pp. 159–160; Alfred De

Grazia, *Public and Republic* (New York, 1951), p. 44; Terry Hoy, "Theories of the Exercise of Suffrage" (unpubl. diss., 1956), p. 92; Harold Foote Gosnell, *Democracy* (New York, 1948), p. 161. Whether or not this was Burke's argument, it was clearly articulated by other British conservatives, both before and after Burke. See, for example, George Grenville, *Regulations Lately Made Concerning the Colonies* (1765), p. 109, cited in De Grazia, *Public and Republic*, p. 75. For a later version see George Cornwall Lewis, *Remarks on the Use and Abuse of Some Political Terms* (Oxford, 1877), p. 105. Lewis justifies extension of the suffrage to disfranchised large towns only on the ground that a large town is "more likely to send a good representative to the national councils." But quite properly he then rejects any distinction between virtual and actual representation, since all places are represented insofar as they are well governed, whether or not they vote.

26 Hogan, *op. cit.*, pp. 159–160; italics mine.

27 *Ibid.*, p. 161. Cf. William Ebenstein, *Great Political Thinkers* (New York, 1956), p. 448.

28 Hogan, *op. cit.*, p. 161.

29 "Speech on the State of the Representation" (1782), *Burke's Politics*, p. 230; italics mine.

30 Hutchins, *op. cit.*, p. 65.

31 "Letter to Langriche" (1792), *Burke's Politics*, p. 495.

32 Hogan, *op. cit.*, p. 160; Hutchins, *op. cit.*, p. 64.

33 "Letter to Langriche," *Burke's Politics*, p. 495.

34 Gibbons, *op. cit.*, p. 37; Beer, *op. cit.*, p. 618.

35 Beer, *op. cit.*, p. 617.

36 *Ibid.*, p. 618.

37 "Letter to Langriche," *Burke's Politics*, p. 495.

38 This point was almost, but not quite, discovered by Macaulay in a parliamentary address cited by Cecil S. Emden, *The People and the Constitution* (Oxford, 1956), p. 190: "A virtual representative is, I presume, a man who acts as a direct representative would act: for surely it would be absurd to say that a man virtually represents the people of Manchester, who is in the habit of saying No, when a man directly representing the people of Manchester would say Aye. The utmost that can be expected from virtual representation is that it may be as good as direct representation. If so, why not grant direct representation to places which, as everybody allows, ought, by some process or other to be represented." (Note the interesting parallel of phrasing to the passage concerning Bethnal Green discussed in Chap. 7, above.)

39 *Oxford English Dictionary*. For two entirely different definitions of virtual representation, see Harvey Walker, *The Legislative Process* (New York, 1948), p. 128; and Gosnell, *op. cit.*, pp. 140–141.

40 "Speech to the Electors," *Burke's Politics*, p. 115.

41 Concerning "opinion" in Burke, see Canavan, *op. cit.*, p. 64.

42 *Ibid.*, p. 155; cf. Parkin, *op. cit.*, p. 43; and Burke's "Speech at the Conclusion of the Poll" (1780), cited in Hogan, *op. cit.*, p. 189.

43 "Speech at the Conclusion," *ibid.*

44 Cited in Parkin, *op. cit.*, pp. 41, 47–48.

45 Canavan points out that "Burke sat during most of his parliamentary career for nomination boroughs and was dependent not on voters, but on

parliamentary patrons. His idea of representation cannot therefore be adequately comprehended without some consideration of his attitude toward his patrons." And Canavan finds that Burke would accord much greater attention to the opinions of a parliamentary patron than to those of constituents, because "the patron was a party leader who also was present on the public scene in the political center of the nation, and with whom the representative had to act if he were to act effectively at all." *Op. cit.*, pp. 151, 155. This would seem to substantiate the view that Burke rejected constituent opinion because he considered it ill informed and likely to be wrong. Had the constituents been well informed and on the scene, as parliamentary patrons were, their opinions might have seemed more relevant to their interest, and the representative might not have been cast in so independent a role.

⁴⁶ Hogan, *op. cit.*, p. 160.

⁴⁷ "Letter to Langriche," *Burke's Politics*, p. 495.

⁴⁸ "Speech on Conciliation with the Colonies" (1775), *ibid.*, p. 85. Cf. also "Observations," *Works*, I, 135. The suggestion that the colonies were virtually represented was made, for example, by Mansfield speaking on the Stamp Act in Parliament in 1766. Cited in Emden, *op. cit.*, p. 189.

⁴⁹ "Letter to Langriche," *Burke's Politics*, p. 495.

⁵⁰ *Ibid.*, p. 482.

⁵¹ "On the State of Ireland" (1792), cited in Canavan, *op. cit.*, p. 159; italics mine.

⁵² "Speech on the State of the Representation," *Burke's Politics*, p. 229.

⁵³ "Reflections," *ibid.*, pp. 285, 304–305, for instance. Cf. Canavan, *op. cit.*, pp. 163, 165; Parkin, *op. cit.*, p. 52.

⁵⁴ Canavan, *op. cit.*, p. 158.

⁵⁵ "Speech on the State of the Representation," *Burke's Politics*, pp. 229-230. A statical chair was a device invented by a Venetian physician, Sanctorius (1561–1636), for weighing people; its purpose was to determine the amount of "insensible perspiration" lost by the body, as after the consumption of certain foods.

⁵⁶ Canavan, *op. cit.*, pp. 163–165; Parkin, *op. cit.*, p. 52.

⁵⁷ Canavan, *op. cit.*, pp. 159, 166–167. See also Hutchins, *op. cit.*; and Gibbons, *op. cit.*, p. 38. Burke never makes explicit how such a criterion might be institutionalized; indeed, he never makes the criterion itself explicit. I think that here again he assumes that reasonable men will agree on the facts.

⁵⁸ Hence Burke can say that elections may be expected to provide men who have "connections" with both "the interest" and "the sentiments" of the people. "Thoughts on the Cause," *Burke's Politics*, p. 21.

⁵⁹ Some interesting but inconclusive support for this parallel may be found in a passage cited by Barker in *Essays on Government*, pp. 230–231: "The votes of a majority of the people . . . cannot alter the moral any more than they can alter the physical essence of things." But the parallel I am suggesting is much broader than this.

⁶⁰ "Speech at the Conclusion," cited in Hogan, *op. cit.*, p. 189.

⁶¹ "Reflections," *Burke's Politics*, p. 348.

⁶² Parkin, *op. cit.*, p. 51.

⁶³ "Speech on the State of the Representation," *Burke's Politics*, p. 227; italics mine.

[64] Barker, *Essays on Government*, p. 199.

[65] Canavan, *op. cit.*, pp. 141–142, 146–147.

[66] "Speech on the State of the Representation," *Burke's Politics*, p. 229.

[67] *Ibid.*, p. 226.

[68] Cited in Parkin, *op. cit.*, p. 53. Cf. Beer, *op. cit.*, pp. 616, 630.

[69] Gibbons, *op. cit.*, p. 36.

[70] Cited in Barker, *Essays on Government*, p. 194.

[71] "Thoughts on the Cause," *Burke's Politics*, p. 28. This passage leads the editors to assert that Burke says the House of Commons "ought to mirror" the nation (p. xxiii). Cf. "Reflections," *ibid.*, pp. 311, 333. Luce treats this "reflection" concept as just one more contradiction in Burke's thought. *Op. cit.*, pp. 199, 313.

[72] "Letter to Langriche," *Burke's Politics*, pp. 492–493. Cf. "Thoughts on the Cause," *ibid.*, p. 8; "Letter to a Member of the Bell Club" (1777), *ibid.*, p. 119; "Appeal," *ibid.*, p. 393; "Fragments of a Tract Relative to the Laws against Popery in Ireland" (1765), *Selected Writings and Speeches*, ed. Peter J. Stanlis (Garden City, 1963), p. 213; Gibbons, *op. cit.*, p. 36; Parkin, *op. cit.*, p. 39.

[73] "Speech on Economic Reform" (1780), cited in Barker, *Essays on Government*, p. 201.

[74] De Grazia, *Public and Republic*, p. 41; cf. p. 39.

[75] *Op. cit.*, p. 617.

[76] Cf. Parkin, *op. cit.*, p. 42.

[77] *Ibid.*, pp. 38, 50. Parkin, however, distorts the Burkean concept of interest when he says that there is a natural harmony between "the true self-interest of the individual" and the general good. Burke never talks about the "self-interest of the individual," true or otherwise. Cf. p. 43.

[78] "Speech on the State of the Representation," *Burke's Politics*, p. 229.

[79] "Speech on the Petition of the Unitarian Society" (1792), *Selected Writings*, p. 315.

[80] Cited in Beer, *op. cit.*, p. 617.

[81] "Speech to the Electors," *Burke's Politics*, p. 116. Cf. Heinz Eulau *et al.*, "The Role of the Representative," *American Political Science Review*, LIII (September 1959), p. 744; Carl J. Friedrich, *Constitutional Government and Democracy* (Boston, 1950), pp. 260, 264–265.

[82] Thus it is misleading to say, as Parkin does, that popular feelings "embody a type of reason" and are "binding" on the government. *Op. cit.*, p. 39. Popular feelings are only the starting point for the representative process, and I think that Burke conceived of them as very primitive, almost inarticulate, like an awareness of physical pain. Anything more discursive would constitute "opinion."

[83] Eulau, *op. cit.*, pp. 744–745.

[84] *The True Theory of Representation in a State* (London, 1857), pp. 9–10.

NOTES TO CHAPTER 9
(Pp. 190–208)

[1] Samuel H. Beer, "The Representation of Interests," *American Political Science Review*, LI (September, 1957), 629–631. The Liberals' belief in the rationality of man has often been exaggerated; see Sheldon S. Wolin, *Politics and Vision* (Boston, 1960), pp. 332–334.

2 Sir William Blackstone, *Commentaries on the Laws of England*, I, 171, cited in Beer, *op. cit.*, p. 630.

3 Alexander Hamilton did express views of representation close to Burke's in an address before the Constitutional Convention of 1787, but he did not speak of virtual representation. Max Farrand, ed., *The Records of the Federal Convention of 1787* (New Haven, 1927), I, 288–289.

4 Alexander Hamilton, James Madison, and John Jay, *The Federalist*, no. 52; I use the Max Beloff edition throughout (Oxford, 1948), p. 270. The original papers appeared in 1787 and 1788. On the disputed authorship of some of the papers, see Beloff's Introduction, pp. lxvii-lxviii.

5 *Federalist*, no. 10, p. 45.

6 *Ibid.*

7 Letter from Madison to Thomas Jefferson, October 24, 1787, cited in Saul K. Padover, *The Complete Madison* (New York, 1953), p. 42.

8 *Ibid.*

9 Speech on June 6, 1787, cited *ibid.*, p. 17.

10 Even where *The Federalist* speaks of "the interest of all," it usually means a like interest held separately by individuals (e.g., no. 60, p. 307); and a "common interest" is a faction! (*e.g.*, no. 60, p. 308).

11 *Ibid.*, no. 6, p. 22; no. 42, p. 215.

12 Cf. Maynard Smith, "Reason, Passion and Political Freedom in the *Federalist*," *Journal of Politics*, XXII (August, 1960), 525–544.

13 *Federalist*, no. 10, p. 42.

14 *Ibid.*, p. 45.

15 For example, Beer, *op. cit.*, p. 629.

16 *Federalist*, no. 10, p. 45.

17 *Ibid.*; cf. no. 63, p. 324.

18 *Ibid.*, no. 10, p. 44.

19 *Ibid.*, p. 47. The same point is made in nos. 51, 60, and 63, pp. 267, 307, 323; in a speech by Madison on June 6, 1787, cited in Padover, *op. cit.*, p. 18; and in Farrand, *op. cit.*, I, 136, 431. Cf. Padover's own interpretation (p. 17); and Neal Riemer, "James Madison's Theory of the Self-Destructive Features of Republican Government," *Ethics*, LXV (October, 1954), 37.

20 Beer, *op. cit.*, p. 629; Padover, *op. cit.*, p. 17; Alfred De Grazia, *Public and Republic* (New York, 1951), pp. 96, 99–100.

21 *Federalist*, no. 63, p. 324.

22 In this respect *The Federalist* is remarkably parallel to the representation theory of the Abbé Siéyès at the time of the French Revolution. Representation is a system for protecting minority rights by reducing the government to inaction. Karl Loewenstein, *Volk und Parlament* (Munich, 1922), pp. 36–37. Cf. John Stuart Mill, *Representative Government*, chap. 6, p. 255, in *Utilitarianism, Liberty, and Representative Government* (London, 1947).

23 *Federalist*, no. 42, p. 215.

24 *Ibid.*, no. 63, p. 323; italics mine.

25 *Ibid.*

26 "The aim of a political organization was not to educate men but to deploy them." Wolin, *op. cit.*, p. 389.

27 De Grazia, *Public and Republic*, p. 96.

28 *Ibid.*; cf. pp. 98–99.

29 Cited in John A. Fairlie, "The Nature of Political Representation,"

American Political Science Review, XXXIV (April, 1940), 244.

30 *Federalist*, no. 10, p. 43.

31 Wolin, *op. cit.*, pp. 388–390.

32 Jeremy Bentham, "A Plan of Parliamentary Reform," *Works*, ed. John Bowring (Edinburgh, 1843), III, 447, 526; "Constitutional Code," IX, 5, 8, 61; "Book of Fallacies," II, 482; "Principles of Judicial Procedure," II, 120; "The Psychology of Economic Man," *Jeremy Bentham's Economic Writings*, ed. W. Stark (London, 1954), III, 421, 423, 429–430, 433. James Mill, *An Essay on Government* (New York, 1955), p. 69; J. S. Mill, *Representative Government*, chap. 3, p. 208; Samuel Bailey, *The Rationale of Political Representation* (London, 1835), p. 68.

33 "Plan of Parliamentary Reform," *Works*, III, 33; "Psychology," *Economic Writings*, III, 438. Cf. James Mill, *op. cit.*, p. 69; J. S. Mill, *Representative Government*, chap. 3, p. 208; *On Liberty*, p. 133 in *Utilitarianism, Liberty and Representative Government* (London, 1947); Bailey, *op. cit.*, p. 68; Adam Smith, *An Inquiry into the Nature and Causes of the Wealth of Nations* (New York, 1937), IV, 497; Elie Halévy, *The Growth of Philosophical Radicalism* (Boston, 1955), p. 491; Harold W. Stoke, "The Paradox of Representative Government," *Essays in Political Science in Honor of W. W. Willoughby*, ed. John M. Mathews (Baltimore, 1937), p. 80.

34 Wolin, *op. cit.*, p. 341; Karl Loewenstein, *Beiträge zur Staatssoziologie* (Tübingen, 1961), p. 149.

35 *Op. cit.*, IV, 421–423, 497. Smith is here speaking primarily about capital allocation.

36 "Plan of Parliamentary Reform," *Works*, III, 33, 35. Recent commentary increasingly stresses the degree to which Bentham abandoned this notion, even in economics, in his later writings. See for example T. W. Hutchinson, "Bentham as an Economist," *Economic Journal*, LXVI (June, 1956), 288–306.

37 It is extremely intriguing, how differently we tend to conceive interests, depending on whether we start from the political or the economic context. An attempt to learn something from this difference is made by Henry M. Oliver, Jr., in "Attitudes toward Market and Political Self-Interest," *Ethics*, LXV (April, 1955), 171–180. This seems a promising area for further work. John P. Plamenatz, "Interests," *Political Studies*, II (February, 1954), should also be relevant.

38 Bentham, "An Introduction to the Principles of Morals and Legislation," *Works*, I, 2; "Leading Principles of a Constitutional Code," II, 269; "Plan of Parliamentary Reform," III, 446, 450–452; James Mill, cited in Henry J. Ford, *Representative Government* (New York, 1924), p. 145; J. S. Mill, *Representative Government*, chap. 6, pp. 248, 255. Bailey, *op. cit.*, pp. 69, 71, 137; Smith, *op. cit.*, IV, 421–423; cf. A. J. Ayer, *Philosophical Essays* (London, 1954), p. 255.

39 Halévy, *op. cit.*, pp. 15–17, 118–119, 405, 489–490.

40 "Plan of Parliamentary Reform," *Works*, III, 453–455; "Constitutional Code," IX, 6, 53, 60–62, 67; "Book of Fallacies," II, 475; "Psychology," *Economic Writings*, III, 428–433. Cf. Mill, *Representative Government*, chap. 6, pp. 248–255; Bailey, *op. cit.*, p. 137.

41 Bentham, "Psychology," *Economic Writings*, III, 432; cf. "Constitutional Code," *Works*, IX, 61.

42 "Constitutional Code," *Works*, IX, 61.

43 Ayer, *op. cit.*, p. 261.

44 *Federalist*, no. 51, p. 265.

45 "Plan of Parliamentary Reform," *Works*, III, 447; cf. Bailey, *op. cit.*, p. 71.

46 "Essay on Political Tactics," *Works*, II, 301n; cf. "Constitutional Code," IX, 4–7, 63; James Mill, *op. cit.*, p. 67.

47 Cited in Ford, *op. cit.*, p. 146; James Mill, *op. cit.*, p. 69.

48 "The case is different . . . when it is considered not from the point-of-view of the individual but from the point-of-view of the community." Ayer, *op. cit.*, p. 255.

49 "Constitutional Code," *Works*, IX, 63, 103, 118, 155.

50 "Plan of Parliamentary Reform," *ibid.*, III, 445–446.

51 *Ibid.*, p. 451; also pp. 450–455; "Essay on Political Tactics," *ibid.*, II, 301.

52 "Plan of Parliamentary Reform," *ibid.*, III, 455.

53 For example, *ibid.*, pp. 455–457; cf. Halévy, *op. cit.*, p. 412.

54 *Representative Government*, chap. 6, p. 252.

55 John Stuart Mill, "Thoughts on Parliamentary Reform," *Dissertations and Discussions* (New York, 1874), IV, 21. Cf. Loewenstein, *Beiträge*, p. 149.

56 *Representative Government*, chap. 4, p. 219. Again, in contrast to Burke, the Utilitarian takes "interest" to be something men "feel."

57 *Ibid.*, chap. 6, pp. 254–255. Cf. Bentham's "sinister interests" in "Plan of Parliamentary Reform," *Works*, III, 446, 450–451.

58 *Representative Government*, chap. 6, p. 255.

59 *Ibid.*

60 Ayer, *op. cit.*, pp. 258–259.

61 For example, "Plan of Parliamentary Reform," *Works*, III, 446, 450–451, 527; "Papers Relative to Codification and Public Instruction," IV, 496; "Constitutional Code," IX, 138–139.

62 Ayer says that Bentham considers selfish action in pursuit of a sinister interest "a course of action which could not intentionally have place." *Op. cit.*, p. 251.

63 *Representative Government*, chap. 6, pp. 250–253.

64 ". . . for the benefits of his ability are certain, while the hypothesis of his being wrong and their being right . . . is a very doubtful one." *Ibid.*, chap. 12, p. 232.

65 *Op. cit.*, p. 254.

66 Cf. e.g., Bentham, "Psychology," *Economic Writings*, III, 422, 438; John Stuart Mill, *Utilitarianism*, chap. 2, p. 10, in *Utilitarianism, Liberty, and Representative Government* (London, 1947).

67 "Theory of Legislation," p. 77, cited in Robert Luce, *Legislative Principles* (Boston, 1930), p. 493.

68 *Representative Government*, chap. 5, p. 239. Cf. his views on the educative function of representative government, chap. 3, pp. 211–218; and "Thoughts on Parliamentary Reform," p. 21.

69 Jean Jacques Rousseau, *Le Contrat Social*, in *Oeuvres Complètes* (Paris, 1905–1912), III, 318: "Le souverain peut bien dire: 'Je veux actuellement ce que veut un tel homme, ou du moins ce qu'il dit vouloir'; mais il ne peut pas dire: 'Ce que cet homme voudra demain, je le voudrai encore'; puisqu'il est absurde que la volonté se donne des chaînes pour l'avenir, et puisqu'il ne dépend d'aucune volonté de consentir à rien de

contraire au bien de l'être qui veut. Si donc le peuple promet simplement d'obéir, il se dissout par cet acte, il perd sa qualité de peuple; à l'instant qu'il y a un maître, il n'y a plus de souverain, et dès lors le corps politique est détruit."

Cf. Bentham: "It is absurd to cause a whole nation to assert this grave foolery: —'We declare that these five hundred individuals, who now possess our confidence, will equally possess it whatever they do during all the rest of their lives.' " "Essay on Political Tactics," *Works*, II, 301.

[70] This accounts for Rousseau's famous condemnation of British representative government: "Le peuple anglois pense être libre, il se trompe fort; il ne l'est que durant l'élection des membres du parlement: sitôt qu'ils sont élus, il est esclave, *il n'est rien.* . . . Quoi qu'il en soit, à l'instant qu'un peuple se donne des représentants, il n'est plus libre; il n'est plus." *Op. cit.,* pp. 361–366.

[71] G. D. H. Cole, *Social Theory* (London, 1920), p. 103.

[72] *Ibid.,* p. 104.

[73] Fairlie, *op. cit.,* p. 466.

[74] Robert E. Dowse, "Representation, General Elections and Democracy," *Parliamentary Affairs*, XV (Summer, 1962), 336.

NOTES TO CHAPTER 10
(Pp. 209–240)

[1] Carl J. Friedrich, "Representation and Constitutional Reform in Europe," *Western Political Quarterly*, I (June, 1948), 128–129.

[2] Lewis Anthony Dexter, "The Representative and His District," *Human Organization*, XVI (Spring, 1957), 3–4; George W. Hartmann, "Judgments," *Journal of Social Psychology*, XXI (February, 1945), 105, 113; Harold Foote Gosnell, *Democracy* (New York, 1948), p. 203.

[3] This is seen most clearly by Warren E. Miller and Donald E. Stokes, "Constituency Influence in Congress," *American Political Science Review*, LVII (March, 1963), 45–56, and by Dexter, "The Representative," pp. 3–4; but also by L. E. Gleeck, "96 Congressmen Make Up Their Minds," *Public Opinion Quarterly*, IV (March, 1940); Heinz Eulau *et al.*, "The Role of the Representative," *American Political Science Review*, LIII (September, 1959), 745, 749; and Julius Turner, *Party and Constituency* (Baltimore, 1951), pp. 70, 79. It is overlooked by studies such as Wilder W. Crane's, which deal with only a single legislative measure. Crane found that "only one" legislator "deliberately voted on the merits" of the issue. But what was the issue? The instituting of Daylight Saving Time! "Do Representatives Represent?" *Journal of Politics*, XXII (May, 1960).

[4] Thus American Congressmen sometimes defend their attention to local needs by saying that the national interest is properly the concern of the Senate and the President. "What snarls up the system is these so-called statesmen—Congressmen who vote for what they think is the country's interest . . . let the Senators do that . . . they're paid to be statesmen; we aren't," says a Congressman cited in Dexter, "The Representative," p. 3. Cf. Gerhard Leibholz, *Das Wesen der Repräsentation* (Berlin, 1929), p. 188.

[5] Constitutions of Germany, Portugal, Belgium, and Italy, cited in Robert Luce, *Legislative Principles* (Boston, 1930), pp. 446–447; cf. Carl

Schmitt, *The Necessity of Politics* (London, 1931), p. 69. Martin Drath points out that such clauses did not originate as moralistic admonitions to the representative, but had a real and practical political significance. *Die Entwicklung der Volksrepräsentation* (Bad Homburg, 1954), pp. 7–10.

6 Siéyès went so far as to argue that even the locally elected representative is really elected by the whole nation, and hence represents it. His speech in the National Assembly of 1789 is cited in Karl Loewenstein, *Volk und Parlament* (Munich, 1922), p. 199. Samuel Bailey, *The Rationale of Political Representation* (London, 1835), p. 137, argues that representatives should be elected nationally at large, if that were practical.

7 Misunderstanding of this distinction is common in the literature. Thus Luce cites the following passage from a speech by a delegate to the New Hampshire convention of 1902 *as an illustration of the way people prefer local to national interest*: "I had just as soon not be represented at all as to be represented by a man whose interests belong to another town, and who does not help our town." *Op. cit.*, pp. 506–507.

8 Cited in Dexter, "The Representative," p. 3.

9 Drath, *op. cit.*, p. 14; see also Sheldon S. Wolin *Politics and Vision* (Boston, 1960), pp. 63–66.

10 *Systematic Politics* (Chicago, 1945), p. 140; also p. 145; Leibholz, *Das Wesen der Repräsentation*, pp. 47–58; Rudolf Smend, *Verfassung und Verfassungsrecht* (Munich, 1928), pp. 39–40.

11 On voting behavior see Joseph A Schumpeter, *Capitalism, Socialism and Democracy* (New York, 1947), p. 261, and these empirical studies: Paul F. Lazarsfeld *et al.*, *The People's Choice* (New York, 1948); Bernard R. Berelson *et al.*, *Voting* (Chicago, 1954); Angus Campbell *et al.*, *The Voter Decides* (White Plains, N. Y., 1954); Eugene Burdick and Arthur J. Brodbeck, eds., *American Voting Behavior* (Glencoe, Ill., 1959); Angus Campbell *et al.*, *The American Voter* (New York, 1960).

12 Dexter, "The Representative," p. 3; John C. Wahlke and Heinz Eulau, eds., *Legislative Behavior* (Glencoe, Ill., 1959), pp. 298–304; John C. Wahlke *et al.*, "American State Legislators' Role Orientation," *Journal of Politics*, XXII (May, 1960); Eulau, *op. cit.*; Charles O. Jones, "Representation in Congress," *American Political Science Review*, LV (December, 1961).

13 Sabine, "What Is the Matter?" in A. N. Christensen and E. M. Kirkpatrick, eds., *The People, Politics and the Politician* (New York, 1941); G. D. H. Cole, *Social Theory* (London, 1920), pp. 103–116; Dexter, "The Representative," pp. 4–5; Howard Lee McBain, *The Living Constitution* (New York, 1948), p. 233; Eulau, *op. cit.*, pp. 747, 751; Schumpeter, *op. cit.*, p. 261; Jones, *op. cit.*, pp. 358–359, 365.

14 Dexter, "The Representative"; and "What Do Congressmen Hear: The Mail," *Public Opinion Quarterly*, XX (Spring, 1956), 16–27; Eulau, *op. cit.*, p. 749; Frank Bonilla, "When Is Petition 'Pressure'?" *Public Opinion Quarterly*, XX (Spring, 1956), 39–48; David B. Truman, *The Governmental Process* (New York, 1959), chap. 11; Jones, *op. cit.*, pp. 366–367.

15 Henry B. Mayo, *An Introduction to Democratic Theory* (New York, 1960), p. 102; Wahlke and Eulau, *op. cit.*, p. 117; Jones, *op. cit.*, p. 359.

16 Robert M. MacIver, *The Modern State* (Oxford, 1926), p. 196; Joseph Tussman, *Obligation and the Body Politic* (New York, 1960), pp. 69, 75; Wahlke, *op. cit.*; Wahlke and Eulau, *op. cit.*, pp. 179–189, 284–293.

[17] Dexter, "The Representative"; Wahlke and Eulau, *op. cit.*, pp. 204–217.

[18] Gleeck, *op. cit.*, p. 7; Turner, *op. cit.*, p. 12; Dexter, "The Representative"; Truman, *op. cit.*, chap. 11.

[19] Dexter, "The Representative," p. 5.

[20] Jones, *op. cit.*, pp. 363–364.

[21] Wahlke and Eulau, *op. cit.*, pp. 298–304.

[22] "Obviously important changes take place which make the substitute assembly far different from the direct meeting of the people." Alfred De Grazia, *Public and Republic* (New York, 1951), p. 126.

"When one person represents a group, and still more when a number of persons represent different groups, the problem becomes much more complicated." John A. Fairlie, "The Nature of Political Representation," *American Political Science Review*, XXXIV (June, 1940), 466.

"My conclusion from this discussion is that the concepts connected with representation of individual persons by individual persons have no simple application to representative government." A. Phillips Griffiths and Richard Wollheim, "How Can One Person Represent Another?" Aristotelian Society, Suppl. Vol. XXXIV (1960), 207.

See also Peter Laslett, "The Face to Face Society," *Philosophy, Politics and Society*, ed. Peter Laslett (New York, 1956).

[23] The first three passages were elicited from New York State legislators by Hartmann, *op. cit.*, p. 111; the fourth passage is from the autobiography of Senator George F. Hoar, pp. 112–113, cited in Luce, *op. cit.*, p. 496; the fifth passage is a statement by a United States Congressman interviewed by Dexter, "The Representative," p. 3; the sixth is by a Congressman interviewed by Bonilla, *op. cit.*, pp. 46–47; the last is a statement by a senior member of the House Agriculture Committee interviewed by Jones, *op. cit.*, p. 365.

[24] Lazarsfeld, *op. cit.*, p. 137. See also Elihu Katz and Paul F. Lazarsfeld, *Personal Influence* (Glencoe, Ill., 1955); Edward C. Banfield, *Political Influence* (Glencoe, Ill., 1961).

[25] Miller and Stokes, *op. cit.*, p. 55; italics mine.

[26] For instance, Karl Loewenstein, *Political Power and the Governmental Process* (Chicago, 1957), pp. 38–39; Eric Voegelin, *The New Science of Politics* (Chicago, 1952), p. 37.

[27] For instance, Georg Jellinek, *Allgemeine Staatslehre* (Berlin, 1905), chap. 17.

[28] For example, James Hogan, *Election and Representation* (1945), p. 114; John P. Plamenatz, *Consent, Freedom and Political Obligation* (London, 1938), p. 12; Eulau, *op. cit.*, p. 743; Fairlie, *op. cit.*, p. 237; Avery Leiserson, *Administrative Regulation* (Chicago, 1942), pp. 3–9; Max Weber, *Wirtschaft und Gesellschaft* (Tübingen, 1956), I, 25, 171–176. Gerhard Leibholz is particularly ambivalent between representation as authority and as effective authority: *Das Wesen der Repräsentation*, pp. 140–141, 163–164; and *Strukturprobleme der modernen Demokratie* (Karlsruhe, 1958), pp. 10–12.

[29] MacIver, *op. cit.*, pp. 197–198.

[30] W. D. Handcock, "What Is Represented in Representative Government?" *Philosophy*, XXII (July, 1947), p. 107; cf. John Dewey, *The Public and Its Problems* (New York, 1927), p. 76.

[31] For instance, Plamenatz, *Consent*, p. 16.

[32] Christian Bay, *The Structure of Freedom* (Stanford, 1958), p. 322.

[33] For representative government to exist, "the *possibility* for opposition must be considered sufficient." Charles William Cassinelli, Jr., "The Concept of Representative Government" (unpubl. thesis, 1950), p. 62.

[34] Five criteria for distinguishing a "process of consent" from a "process of manipulation" in political elections are suggested by Morris Janowitz and Dwaine Marvick, "Competitive Pressure and Democratic Consent," *Public Opinion Quarterly*, XIX (Winter, 1955–56), 381–400. See also their book of the same title (Ann Arbor, 1956) for an application. A useful discussion of the criteria of "free" elections is given in W. J. M. Mackenzie, *Free Elections* (New York, 1958), esp. the introduction and Part IV.

[35] One must be cautious about the recent "economic" theories of democracy. Starting with Schumpeter, a number of writers have suggested that democracy may be regarded as a sort of economic marketplace in which votes constitute money, and would-be representatives are competitively trying to sell themselves to the buyers. Schumpeter defines democracy as "that institutional arrangement for arriving at political decisions in which individuals acquire the power to decide by means of a competitive struggle for the people's vote." *Op. cit.*, p. 269. Issues thus are not decided by the voters; the voters merely choose the "men who are to do the deciding." Marvick and Janowitz suggest that elections should not be considered as giving a mandate for certain action on issues, but as "a process of selecting and rejecting candidates . . . in competition for public office." "Competitive Pressure," p. 382.

A full theoretical development of this model has most recently been made by Anthony Downs, for whom, again, "the central purpose of elections in a democracy is to select a government." *An Economic Theory of Democracy* (New York, 1957), p. 24. Policy decisions and ideologies are strictly secondary concepts in these theories. As Downs says, politicians in his model "never seek office as a means of carrying out particular policies; their only goal is to reap the rewards of holding office *per se*. They treat policies purely as a means to the attainment of their private ends, which they can reach only by being elected. . . . Parties formulate policies in order to win elections, rather than win elections in order to formulate policies." *Ibid.*, p. 28.

This idea is derived from Schumpeter, who compares the competition of political parties to war: the decision of political issues is like the taking of a strategic position, not an end but a means. "Victory over the opponent" is "the essence of both games." *Op. cit.*, p. 279. The voters are conceived as being at the mercy of what the parties offer them by way of programs and candidates; "If the alternative is a choice between demagogues, the electorate suffers; if the choice is between statesmen, the electorate gains. The quality of results is not guaranteed by the presence of competition." Janowitz and Marvick, "Competitive Pressure," p. 382.

A political system defined in this way is not necessarily a representative one, however; if our politics really corresponded to these models we would not call it representation. We have merely to imagine a situation in which the electorate has a fairly explicit, articulate wish, but none of the political parties is willing to enact it. We can imagine such a situation, for example, in a society strongly divided on class lines, where a few parties, all from a single class, monopolize access to the legislature. Or we can imagine it in a colonial society in which nonwhites are permitted to vote, but only whites may sit in the legislature. In such situations a competitive selection of rulers might repeatedly fail to result in the enactment of a widely desired measure. We would be reluctant to call such a system representative government.

Now in all justice to Downs and Schumpeter one must add that they also wish to exclude such cases. They require that the candidate or parties seeking office engage in free competition, in the economic sense. Schumpeter, *op. cit.*, p. 272. (Janowitz and Marvick apparently do not understand Schumpeter's use of the term "free competition," for they argue that competition is no guarantee of good political results. They themselves require effective deliberation on the issues in the electoral campaign, but it is not clear whether they mean this to be a prerequisite for representation or merely for desirable, good representation. See also George Cornwall Lewis, *Remarks on the Use and Abuse of Some Political Terms* (Oxford, 1877), pp. 98–99. Downs makes it clear that in his model new parties must arise whenever the old ones are not offering the people what they want. The concept is thus an analogue to economic free competition, in which the producer must supply what consumers want lest he be put out of business by a more responsive competitor. But such free competition on the political scene seems so farfetched as to raise doubts about the usefulness of the model. A second objection, more to the point of our concerns, is that, whether or not these models give an account of how democracy actually works, they are misleading if applied to the meaning of representation and representative government. The power to select one's rulers may result in representation, but it does not constitute representation (except possibly in the formal sense). What constitutes representation is the very responsiveness on issues which these models relegate to a secondary position. Mere selection of one man for a job by others need not make him their representative.

36 Cassinelli, "The Concept of Representative Government," and "Representative Government" (unpubl. diss., 1953). See also Bay, *op. cit.*; Mackenzie, *Free Elections*; Janowitz and Marvick, "Competitive Pressure."

37 "Now in this more conventional sense a monarch is not a representative. He is a ruler. The president is not a representative. . . . To catch our representative we have got to look where one group of people, formal or fundamental, has one member in some common body, and other groups have other members." Arthur F. Bentley, *The Process of Government* (Evanston, Ill., 1949), p. 450. See also Friedrich Glum, *Der deutsche und der französische Reichswirtschaftsrat* (Berlin, 1929), p. 33.

38 For some astute recent philosophical treatments of the problem of punishment, see John Rawls, "Two Concepts of Rules," *Philosophical Review*, LXIV (January, 1955), 3–32; Quinton, "On Punishment," in Laslett, *op. cit.*; J. D. Mabbott, "Punishment," *Mind*, XLVIII (1939), 152–167.

39 Jean Piaget, *The Moral Judgment of the Child* (New York, 1962).

40 *Ibid.*, pp. 42, 65–76, 98. Piaget's own findings thus cast doubt on his categorical assertion that "procedure alone is obligatory." *Ibid.*, p. 71.

41 It is clearly articulated also by Drath, *op. cit.*, pp. 3, 15, 19–21.

42 *Obligation*, p. 86. Tussman calls them "the two great moods of deliberative life."

43 For a similar critique of liberalism and constitutionalism, see Wolin, *op. cit.*, esp. chap. 9.

44 *The Federalist*, No. 51, p. 265; Tussman, *Obligation*, p. 108.

45 Hans J. Wolff says that representation is neither a "zueinander" nor a "miteinander," but a "für einander," "und zwar nicht nur des Vertreters für die Vertretenen, sondern ebenso entsprechend der Vertretenen für den Vertreter. Darin liegt der tiefe ethische und soziale Gehalt der Vertretung, die grundsätzlich den Eigennutz überwindet und tiefer als im Versprechen und in der Gemeinsamkeit wurzelt in der gegenseitigen Treue." *Organschaft und juristische Person* (Berlin, 1934), pp. 5–6.

46 Drath, *op. cit.*, p. 24. Drath reduces the force of his insight by confusing the substance of representation with a De Grazia-Gosnell sort of acceptance-of-the-government-by-the-people or the-people's-identifying-themselves-with-the-government. *Ibid.*, pp. 24–27.

47 This point is nowhere made better than in the writings of Michael Oakeshott, *Rationalism in Politics* (New York, 1962), esp. pp. 118–126. But it is only half of the truth; Oakeshott robs us of the possibility of using an ideal abstracted from our institutions to criticize and change them.

48 Drath, *op. cit.*, p. 13; Weber, *Wirtschaft*, II, 675; Merriam, *op. cit.*, p. 139; Harold D. Lasswell and Abraham Kaplan, *Power and Society* (New Haven, 1950), p. 165; Glum, *op. cit.*, p. 25; Leibholz, *Das Wesen der Repräsentation*, pp. 157–158.

49 Drath, *op. cit.*, pp. 7, 27–28. For a discussion of the American Revolution in this light, see Leibholz, *Das Wesen der Repräsentation*, pp. 157–158; De Grazia, *Public and Republic*, pp. 14, 22. The same kind of conflict is traced in medieval thought by Georges de Lagarde, "L'Idee de Représentation," International Committee of the Historical Sciences, *Bulletin*, IX (December, 1937), 426, 435. It is traced during the crucial Civil War period in England by Louise Fargo Brown, "Ideas of Representation from Elizabeth to Charles II," *Journal of Modern History*, XI (March, 1939), 23–40. See also Appendix, below; for a more recent instance see Mackenzie, *Free Elections*, p. 175.

50 Henry J. Ford, *Representative Government* (New York, 1924), pp. 145–146. Ford attributes the view to John Stuart Mill.

NOTES TO APPENDIX ON ETYMOLOGY
(Pp. 241–252)

1 Georges de Lagarde, "L'Idée de Représentation," International Committee of the Historical Sciences, *Bulletin*, IX (December, 1937), 425–451; Albert Hauck, "Die Rezeption und Umbildung der allgemeinen Synode im Mittelalter," *Historische Vierteljahrschrift*, X (1907), 479.

2 Lagarde, p. 429n; my translation. See also Brian Tierney, *Foundations of the Conciliar Theory* (1955), pp. 4, 34–36, 45.

3 My information in this and the following paragraph comes from Lagarde.

4 Roffredus, *Quaestiones Sabbathinae*, cited in Lagarde, p. 429n.

5 *Ibid.*, p. 433 and n. Tierney suggests that the concept of a proctor may figure significantly in the transition from image or embodiment to authoritative action. *Op. cit.*, p. 126.

6 E. Littré, *Dictionnaire de la Langue Française* (Paris, 1875). The

Latin development probably had a greater influence on French than it did on English. C. H. MacIlwain cites an early-fourteenth-century summons from the French king to the clergy of Tours, ordering them to come in person or send "ex vobis unum nobis ad premissa mittatis, qui vicem omnium representet et omnium habeat plenariam potestatem." Corresponding documents in England do not seem to use *repraesentare*. "Medieval Estates," *Cambridge Medieval History*, VII: *The Decline of Empire and Papacy* (Cambridge, England, 1932), 689.

[7] When a word of Latin origin was introduced into English fairly late by way of Old French, it was often used particularly in formal contexts, especially if the new word paralleled an older Anglo-Saxon word already in use, with nearly the same meaning. Thus "liberty" and "freedom," "commence" and "begin," "initiate" and "start." See Paul Ziff, *Semantic Analysis* (Ithaca, 1960), p. 190.

[8] The statute is in Eleanor C. Lodge and Gladys A. Thornton, eds., *English Constitutional Documents 1307–1485* (1935), p. 268. Stanley Bertram Chrimes presents excerpts from Year Book Cases throughout the fifteenth century, all still in French. *English Constitutional Ideas* (Cambridge, England, 1936).

[9] For example, those cited in Lodge and Thornton.

[10] Chrimes, *op. cit.*, p. 132.

[11] For a clear discussion of the rival theories, see MacIlwain, *op. cit.*, and Helen M. Cam, *Liberties and Communities*, (Cambridge, England, 1944), chap. 15. The fact is substantiated by the reluctance of early knights and burgesses to serve in Parliament: A. F. Pollard, *The Evolution of Parliament* (London, 1926), pp. 109, 158–159; Charles A. Beard and John D. Lewis, "Representative Government in Evolution," *American Political Science Review*, XXVI (April, 1932), 230–233; Henry J. Ford, *Representative Government* (New York, 1924), p. 101n; James Hogan, *Election and Representation* (1945), pp. 142–143.

[12] Cam, *Liberties and Communities*, chap. 15; MacIlwain, *op. cit.*, p. 669; Chrimes, *op. cit.*, pp. 142–145.

[13] Cam, *Liberties and Communities*, chap. 15; Pollard, *op. cit.*, pp. 158–159.

[14] Cam, *Liberties and Communities*, chaps. 15 and 16, esp. pp. 230–232; May McKisack, *Representation of the English Boroughs during the Middle Ages* (London, 1932), pp. 82–99; Louise Fargo Brown, "Ideas of Representation," *Journal of Modern History*, XI (March, 1939), 23–24; Cecil S. Emden, *The People and the Constitution* (Oxford, 1956), p. 12.

[15] McKisack, *op. cit.*, p. 130.

[16] On this development see MacIlwain, *op. cit.*, pp. 671–673; Brown, *op. cit.*, pp. 25, 32, 36; Alfred De Grazia, *Public and Republic* (New York, 1951), pp. 14–18; Chrimes, *op. cit.*, p. 131; Samuel Bailey, *The Rationale of Political Representation* (London, 1835), p. 3; Gerhard Leibholz, *Das Wesen der Repräsentation* (Berlin, 1929), pp. 54–55; T. C. Pease, *The Leveller Movement* (Washington, D.C., 1916), pp. 25–26; Julius Hatschek, *Englisches Staatsrecht* (Tübingen, 1905), I, 241.

[17] Cam, *Liberties and Communities*, chaps. 15, 16; Chrimes, *op. cit.*, pp. 131–133; Robert Luce, *Legislative Principles* (Boston, 1930), p. 434.

[18] Chrimes, *op. cit.*, p. 131; the citation dates from 1407.

[19] *Ibid.*, p. 132; from about 1470.

20 Sir Edward Coke, *The Fourth Part of the Institutes of the Laws of England* (London, 1809), chap. 1, p. 14. There is (understandably) much disagreement about just when this doctrine originated. Hatschek produces a passage of parliamentary history from 1415 that seems to articulate it. *Op. cit.*, I, 238. Henry Hallam dates it from a parliamentary debate of 1571. *Constitutional History of England* (New York, 1871), I, 265. Writers who do not cite a single specific instance nevertheless vary considerably as to the period in which members of Parliament first thought of themselves as each acting for the whole nation. Chrimes suggests the fifteenth century (*op. cit.*, p. 131); Brown, the seventeenth (*op. cit.*, pp. 24–25); Emden, the eighteenth (*op. cit.*, p. 5). The idea must have emerged gradually, and we might expect to find instances of it when it was by no means the main constitutional doctrine. Hatschek and Hallam's early instances seem limited because each occurs in a rather specialized context. Coke's is the first I have found in which the doctrine is clearly and broadly articulated as constitutional principle.

21 See Chap. 4, above, esp. note 89.

22 Chap. 4, above, note 90.

23 Otto von Gierke, *Johannes Althusius* (Breslau, 1913), Part II, chap. 4; also, more generally, his *Das deutsche Genossenschaftsrecht* (Berlin, 1881), Vol. III; Fritz Kern, *Kingship and Law in the Middle Ages*, trans. S. B. Chrimes (Oxford, 1939), Part I; Hauck, *op. cit.*; Otto Hintze, "Typologie der ständischen Verfassungen," *Historische Zeitschrift*, CXLI (1929–1930), 230; Lagarde, *op. cit.*, Ewart Lewis, *Medieval Political Ideas* (New York, 1954), I, 195, 242, 263–264; II, 415; Ernst Kantorowicz, *The King's Two Bodies* (Princeton, 1957).

24 Kern, *op. cit.*, p. 141. Cf. Maude V. Clarke, *Medieval Representation and Consent* (London, 1936), p. 290, who says the idea "resists analysis"; and Hans J. Wolff, *Organschaft und juristische Person* (Berlin, 1934), II, 13–16.

25 B. Wilkinson, "The Political Revolution of the Thirteenth and Fourteenth Centuries in England," *Speculum*, XXIV (October, 1949), 502–509; Brown, *op. cit.*, p. 29; Hatschek, *op. cit.*, I, 239.

26 Chrimes, *op. cit.*, pp. 81–126.

27 The work was actually completed in 1565.

28 Sir Thomas Smith, *De Republica Anglorum* (1906), p. 49.

29 *Ibid.*

30 Sir Edward Coke, *The Fourth Part of the Institutes of the Laws of England* (London, 1809), chap. 1, p. 1; italics mine.

31 *Ibid.*, p. 26.

32 From G. P. Gooch, *English Democratic Ideas in the Seventeenth Century*, ed. Harold J. Laski (1954), p. 91. Gooch, however, writes: "Amongst the instructions to the committee was that to urge on the Lords that the Commons were 'representatives of the whole Kingdom,' but the Lords only 'particular persons.' " If this citation were correct, it would be a counterexample to my argument, an application of the word to members of Parliament. In fact, however, the *Journals of the House of Commons* (II, 330) read: "And that this House being the Representative Body of the whole Kingdom, and their Lordships being but as particular Persons, and coming to Parliament in their particular capacity. . . ."

33 Brown, *op. cit.*, p. 34; italics mine.

[34] Cited in John A. Fairlie, "The Nature of Political Representation," *American Political Science Review*, XXXIV (April, 1940), 239. But Charles I is supposed to have referred to himself as the representative of his people as he stood on the scaffold. Pollard, *op. cit.*, p. 151.

[35] Cited in Hugh Chisholm, "Representation," *Encyclopaedia Britannica*, XXIII, 109. Cf. also a Leveller petition of September, 1648, cited in A. S. P. Woodhouse, *Puritanism and Liberty* (London, 1951), pp. 338–339; and references to the "Representative of the Army," a general council set up in June, 1647, in Charles F. Firth, ed., *The Clarke Papers* (1891), I, 293–294.

[36] Chisholm, *op. cit.*, p. 109; Hintze, *op. cit.*, p. 235. But see note 43, below.

[37] There is also "representator," but this word apparently was never applied to politics or to "acting for" others.

[38] Firth, *op. cit.*, I, 293, 300–303, 317, 324, 351; III, 6–7. In I, 324, Firth has interpolated an "s" that would contradict my argument; but I suggest that the passage was probably correct without the addition: "if all the people in this Kingdome, or (the) Representative(s) of them all together, should meete. . . ."

[39] Cited in Chisholm, *op. cit.*, p. 109; italics mine.

[40] According to the *Oxford English Dictionary*, none survives the seventeenth century. For examples of the new usage in the Protectorate parliaments and after, see Brown, *op. cit.*; Emden, *op. cit.*, p. 15.

[41] English Works, ed. Sir William Molesworth (London, 1839–1845), III, 149, 151.

[42] *Ibid.*, p. 151.

[43] Some writers, however, argue that the term "representation" was applied first to the activities of attorneys and agents, and hence to individual members of Parliament insofar as they were thought of as agents or attorneys, and only derivately to Parliament as a whole. See esp. F. A. Hermens, *Democracy or Anarchy?* (Notre Dame, Ind., 1941), p. 5; George Cornwall Lewis, *Remarks on the Use and Abuse of Some Political Terms* (Oxford, 1877), pp. 97–98. Perhaps these disagreements involve some confusion as to how the Latin word was used and how the English word was used during the time when both were in use in England.

[44] *Op. cit.*, pp. 426, 435. See also Tierney, *op. cit.*, pp. 47, 53, 176, 235.

[45] Brown, *op. cit.*, p. 27; Leibholz, *Das Wesen der Repräsentation*, p. 147.

[46] "An Appeal," cited in Woodhouse, *op. cit.*, p. 329.

[47] *Ibid.*, p. 330.

Bibliography

Abell, Walter. *Representation and Form*. New York: Charles Scribner's Sons, 1936.

Adams, John. *Works*. Boston: Little, Brown and Co., 1852–1865.

Adams, Randolph G. *Political Ideas of the American Revolution*. 3d ed. New York: Barnes and Noble, 1958.

Allport, Gordon W. *Personality*. New York: Henry Holt and Co., 1937.

Anson, William R. *Principles of the English Law of Contract, and of Agency in Its Relation to Contract*. 21st ed. Ed. A. G. Guest. Oxford: Clarendon Press, 1959.

Appleby, Paul H. *Morality and Administration*. Baton Rouge: Louisiana State University Press, 1952.

Arendt, Hannah. *Between Past and Future*. Cleveland: World Publishing, 1963.

Arneson, Ben A. "Do Representatives Represent?" *National Municipal Review*, XVI (December, 1927), 751–754.

Austin, J. L. *Philosophical Papers*. Oxford: Clarendon Press, 1960.

Ayer, A. J. *Philosophical Essays*. London: Macmillan & Co., Ltd., 1954.

Bagehot, Walter. *The English Constitution*. London: Oxford University Press, 1928.

Bailey, Samuel. *The Rationale of Political Representation*. London: R. Hunter, 1835.

Banfield, Edward C. *Political Influence*. Glencoe, Ill.: Free Press, 1961.

Barker, Ernest. *Essays on Government*. 2d ed. Oxford: Clarendon Press, 1951.

———. *Reflections on Government*. London: Oxford University Press, 1942.

Barrows, Herbert. *Reading the Short Story.* Boston: Houghton Mifflin Co., 1959.

Bay, Christian. *The Structure of Freedom.* Stanford University Press, 1958.

Beard, Charles A., and John D. Lewis. "Representative Government in Evolution," *American Political Science Review,* XXVI (April, 1932), 223–240.

Beer, Samuel H. "The Representation of Interests in British Government: Historical Background," *American Political Science Review,* LI (September, 1957), 613–650.

Belloc, H., and G. K. Chesterton. *The Party System.* London: S. Swift, 1911.

Bentham, Jeremy. *Jeremy Bentham's Economic Writings.* Ed. W. Stark. London: George Allen and Unwin, 1954.

———. *Works.* Ed. John Bowring. Edinburgh: William Tait, 1843.

Bentley, Arthur F. *The Process of Government.* Evanston, Ill.: Principia, 1949.

Berelson, Bernard R., Paul F. Lazarsfeld, and William N. McPhee. *Voting.* University of Chicago Press, 1954.

Bernheimer, Richard, *et al. Art: A Bryn Mawr Symposium.* Bryn Mawr Monographs, IX. Bryn Mawr, 1940.

Blaisdell, Donald C., ed., *Unofficial Government: Pressure Groups and Lobbies.* American Academy of Political and Social Science, *Annals,* Vol. 319 (September, 1958).

Bluntschli, J. C. *Die Lehre vom modernen Staat.* Vol. II: *Allgemeines Staatsrecht.* Stuttgart: J. G. Cotta, 1876.

Bonilla, Frank. "When Is Petition 'Pressure'?" *Public Opinion Quarterly,* XX (Spring, 1956), 39–48.

Bornhak, Conrad. *Allgemeine Staatslehre.* 2d ed. Berlin: Carl Heymanns, 1909.

Bromage, Arthur W. *Political Representation in Metropolitan Agencies.* Michigan Governmental Studies No. 42. Ann Arbor: University of Michigan, 1962.

———. "Political Representation in Metropolitan Areas," *American Political Science Review,* LII (June, 1958), 406–418.

Brown, Louise Fargo. "Ideas of Representation from Elizabeth to Charles II," *Journal of Modern History,* XI (March, 1939), 23–40.

Burdick, Eugene, and Arthur J. Brodbeck, eds. *American Voting Behavior.* Glencoe, Ill.: Free Press, 1959.

Burke, Edmund. *Burke's Politics.* Eds. Ross J. S. Hoffman and Paul Levack. New York: Alfred A. Knopf, Inc., 1949.

———. *Selected Writings and Speeches.* Ed. Peter J. Stanlis. Garden City: Doubleday, 1963.

———. *Works.* Vol. I. New York: Harpers, 1847.

Callender, Clarence N., and James C. Charlesworth, eds. *Ethical Standards in American Public Life*. American Academy of Political and Social Science, *Annals*, Vol. 280 (March, 1952).

Cam, Helen M. *Liberties and Communities in Medieval England*. Cambridge, England: Cambridge University Press, 1944.

———. "The Theory and Practice of Representation in Medieval England," *History*, XXXVIII (February, 1953), 11–26.

Campbell, Angus, Philip E. Converse, Warren E. Miller, and Donald E. Stokes. *The American Voter*. New York: John Wiley and Sons, 1960.

———, Gerald Gurin, and Warren E. Miller. *The Voter Decides*. White Plains, N. Y.: Row, Peterson and Co., 1954.

Canavan, Francis P. *The Political Reason of Edmund Burke*. Durham, N. C.: Duke University Press, 1960.

Cantril, Hadley. *Public Opinion 1935–46*. Princeton University Press, 1951.

Carney, Francis M. "Concepts of Political Representation in the United States Today." Unpubl. diss., University of California at Los Angeles, 1956.

Carpenter, William Seal. *Democracy and Representation*. Princeton University Press, 1925.

Carr, Robert H., Marven H. Bernstein, and Donald H. Morrison. *American Democracy in Theory and Practice*. 3d ed. New York: Rinehart, 1959.

Cary, Joyce. *Art and Reality*. New York: Harper and Bros., 1958.

Cassinelli, Charles William, Jr. "The Concept of Representative Government." Unpubl. thesis, University of California, Berkeley, 1950.

———. "Representative Government: The Concept and Its Implications." Unpubl. diss., Harvard University, 1953.

———. "Some Reflections on the Concept of the Public Interest," *Ethics*, LXIX (October, 1958), 48–61.

Cavell, Stanley. "The Availability of Wittgenstein's Later Philosophy," *Philosophical Review*, LXXI (1962), 67–93.

———. "Must We Mean What We Say?" *Inquiry*, I (1958), 172–212.

Chisholm, Hugh. "Representation," *Encyclopaedia Britannica*, 11th ed. (1910–1911), XXIII, 108–116.

Chrimes, Stanley Bertram. *English Constitutional Ideas in the Fifteenth Century*. Cambridge, England: Cambridge University Press, 1936.

Christensen, A. N., and E. M. Kirkpatrick, eds. *The People, Politics and the Politician*. New York: Henry Holt and Co., 1941.

Chubb, Basil. "Vocational Representation," *Political Studies*, II (June, 1954), 97.

Cicero, Marcus Tullius. *De Oratore, libri tres.* Ed. Augustus S. Wilkins. Oxford: Clarendon Press, 1879–1892.

Clark, Carroll D. "The Concept of the Public," *Southwestern Social Science Quarterly,* XIII (March, 1933), 311–320.

Clarke, Maude V. *Medieval Representation and Consent.* London: Longmans, Green and Co., 1936.

Coke, Sir Edward. *The Fourth Part of the Institutes of the Laws of England.* London: W. Clarke and Sons, 1809.

Coker, Francis W., and Carlton C. Rodee. "Representation," *Encyclopaedia of the Social Sciences,* XIII (1935), 309–315.

Cole, G. D. H. *Social Theory.* London: Methuen, 1920.

Commons, John Roger. *Proportional Representation.* New York: Thomas Y. Crowell Co., 1896.

Congar, Yves M.-J. "Quod Omnes Tangit ab Omnibus Tractari et Approbatur Debet," *Revue Historique de Droit Français et Etranger,* 4th ser., XXXVI (April–June, 1958), 210–259.

Crane, Wilder W., Jr. "Do Representatives Represent?" *Journal of Politics,* XXII (May, 1960), 295–299.

Dahl, Robert A., and Charles E. Lindblom. *Politics, Economics and Welfare.* New York: Harpers, 1953.

Davy, Georges. *Thomas Hobbes et Jean Jacques Rousseau.* Oxford: Clarendon Press, 1953.

De Grazia, Alfred. "General Theory of Apportionment," *Law and Contemporary Problems,* XVII (Spring, 1952), 256–267.

———. "The Nature and Prospects of Political Interest Groups," American Academy of Political and Social Science, *Annals,* Vol. 319 (September, 1958).

———. *Public and Republic.* New York: Alfred A. Knopf, Inc., 1951.

De Grazia, Sebastian. "What Authority Is *Not.*" *American Political Science Review,* LIII (June, 1959), 321–331.

Dewey, John. *Art as Experience.* New York: Minton, Balch and Co., 1934.

———. *Interest as Related to Will.* Second Supplement, Herbart Yearbook for 1895, reprinted by National Herbart Society. University of Chicago Press, 1899.

———. *The Public and Its Problems.* New York: Henry Holt and Co., 1927.

Dexter, Lewis Anthony. "Candidates Must Make the Issues and Give Them Meaning," *Public Opinion Quarterly,* XIX (Winter, 1955–56), 408–414.

———. "The Representative and His District," *Human Organization,* XVI (Spring, 1957), 2–13.

———. "What Do Congressmen Hear: The Mail," *Public Opinion Quarterly,* XX (Spring, 1956), 16–27.

Dicey, Albert V. *Introduction to the Study of the Law of the Constitution.* 8th ed. London: Macmillan & Co., Ltd., 1924.

Diggs, Bernard J. "Practical Representation," *Representation* (Nomos X). Eds. Roland Pennock and John Chapman. New York: Atherton (in press).

Douglas, Paul H. "Occupational vs. Proportional Representation," *American Journal of Sociology*, XXIX (September, 1923), 129–157.

Downs, Anthony. *An Economic Theory of Democracy.* New York: Harpers, 1957.

Dowse, Robert E. "Representation, General Elections and Democracy," *Parliamentary Affairs*, XV (Summer, 1962), 331–346.

Drath, Martin. *Die Entwicklung der Volksrepräsentation.* Bad Homburg v.d. H.: Gehlen, 1954.

Duguit, Léon. *Traité de Droit Constitutionnel.* Vol. II. 3d ed. Paris: Boccard, 1928.

Ebenstein, William. *Great Political Thinkers: Plato to the Present.* 2d ed. New York: Rinehart, 1956.

Edward, J. G. "The *Plena Potestas* of English Parliamentary Representatives," *Oxford Essays in Medieval History Presented to H. E. Salter.* Oxford: Clarendon Press, 1934.

Emden, Cecil S. *The People and the Constitution.* 2d ed. Oxford: Clarendon Press, 1956.

Emerson, Ralph Waldo. *Representative Men.* Boston: Phillips, Sampson, 1852.

England, Leonard: "The Personal Impact of British M.P.'s on Their Constituencies," *International Journal of Opinion and Attitude Research*, IV (Fall, 1950), 412–414.

Epstein, Leon D. "British M. P.'s and Their Local Parties: The Suez Cases," *American Political Science Review*, LIV (June, 1960), 371–390.

Esmein, A., and H. Nézard. *Eléments de Droit Constitutionel Français et Comparé.* Vol. I. 8th ed. Paris: Recueil Sirey, 1927.

Eulau, Heinz, *et al.* "The Role of the Representative: Some Empirical Observations on the Theory of Edmund Burke," *American Political Science Review*, LIII (September, 1959), 742–756.

Fairlie, John A. "The Nature of Political Representation," *American Political Science Review*, XXXIV (April, June, 1940), 236–248, 456–466.

Farrand, Max, ed. *The Records of the Federal Convention of 1787.* New Haven: Yale University Press, 1927.

Ferguson, George. *Signs and Symbols in Christian Art.* New York: Oxford University Press, 1954.

Fergusson, Francis. *The Idea of a Theater.* Princeton University Press, 1949.

Field, Guy C. *Political Theory.* London: Methuen, 1956.

Finer, Herman. *The Theory and Practice of Modern Government.* Rev. ed. New York: Henry Holt and Co., 1949.

Firth, Charles, ed. *The Clarke Papers*. Vols. I, III. Camden Society, 1891.

Ford, Henry J. *Representative Government*. New York: Henry Holt and Co., 1924.

Frankel, Charles. "Introduction," to Jean Jacques Rousseau, *The Social Contract*. Ed. Charles Frankel. New York: Hafner, 1951.

Friedrich, Carl J., ed. *Authority* (Nomos I). Cambridge: Harvard University Press, 1958.

————. *Constitutional Government and Democracy*. Boston: Ginn and Co., 1950.

————. "Representation," *Encyclopaedia Britannica*, XIX (1960), 163–167.

————. "Representation and Constitutional Reform in Europe," *Western Political Quarterly*, I (June, 1948), 124–130.

————, ed. *Responsibility* (Nomos III). New York: Liberal Arts Press, 1960.

Fryer, Douglas. *The Measurement of Interests in Relation to Human Adjustment*. New York: Henry Holt and Co., 1931.

Gadave, René. *Thomas Hobbes, et Ses Théories du Contrat Social et de la Souveraineté*. Toulouse: Ch. Marqués, 1907.

Gage, Nathaniel L. *Judging Interests from Expressive Behavior*. Washington, D. C.: American Psychological Association, 1952.

Garner, James Wilford. *Political Science and Government*. New York: American Book Co., 1928.

Gibbons, Philip Arnold. *Ideas of Political Representation in Parliament 1651–1832*. Oxford: Blackwell, 1914.

Gierke, Otto von. *Das deutsche Genossenschaftsrecht*. Vol. III: *Die Staats- und Korporationslehre des Alterthums und des Mittelalters und ihre Aufnahme in Deutschland*. Berlin: Weidmann, 1881.

————. *Johannes Althusius*. Breslau: M. and H. Marcus, 1913.

Gleeck, L. E. "96 Congressmen Make Up Their Minds," *Public Opinion Quarterly*, IV (March, 1940), 3–24.

Glickman, Harvey. "Viewing Public Opinion in Politics: A Common Sense Approach," *Public Opinion Quarterly*, XXIII (Winter, 1959–60), 495–504.

Glum, Friedrich. *Der deutsche und der französische Reichswirtschaftsrat*. Berlin: Walter de Gruyter, 1929.

Godwin, Parke. *Political Essays*. New York: Dix, Edwards, 1856.

Goffman, Erving. *The Presentation of Self in Everyday Life*. University of Edinburgh, 1958.

Gombrich, Ernst H. *Art and Illusion*. New York: Pantheon, 1960.

Gooch, G. P. *English Democratic Ideas in the Seventeenth Century*. 2d ed. Ed. Harold J. Laski. Cambridge, England: Cambridge University Press, 1954.

Gosnell, Harold Foote. *Democracy, The Threshold of Freedom*. New York: Ronald Press Co., 1948.

Graham, George A. *Morality in American Politics*. New York: Random House, 1952.

Great Britain. Parliament. House of Commons. *Journal of the House of Commons*. Vol. II.

Griffiths, A. Phillips, and Richard Wollheim. "How Can One Person Represent Another?" Aristotelian Society, Supplementary Vol. XXXIV (1960), 187–224.

Guilford, J. P., *et al.* "A Factor Analysis Study of Human Interests," *Psychological Monographs: General and Applied*, LXVIII (1954), no. 4.

Guizot, M. *Representative Government in Europe*. Trans. Andrew R. Scoble. London: Henry G. Bohn, 1861.

Hadley, Arthur T. *Standards of Public Morality*. New York: The Macmillan Co., 1907.

Halévy, Elie. *The Growth of Philosophical Radicalism*. Boston: The Beacon Press, 1955.

Hallam, Henry. *Constitutional History of England*. Vol. I. New York: Widdleton, 1871.

Hamilton, Alexander, James Madison, and John Jay. *The Federalist*. Ed. Max Beloff. Oxford: Blackwell, 1948.

Hamilton, Howard D. *Legislative Apportionment, Key to Power*. New York: Harper and Row, 1964.

Handcock, W. D. "What Is Represented in Representative Government?" *Philosophy*, XXII (July, 1947), 99–111.

Hare, R. M., *et al.* "Symposium on the Nature of Analysis," *Journal of Philosophy*, LIV (November, 1957), 741–765.

Hare, Thomas. *The Election of Representatives, Parliamentary and Municipal*. 4th ed. London: Longmans, Green, 1873.

Harris, Errol E. "Political Power," *Ethics*, LXVIII (October, 1957), 1–10.

Harris, George. *The True Theory of Representation in a State*. London: Longmans, Green and Co., 1857.

Hartmann, George W. "Judgments of State Legislators Concerning Public Opinion," *Journal of Social Psychology*, XXI (February, 1945), 105–114.

Haskins, George L. *The Growth of English Representative Government*. Philadelphia: University of Pennsylvania Press, 1948.

Hatschek, Julius. *Englisches Staatsrecht*. Vol. I. Tübingen: J. C. B. Mohr, 1905.

Hauck, Albert. "Die Rezeption und Umbildung der allgemeinen Synode in Mittelalter," *Historische Vierteljahrschrift*, X (1907), 465–482.

Hermens, F. A. *Democracy and Proportional Representation*. Public Policy Pamphlet No. 31. University of Chicago Press, 1940.

———. *Democracy or Anarchy?* Notre Dame, Ind.: Notre Dame University Press, 1941.

Herring, E. Pendleton. *Group Representation before Congress*. Baltimore: Johns Hopkins Press, 1929.

Hintze, Otto. "Typologie der ständischen Verfassungen des Abendlandes," *Historische Zeischrift*, CXLI (1929–1930), 229–248.

Hoag, Clarence Gilbert, and George Hervey Hallett, Jr. *Proportional Representation*. New York: The Macmillan Co., 1926.

Hobbes, Thomas. *The Elements of Law*. Ed. Ferdinand Tönnies. Cambridge, England: Cambridge University Press, 1928.

——. *English Works*. Ed. Sir William Molesworth. London: Longmans, Brown, Green and Longmans, 1839–1845.

Hogan, James. *Election and Representation*. Cork University Press, 1945.

Holdsworth, William S. *A History of English Law*. Boston: Little, Brown and Co., 1922–1938.

Horwill, G. *Proportional Representation, Its Dangers and Defects*. London: G. Allen and Unwin, 1925.

Hospers, J. *Meaning and Truth in the Arts*. Chapel Hill: University of North Carolina Press, 1946.

Hoy, Terry. "Theories of the Exercise of Suffrage in the United States: A Critical Analysis." Unpubl. diss., University of California, Berkeley, 1956.

Hume, David. "Of the Original Contract," *The Social Contract*. Ed. by Ernest Barker. New York: Oxford University Press, 1960.

——. *A Treatise of Human Nature*. Everyman's ed. New York: E. P. Dutton and Co. [1920].

Hutchins, Robert M. "The Theory of Oligarchy: Edmund Burke," *The Thomist*, V (January, 1943), 61–78.

Hutchison, T. W. "Bentham as an Economist," *Economic Journal*, LXVI (June, 1956), 288–306.

Hyneman, Charles S. "Who Makes Our Laws?" *Political Science Quarterly*, LV (December, 1940), 556–581.

Isenberg, Arnold. "Perception, Meaning and the Subject-Matter of Art," *Journal of Philosophy*, XLI (1944), 561–575.

Jacob, E. F. "English Documents of the Conciliar Movement," *Rylands Library Bulletin*, XV (July, 1931), 358–394.

Janowitz, Morris, and Dwaine Marvick. "Competitive Pressure and Democratic Consent," *Public Opinion Quarterly*, XIX (Winter, 1955–56), 381–400.

——. *Competitive Pressure and Democratic Consent*. Ann Arbor: University of Michigan Press, 1956.

Jellinek, Georg. *Allgemeine Staatslehre*. 2d ed. Berlin: O. Häring, 1905.

Jones, Charles O. "Representation in Congress," *American Political Science Review*, LV (December, 1961), 358–367.

Kantorowicz, Ernst. *The King's Two Bodies*. Princeton University Press, 1957.

Kaplan, Morton. "How Sovereign Is Hobbes' Sovereign?" *Western Political Quarterly*, IX (June, 1956), 389–405.

Katz, Elihu, and Paul F. Lazarsfeld. *Personal Influence*. Glencoe, Ill.: Free Press, 1955.

Kelsen, Hans. *The Pure Theory of Law*. Berkeley and Los Angeles: University of California Press, 1967.

———. *Vom Wesen und Wert der Demokratie*. 2d ed. Tübingen: J. C. B. Mohr, 1929.

Kern, Fritz. *Kingship and Law in the Middle Ages*. Trans. S. B. Chrimes. Oxford: Blackwell, 1939.

Klöti, Emil. *Die Proportionwahl in der Schweitz*. Bern: Schmid and Francke, 1901.

Knight, F. H. *Intelligence and Democratic Action*. Cambridge: Harvard University Press, 1960.

Koellreutter, Otto. *Grundriss der allgemeinen Staatslehre*. Tübingen: J. C. B. Mohr, 1933.

Korzybski, Alfred. *Science and Sanity*. New York: International Non-Aristotelian Library, 1933.

Lagarde, Georges de. "L'Idée de Représentation dans les Oeuvres de Guillaume d'Ockham," International Committee of the Historical Sciences, *Bulletin*, IX (December, 1937), 425–451.

Laird, John. "The Conception of Authority," Aristotelian Society, *Proceedings*, XXXIV (1934), 87–110.

Landry, Bernard. *Hobbes*. Paris: F. Alcan, 1930.

Langer, Susan. *Philosophy in a New Key*. Mentor, 1942.

Larsen, J. A. O. *Representative Government in Greek and Roman History*. Berkeley and Los Angeles: University of California, 1955.

Laski, Harold J. *Democracy in Crisis*. Chapel Hill: University of North Carolina Press, 1933.

Laslett, Peter, ed. *Philosophy, Politics and Society*. New York: The Macmillan Co., 1956.

Lasswell, Harold D., and Abraham Kaplan. *Power and Society*. New Haven: Yale University Press, 1950.

Lazarsfeld, Paul F., Bernard Berelson, and Hazel Gaudet. *The People's Choice*. New York: Columbia University Press, 1948.

Leibholz, Gerhard. *Strukturprobleme der modernen Demokratie*. Karlsruhe: C. F. Müller, 1958.

———. *Das Wesen der Repräsentation*. Berlin: Walter de Gruyter, 1929.

Leiserson, Avery. *Administrative Regulation*. University of Chicago Press, 1942.

———. "Problems of Representation in the Government of Private Groups," *Journal of Politics*, XI (August, 1949), 566–577.

Lewis, Ewart. *Medieval Political Ideas*. New York: Alfred A. Knopf, Inc., 1954.

Lewis, George Cornwall. *Remarks on the Use and Abuse of Some Political Terms.* Oxford: James Thornton, 1877.

Lieber, Francis. *Manual of Political Ethics.* Vol. II. Boston: Little, Brown and Co., 1839.

Littré, E. *Dictionnaire de la Langue Française.* Paris: Libraire Hachette, 1875.

Locke, John. *Two Treatises of Government.* Ed. Peter Laslett. Cambridge, England: Cambridge University Press, 1960.

Lodge, Eleanor C., and Gladys A. Thornton, eds. *English Constitutional Documents 1307–1485.* Cambridge, England: Cambridge University Press, 1935.

Loewenstein, Karl. *Beiträge zur Staatssoziologie.* Tübingen: J. C. B. Mohr, 1961.

———. *Political Power and the Governmental Process.* University of Chicago Press, 1957.

———. *Volk und Parlament.* Munich: Dreimasken, 1922.

Lowell, A. Lawrence. *Public Opinion and Popular Government.* New York: Longmans, Green and Co., 1921.

Luce, Robert. *Legislative Principles.* Boston: Houghton Mifflin Co., 1930.

Luepp, Francis. "Do Our Representatives Represent?" *Atlantic Monthly,* CXIV (October, 1944), 433–443.

Mabbott, J. D. "Punishment," *Mind,* XLVIII (1939), 152–167.

McBain, Howard Lee. *The Living Constitution.* New York: The Macmillan Co., 1948.

Machiavelli, Niccolò. *The Prince and the Discourses.* Ed. Max Lerner. New York: Modern Library, 1940.

MacIlwain, C. H. "Medieval Estates," *Cambridge Medieval History.* Vol. VII: *The Decline of Empire and Papacy.* Cambridge, England: Cambridge University Press, 1932.

MacIver, Robert M. "Interests," *Encyclopaedia of the Social Sciences,* VIII (1935), 144–148.

———. *The Modern State.* Oxford: Clarendon, 1926.

———. *Society, Its Structure and Changes.* New York: Ray Long and Richard R. Smith, 1931.

Mackenzie, W. J. M. *Free Elections.* New York: Rinehart, 1958.

———. "Representation in Plural Societies," *Political Studies,* II (February, 1954), 54–69.

McKisack, May. *Representation of the English Boroughs during the Middle Ages.* London: Oxford University Press, 1932.

MacRae, Duncan, Jr. *Dimensions of Congressional Voting.* Berkeley and Los Angeles: University of California, 1958.

———. "Roll Call Votes and Leadership," *Public Opinion Quarterly,* XX (Fall, 1956), 543–558.

Maitland, Frederick William. *Roman Canon Law in the Church of England.* London: Methuen, 1898.

————. *Selected Essays*. Ed. H. D. Hazeltine *et al.* Cambridge, England: Cambridge University Press, 1936.

Malé, Émil. *Religious Art in France XIII Century*. Trans. from 3d ed. by Dora Nussey. New York: E. P. Dutton and Co., 1913.

Mayo, Bernard. *Ethics and the Moral Life*. London: Macmillan & Co., Ltd., 1958.

Mayo, Henry B. *An Introduction to Democratic Theory*. New York: Oxford University Press, 1960.

"Medieval Representation in Theory and Practice," *Speculum*, XXIX (April, 1954), Part 2.

Merriam, Charles E. *Systematic Politics*. University of Chicago Press, 1945.

Michels, Robert. *Political Parties*. Trans. Eden and Cedar Paul. Chicago: Free Press, 1915.

Mill, James. *An Essay on Government*. New York: Library of Liberal Arts, 1955.

Mill, John Stuart. "Thoughts on Parliamentary Reform," *Dissertations and Discussions*. Vol. IV. New York: Henry Holt and Co., 1874.

————. *Utilitarianism, Liberty, and Representative Government*. Everyman's ed. London: J. M. Dent and Sons, 1947.

Miller, Warren E., and Donald E. Stokes. "Constituency Influence in Congress," *American Political Science Review*, LVII (March, 1963), 45–56.

Milrath, L. W. "Lobbying as a Communications Process," *Public Opinion Quarterly*, XXIV (Spring, 1960), 32–53.

Mirabeau, Honoré Gabriel Riquetti. *Oeuvres*. Vol. I. Paris: Lecointe et Pougin, Didier, 1834–1835.

Müller, F. Max. *Biographies of Words*. London: Longmans, Green and Co., 1888.

The New Yorker, XXXVII (April 29, 1961).

Oakeshott, Michael. "Introduction" to Thomas Hobbes. *The Leviathan*. Ed. by Michael Oakeshott. Oxford: Blackwell, 1957.

————. *Rationalism in Politics*. New York: Basic Books, 1962.

Oliver, Henry M., Jr., "Attitudes toward Market and Political Self-Interest," *Ethics*, LXV (April, 1955), 171–180.

Oxford English Dictionary. Oxford: Clarendon Press, 1937.

Padover, Saul K. *The Complete Madison*. New York: Harpers, 1953.

Parkin, Charles. *The Moral Basis of Burke's Political Thought*. Cambridge, England: Cambridge University Press, 1956.

Pasquet, D. *An Essay on the Origins of the House of Commons*. Trans. R. G. D. Laffan. Cambridge, England: Cambridge University Press, 1925.

Pease, T. C. *The Leveller Movement*. Washington, D. C.: American Historical Association, 1916.

Peters, R. S., P. G. Winch, and A. E. Duncan-Jones. "Symposium on Authority," Aristotelian Society, Supplementary Volume, XXXII (1958), 207–260.

Piaget, Jean. *The Moral Judgment of the Child.* Trans. Marjorie Gabain. New York: Collier, 1962.

Pinney, Harvey. "Government—by Whose Consent?" *Social Science,* XIII (October, 1938), 296–302.

Pitkin, Hanna. "Hobbes' Concept of Representation," *American Political Science Review,* LVIII (June, December, 1964), 328–340, 902–918.

Plamenatz, John P. *Consent, Freedom and Political Obligation.* London: Oxford University Press, 1938.

————. "Interests," *Political Studies,* II (February, 1954), 1–8.

Polin, Raymond. *Politique et Philosophie chez Thomas Hobbes.* Paris: Presses Universitaires de France, 1953.

Pollard, A. F. *The Evolution of Parliament.* 2d ed. London: Longmans, Green and Co., 1926.

Post, Gaines. "*Plena Potestas* and Consent in Medieval Assemblies," *Traditio,* I (1943), 355–408.

————. "Roman Law and Early Representation in Spain and Italy 1150–1250," *Speculum,* XVIII (1943), 211–232.

————. "A Roman Legal Theory of Consent, *Quod Omnes Tangit* in Medieval Representation," *Wisconsin Law Review,* January, 1950, pp. 66–78.

Pufendorf, Samuel. *Of the Law of Nature and Nations.* Trans. by Basil Kennett. London, 1729.

Rader, Melvin, ed. *A Modern Book of Esthetics.* New York: Henry Holt and Co., 1952.

Ranney, Austin, and Willmoore Kendall. *Democracy and the American Party System.* New York: Harcourt, Brace and Co., 1956.

Ranney, John C., and Gwendolen M. Carter. *The Major Foreign Powers.* New York: Harcourt, Brace and Co., 1949.

Rawls, John. "Two Concepts of Rules," *Philosophical Review,* LXIV (January, 1955), 3–32.

Redslob, Robert. *Die Staatstheorien der französischen Nationalversammlung von 1789.* Leipzig: Von Veit, 1912.

Rheinfelder, H. "Das Wort 'Persona,'" *Beihefte zur Zeitschrift für Romanische Philologie,* LXXVII (1928).

Rice, Stuart. *Quantitative Methods in Politics.* New York: Alfred A. Knopf, Inc., 1928.

Riemer, Neal. "James Madison's Theory of the Self-Destructive Features of Republican Government," *Ethics,* LXV (October, 1954), 34–43.

Ross, J. F. S. *Parliamentary Representation.* New Haven: Yale University Press, 1944.

Rossiter, Clinton. *The American Presidency.* Mentor, 1956.

Rousseau, Jean Jacques. *Oeuvres Complètes.* Paris: Libraire Hachette, 1905–1912.

Royce, Josiah. *War and Insurance.* New York: The Macmillan Co., 1914.

Sait, Edward McChesney. *Political Institutions.* New York: D. Appleton-Century, 1938.

Saussure, Ferdinand de. *Course in General Linguistics.* Trans. Wade Baskin. New York: Philosophical Library, 1959.

Schlesinger, Arthur M. *New Viewpoints in American History.* New York: The Macmillan Co., 1948.

Schlossmann, Siegmund. *Persona und πρόσωπον im Recht und im Christlichen Dogma.* Kiel, 1906.

Schmitt, Carl. *The Necessity of Politics.* London: Sheed and Ward, 1931.

———. *Verfassungslehre.* Berlin: Duncker and Humblot, 1954.

Schumpeter, Joseph A. *Capitalism, Socialism and Democracy.* 2d ed. New York: Harpers, 1947.

Small, Albion W. *General Sociology.* University of Chicago Press, 1905.

Smend, Rudolf. *Verfassung und Verfassungsrecht.* Munich: Duncker and Humblot, 1928.

Smith, Adam. *An Inquiry into the Nature and Causes of the Wealth of Nations.* New York: Modern Library, 1937.

Smith, E. Baldwin. *Early Christian Iconography.* Princeton University Press, 1918.

Smith, Maynard. "Reason, Passion and Political Freedom in the *Federalist*," *Journal of Politics*, XXII (August, 1960), 525–544.

Smith, Sir Thomas. *De Republica Anglorum.* Ed. L. Alston. Cambridge, England: Cambridge University Press, 1906.

Smith, T. V. *The Promise of American Politics.* University of Chicago Press, 1936.

Sorauf, Frank J. "The Public Interest Reconsidered," *Journal of Politics*, XIX (November, 1957), 616–639.

Sterne, Simon. *Representative Government and Personal Representation.* Philadelphia: J. B. Lippincott Co., 1871.

Stevenson, Charles L. *Ethics and Language.* New Haven: Yale University Press, 1944.

Stoke, Harold W. "The Paradox of Representative Government," *Essays in Political Science in Honor of W. W. Willoughby.* Ed. John M. Mathews. Baltimore: Johns Hopkins Press, 1937.

Stout, Hiram Miller. *British Government.* New York: Oxford University Press, 1953.

Stout, Rex. *Three at Wolfe's Door.* New York: Viking Press, 1960.

Strauss, Leo. *The Political Philosophy of Hobbes.* University of Chicago Press, 1952.

Sutton, Francis X. "Representation and the Nature of Political Systems," *Comparative Studies in Society and History*, II (October, 1959), 1–10.

Swabey, Marie Collins. *Theory of the Democratic State*. Cambridge: Harvard University Press, 1937.

Taylor, John. *An Inquiry into the Principles and Policy of the Government of the United States*. Fredericksburg: Green and Cady, 1814.

Tierney, Brian. *Foundations of the Conciliar Theory*. Cambridge, England: Cambridge University Press, 1955.

Tindall, William York. *The Literary Symbol*. New York: Columbia University Press, 1955.

Tönnies, Ferdinand. *Thomas Hobbes, Leben und Lehre*. Stuttgart: Fr. Frommanns (H. Kurtz), 1925.

Trendlenburg. "Zur Geschichte des Wortes 'Person,' " *Kantstudien*, XIII (1908), 1.

Truman, David B. *The Governmental Process*. New York: Alfred A. Knopf, Inc., 1959.

Tsarnoff, Radoslav A. "Moral Principles and National Interests," *Ethics*, LXII (October, 1951), 11–15.

Turner, Julius. *Party and Constituency: Pressures on Congress*. Baltimore: Johns Hopkins Press, 1951.

Tussman, Joseph. *Obligation and the Body Politic*. New York: Oxford University Press, 1960.

———. "The Political Theory of Thomas Hobbes." Unpubl. diss., University of California, Berkeley, 1947.

Voegelin, Eric. *The New Science of Politics*. University of Chicago Press, 1952.

Wahlke, John C., *et al.* "American State Legislators' Role Orientation toward Pressure Groups," *Journal of Politics*, XXII (May, 1960), 203–227.

———, and Heinz Eulau, eds. *Legislative Behavior*. Glencoe, Ill.: Free Press, 1959.

Waldman, Theodore. "A Reëxamination of the Notion of Consent and Political Obligation." Unpubl. diss., University of California, Berkeley, 1956.

Walker, Harvey. *The Legislative Process*. New York: Ronald Press Co., 1948.

Warrender, Howard. *The Political Philosophy of Hobbes*. Oxford: Clarendon Press, 1957.

Webb, Sidney, and Beatrice Webb. "Representative Institutions in British Trade-Unionism," *Political Science Quarterly*, XI (1896), 640–671.

Weber, Max. *The Theory of Social and Economic Organization*. Trans. A. M. Henderson and Talcott Parsons. Glencoe, Ill.: Free Press, 1947.

————. *Wirtschaft und Gesellschaft.* Tübingen: J. C. B. Mohr, 1956.

Weldon, T. D. *The Vocabulary of Politics.* London: Penguin, 1953.

Wilkinson, B. "The Political Revolution of the Thirteenth and Fourteenth Centuries in England," *Speculum,* XXIV (October, 1949), 502–509.

Williamson, René de Visme. "The Fascist Concept of Representation," *Journal of Politics,* III (February, 1941), 29–41.

Wilson, Francis Graham. *The Elements of Modern Politics.* New York: McGraw-Hill Book Co., 1936.

Wilson, James. *Works.* Ed. James DeWitt Andrews. Chicago: Callaghan, 1896.

Wittgenstein, Ludwig. *Philosophical Investigations.* Trans. G. E. M. Anscombe. New York: The Macmillan Co., 1953.

Wolfe, Don M., ed. *Leveller Manifestoes of the Puritan Revolution.* New York: Thomas Nelson and Sons, 1944.

Wolff, Hans J. *Organschaft und juristische Person.* Vol. II: *Theorie der Vertretung.* Berlin: Carl Heymanns, 1934.

Wolin, Sheldon S. *Politics and Vision.* Boston: Little, Brown and Co., 1960.

Woodhouse, A. S. P. *Puritanism and Liberty.* London: J. M. Dent, 1951.

Ziff, Paul. *Semantic Analysis.* Ithaca: Cornell University Press, 1960.

Index

trusteeship, 128, 129, 171–172,
173; on parliamentary deliberation, 147, 170, 171, 181–188,
passim, 195; on role of representative, 147, 169–171, 174–
176, 182–183, 188–189, 195,
210–211; on representation of
interests, 167, 168, 171, 174–
182, 184, 185; on concept of interest, 168, 174–175, 180, 186–
187; on democracy, 168, 170–
181, 182, 189; on rights, 168,
179; elite view of representation,
169–174, 185, 188, 193, 211; on
natural aristocracy, 169, 171–
173, 185; on role of reason, 169–
171, 176, 179–189 *passim*, 193,
195–197; on will, 169–171, 176,
181, 183, 186, 187, 188, 189,
192; on national interest, 170–
172, 185–188, 217; on opinion,
170, 176, 180–183, 187, 189, 192,
205–206; on elections, 171–173,
175, 177, 178, 180, 182, 184; on
virtual representation, 171–180,
184–186, 188, 237–239; on substance and form, 175–176, 179–
180, 182, 184, 197; on representation of persons, 182–183,
185, 189; views compared to
those of Liberalism, 191–198
passim, 205–206; relation to parliamentary patron, 282–283 n.
45; mentioned, 12, 56, 209, 214

Canning, George, 164
Ceremonial. *See* Ritual
Characteristics of representative:
likeness of, to those of repre-
sented, 61, 75–78, 84; in De
Grazia and Gosnell, 77–79, 104;
not all politically relevant, 87–
90, 142; in symbolic represen-
tation, 94, 99, 100; in Burke, 185.
See also Correspondence; Like-
ness; Reflection; Resemblance;
Representativeness
Charles I, King of England, 248
Chesterton, G. K., 150, 152
Christ, representation of: by sym-
bol, 69, 94, 101; by Pope, 105,

241–242, 246; by persons, 247
Christian symbolism: exemplified,
69, 94, 99, 101; independent of
speaker's belief, 100, 110; requires community of believers,
105; medieval, 241
Cicero, 24, 25, 27
Civil War, English, development of
representation during, 245–252
passim
Clarke, Maude, 93
Coke, Sir Edward, 245, 248
Cole, G. D. H., 207
Commissioner, representative as,
119, 121, 133–134, 221
Common good. *See* Interest, Public
Commonwealth, creation of, in
Hobbes, 29–32
Concepts: significance of, 1–2, 225–
226; common, not defined, 3; not
easily abandoned, 6; in relation
to practice, institutionalization,
235, 237, 240. *See also* Definition; Meaning; Words
Conceptual problems, 58, 145, 149–
150; in mandate-independence
controversy, 145, 149–150, 153,
154, 165–166, 215. *See also*
Meaning
Condensation. *See* Miniature
Congress, U.S., 26, 43, 75, 76, 115,
134, 142, 190, 195, 217, 219,
223, 227
Constituency, distinguished from
Principal, 144–145, 147, 214–
215, 219–221. *See also* Public
Context: function in defining representation, 6–8, 10–11, 120,
226–228; of authorization view,
47–55; of "acting for" view, 51,
112–118, 141–143; of accountability view, 56–57; of descriptive representation, 81–91, 142;
of symbolic representation, 99,
103, 109–111, 142
Conventional symbol, 71, 72, 95–
97, 100, 101, 102
Corporation, representative of: in
Hobbes, 15–16, 250; is under
authority, 53; distinguished from
agent, 123, 125, 153; distin-